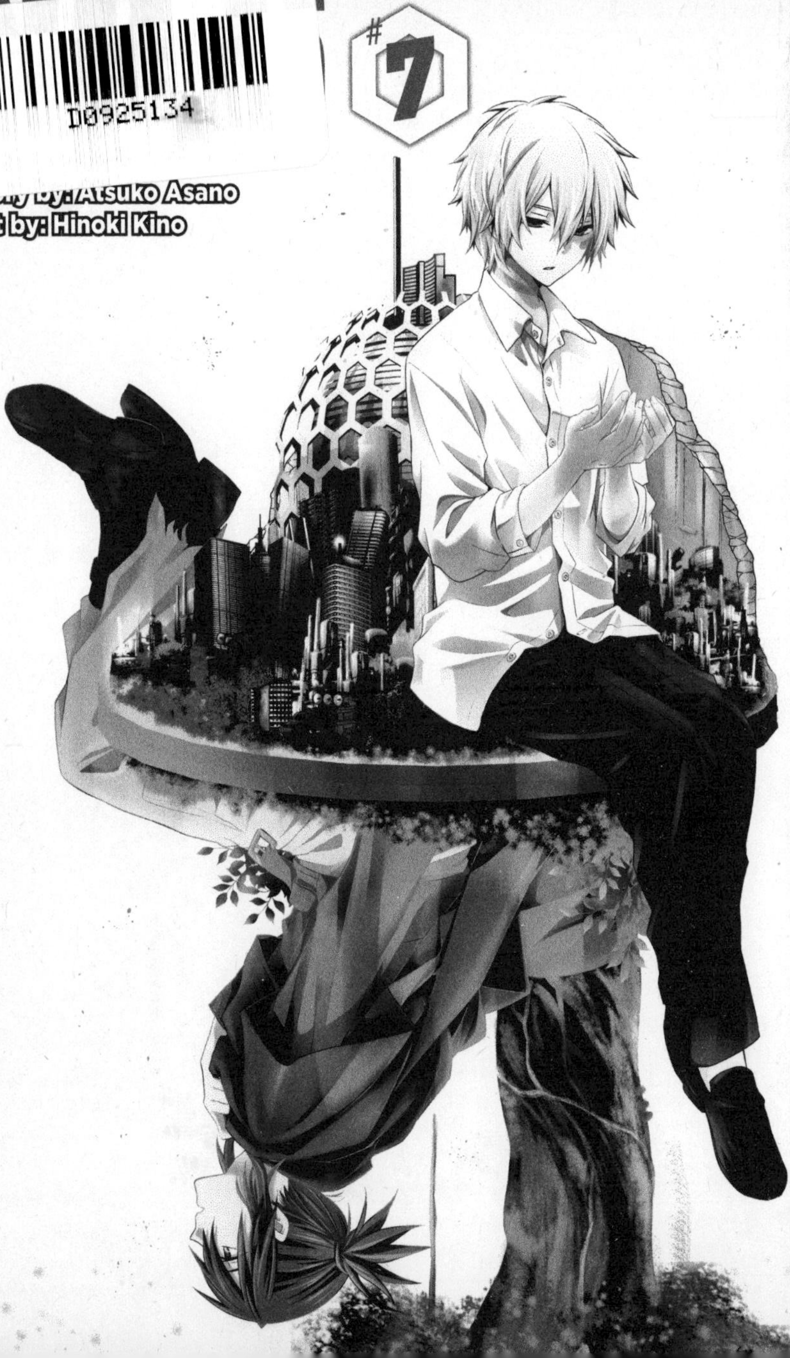
#7

Story by: Atsuko Asano
Art by: Hinoki Kino

NO.6

#7

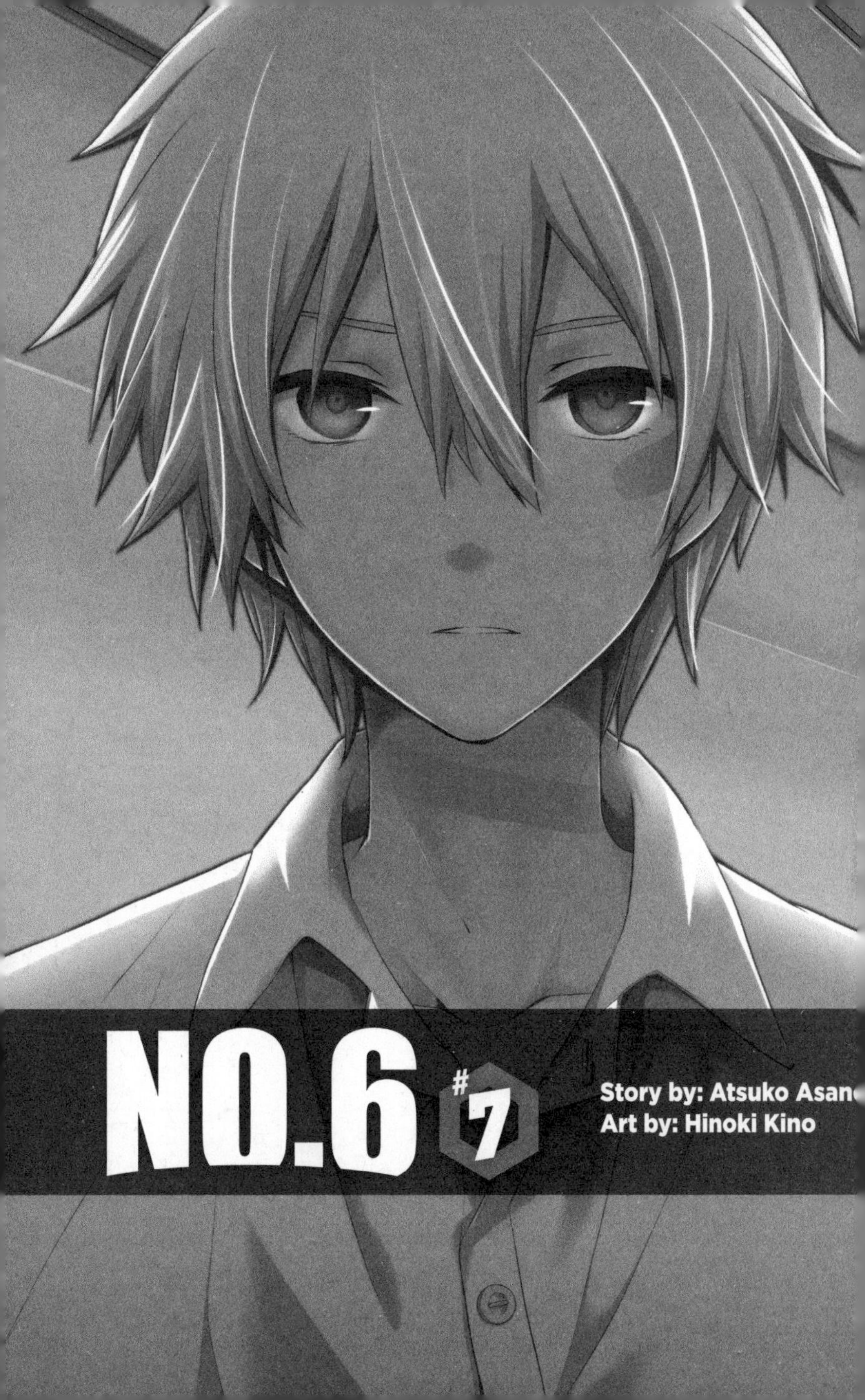
NO.6
#7
Story by: Atsuko Asan
Art by: Hinoki Kino

STORY and CHARACTERS

Shion was raised as a privileged elite in the holy city of No. 6. As the Public Security Bureau was arresting him on charges of murder, a boy named Rat, whom Shion helped during a storm four years earlier, stepped in to save him. Together they escaped No. 6 and fled to West Block, a place of violence and chaos. Shion was infected by a mysterious parasitic bee, but survived, living together with Rat in West Block. After hearing that his childhood friend Safu had been detained and taken to the Correctional Facility, Shion decided to go free her. With assistance from Dogkeeper and Rikiga, Shion and Rat snuck into the Correctional Facility. Following Rat's lead into the depths of the underground, Shion met the Elder — a founder of No. 6 —from whom he heard of the city's creation, and learned that Rat was the sole survivor of the land's previous inhabitants. Now, they carry on to fulfill their vow to free Safu!

Chronos

The top-class residential area, open only to special elite citizens.

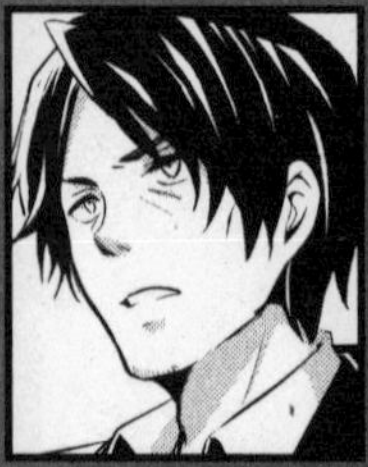

YOMIN

He's doubted No. 6 since his wife and child died.

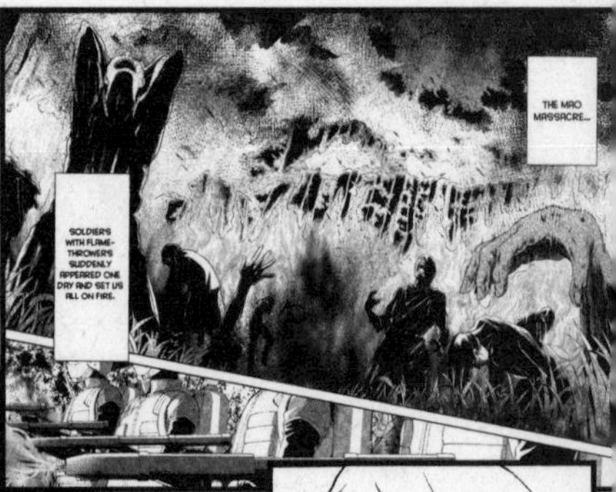
THE MAO MASSACRE...
SOLDIERS WITH FLAME-THROWERS SUDDENLY APPEARED ONE DAY AND SET US ALL ON FIRE.

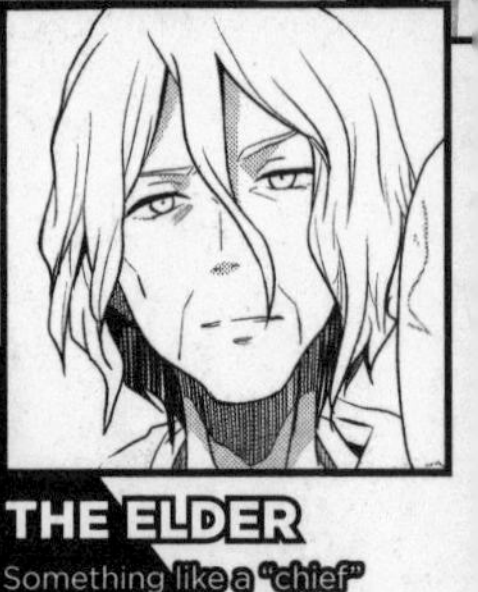

THE ELDER

Something like a "chief" to the people living in the caverns beneath the Correctional Facility.

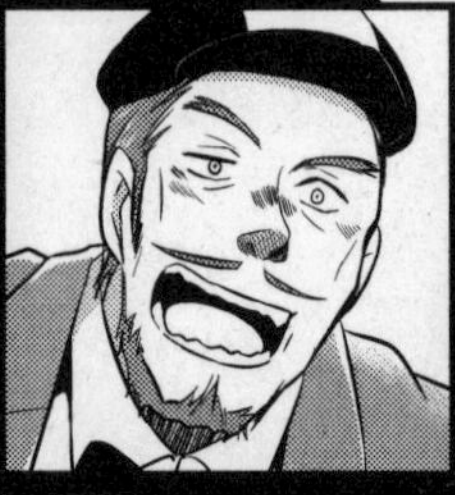

RIKIGA

A former journalist who now publishes a porno magazine in West Block. An old friend of Karan.

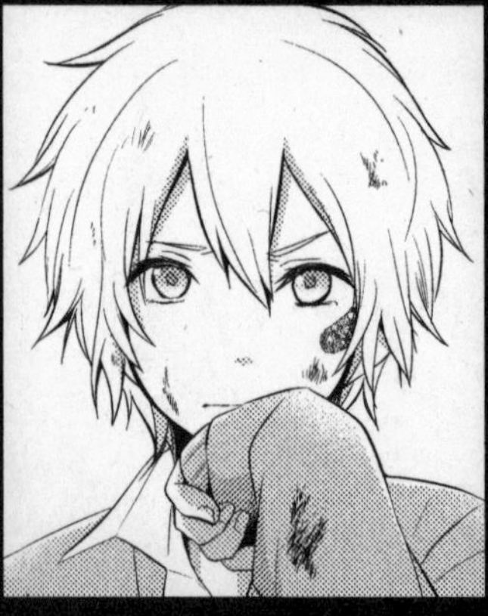

SHION

A former elite candidate, he was a kind, gentle youth, but as his life has grown harsher, he has begun to change.

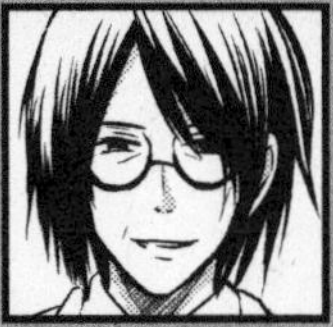

The Man in White

An ambitious research scientist.

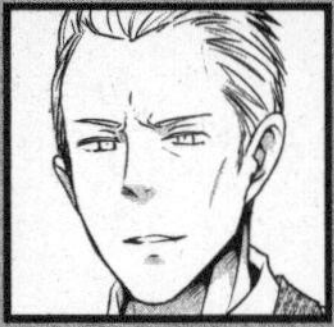

The Mayor

The most powerful man in No. 6.

Inside No. 6

Upper Class

The center of the city, with the Moondrop (City Hall) at its apex.

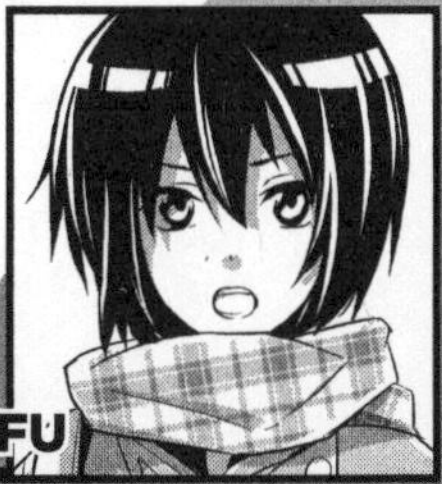

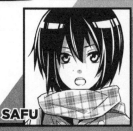

SAFU

A childhood friend who loves Shion. An elite researcher who specializes in neuroscience.

Arrested

The Correctional Facility

The prison for criminals from No. 6. Located in West Block.

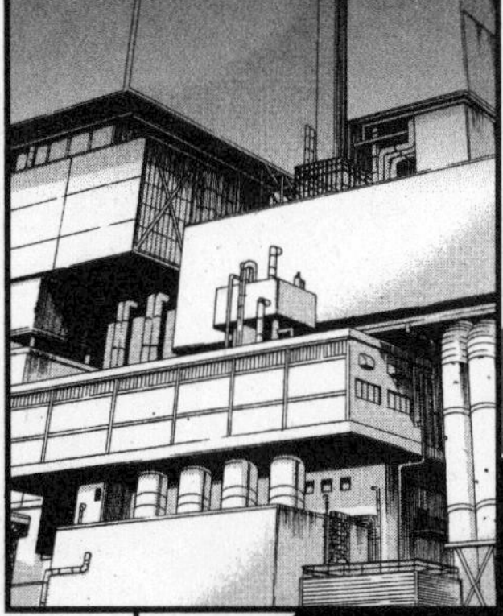

Lost Town

The lower-class residential area for the city's disenfranchised.

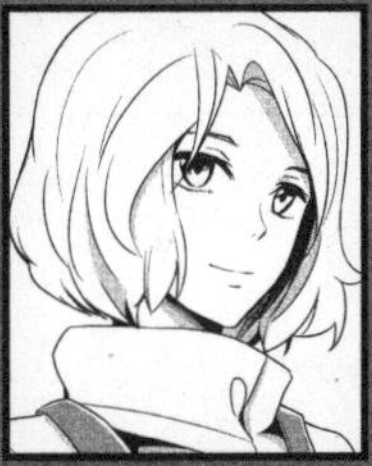

KARAN

Shion's mother. Operates a bakery in Lost Town.

The Outskirts

West Block

The dangerous special zone outside the walls of the city.

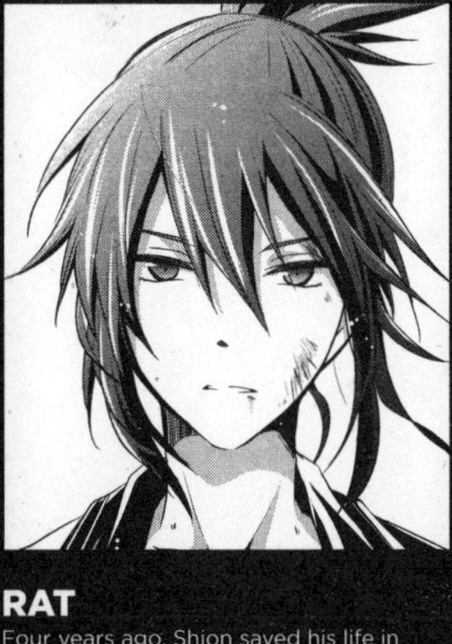

RAT

Four years ago, Shion saved his life in Chronos. In return, he helped Shion escape from No. 6.

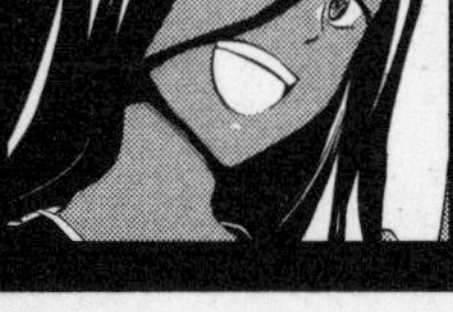

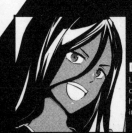

DOGKEEPER

Lives with dogs and operates a dilapidated hotel. Also gathers information for a price.

NO.6

Chapter 24: The Final Embrace

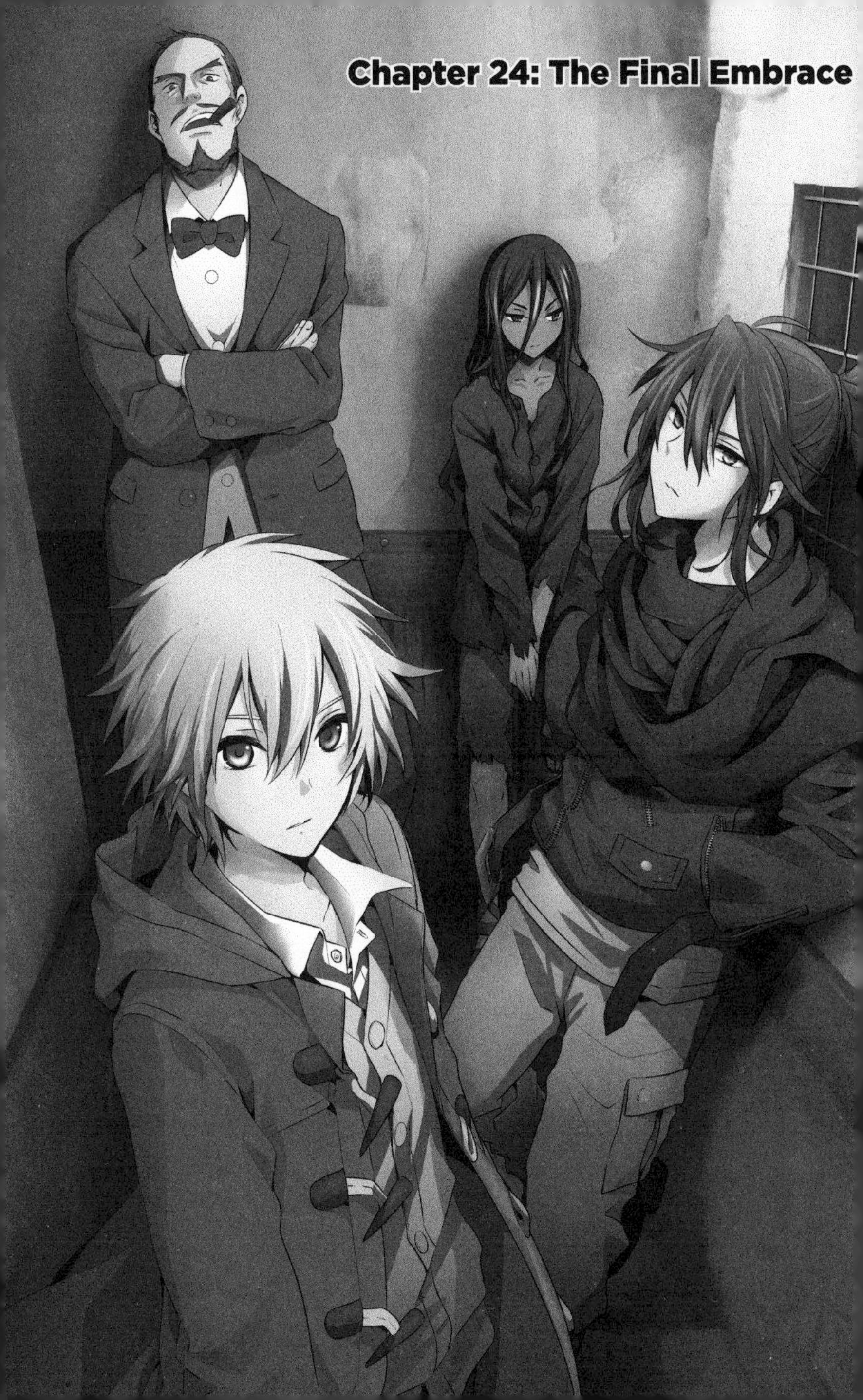

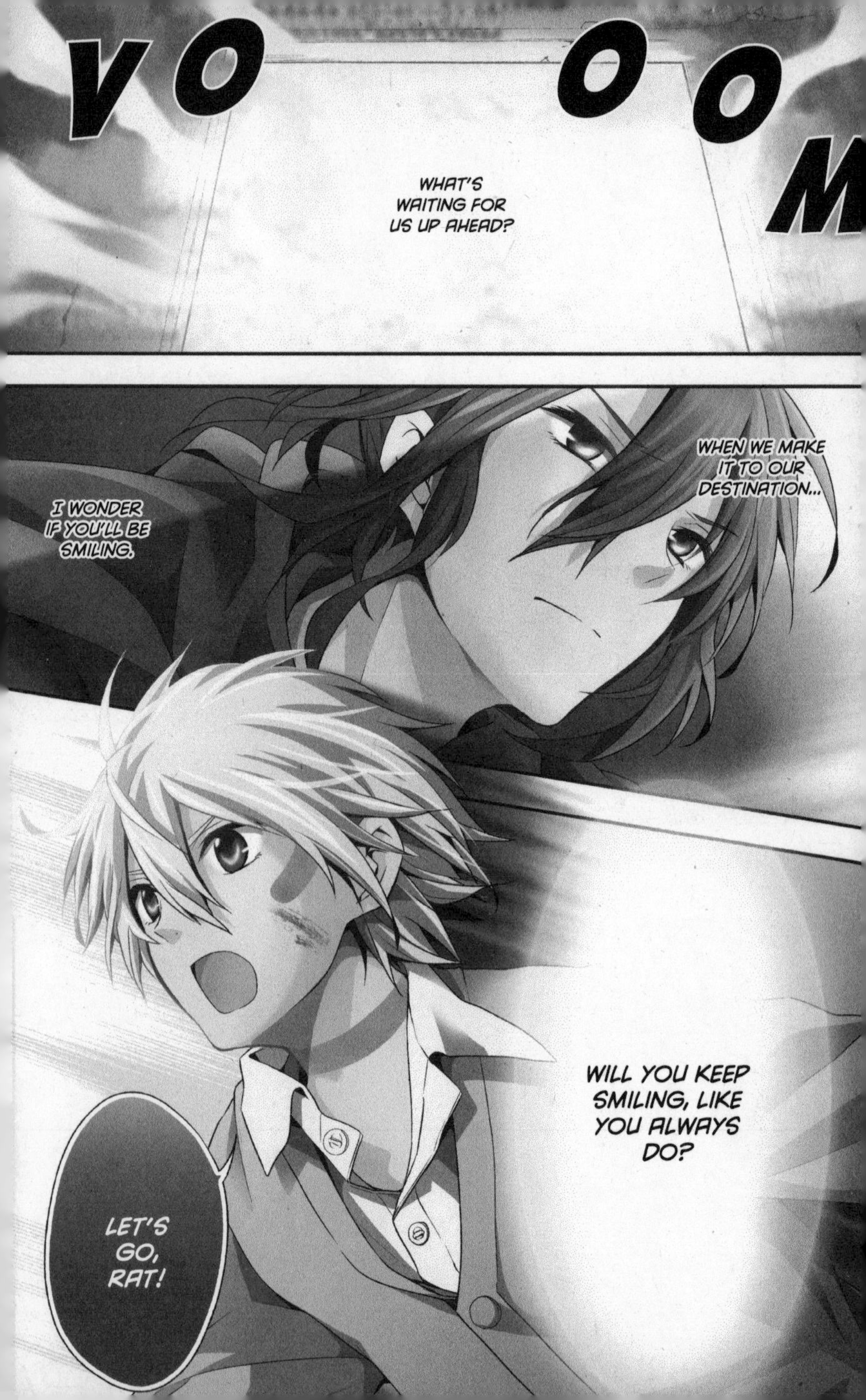
VOOOOM
WHAT'S WAITING FOR US UP AHEAD?
WHEN WE MAKE IT TO OUR DESTINATION...
I WONDER IF YOU'LL BE SMILING.
WILL YOU KEEP SMILING, LIKE YOU ALWAYS DO?
LET'S GO, RAT!

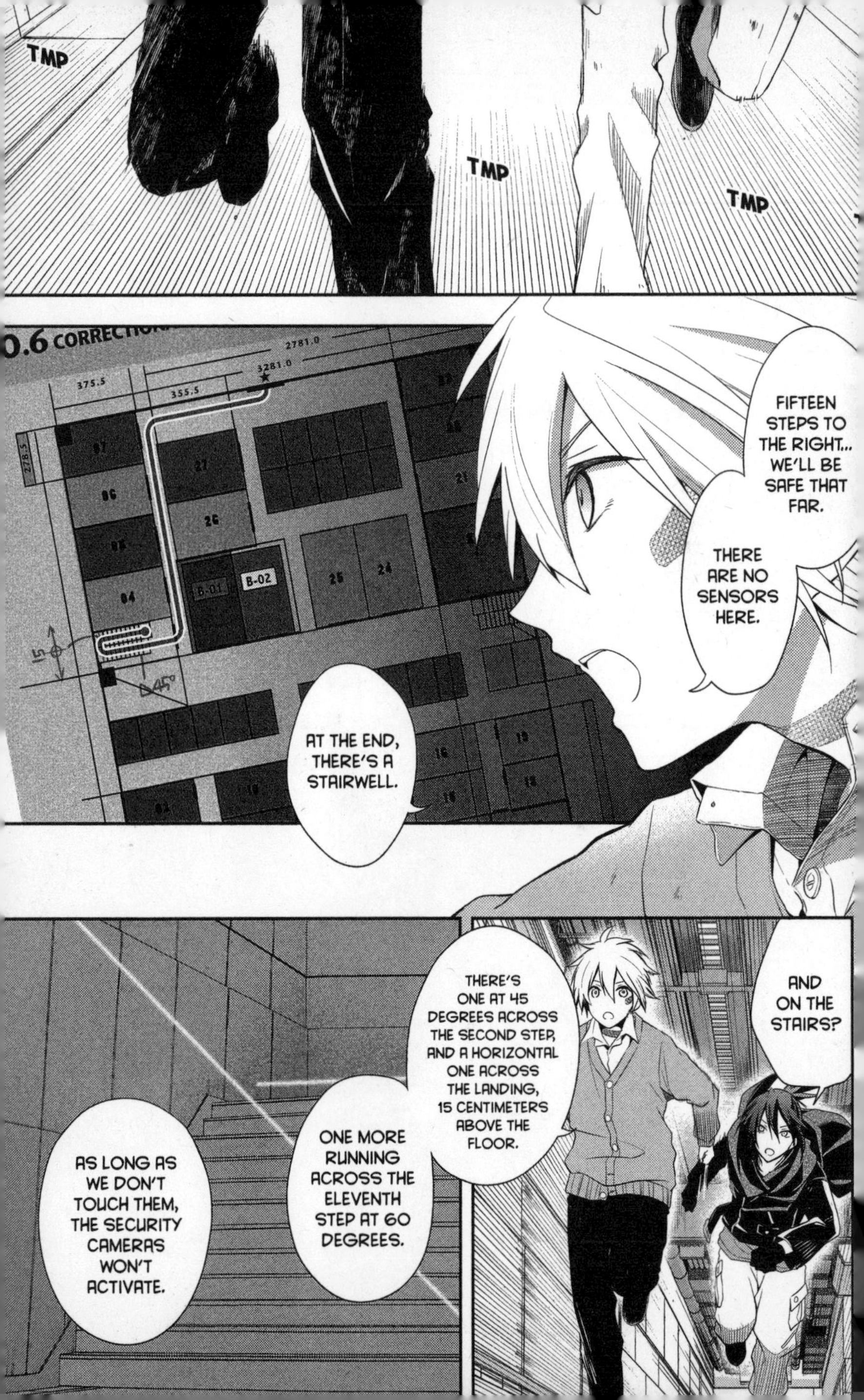
TMP
TMP
TMP
FIFTEEN STEPS TO THE RIGHT... WE'LL BE SAFE THAT FAR.
THERE ARE NO SENSORS HERE.
AT THE END, THERE'S A STAIRWELL.
AND ON THE STAIRS?
THERE'S ONE AT 45 DEGREES ACROSS THE SECOND STEP, AND A HORIZONTAL ONE ACROSS THE LANDING, 15 CENTIMETERS ABOVE THE FLOOR.
ONE MORE RUNNING ACROSS THE ELEVENTH STEP AT 60 DEGREES.
AS LONG AS WE DON'T TOUCH THEM, THE SECURITY CAMERAS WON'T ACTIVATE.

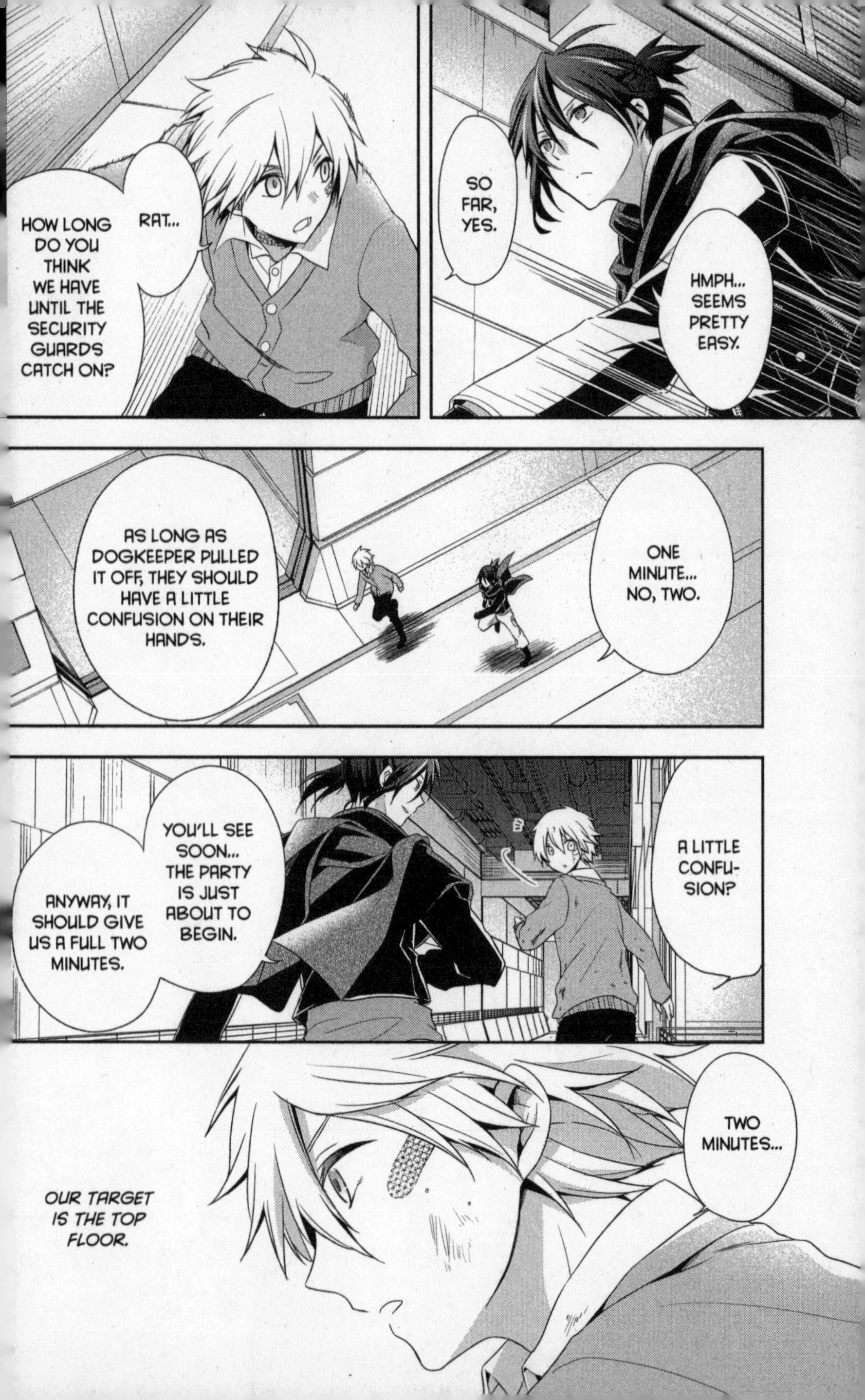
HMPH... SEEMS PRETTY EASY.
SO FAR, YES.
RAT...
HOW LONG DO YOU THINK WE HAVE UNTIL THE SECURITY GUARDS CATCH ON?
ONE MINUTE... NO, TWO.
AS LONG AS DOGKEEPER PULLED IT OFF, THEY SHOULD HAVE A LITTLE CONFUSION ON THEIR HANDS.
A LITTLE CONFU-SION?
YOU'LL SEE SOON... THE PARTY IS JUST ABOUT TO BEGIN.
ANYWAY, IT SHOULD GIVE US A FULL TWO MINUTES.
TWO MINUTES...
OUR TARGET IS THE TOP FLOOR.

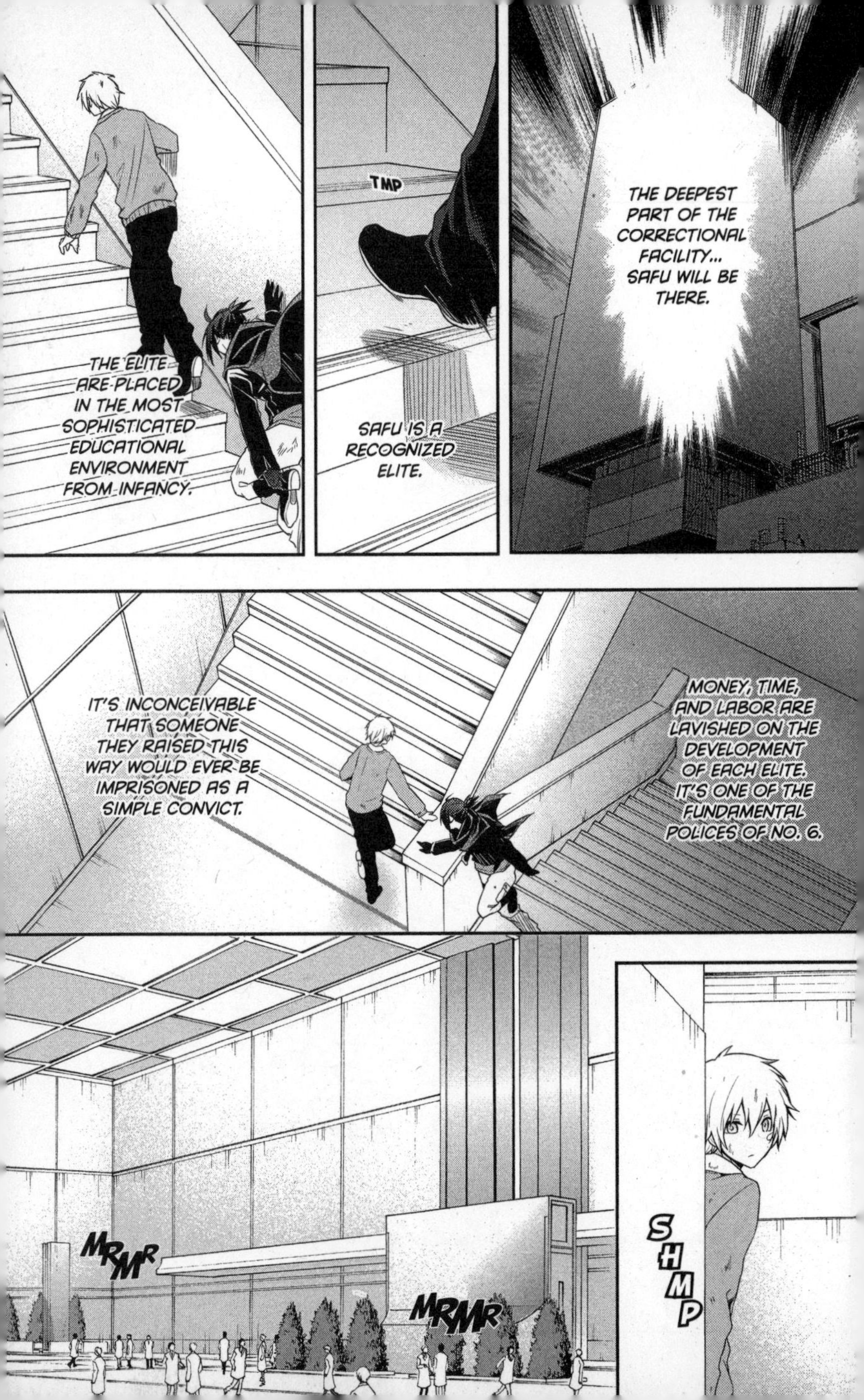
THE DEEPEST PART OF THE CORRECTIONAL FACILITY... SAFU WILL BE THERE.
TMP
SAFU IS A RECOGNIZED ELITE.
THE ELITE ARE PLACED IN THE MOST SOPHISTICATED EDUCATIONAL ENVIRONMENT FROM INFANCY.
MONEY, TIME, AND LABOR ARE LAVISHED ON THE DEVELOPMENT OF EACH ELITE. IT'S ONE OF THE FUNDAMENTAL POLICES OF NO. 6.
IT'S INCONCEIVABLE THAT SOMEONE THEY RAISED THIS WAY WOULD EVER BE IMPRISONED AS A SIMPLE CONVICT.
SHMP
MRMR
MRMR

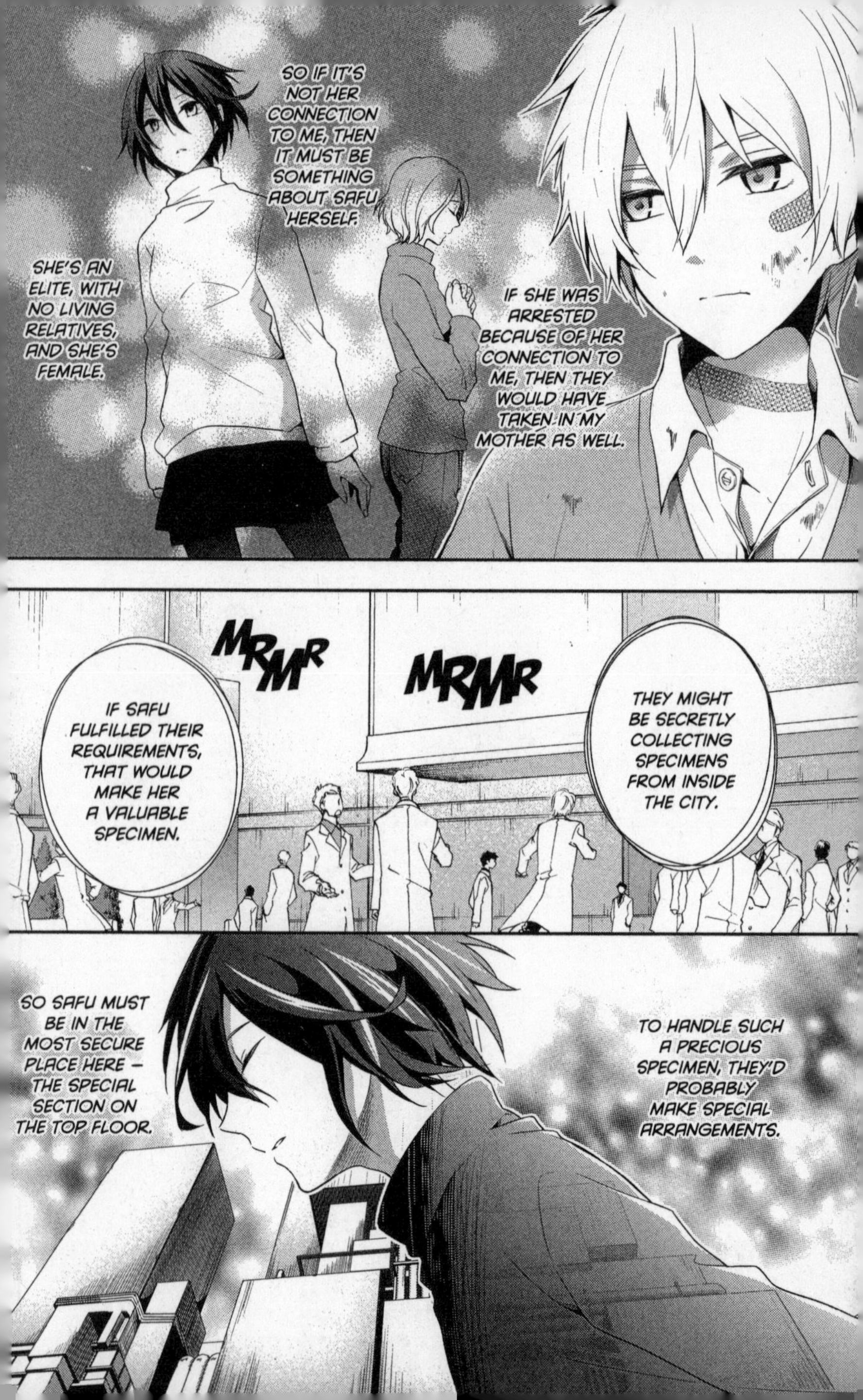
IF SHE WAS ARRESTED BECAUSE OF HER CONNECTION TO ME, THEN THEY WOULD HAVE TAKEN IN MY MOTHER AS WELL.
SO IF IT'S NOT HER CONNECTION TO ME, THEN IT MUST BE SOMETHING ABOUT SAFU HERSELF.
SHE'S AN ELITE, WITH NO LIVING RELATIVES, AND SHE'S FEMALE.
MRMR
MRMR
THEY MIGHT BE SECRETLY COLLECTING SPECIMENS FROM INSIDE THE CITY.
IF SAFU FULFILLED THEIR REQUIREMENTS, THAT WOULD MAKE HER A VALUABLE SPECIMEN.
TO HANDLE SUCH A PRECIOUS SPECIMEN, THEY'D PROBABLY MAKE SPECIAL ARRANGEMENTS.
SO SAFU MUST BE IN THE MOST SECURE PLACE HERE – THE SPECIAL SECTION ON THE TOP FLOOR.

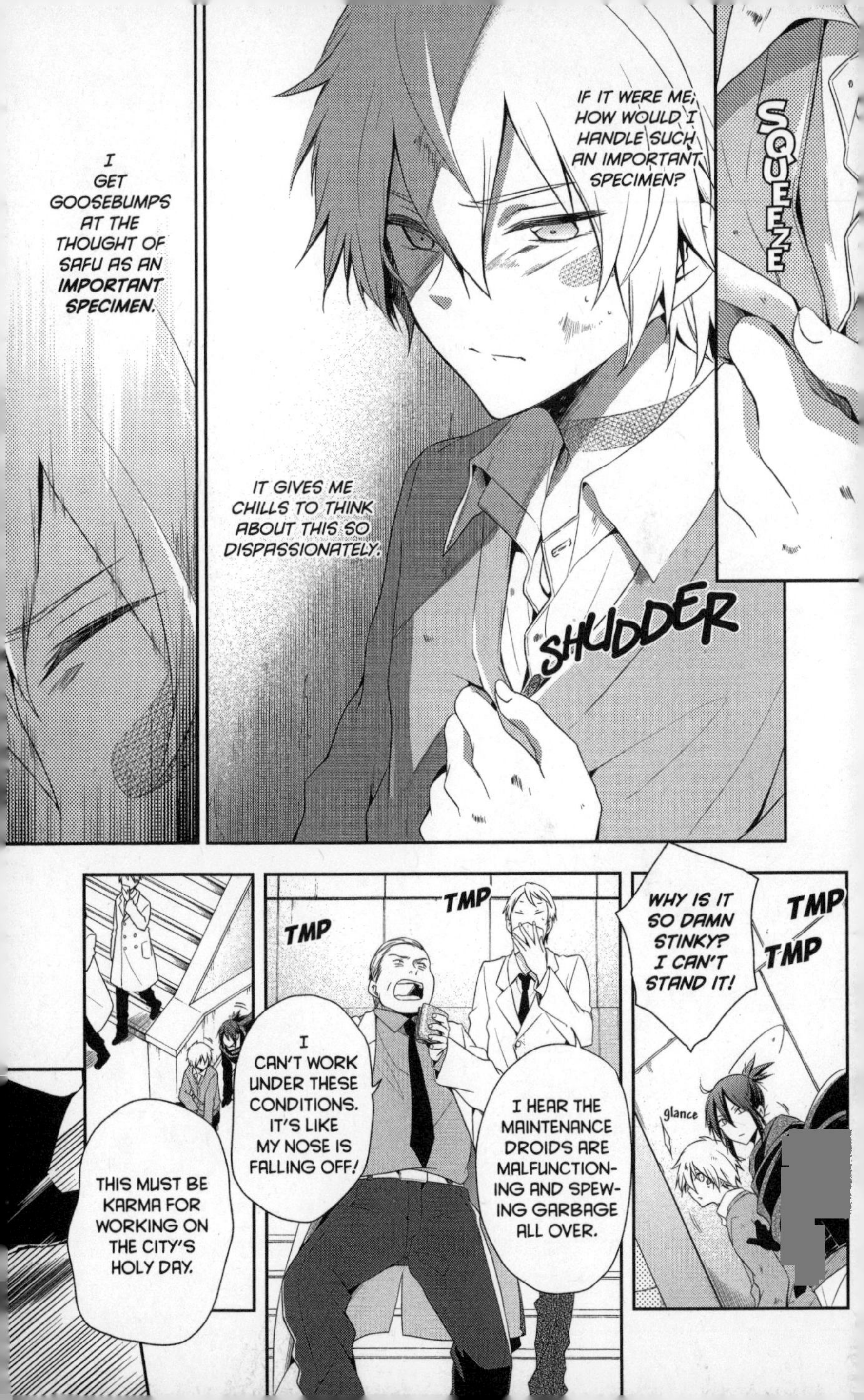
SQUEEZE
IF IT WERE ME, HOW WOULD I HANDLE SUCH AN IMPORTANT SPECIMEN?
IT GIVES ME CHILLS TO THINK ABOUT THIS SO DISPASSIONATELY.
SHUDDER
I GET GOOSEBUMPS AT THE THOUGHT OF SAFU AS AN IMPORTANT SPECIMEN.
WHY IS IT SO DAMN STINKY? I CAN'T STAND IT!
TMP
TMP
glance
TMP
TMP
I CAN'T WORK UNDER THESE CONDITIONS. IT'S LIKE MY NOSE IS FALLING OFF!
I HEAR THE MAINTENANCE DROIDS ARE MALFUNCTIONING AND SPEWING GARBAGE ALL OVER.
THIS MUST BE KARMA FOR WORKING ON THE CITY'S HOLY DAY.

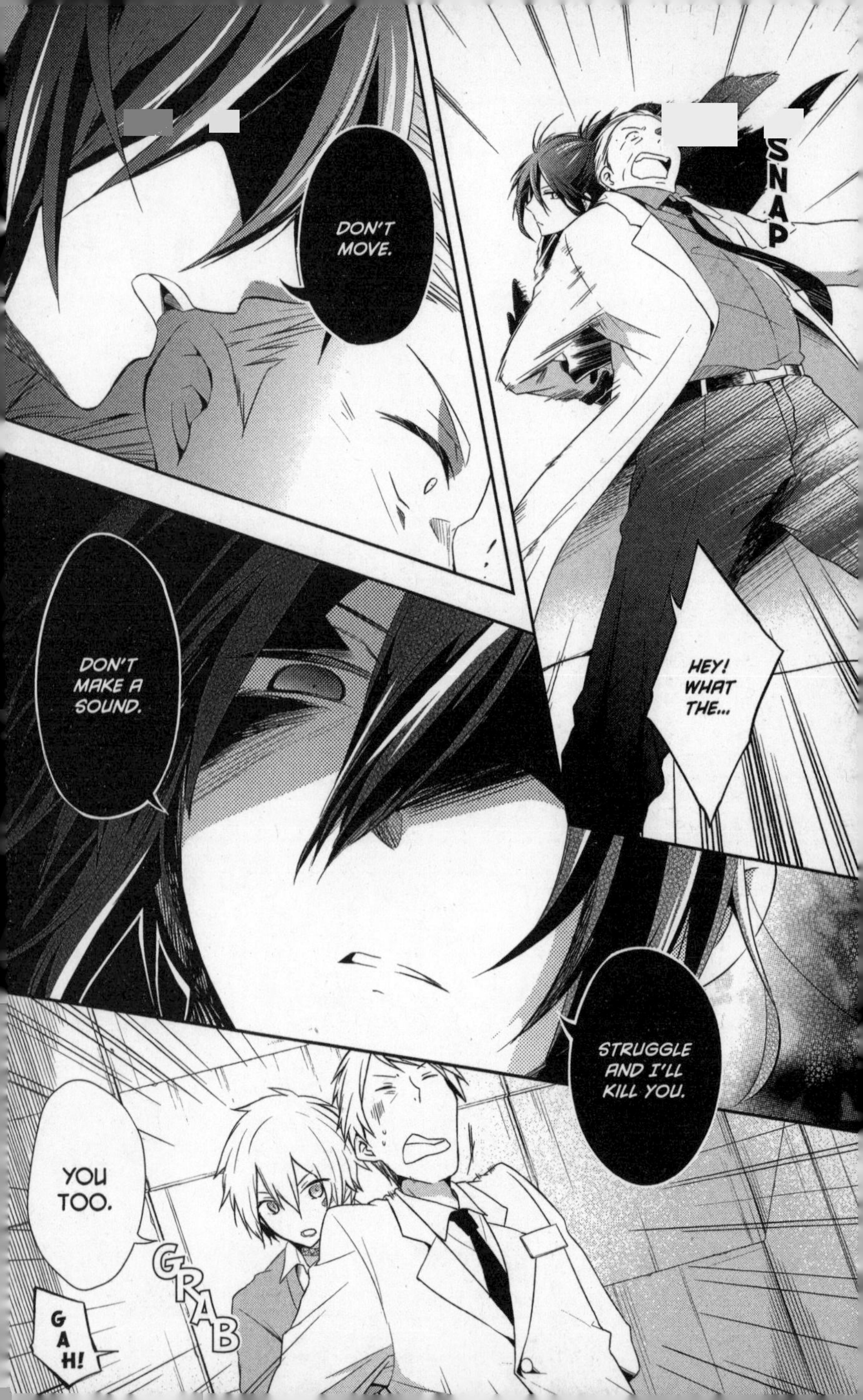
SNAP
HEY! WHAT THE...
DON'T MOVE.
DON'T MAKE A SOUND.
STRUGGLE AND I'LL KILL YOU.
GRAB
GAH!
YOU TOO.

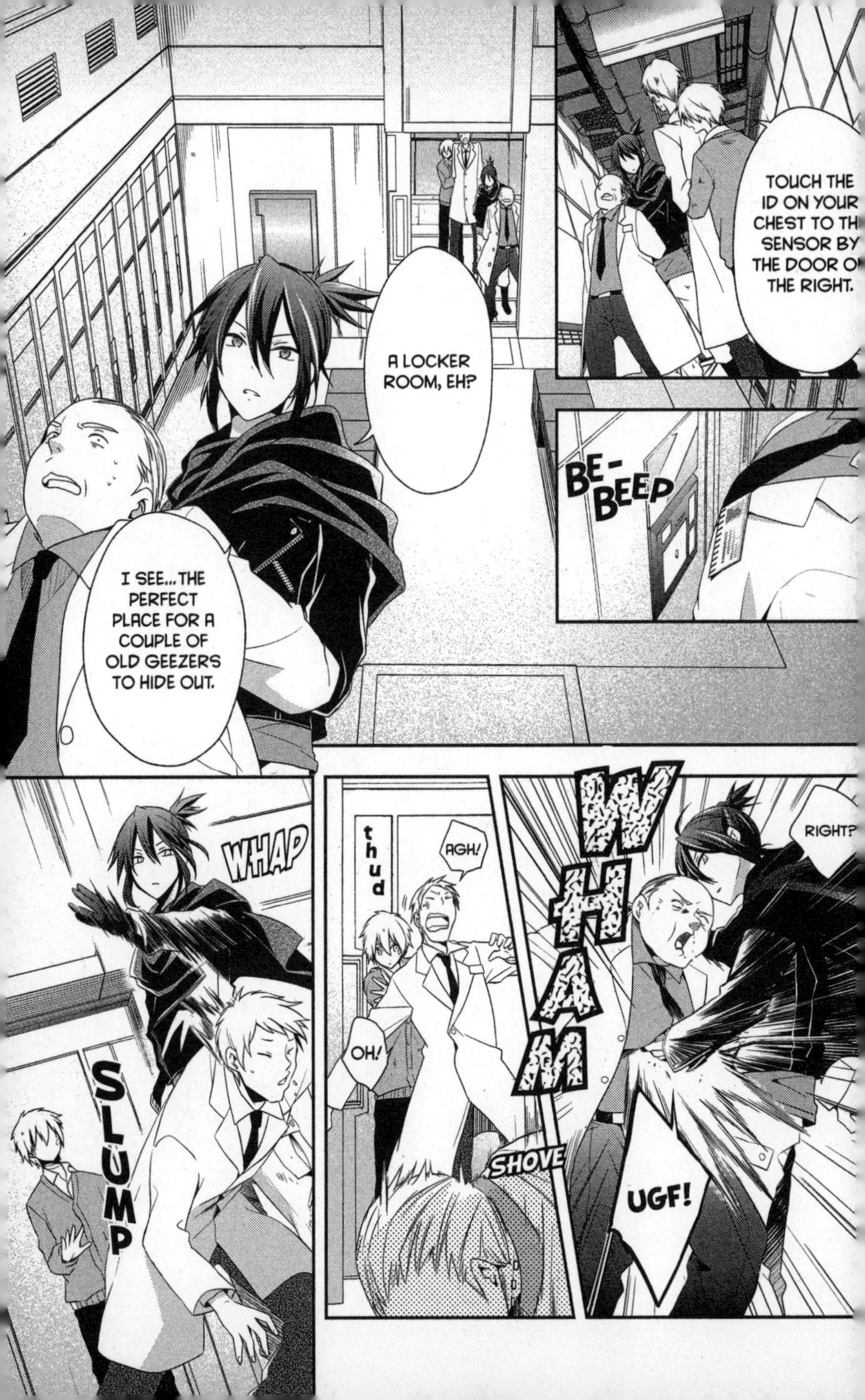
TOUCH THE ID ON YOUR CHEST TO TH SENSOR BY THE DOOR O THE RIGHT.
BE-BEEP
A LOCKER ROOM, EH?
I SEE... THE PERFECT PLACE FOR A COUPLE OF OLD GEEZERS TO HIDE OUT.
RIGHT?
WHAM
UGF!
SHOVE
AGH!
thud
OH!
WHAP
SLUMP

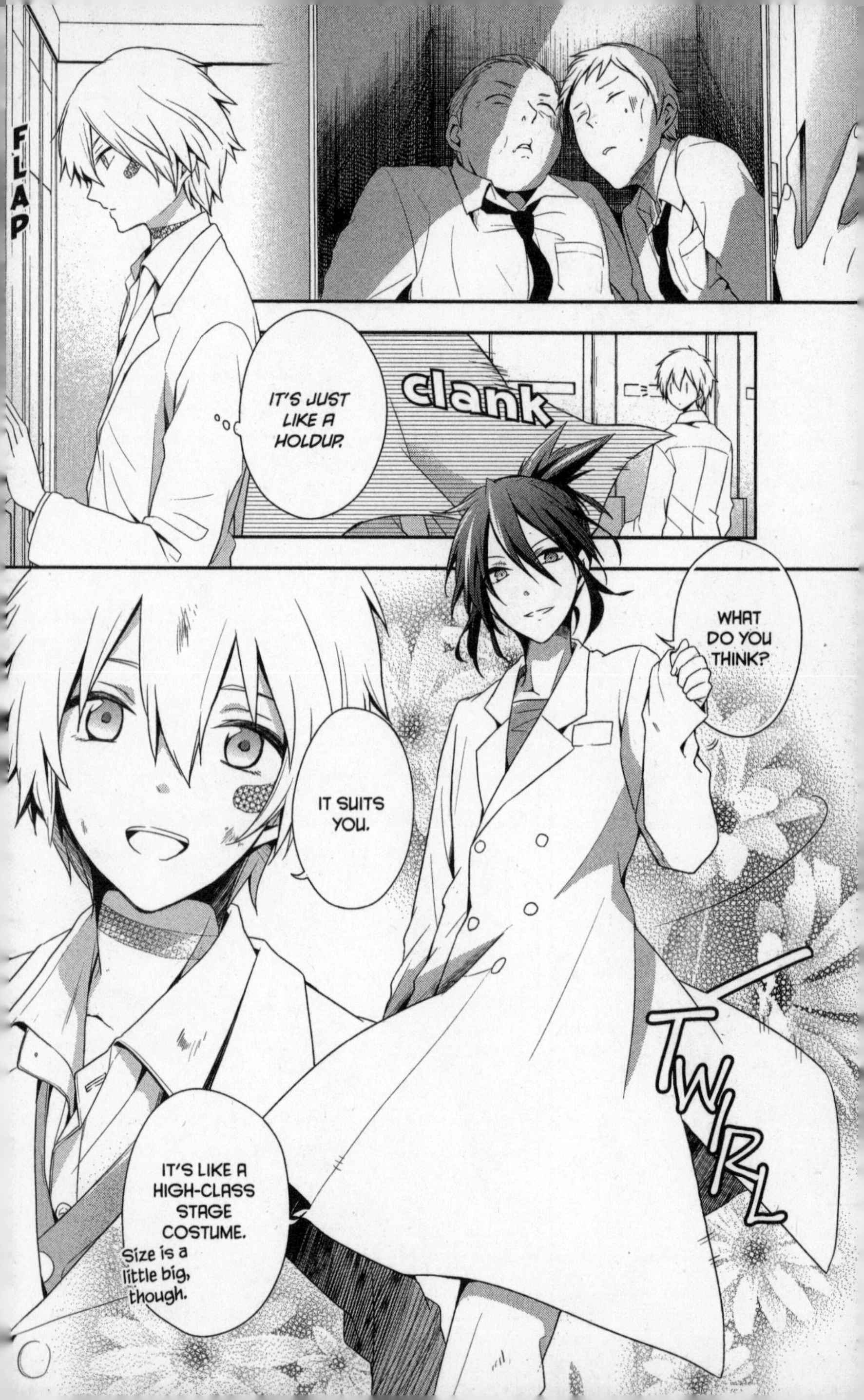
clank
FLAP
IT'S JUST LIKE A HOLDUP.
WHAT DO YOU THINK?
TWIRL
IT SUITS YOU.
IT'S LIKE A HIGH-CLASS STAGE COSTUME.
Size is a little big, though.

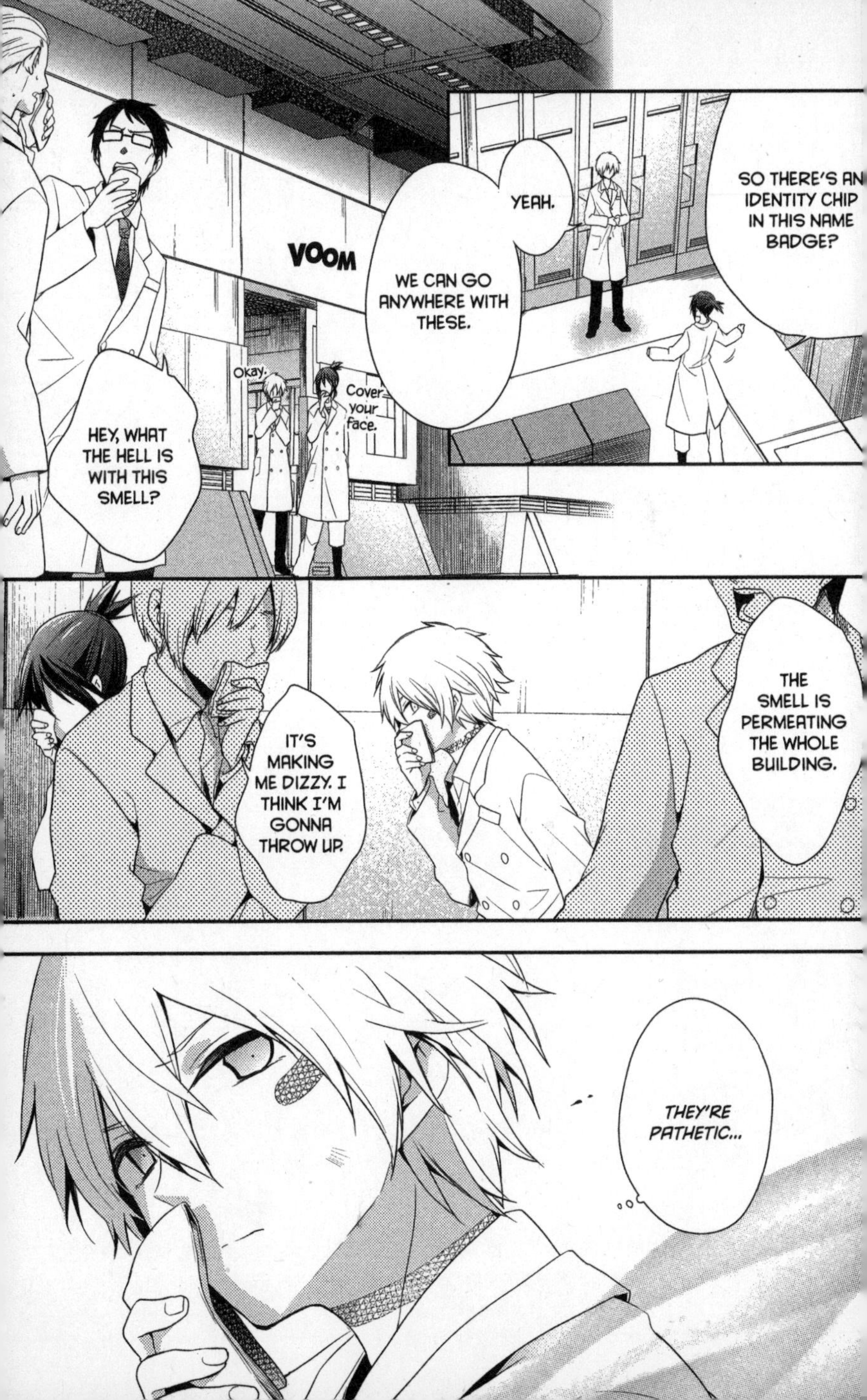
SO THERE'S AN IDENTITY CHIP IN THIS NAME BADGE?
YEAH.
WE CAN GO ANYWHERE WITH THESE.
VOOM
Cover your face.
Okay.
HEY, WHAT THE HELL IS WITH THIS SMELL?
THE SMELL IS PERMEATING THE WHOLE BUILDING.
IT'S MAKING ME DIZZY. I THINK I'M GONNA THROW UP.
THEY'RE PATHETIC...

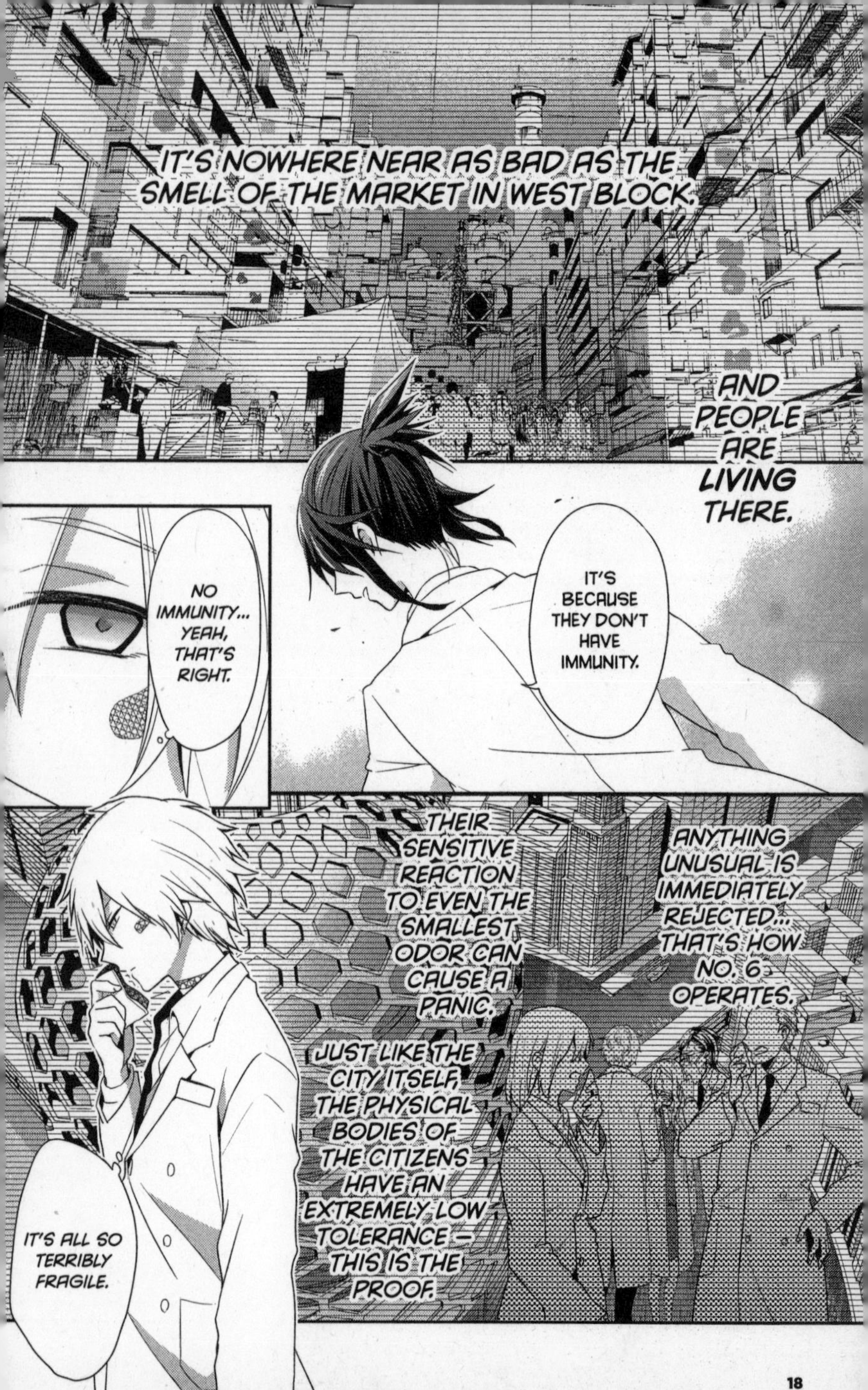
IT'S NOWHERE NEAR AS BAD AS THE SMELL OF THE MARKET IN WEST BLOCK.
AND PEOPLE ARE LIVING THERE.
IT'S BECAUSE THEY DON'T HAVE IMMUNITY.
NO IMMUNITY... YEAH, THAT'S RIGHT.
ANYTHING UNUSUAL IS IMMEDIATELY REJECTED... THAT'S HOW NO. 6 OPERATES.
THEIR SENSITIVE REACTION TO EVEN THE SMALLEST ODOR CAN CAUSE A PANIC.
JUST LIKE THE CITY ITSELF, THE PHYSICAL BODIES OF THE CITIZENS HAVE AN EXTREMELY LOW TOLERANCE – THIS IS THE PROOF.
IT'S ALL SO TERRIBLY FRAGILE.

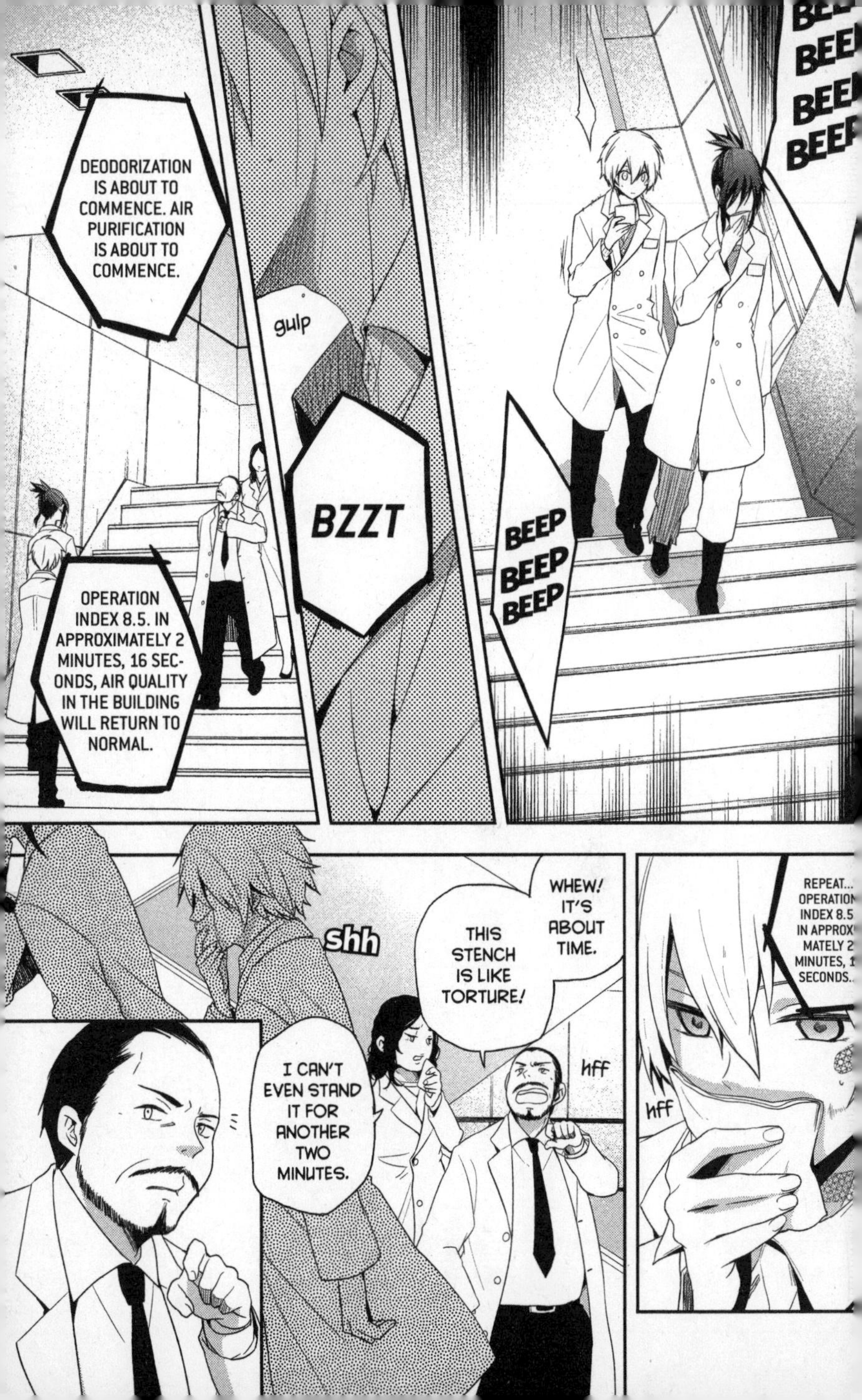
BEEP BEEP BEEP
gulp
BZZT
DEODORIZATION IS ABOUT TO COMMENCE. AIR PURIFICATION IS ABOUT TO COMMENCE.
OPERATION INDEX 8.5. IN APPROXIMATELY 2 MINUTES, 16 SECONDS, AIR QUALITY IN THE BUILDING WILL RETURN TO NORMAL.
REPEAT... OPERATION INDEX 8.5 IN APPROX MATELY 2 MINUTES, 1 SECONDS...
hff
WHEW! IT'S ABOUT TIME.
THIS STENCH IS LIKE TORTURE!
shh
hff
I CAN'T EVEN STAND IT FOR ANOTHER TWO MINUTES.

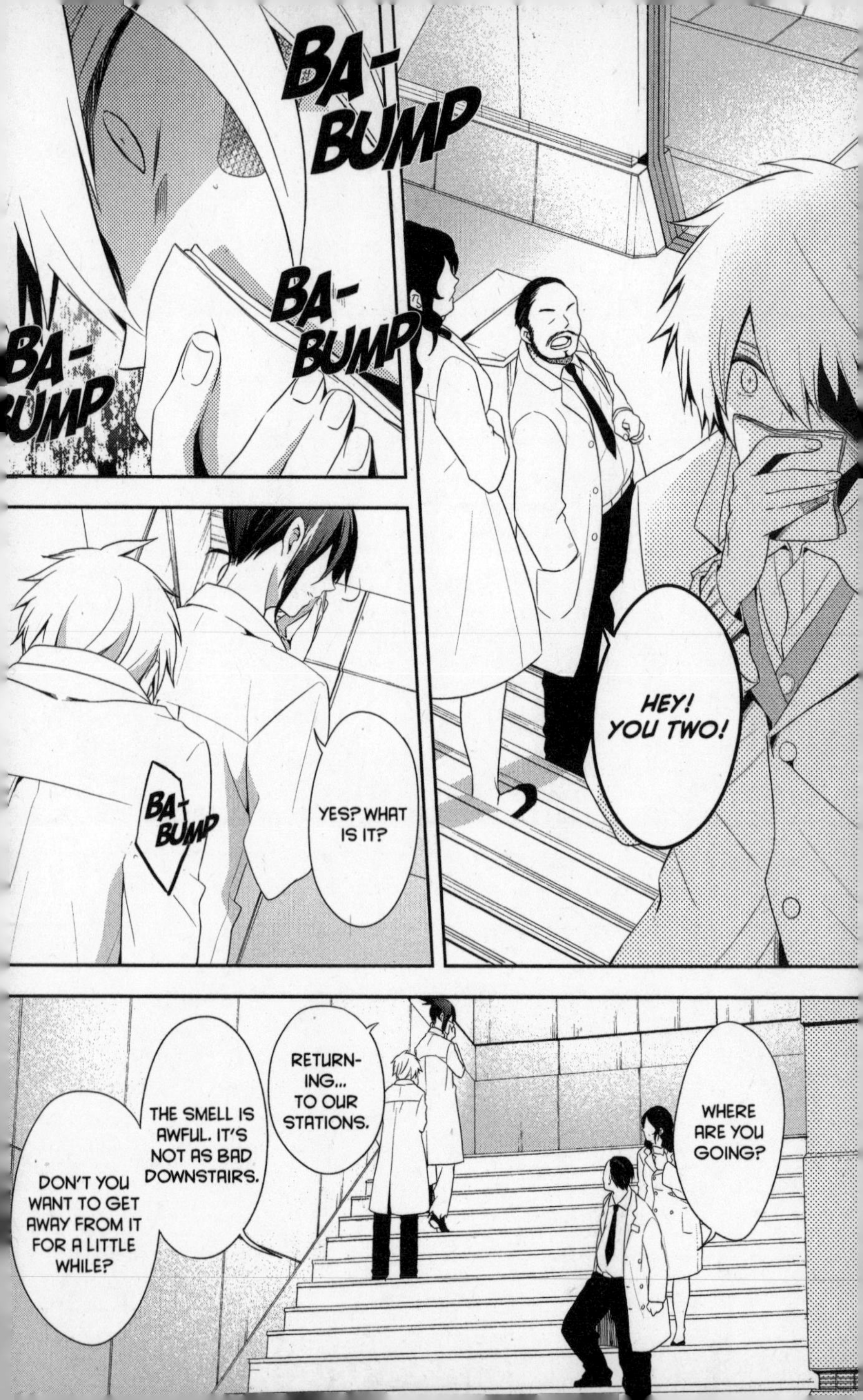
HEY! YOU TWO!
BA-BUMP
BA-BUMP
BA-UMP
BA-BUMP
YES? WHAT IS IT?
WHERE ARE YOU GOING?
RETURNING... TO OUR STATIONS.
THE SMELL IS AWFUL. IT'S NOT AS BAD DOWNSTAIRS.
DON'T YOU WANT TO GET AWAY FROM IT FOR A LITTLE WHILE?

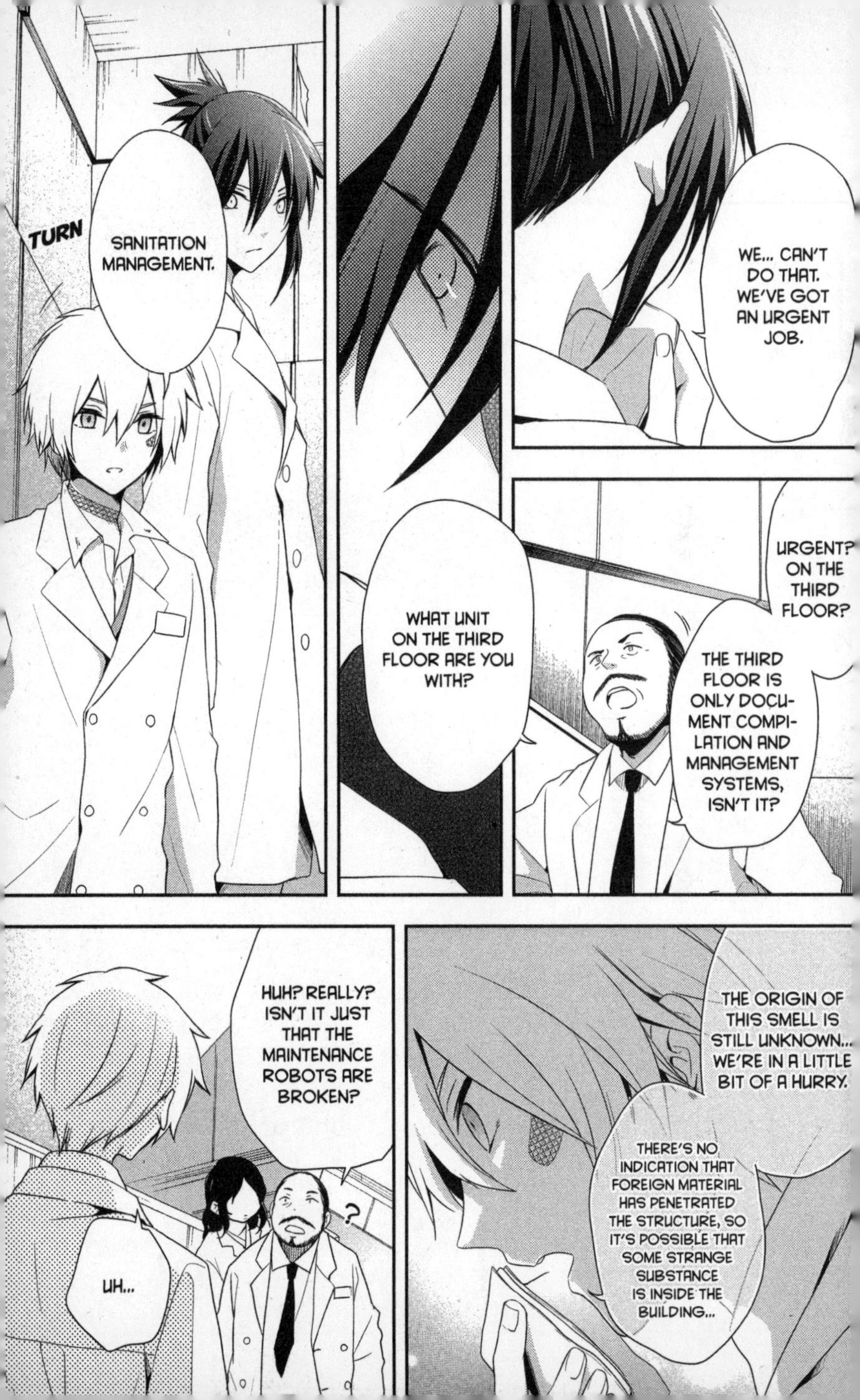
WE... CAN'T DO THAT. WE'VE GOT AN URGENT JOB.
URGENT? ON THE THIRD FLOOR?
THE THIRD FLOOR IS ONLY DOCU-MENT COMPI-LATION AND MANAGEMENT SYSTEMS, ISN'T IT?
WHAT UNIT ON THE THIRD FLOOR ARE YOU WITH?
TURN
SANITATION MANAGEMENT.
THE ORIGIN OF THIS SMELL IS STILL UNKNOWN... WE'RE IN A LITTLE BIT OF A HURRY.
THERE'S NO INDICATION THAT FOREIGN MATERIAL HAS PENETRATED THE STRUCTURE, SO IT'S POSSIBLE THAT SOME STRANGE SUBSTANCE IS INSIDE THE BUILDING...
HUH? REALLY? ISN'T IT JUST THAT THE MAINTENANCE ROBOTS ARE BROKEN?
?
UH...

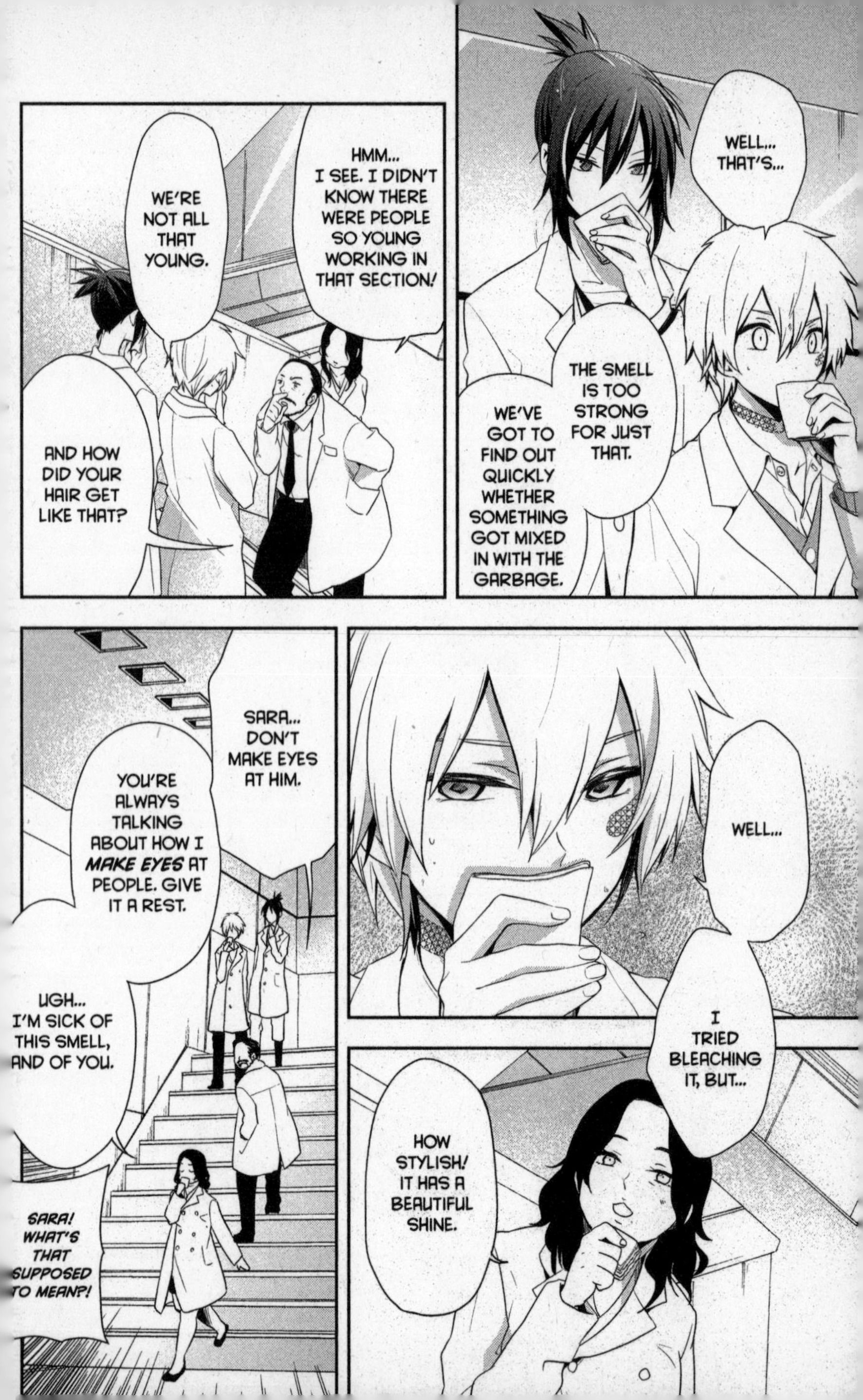
WELL... THAT'S...
THE SMELL IS TOO STRONG FOR JUST THAT.
WE'VE GOT TO FIND OUT QUICKLY WHETHER SOMETHING GOT MIXED IN WITH THE GARBAGE.
HMM... I SEE. I DIDN'T KNOW THERE WERE PEOPLE SO YOUNG WORKING IN THAT SECTION!
WE'RE NOT ALL THAT YOUNG.
AND HOW DID YOUR HAIR GET LIKE THAT?
WELL...
I TRIED BLEACHING IT, BUT...
HOW STYLISH! IT HAS A BEAUTIFUL SHINE.
SARA... DON'T MAKE EYES AT HIM.
YOU'RE ALWAYS TALKING ABOUT HOW I *MAKE EYES* AT PEOPLE. GIVE IT A REST.
UGH... I'M SICK OF THIS SMELL, AND OF YOU.
SARA! WHAT'S THAT SUPPOSED TO MEAN?!

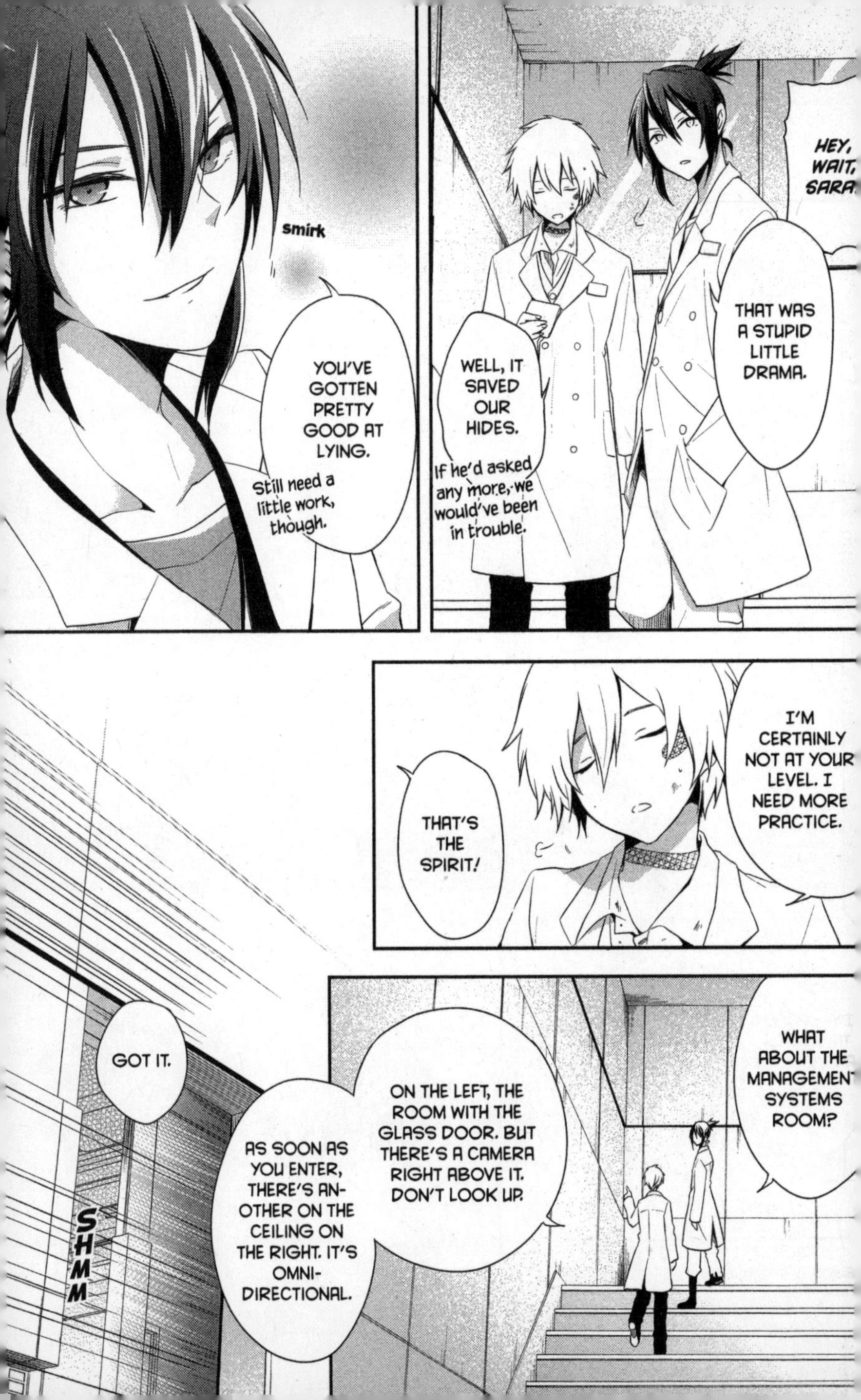
HEY, WAIT, SARA
THAT WAS A STUPID LITTLE DRAMA.
WELL, IT SAVED OUR HIDES.
If he'd asked any more, we would've been in trouble.
smirk
YOU'VE GOTTEN PRETTY GOOD AT LYING.
Still need a little work, though.
I'M CERTAINLY NOT AT YOUR LEVEL. I NEED MORE PRACTICE.
THAT'S THE SPIRIT!
WHAT ABOUT THE MANAGEMENT SYSTEMS ROOM?
ON THE LEFT, THE ROOM WITH THE GLASS DOOR. BUT THERE'S A CAMERA RIGHT ABOVE IT. DON'T LOOK UP.
AS SOON AS YOU ENTER, THERE'S AN-OTHER ON THE CEILING ON THE RIGHT. IT'S OMNI-DIRECTIONAL.
GOT IT.
SHMM

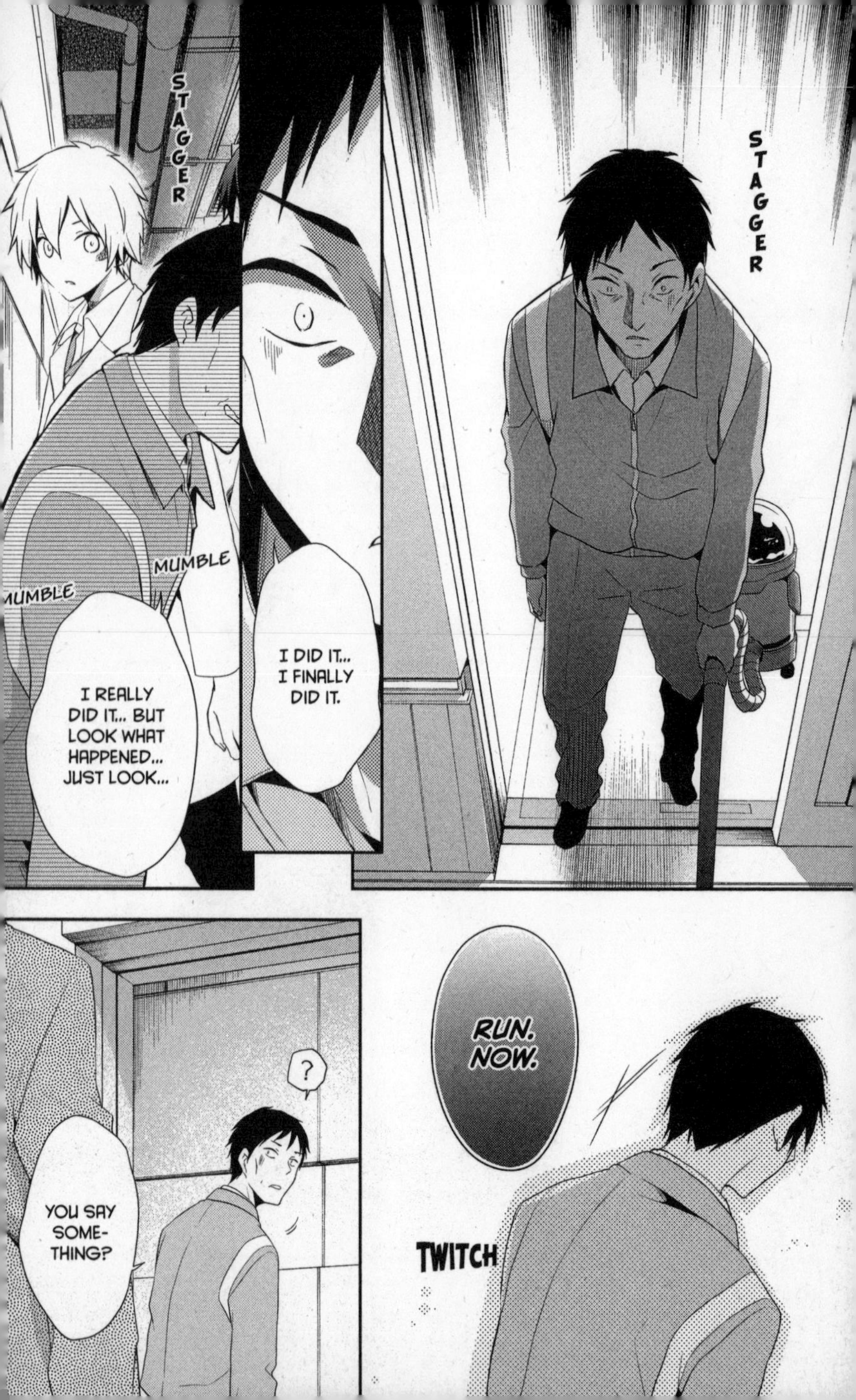
STAGGER
I DID IT... I FINALLY DID IT.
STAGGER
MUMBLE
MUMBLE
I REALLY DID IT... BUT LOOK WHAT HAPPENED... JUST LOOK...
RUN. NOW.
TWITCH
?
YOU SAY SOME-THING?

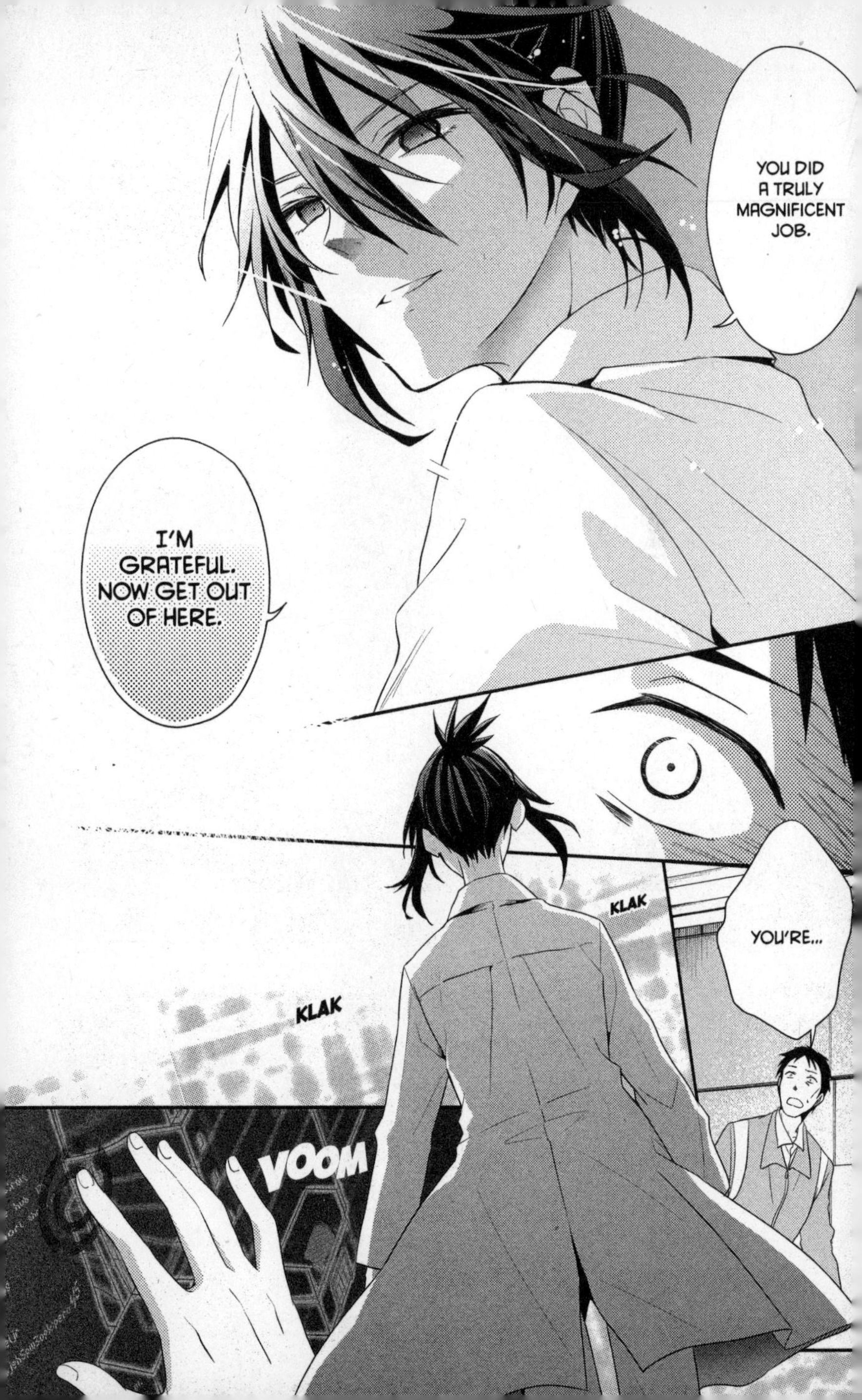
YOU DID A TRULY MAGNIFICENT JOB.
I'M GRATEFUL. NOW GET OUT OF HERE.
YOU'RE...
KLAK
KLAK
VOOM

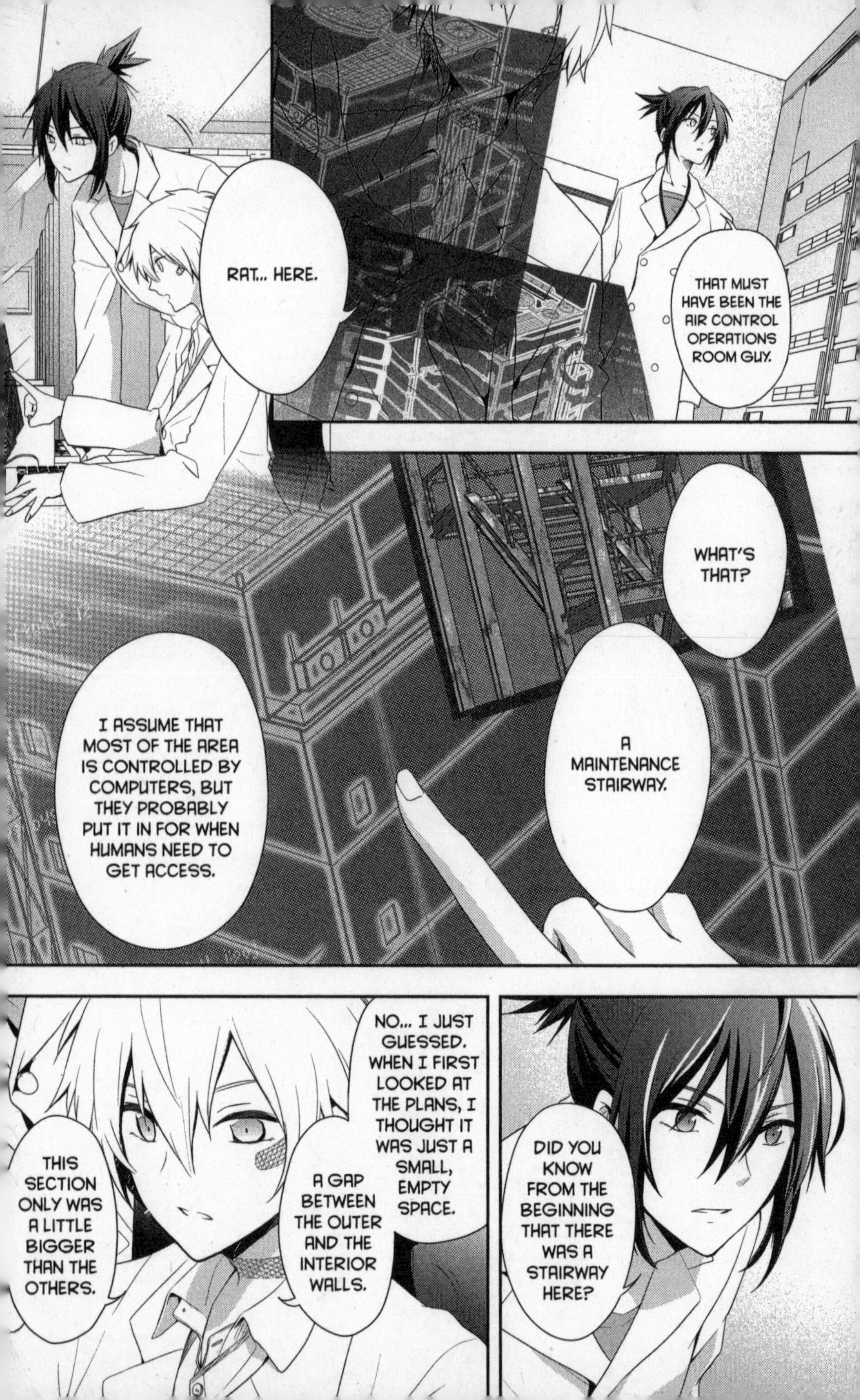
THAT MUST HAVE BEEN THE AIR CONTROL OPERATIONS ROOM GUY.
RAT... HERE.
WHAT'S THAT?
A MAINTENANCE STAIRWAY.
I ASSUME THAT MOST OF THE AREA IS CONTROLLED BY COMPUTERS, BUT THEY PROBABLY PUT IT IN FOR WHEN HUMANS NEED TO GET ACCESS.
DID YOU KNOW FROM THE BEGINNING THAT THERE WAS A STAIRWAY HERE?
NO... I JUST GUESSED. WHEN I FIRST LOOKED AT THE PLANS, I THOUGHT IT WAS JUST A SMALL, EMPTY SPACE.
A GAP BETWEEN THE OUTER AND THE INTERIOR WALLS.
THIS SECTION ONLY WAS A LITTLE BIGGER THAN THE OTHERS.

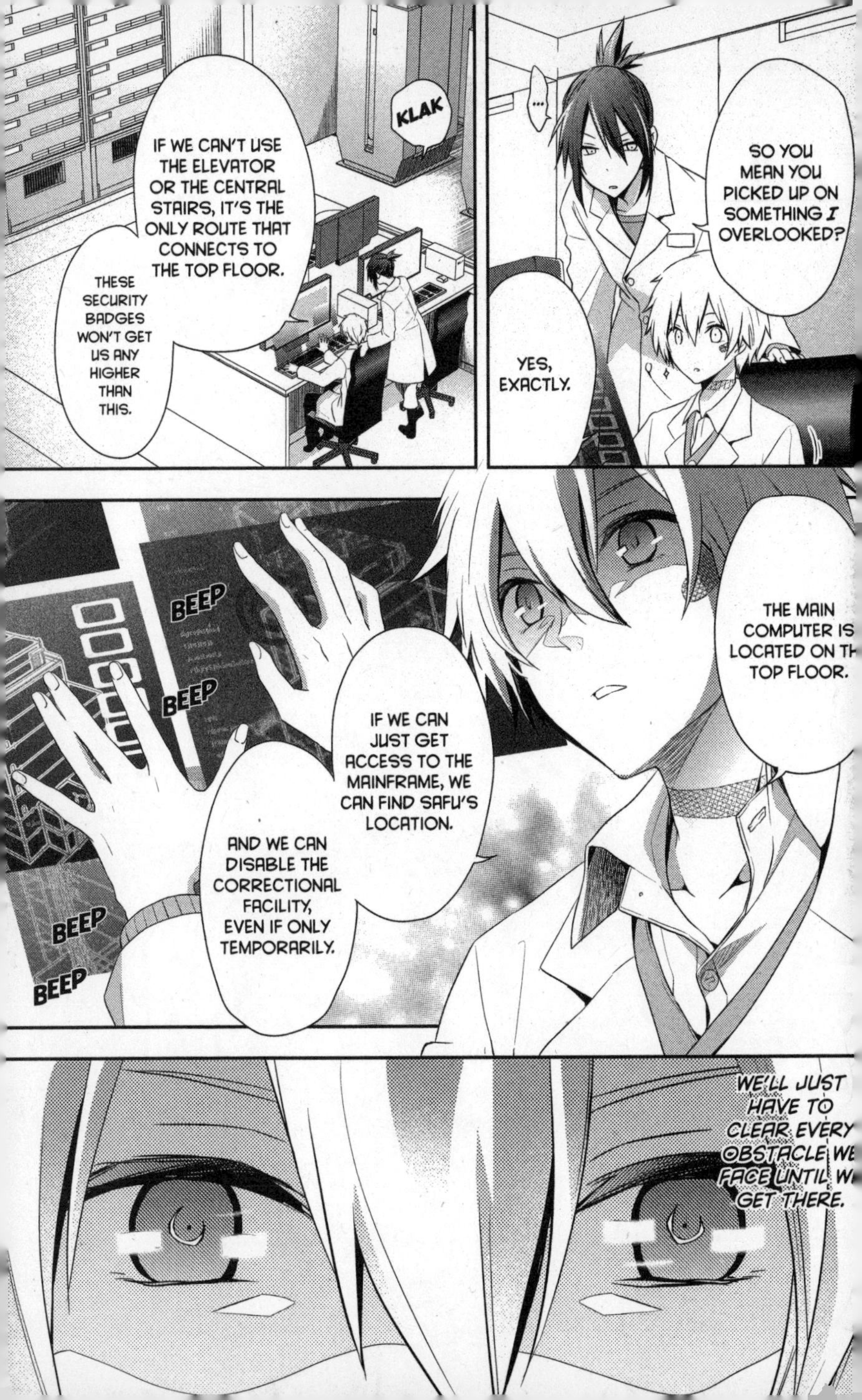

SO YOU MEAN YOU PICKED UP ON SOMETHING *I* OVERLOOKED?
...
YES, EXACTLY.
KLAK
IF WE CAN'T USE THE ELEVATOR OR THE CENTRAL STAIRS, IT'S THE ONLY ROUTE THAT CONNECTS TO THE TOP FLOOR.
THESE SECURITY BADGES WON'T GET US ANY HIGHER THAN THIS.
THE MAIN COMPUTER IS LOCATED ON TH TOP FLOOR.
IF WE CAN JUST GET ACCESS TO THE MAINFRAME, WE CAN FIND SAFU'S LOCATION.
BEEP
BEEP
AND WE CAN DISABLE THE CORRECTIONAL FACILITY, EVEN IF ONLY TEMPORARILY.
BEEP
BEEP
WE'LL JUST HAVE TO CLEAR EVERY OBSTACLE WE FACE UNTIL W GET THERE.

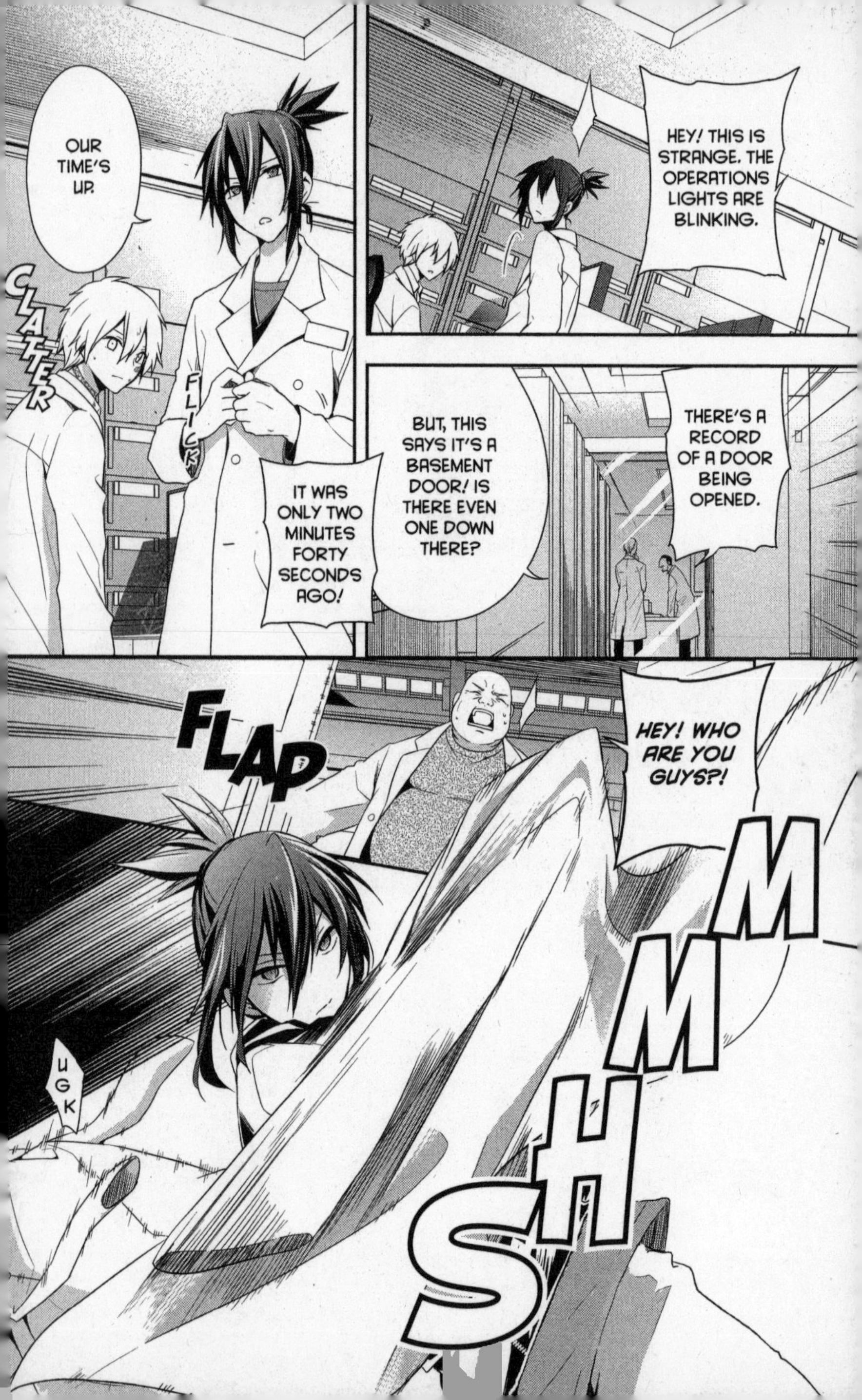
HEY! THIS IS STRANGE. THE OPERATIONS LIGHTS ARE BLINKING.
THERE'S A RECORD OF A DOOR BEING OPENED.
BUT, THIS SAYS IT'S A BASEMENT DOOR! IS THERE EVEN ONE DOWN THERE?
OUR TIME'S UP.
CLATTER
FLICK
IT WAS ONLY TWO MINUTES FORTY SECONDS AGO!
HEY! WHO ARE YOU GUYS?!
FLAP
SHHMMM
UGK

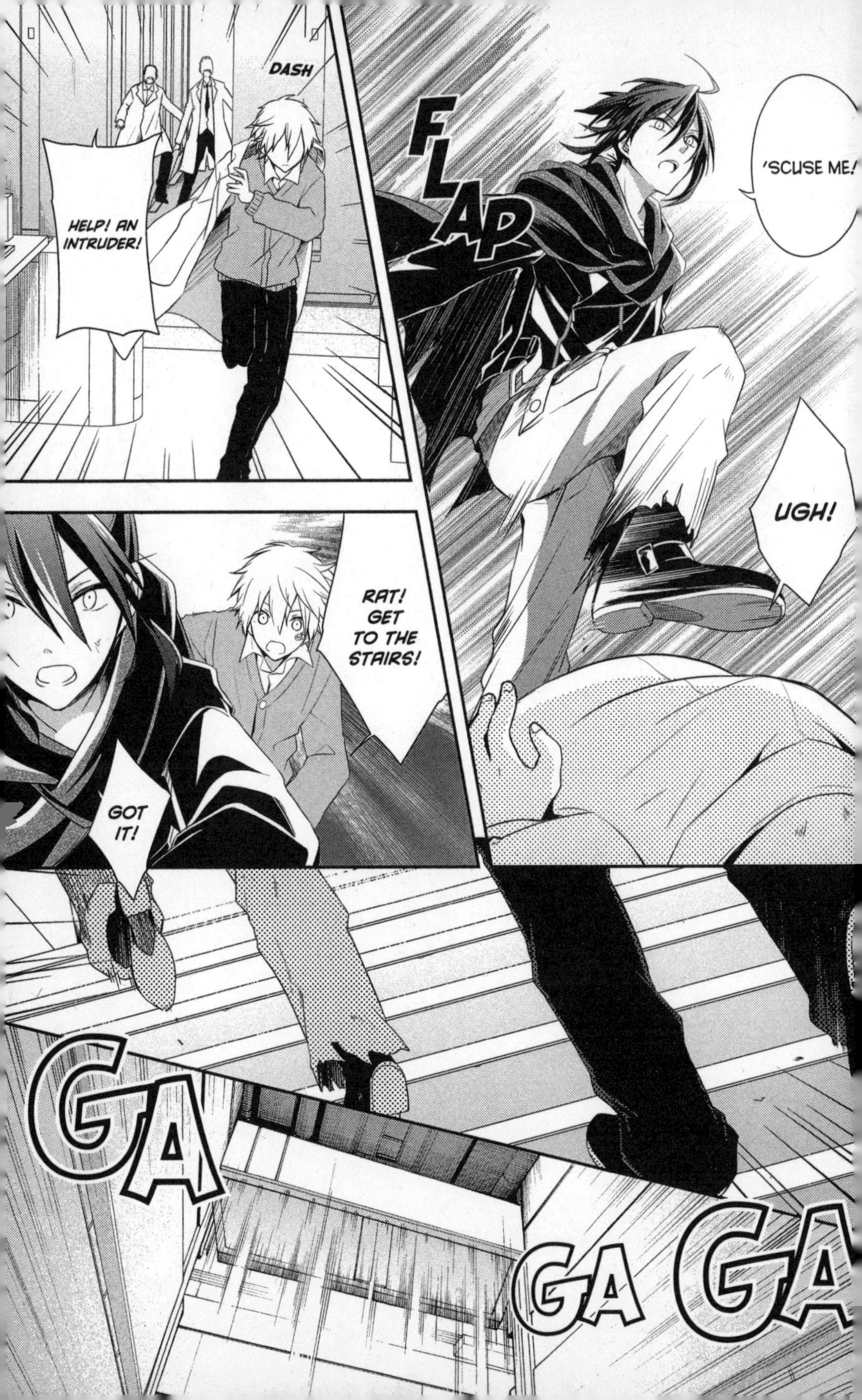
FLAP
'SCUSE ME!
UGH!
DASH
HELP! AN INTRUDER!
RAT! GET TO THE STAIRS!
GOT IT!
GA GA
GA

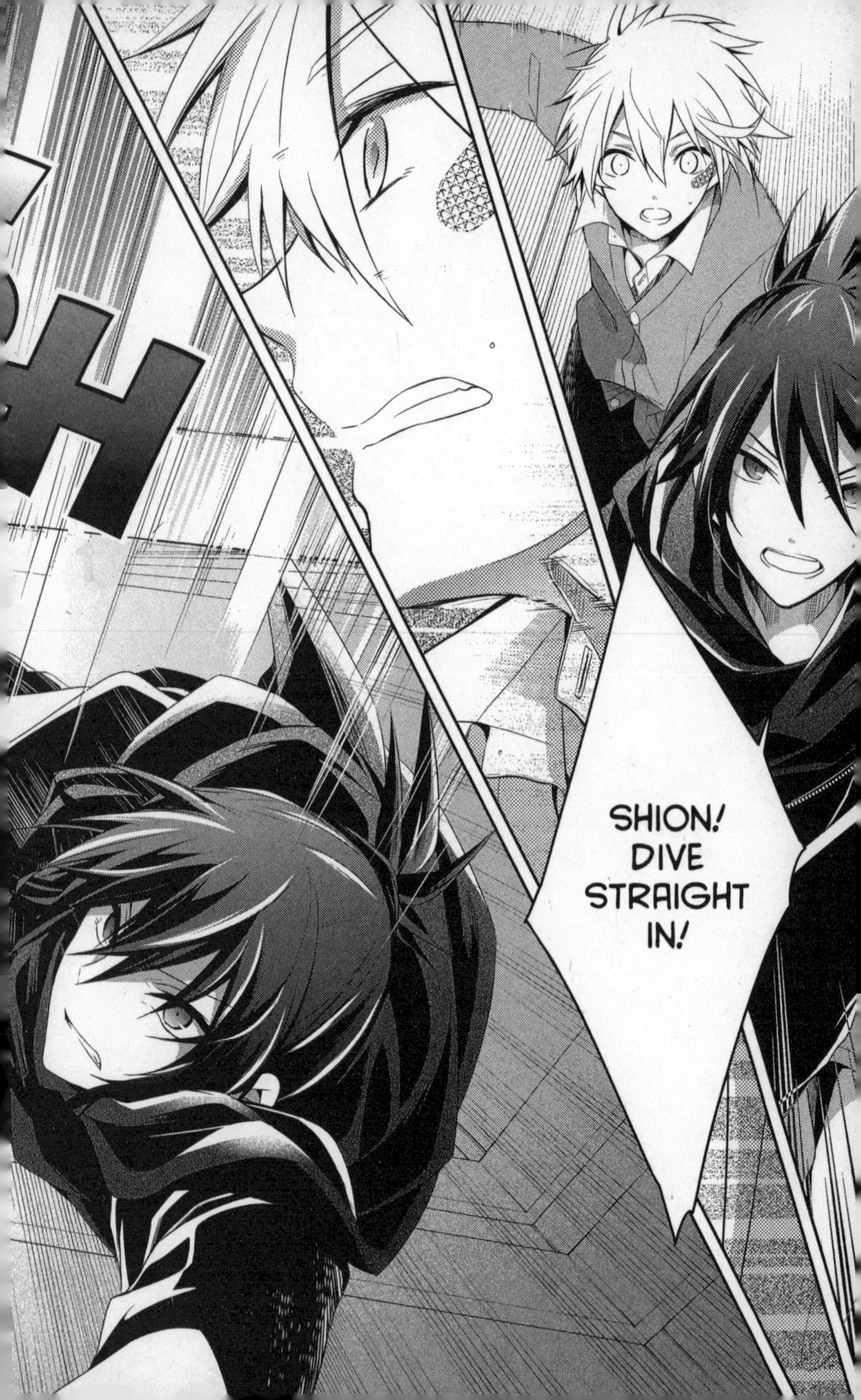
SHION! DIVE STRAIGHT IN!

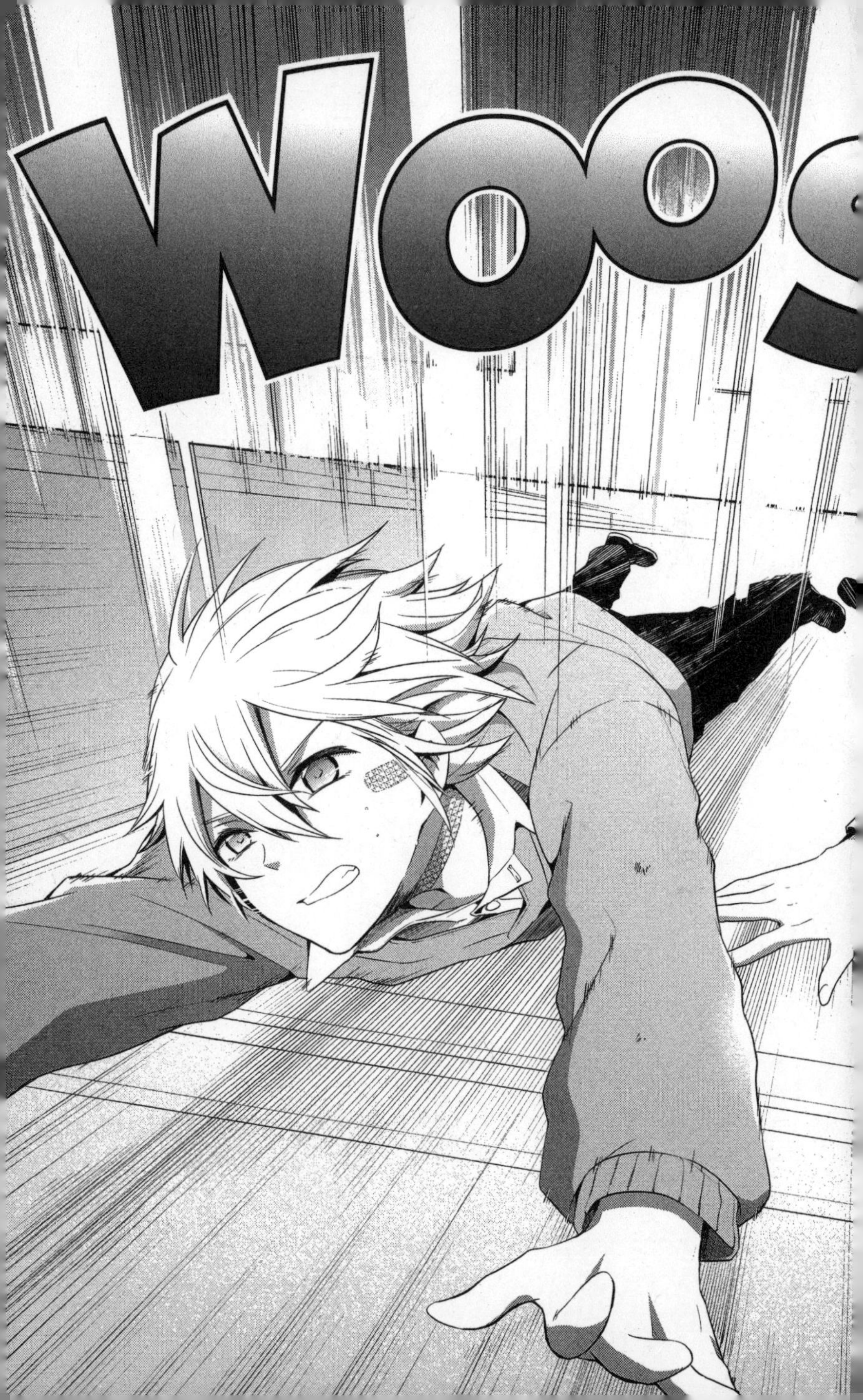
WOO

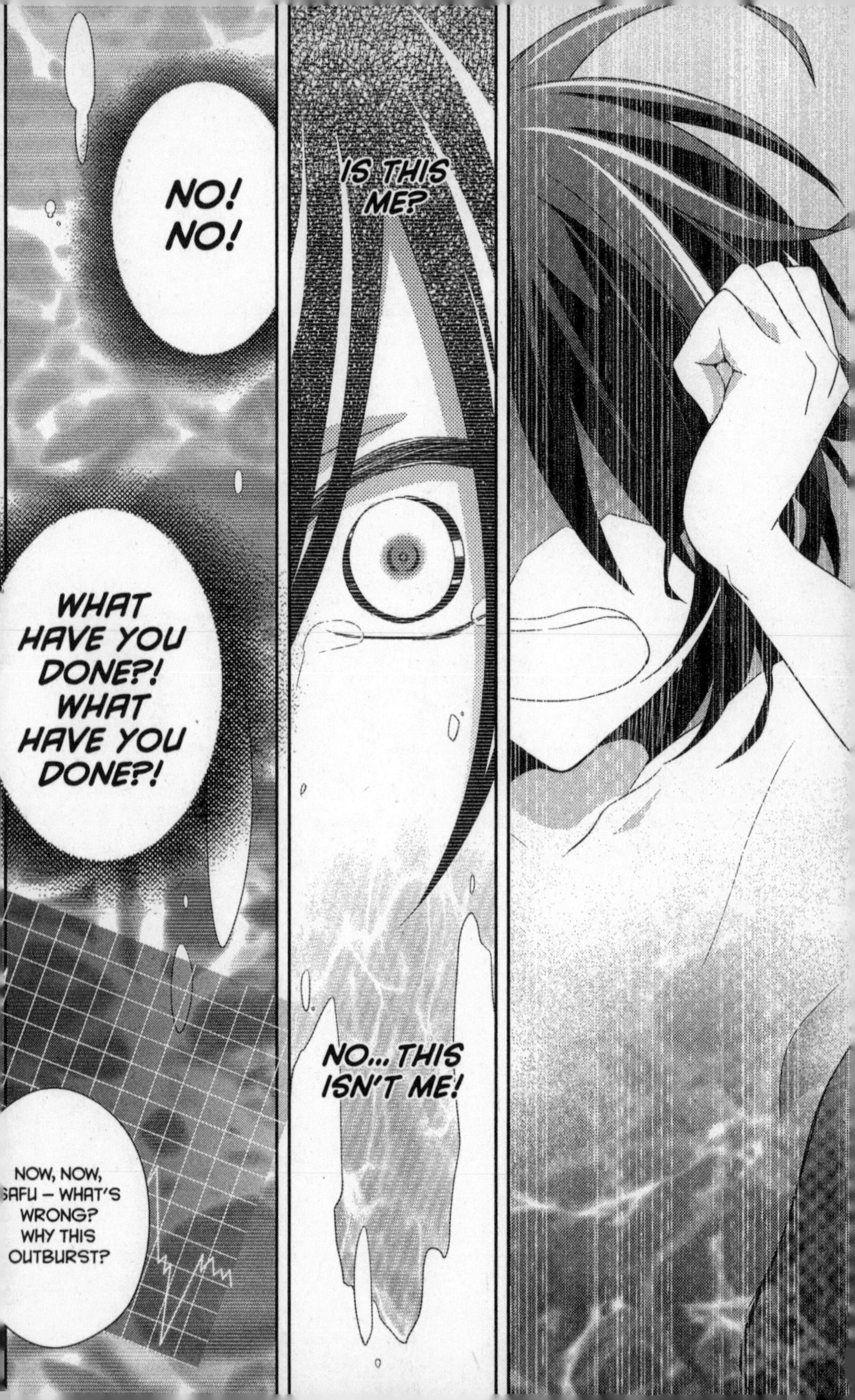
IS THIS ME?
NO... THIS ISN'T ME!
NO! NO!
WHAT HAVE YOU DONE?! WHAT HAVE YOU DONE?!
NOW, NOW, SAFU – WHAT'S WRONG? WHY THIS OUTBURST?

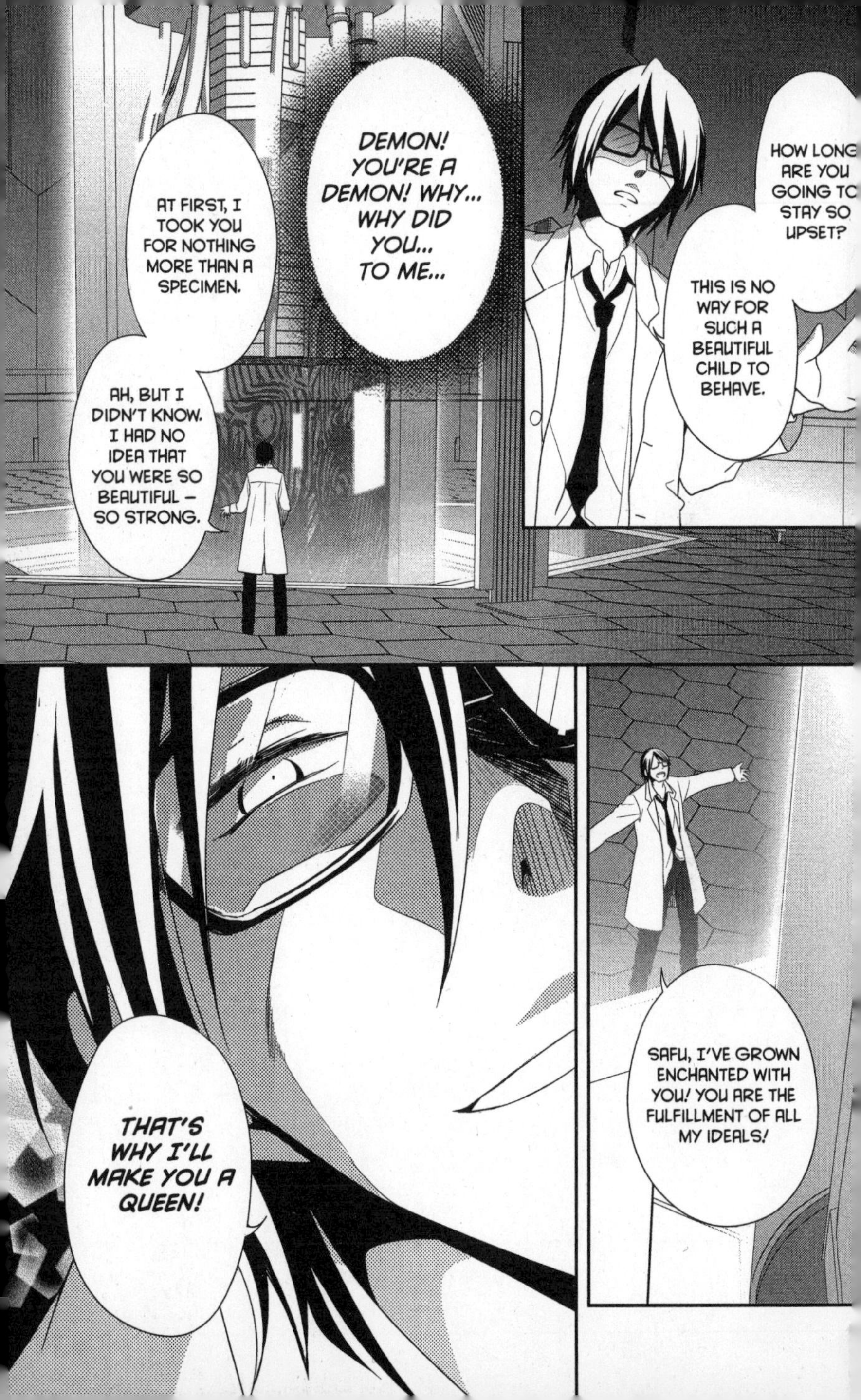
HOW LONG ARE YOU GOING TO STAY SO UPSET?
THIS IS NO WAY FOR SUCH A BEAUTIFUL CHILD TO BEHAVE.
DEMON! YOU'RE A DEMON! WHY... WHY DID YOU... TO ME...
AT FIRST, I TOOK YOU FOR NOTHING MORE THAN A SPECIMEN.
AH, BUT I DIDN'T KNOW. I HAD NO IDEA THAT YOU WERE SO BEAUTIFUL — SO STRONG.
SAFU, I'VE GROWN ENCHANTED WITH YOU! YOU ARE THE FULFILLMENT OF ALL MY IDEALS!
THAT'S WHY I'LL MAKE YOU A QUEEN!

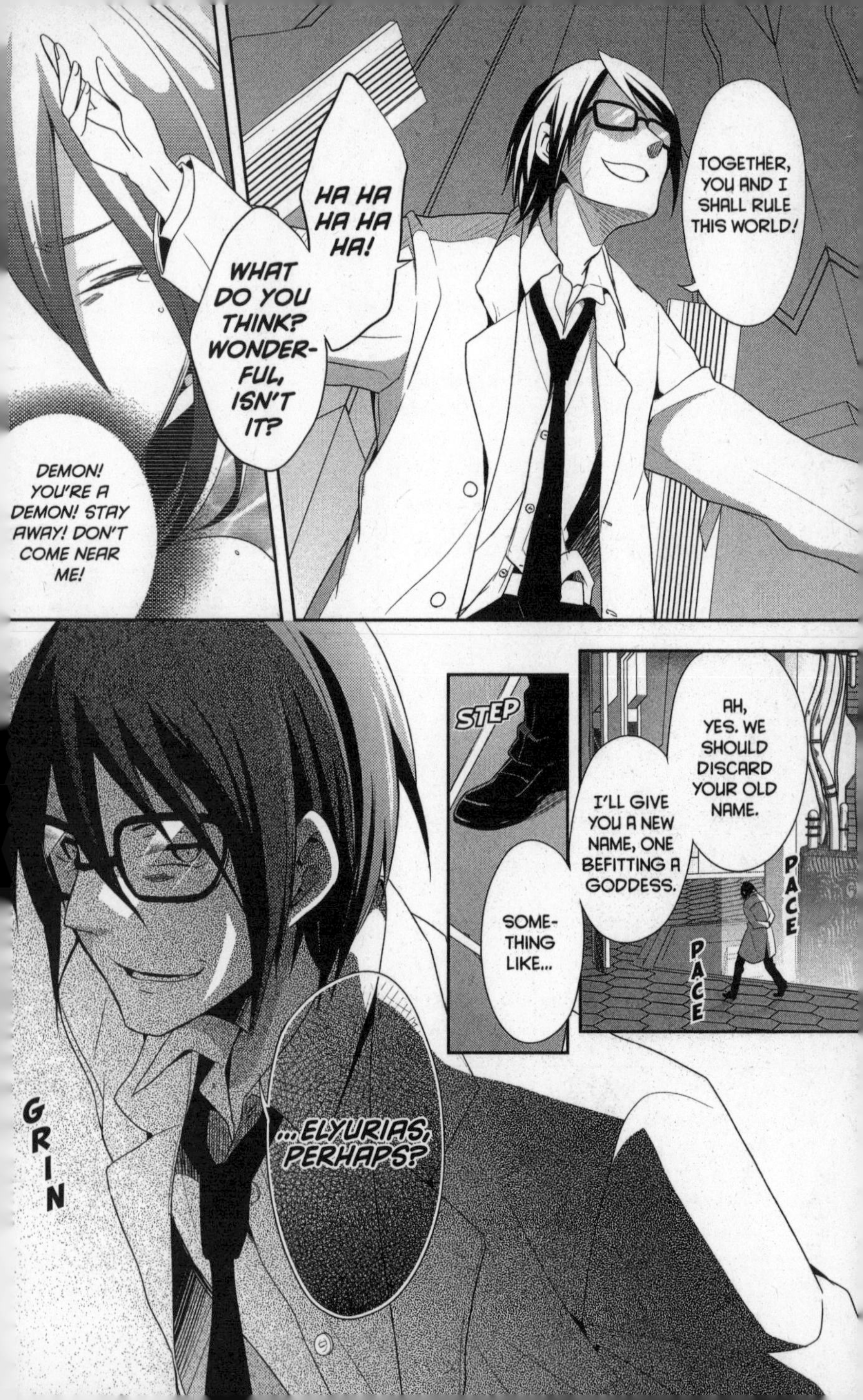
TOGETHER, YOU AND I SHALL RULE THIS WORLD!
HA HA HA HA HA!
WHAT DO YOU THINK? WONDERFUL, ISN'T IT?
DEMON! YOU'RE A DEMON! STAY AWAY! DON'T COME NEAR ME!
AH, YES. WE SHOULD DISCARD YOUR OLD NAME.
I'LL GIVE YOU A NEW NAME, ONE BEFITTING A GODDESS.
SOME-THING LIKE...
PACE
PACE
STEP
...ELYURIAS, PERHAPS?
GRIN

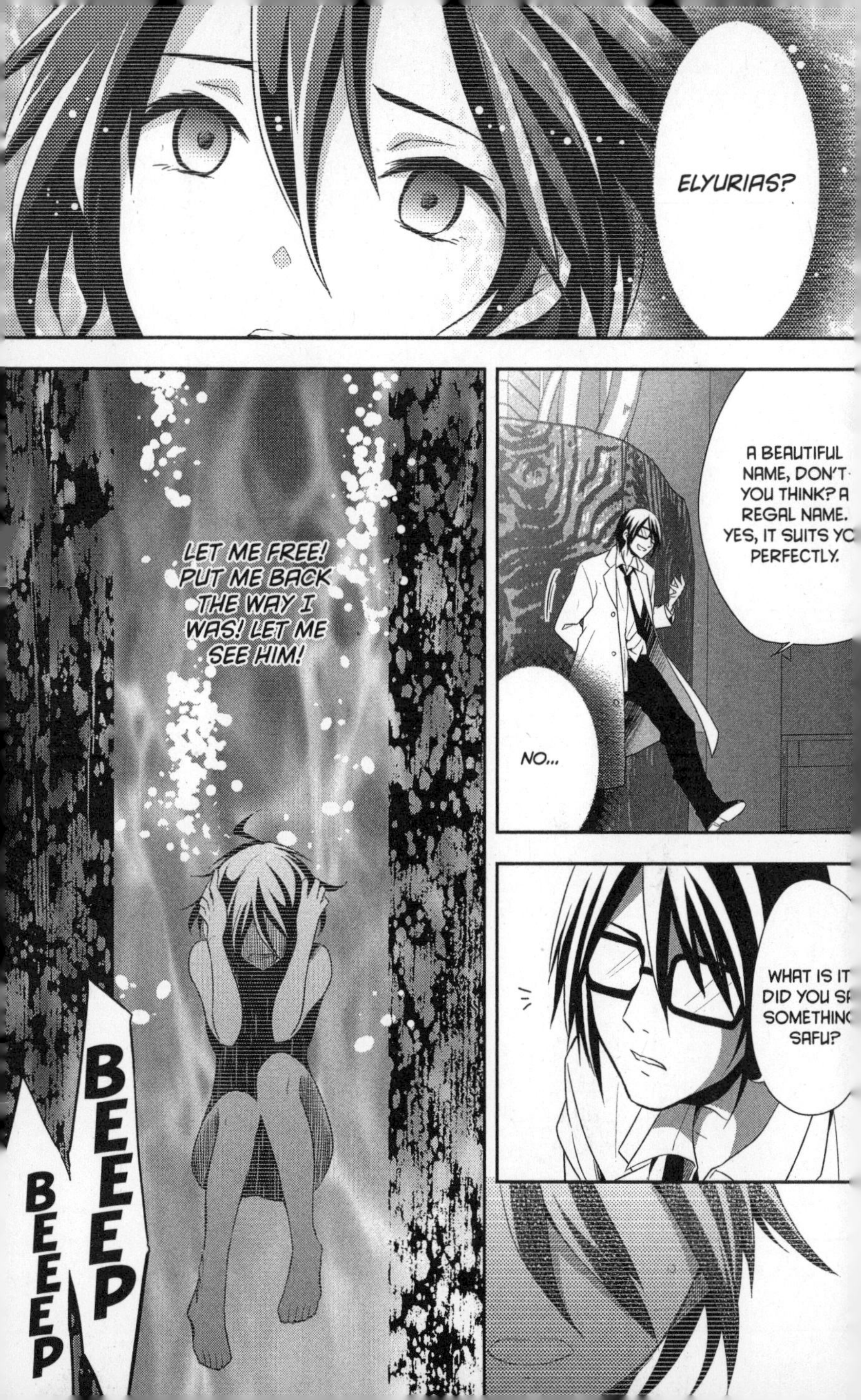
ELYURIAS?
A BEAUTIFUL NAME, DON'T YOU THINK? A REGAL NAME. YES, IT SUITS Y PERFECTLY.
NO...
WHAT IS IT DID YOU S SOMETHIN SAFU?
LET ME FREE! PUT ME BACK THE WAY I WAS! LET ME SEE HIM!
BEEEP
BEEEP

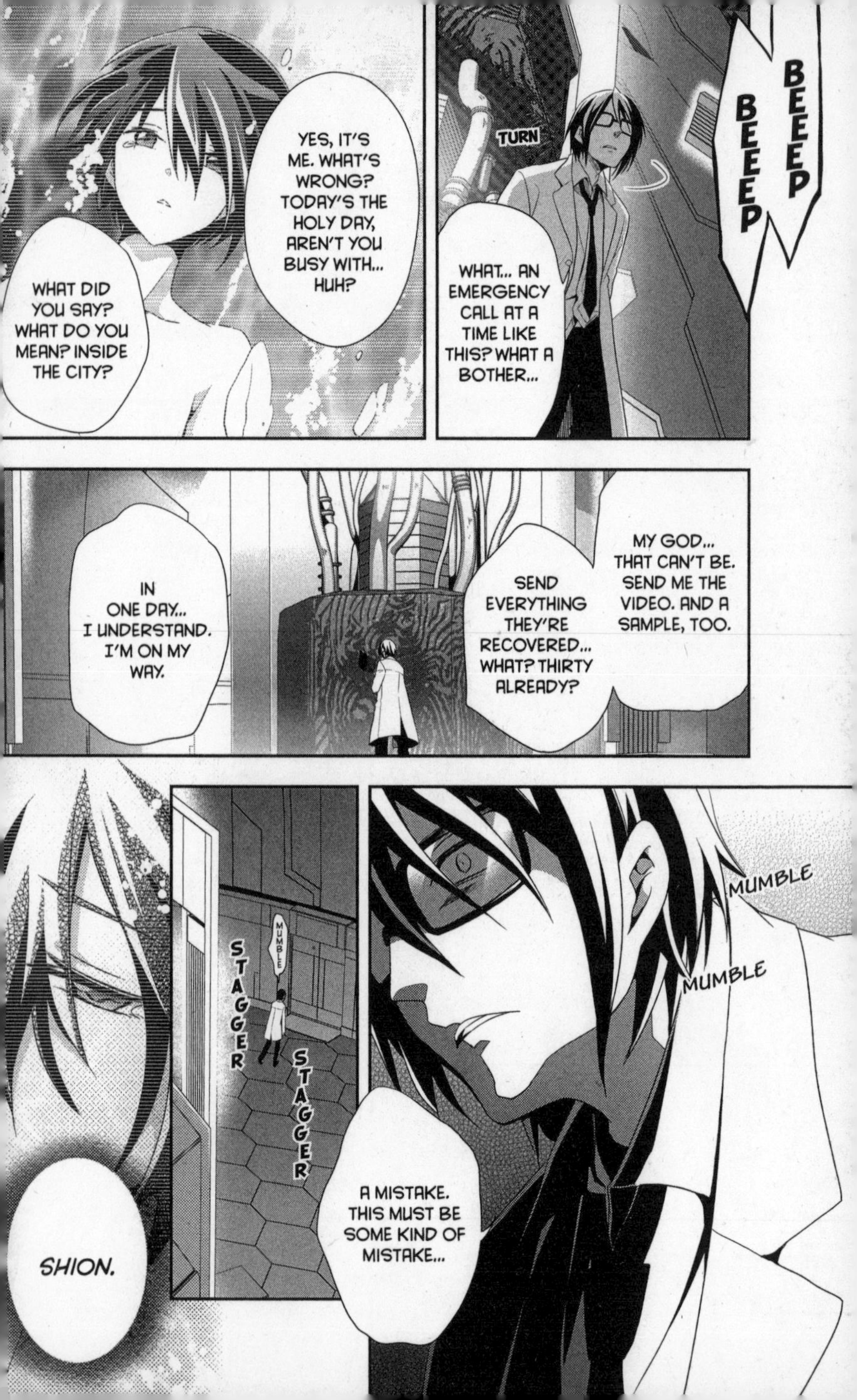
BEEEP
BEEEP
TURN
WHAT... AN EMERGENCY CALL AT A TIME LIKE THIS? WHAT A BOTHER...
YES, IT'S ME. WHAT'S WRONG? TODAY'S THE HOLY DAY, AREN'T YOU BUSY WITH... HUH?
WHAT DID YOU SAY? WHAT DO YOU MEAN? INSIDE THE CITY?
MY GOD... THAT CAN'T BE. SEND ME THE VIDEO. AND A SAMPLE, TOO.
SEND EVERYTHING THEY'RE RECOVERED... WHAT? THIRTY ALREADY?
IN ONE DAY... I UNDERSTAND. I'M ON MY WAY.
MUMBLE
MUMBLE
A MISTAKE. THIS MUST BE SOME KIND OF MISTAKE...
MUMBLE
STAGGER
STAGGER
SHION.

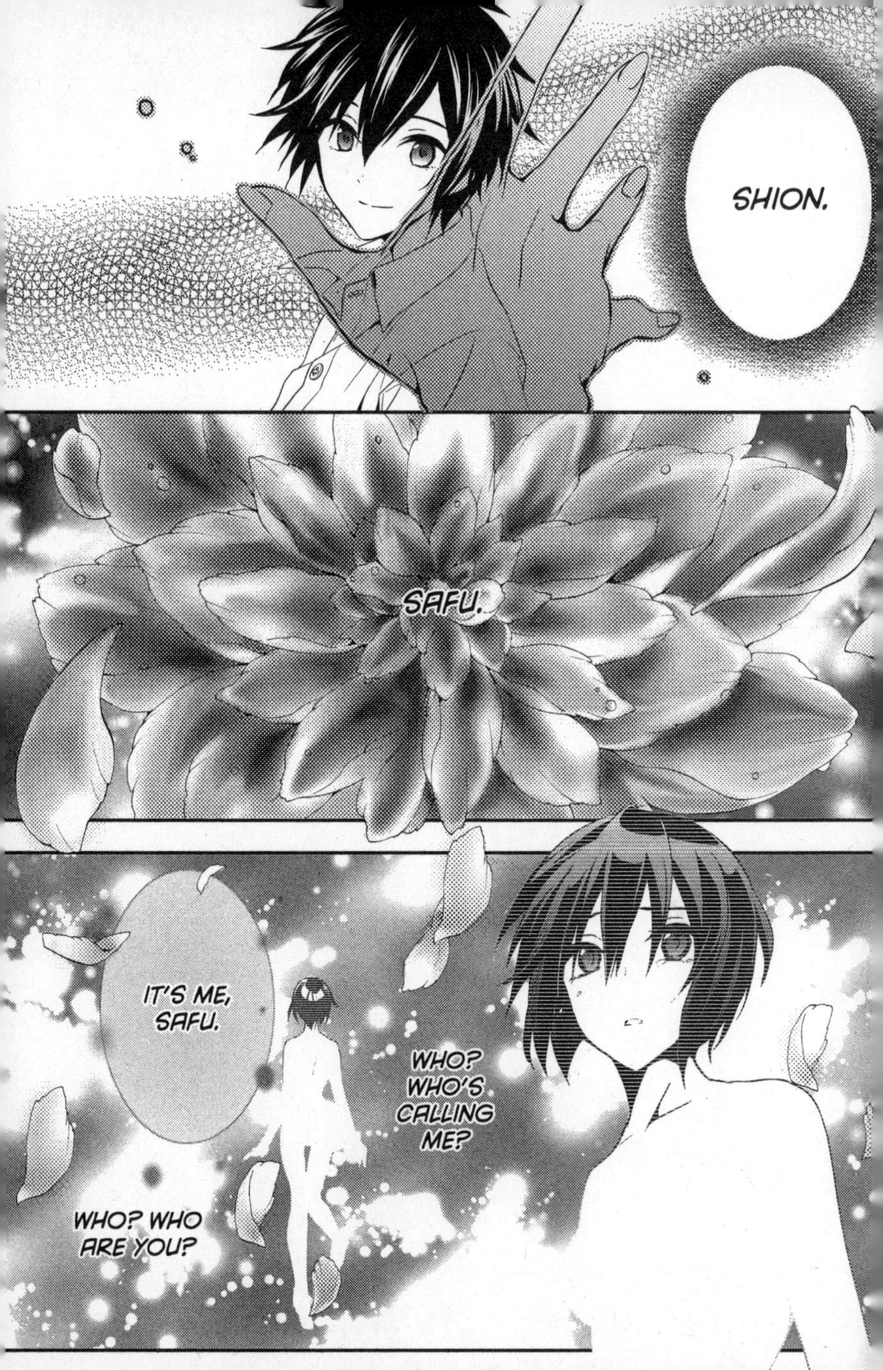
SHION.
SAFU.
WHO? WHO'S CALLING ME?
IT'S ME, SAFU.
WHO? WHO ARE YOU?

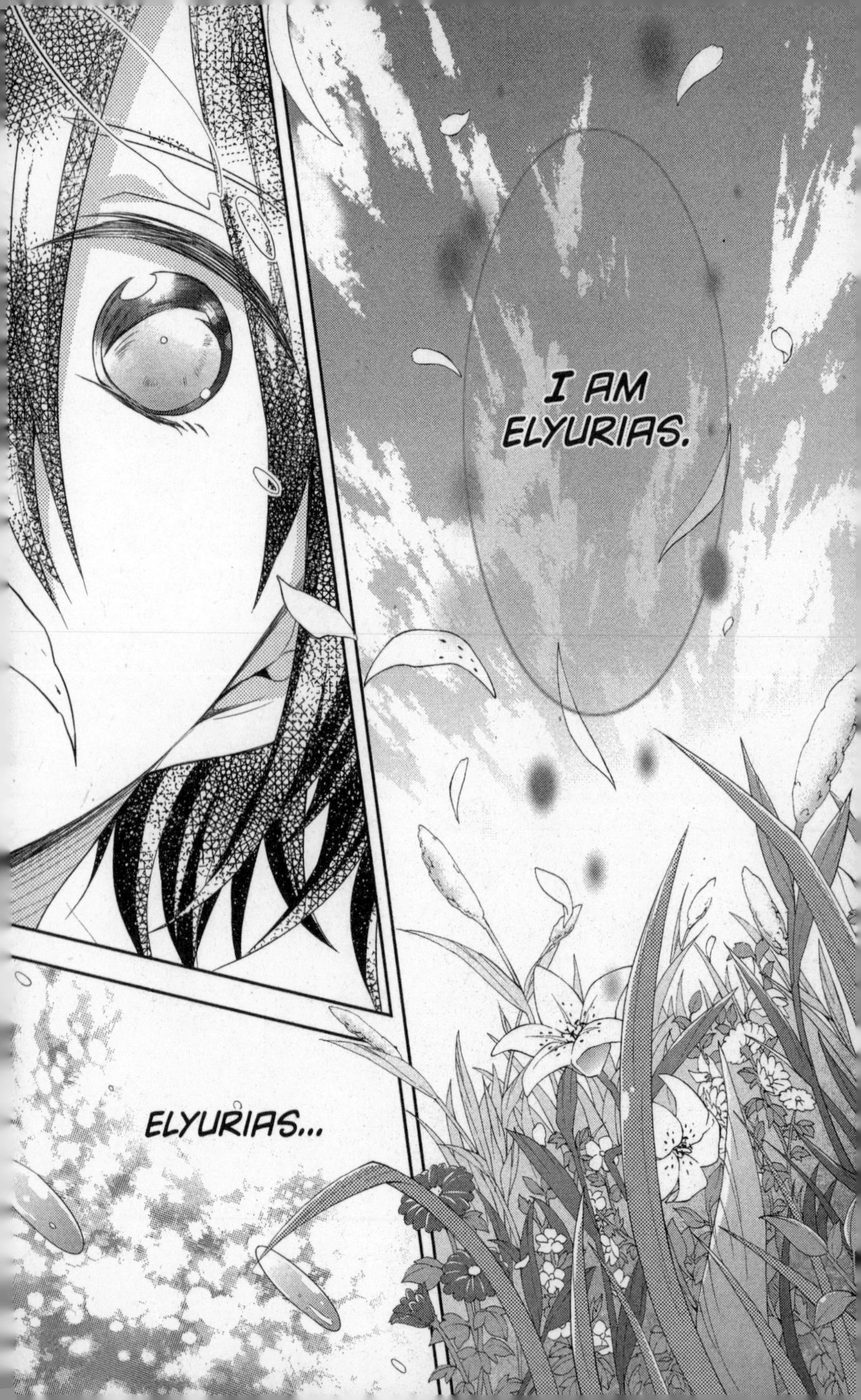
I AM ELYURIAS.
ELYURIAS...

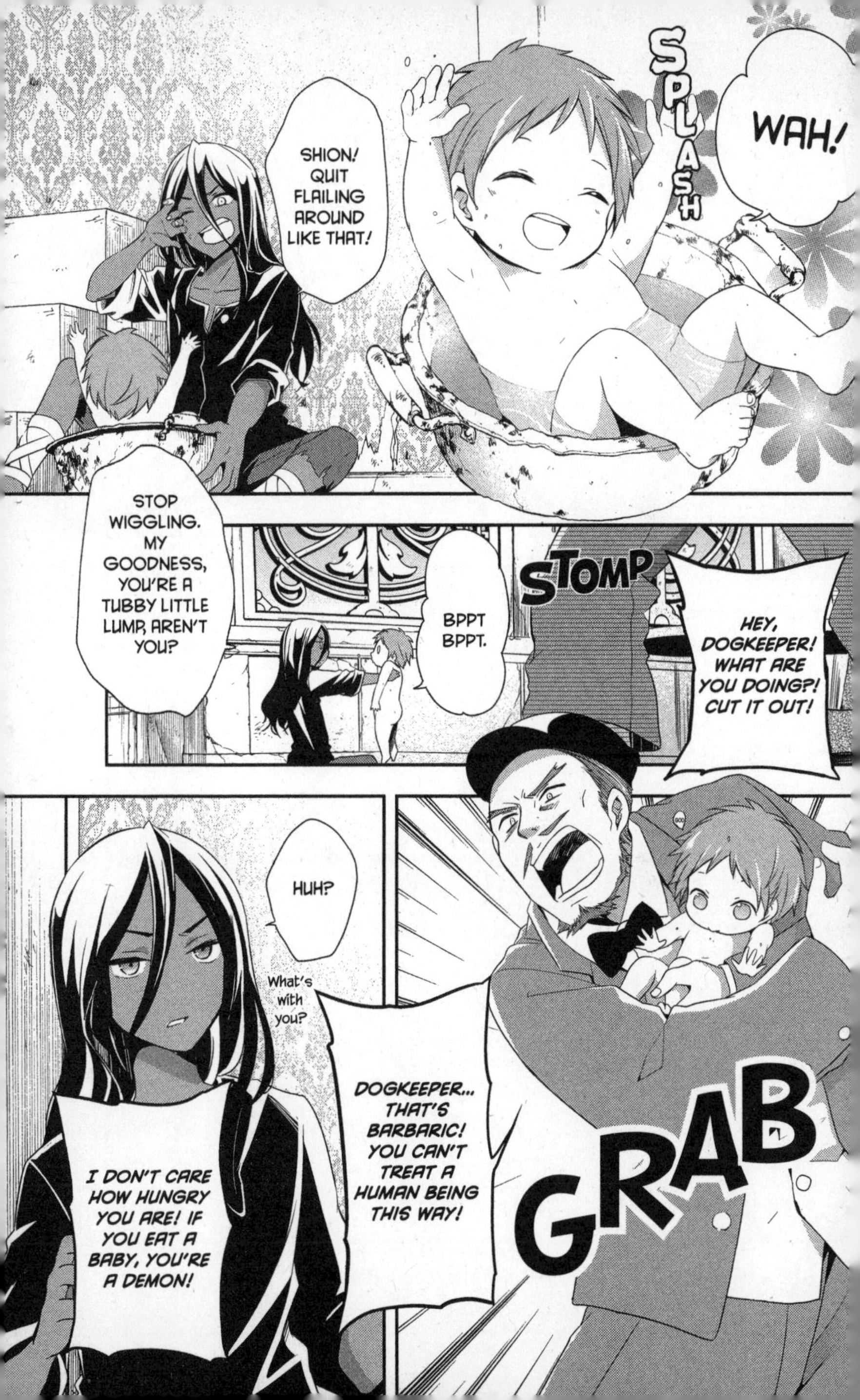
WAH!
SPLASH
SHION! QUIT FLAILING AROUND LIKE THAT!
STOMP
HEY, DOGKEEPER! WHAT ARE YOU DOING?! CUT IT OUT!
STOP WIGGLING. MY GOODNESS, YOU'RE A TUBBY LITTLE LUMP, AREN'T YOU?
BPPT BPPT.
GRAB
DOGKEEPER... THAT'S BARBARIC! YOU CAN'T TREAT A HUMAN BEING THIS WAY!
HUH?
What's with you?
I DON'T CARE HOW HUNGRY YOU ARE! IF YOU EAT A BABY, YOU'RE A DEMON!

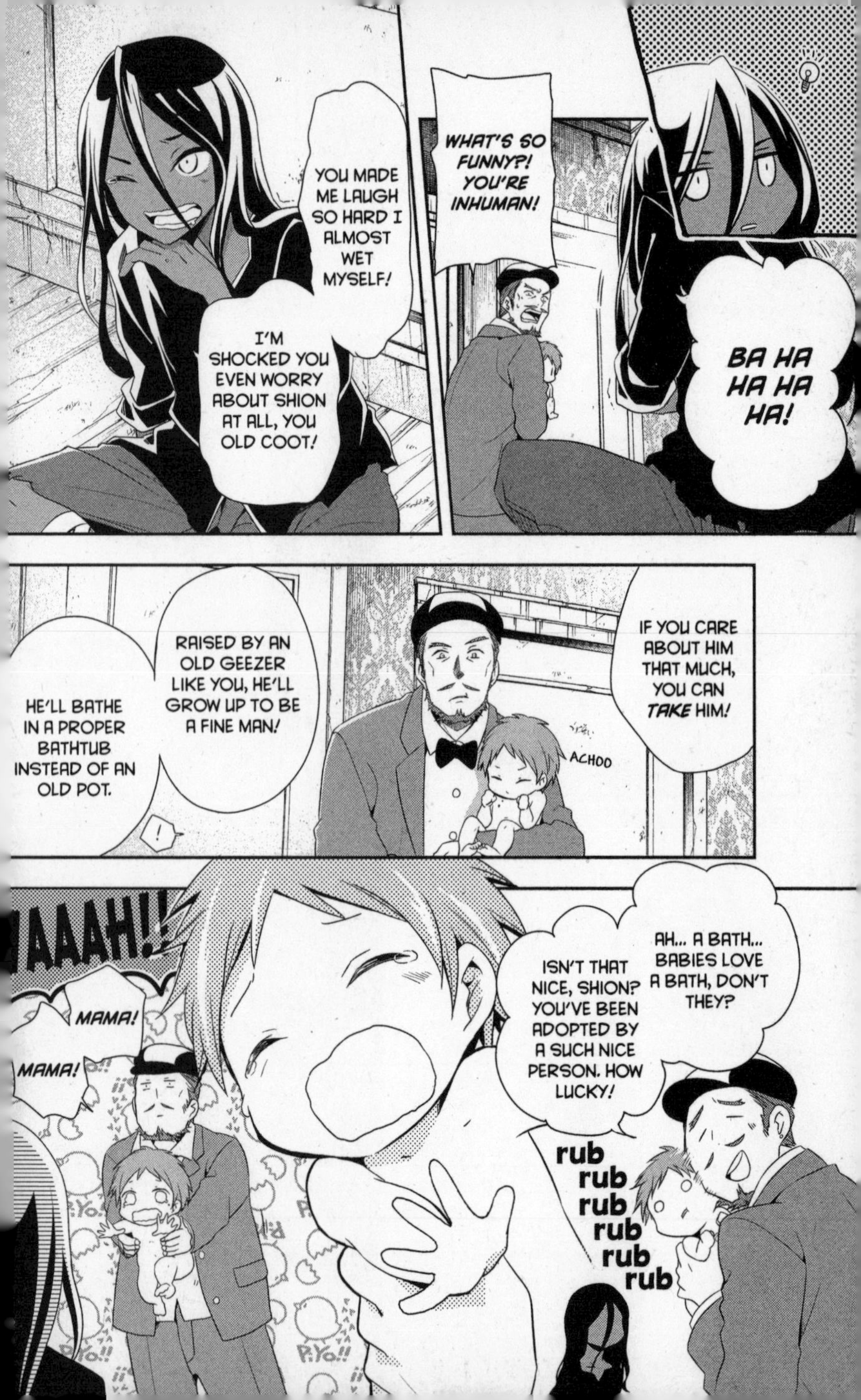
BA HA HA HA HA!
WHAT'S SO FUNNY?! YOU'RE INHUMAN!
YOU MADE ME LAUGH SO HARD I ALMOST WET MYSELF!
I'M SHOCKED YOU EVEN WORRY ABOUT SHION AT ALL, YOU OLD COOT!
IF YOU CARE ABOUT HIM THAT MUCH, YOU CAN *TAKE* HIM!
ACHOO
RAISED BY AN OLD GEEZER LIKE YOU, HE'LL GROW UP TO BE A FINE MAN!
HE'LL BATHE IN A PROPER BATHTUB INSTEAD OF AN OLD POT.
!
AH... A BATH... BABIES LOVE A BATH, DON'T THEY?
ISN'T THAT NICE, SHION? YOU'VE BEEN ADOPTED BY A SUCH NICE PERSON. HOW LUCKY!
rub rub rub rub rub rub
AAAH!!
MAMA!
MAMA!

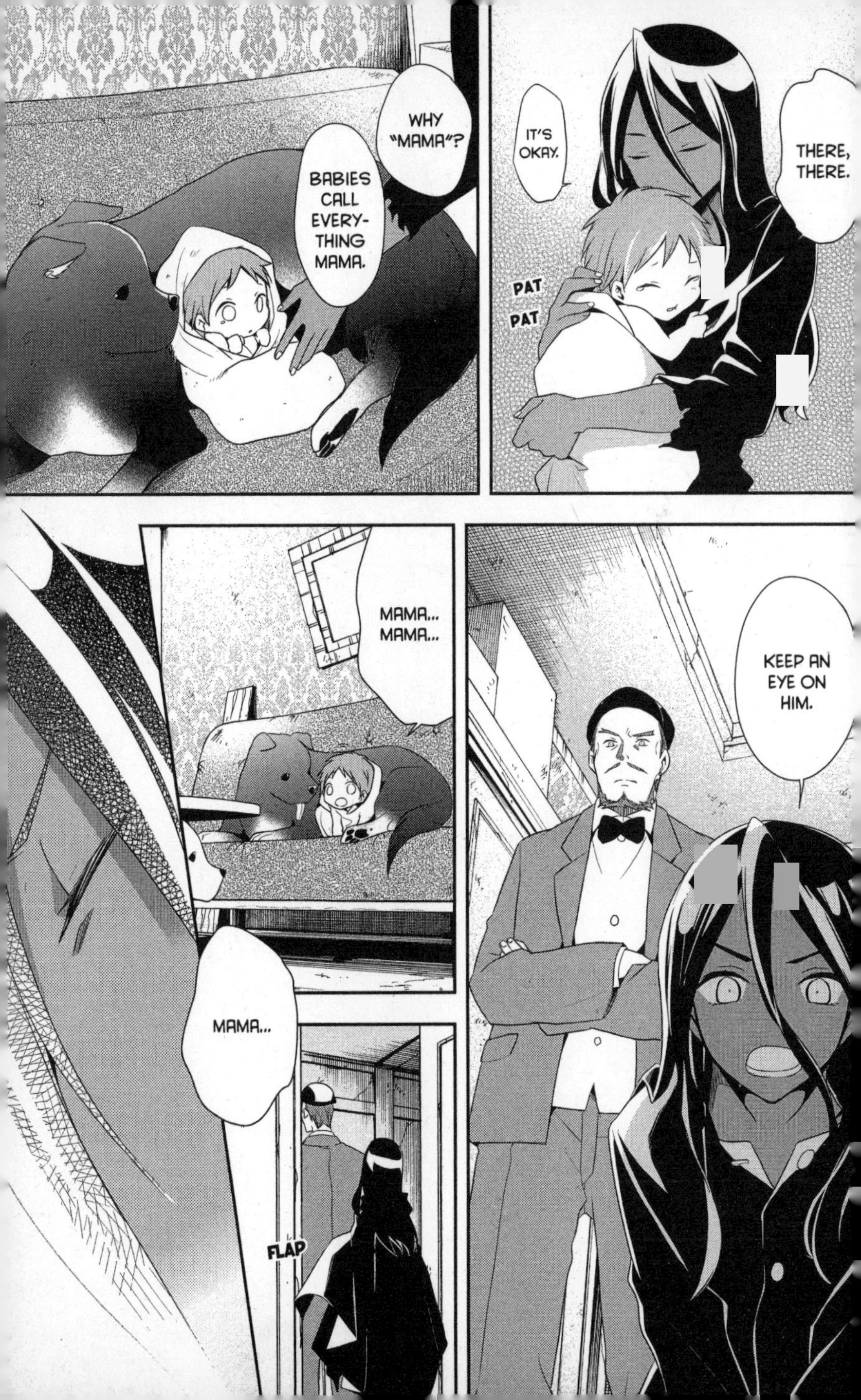
THERE, THERE.
IT'S OKAY.
PAT
PAT
WHY "MAMA"?
BABIES CALL EVERY-THING MAMA.
KEEP AN EYE ON HIM.
MAMA... MAMA...
MAMA...
FLAP

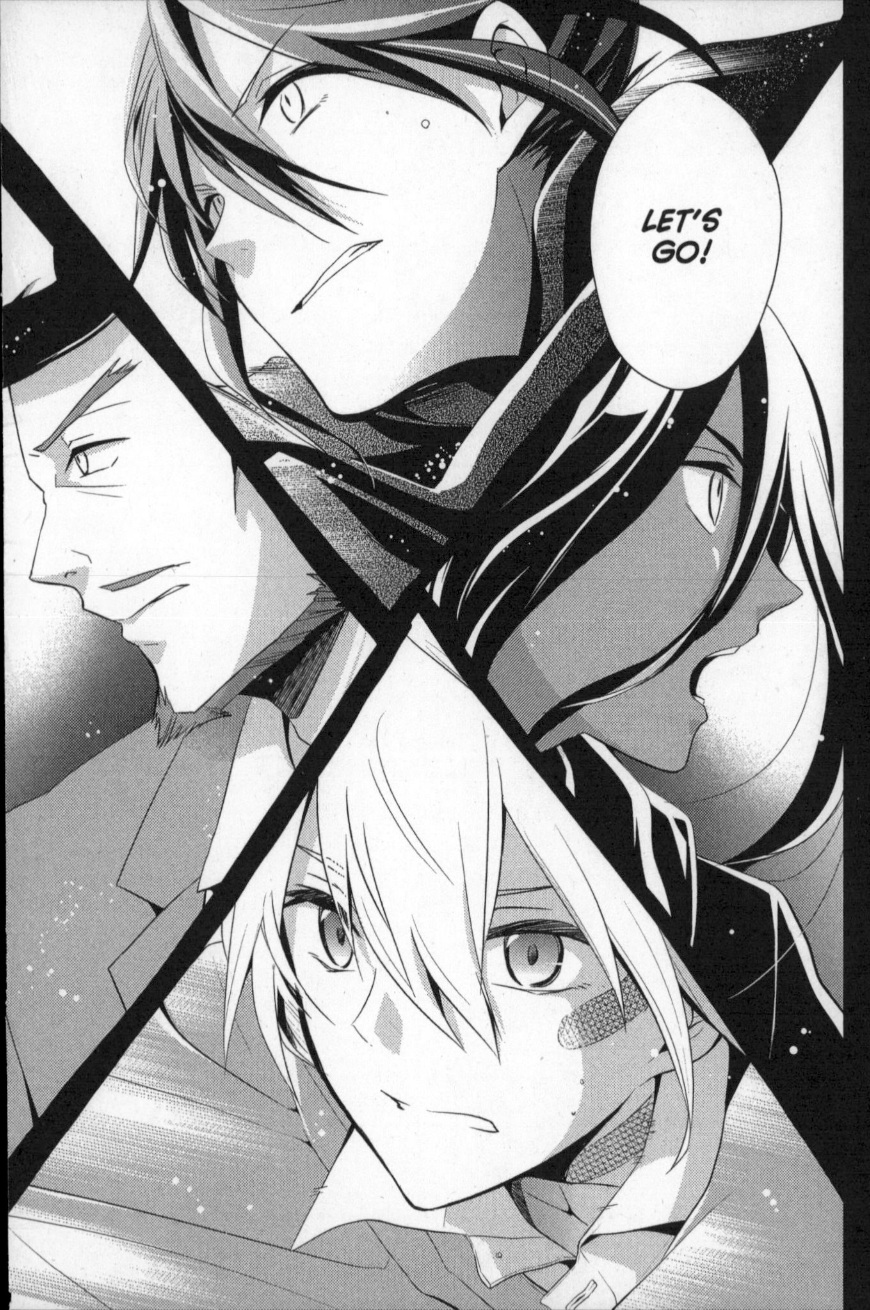
LET'S GO!

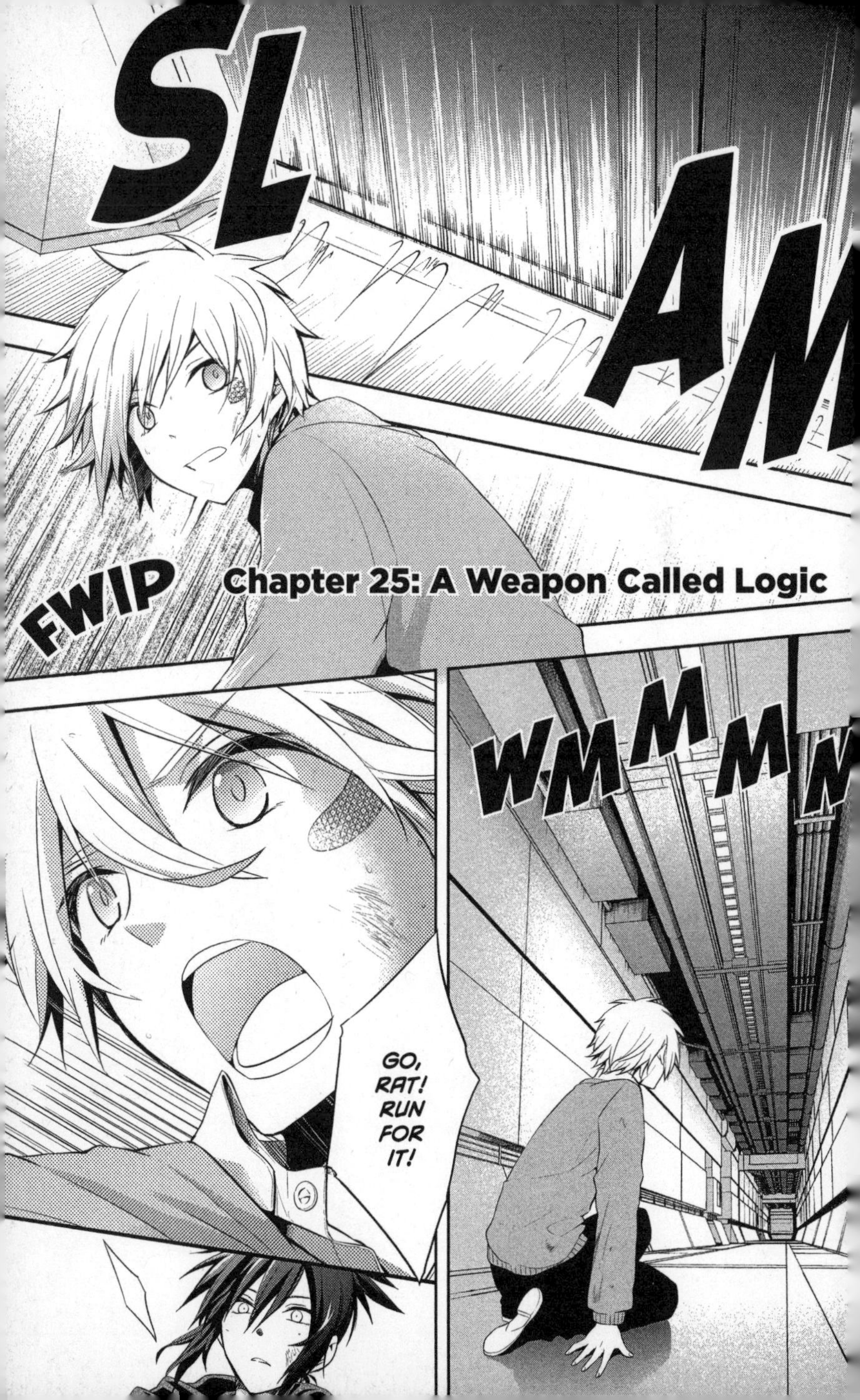
SLAM
FWIP
Chapter 25: A Weapon Called Logic
WMMMN
GO, RAT! RUN FOR IT!

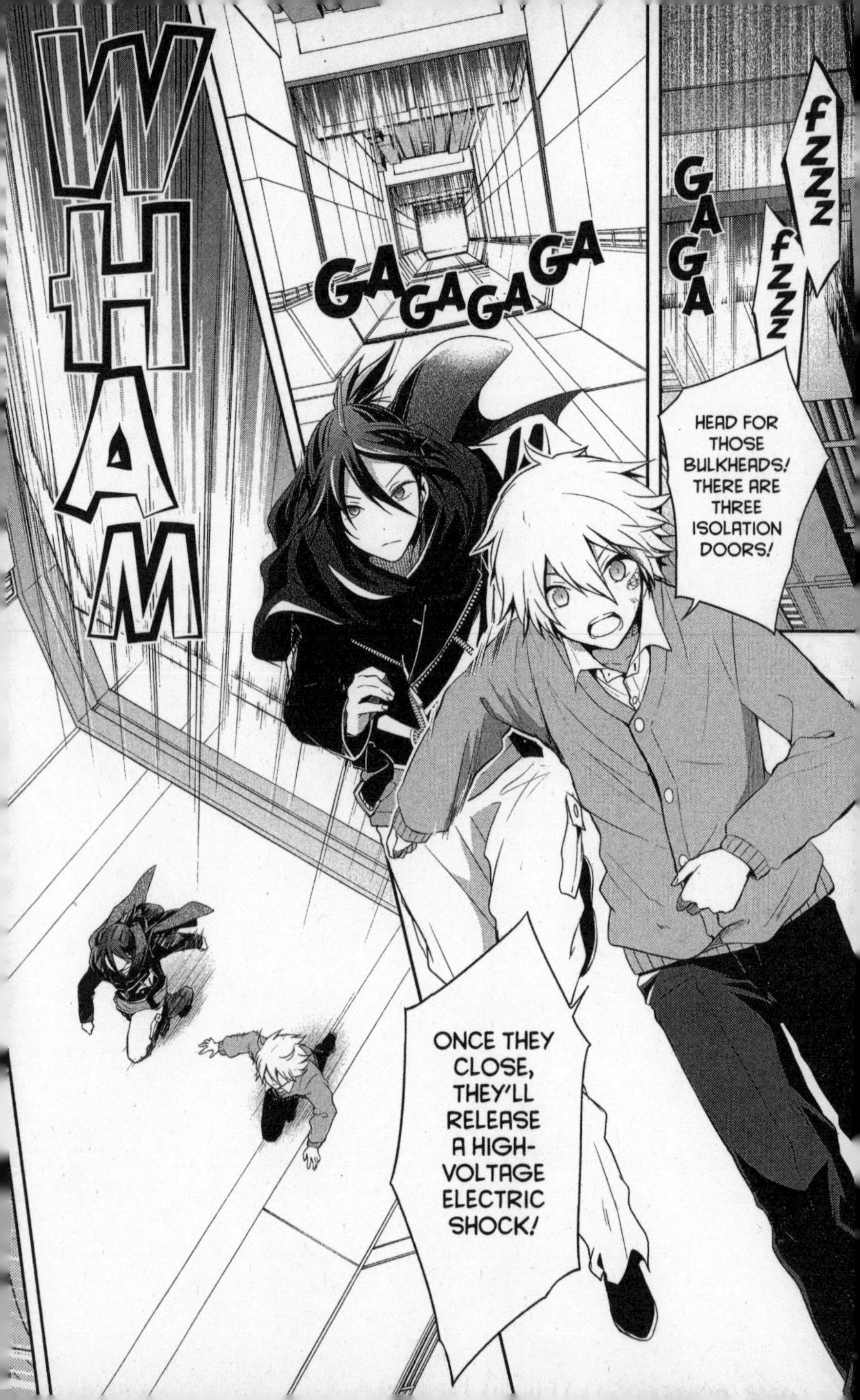
fzzz
fzzz
GAGA
GAGAGAGA
WHAM
HEAD FOR THOSE BULKHEADS! THERE ARE THREE ISOLATION DOORS!
ONCE THEY CLOSE, THEY'LL RELEASE A HIGH-VOLTAGE ELECTRIC SHOCK!

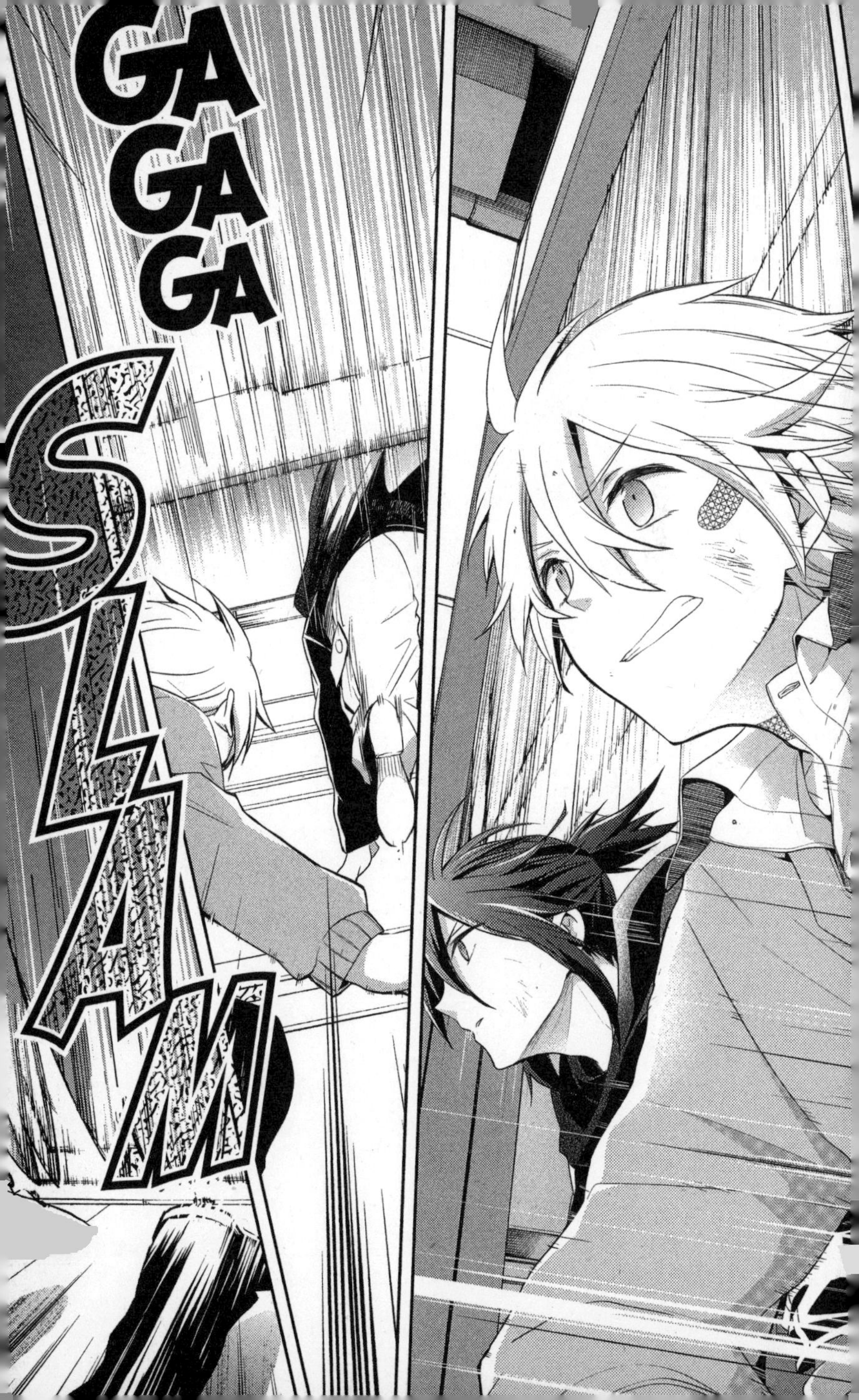
GA GA GA
SLAM

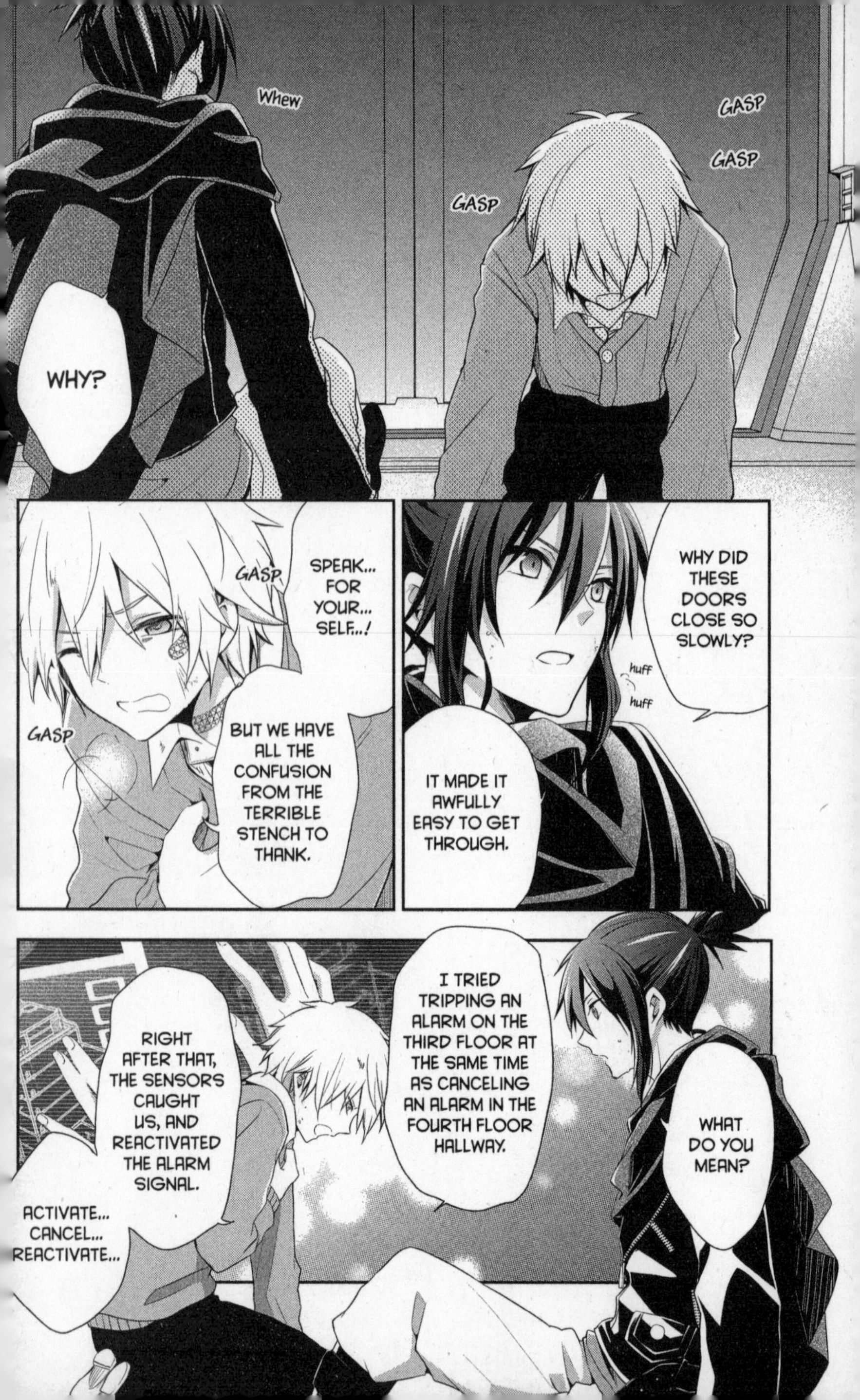
GASP
GASP
Whew
GASP
WHY?
WHY DID THESE DOORS CLOSE SO SLOWLY?
huff
huff
IT MADE IT AWFULLY EASY TO GET THROUGH.
SPEAK... FOR YOUR... SELF...!
GASP
BUT WE HAVE ALL THE CONFUSION FROM THE TERRIBLE STENCH TO THANK.
GASP
WHAT DO YOU MEAN?
I TRIED TRIPPING AN ALARM ON THE THIRD FLOOR AT THE SAME TIME AS CANCELING AN ALARM IN THE FOURTH FLOOR HALLWAY.
RIGHT AFTER THAT, THE SENSORS CAUGHT US, AND REACTIVATED THE ALARM SIGNAL.
ACTIVATE... CANCEL... REACTIVATE...

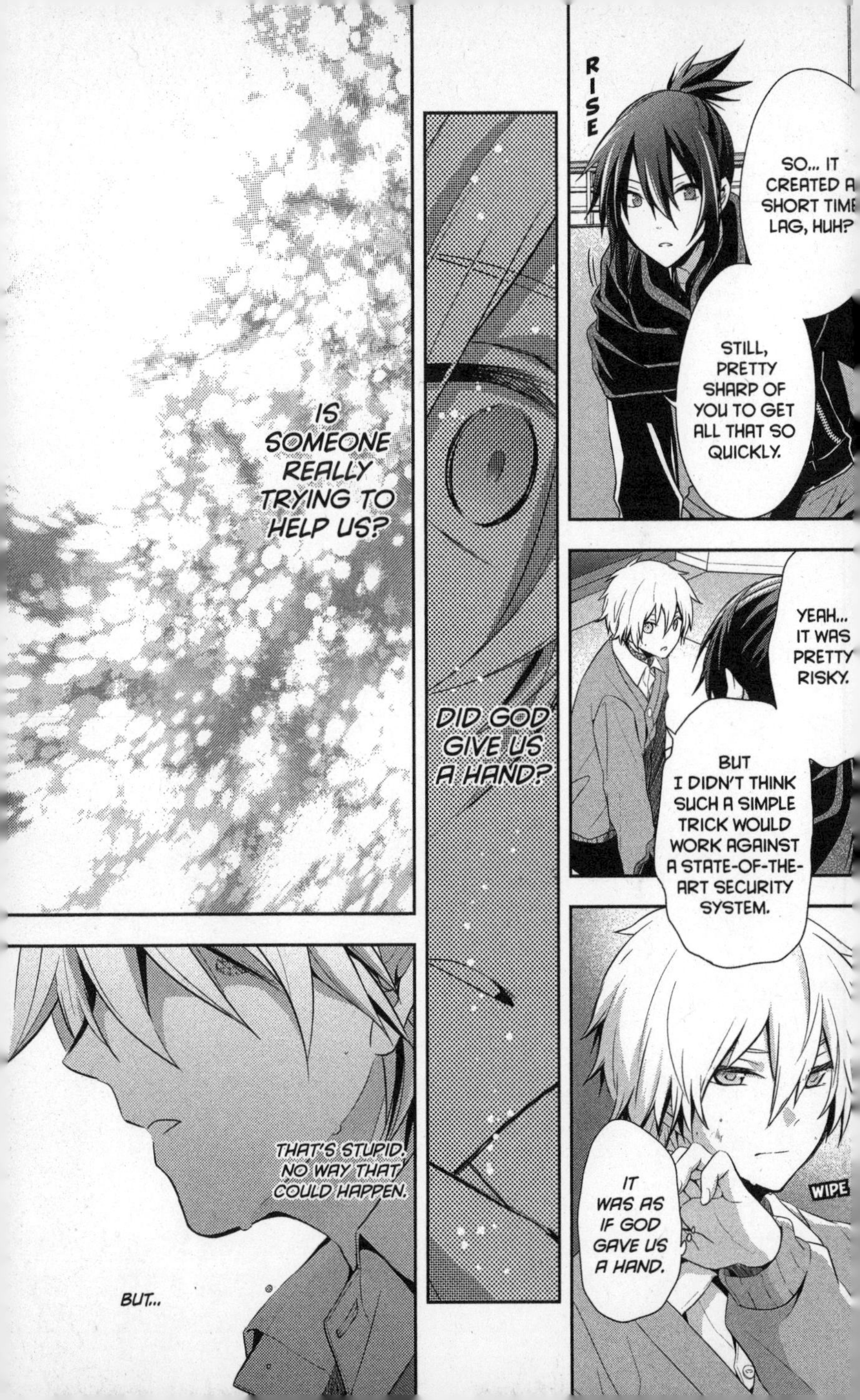
RISE
SO... IT CREATED A SHORT TIME LAG, HUH?
STILL, PRETTY SHARP OF YOU TO GET ALL THAT SO QUICKLY.
YEAH... IT WAS PRETTY RISKY.
BUT I DIDN'T THINK SUCH A SIMPLE TRICK WOULD WORK AGAINST A STATE-OF-THE-ART SECURITY SYSTEM.
WIPE
IT WAS AS IF GOD GAVE US A HAND.
DID GOD GIVE US A HAND?
IS SOMEONE REALLY TRYING TO HELP US?
THAT'S STUPID. NO WAY THAT COULD HAPPEN.
BUT...

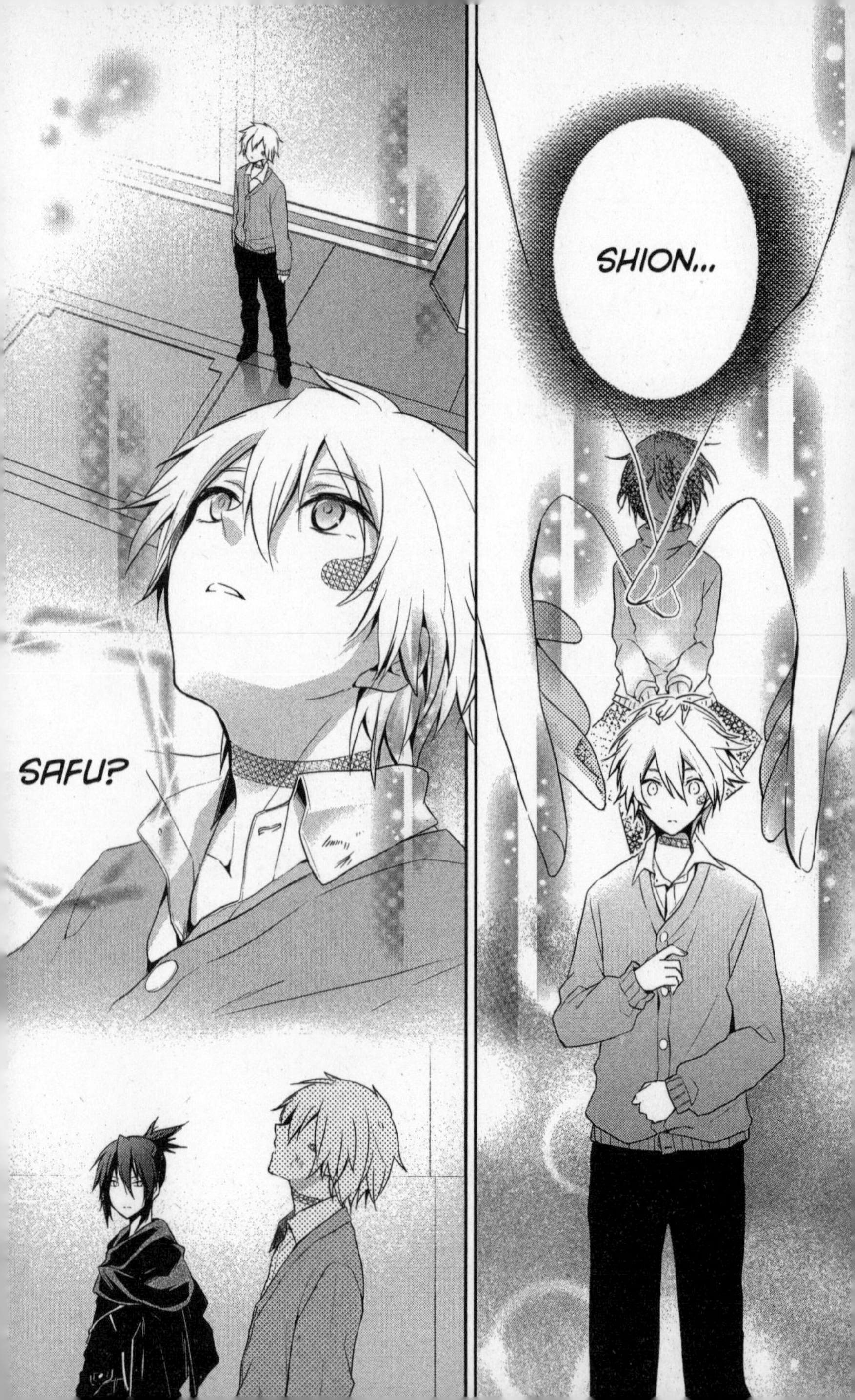
SHION...
SAFU?

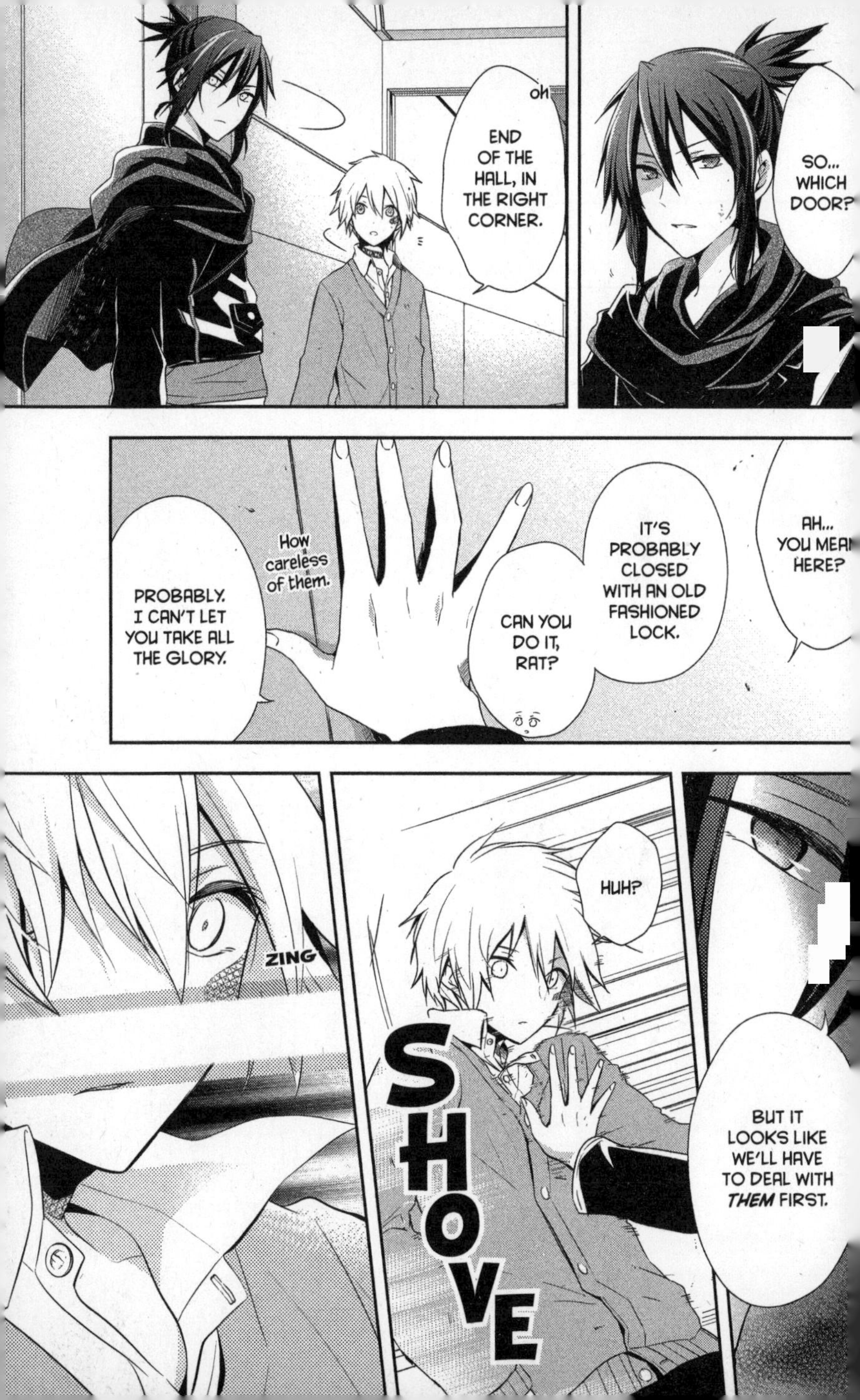
SO... WHICH DOOR?
oh
END OF THE HALL, IN THE RIGHT CORNER.
AH... YOU MEA HERE?
IT'S PROBABLY CLOSED WITH AN OLD FASHIONED LOCK.
CAN YOU DO IT, RAT?
How careless of them.
PROBABLY. I CAN'T LET YOU TAKE ALL THE GLORY.
BUT IT LOOKS LIKE WE'LL HAVE TO DEAL WITH *THEM* FIRST.
HUH?
SHOVE
ZING

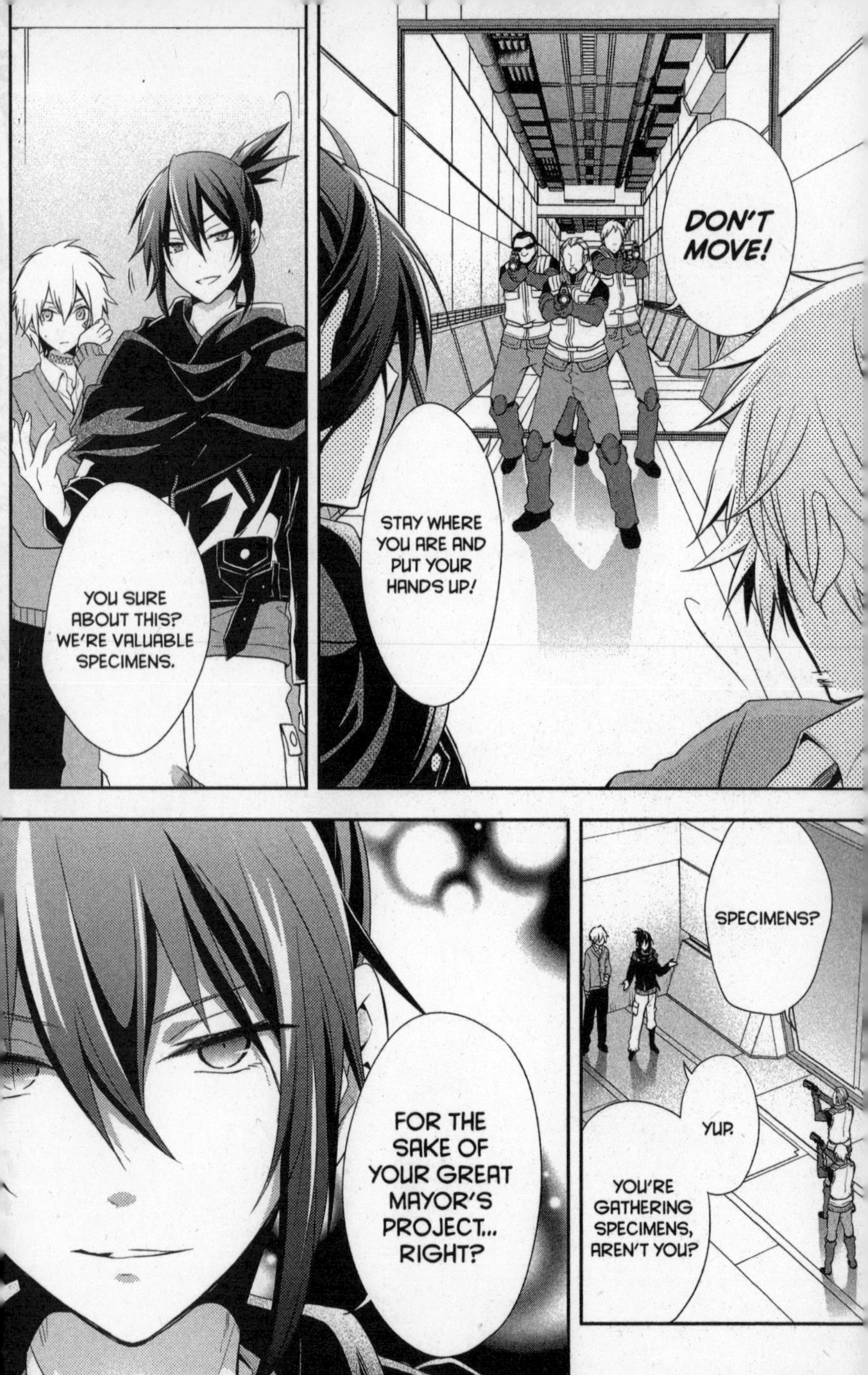
DON'T MOVE!
STAY WHERE YOU ARE AND PUT YOUR HANDS UP!
YOU SURE ABOUT THIS? WE'RE VALUABLE SPECIMENS.
SPECIMENS?
YUP.
YOU'RE GATHERING SPECIMENS, AREN'T YOU?
FOR THE SAKE OF YOUR GREAT MAYOR'S PROJECT... RIGHT?

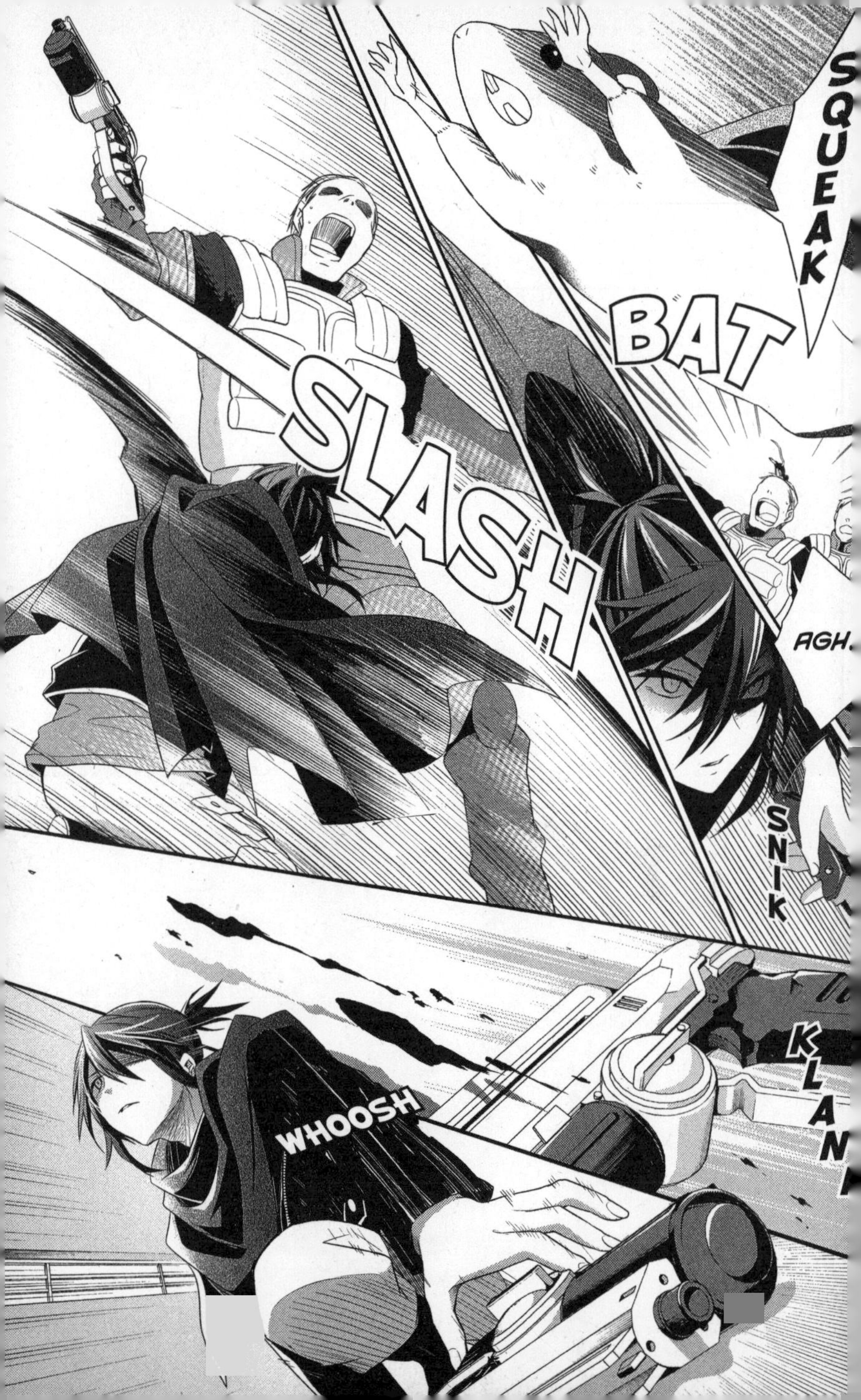
SQUEAK
BAT
AGH.
SNIK
SLASH
KLAN
WHOOSH

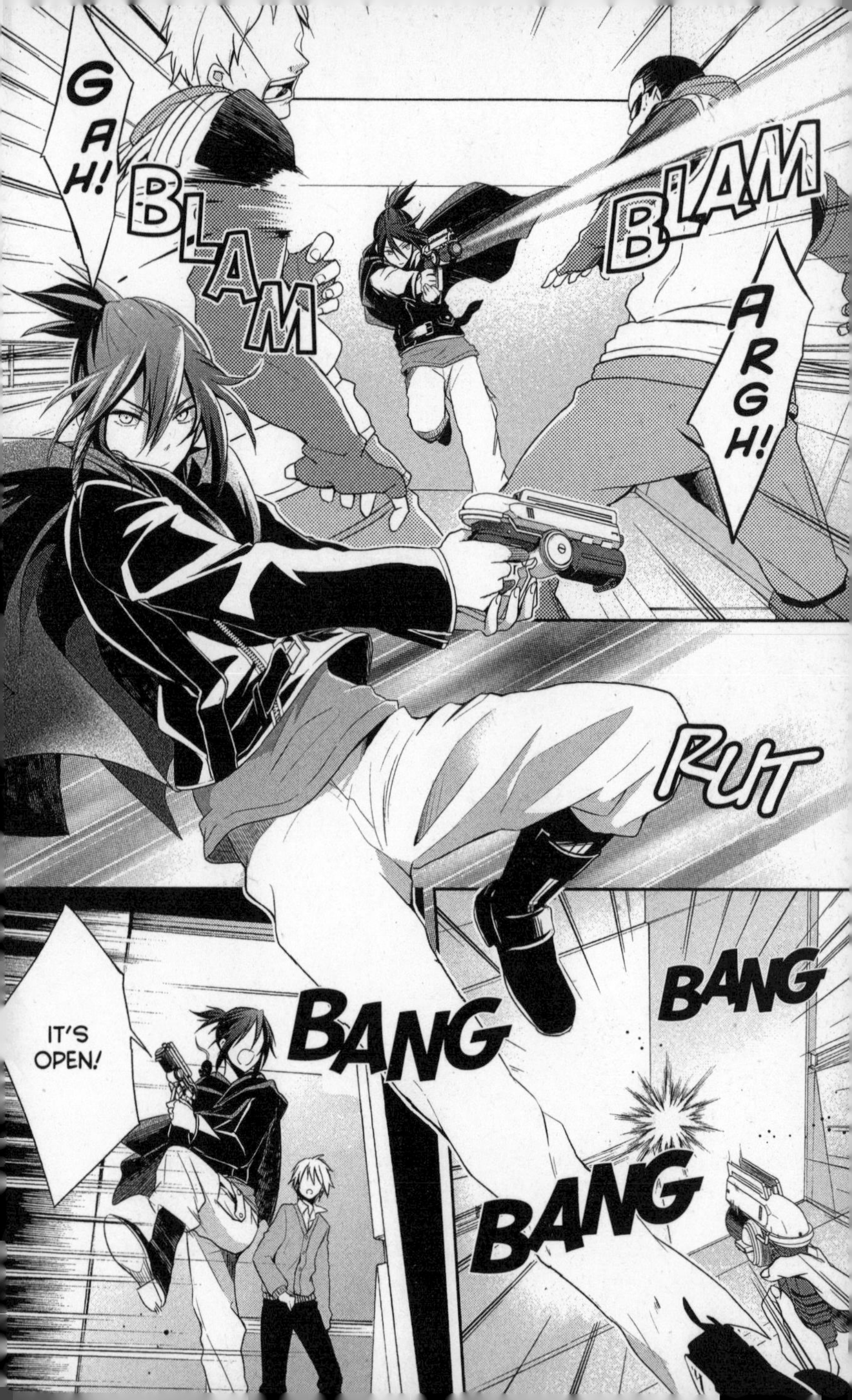
BLAM
ARGH!
GAH!
BLAM
RUT
BANG
BANG
BANG
IT'S OPEN!

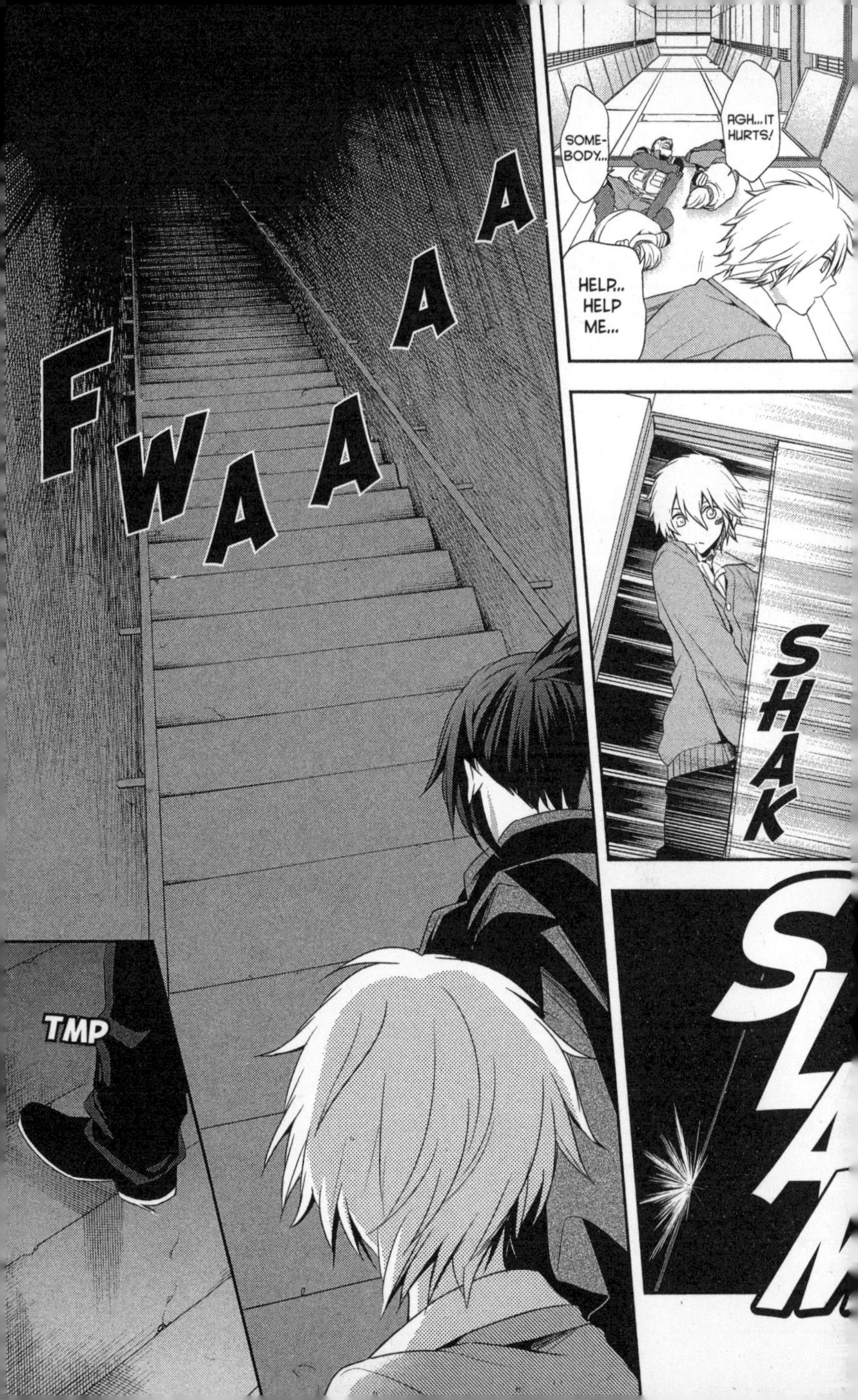
AGH... IT HURTS!
SOME-BODY...
HELP... HELP ME...
SHAK
SLAM
FWAAAAA
TMP

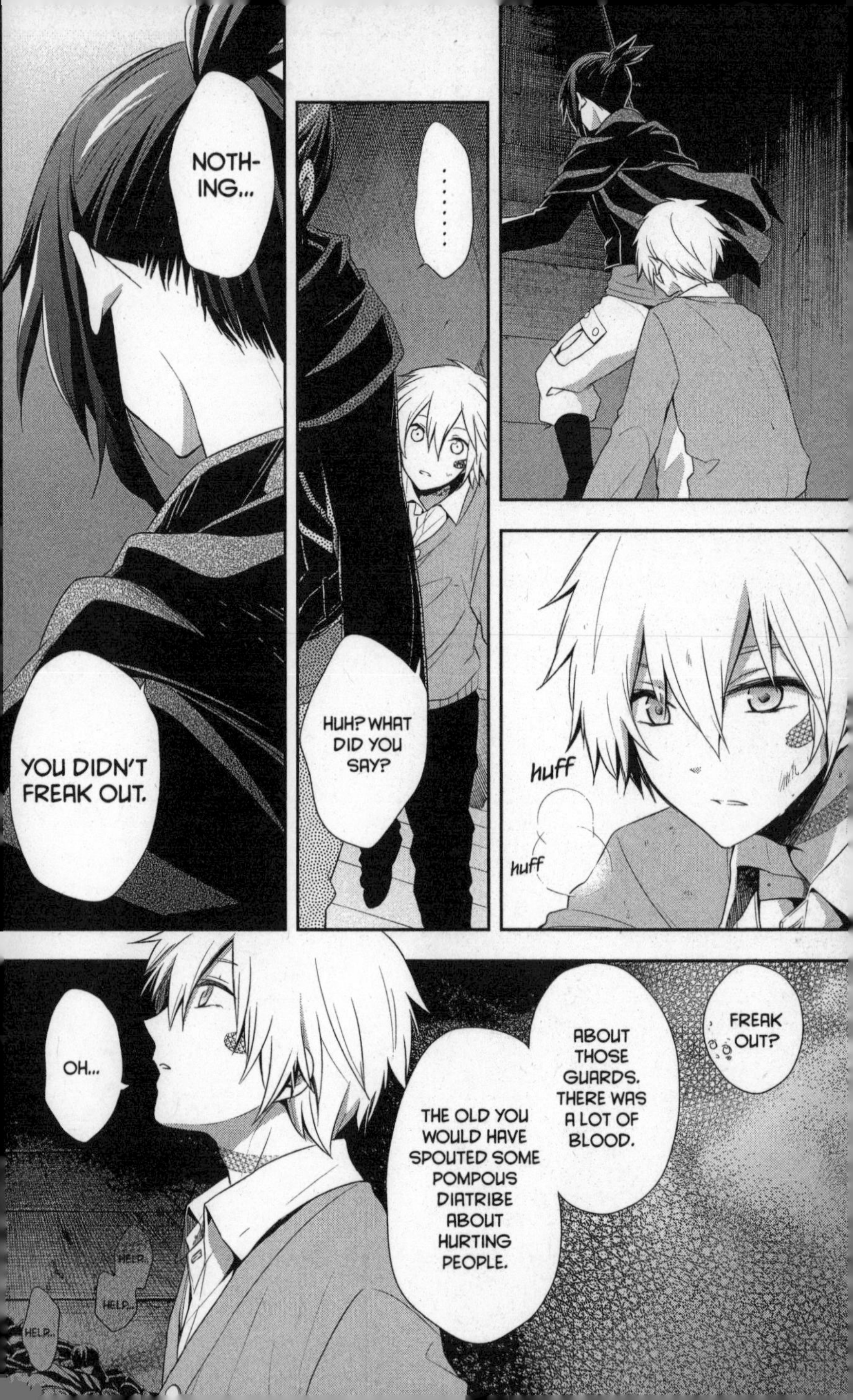
huff
huff
......
HUH? WHAT DID YOU SAY?
NOTH-ING...
YOU DIDN'T FREAK OUT.
FREAK OUT?
ABOUT THOSE GUARDS. THERE WAS A LOT OF BLOOD.
THE OLD YOU WOULD HAVE SPOUTED SOME POMPOUS DIATRIBE ABOUT HURTING PEOPLE.
OH...
HELP...
HELP...
HELP...

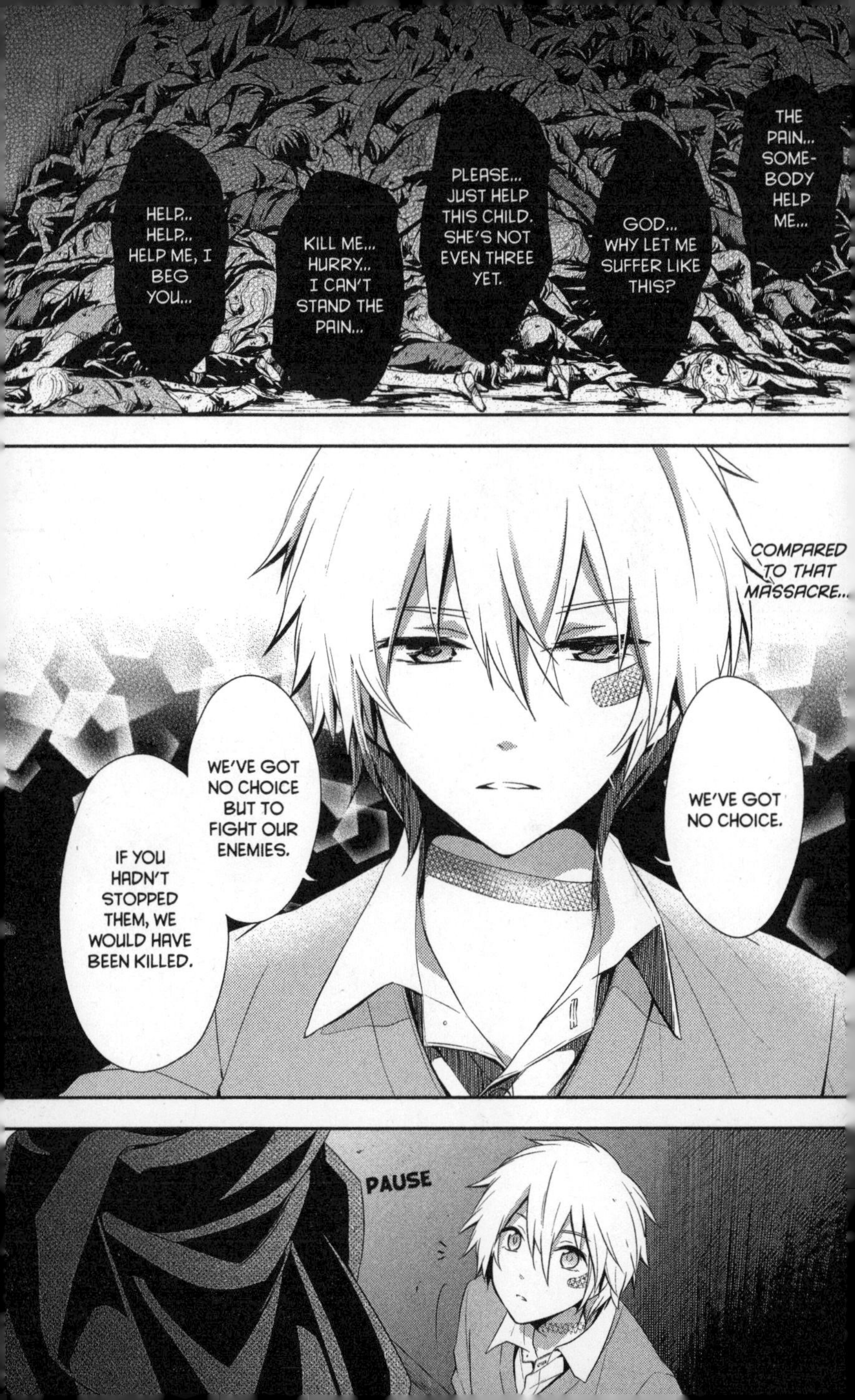
THE PAIN... SOME-BODY HELP ME...
GOD... WHY LET ME SUFFER LIKE THIS?
PLEASE... JUST HELP THIS CHILD. SHE'S NOT EVEN THREE YET.
KILL ME... HURRY... I CAN'T STAND THE PAIN...
HELP... HELP... HELP ME, I BEG YOU...
COMPARED TO THAT MASSACRE...
WE'VE GOT NO CHOICE.
WE'VE GOT NO CHOICE BUT TO FIGHT OUR ENEMIES.
IF YOU HADN'T STOPPED THEM, WE WOULD HAVE BEEN KILLED.
PAUSE

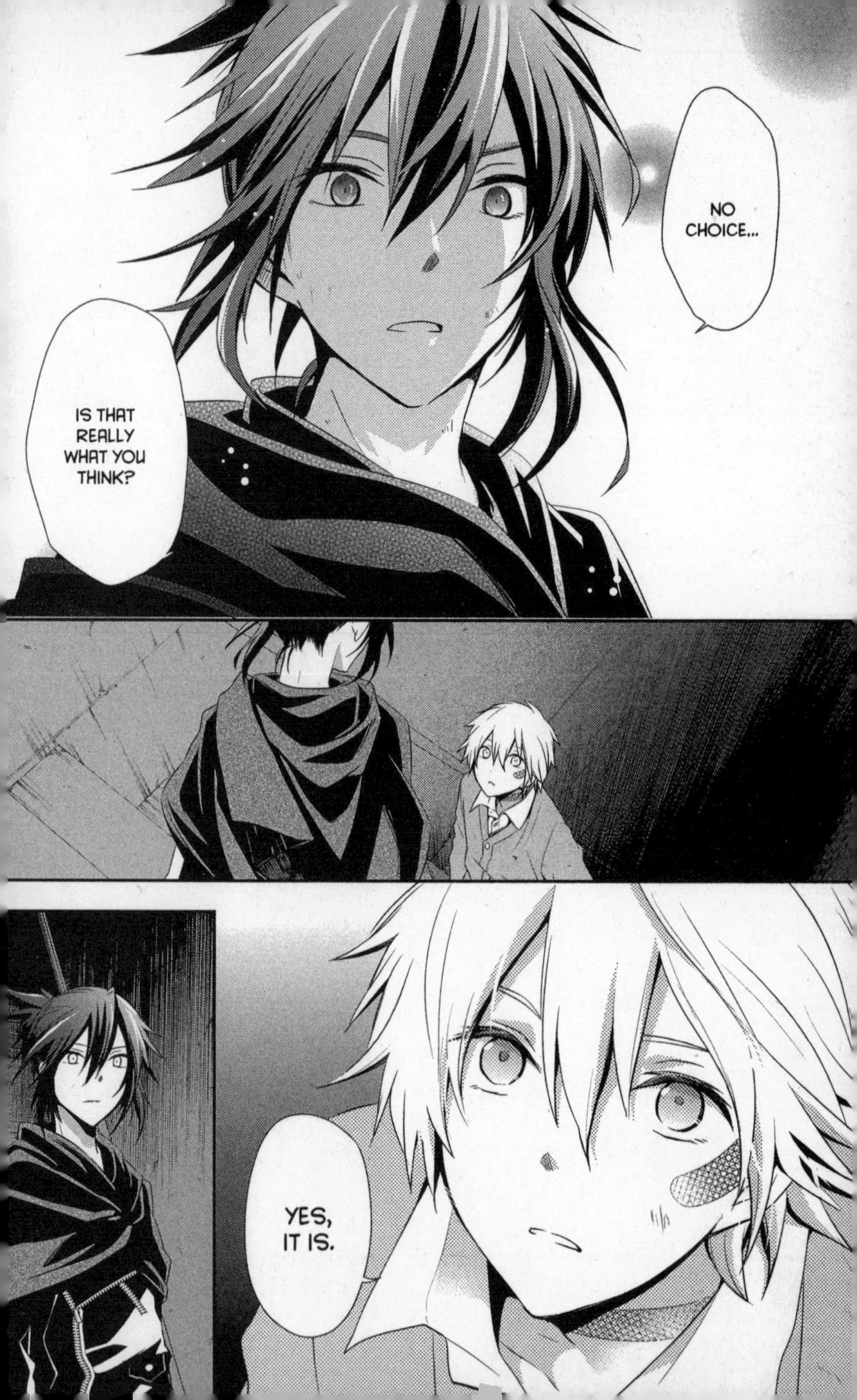
NO CHOICE...
IS THAT REALLY WHAT YOU THINK?
YES, IT IS.

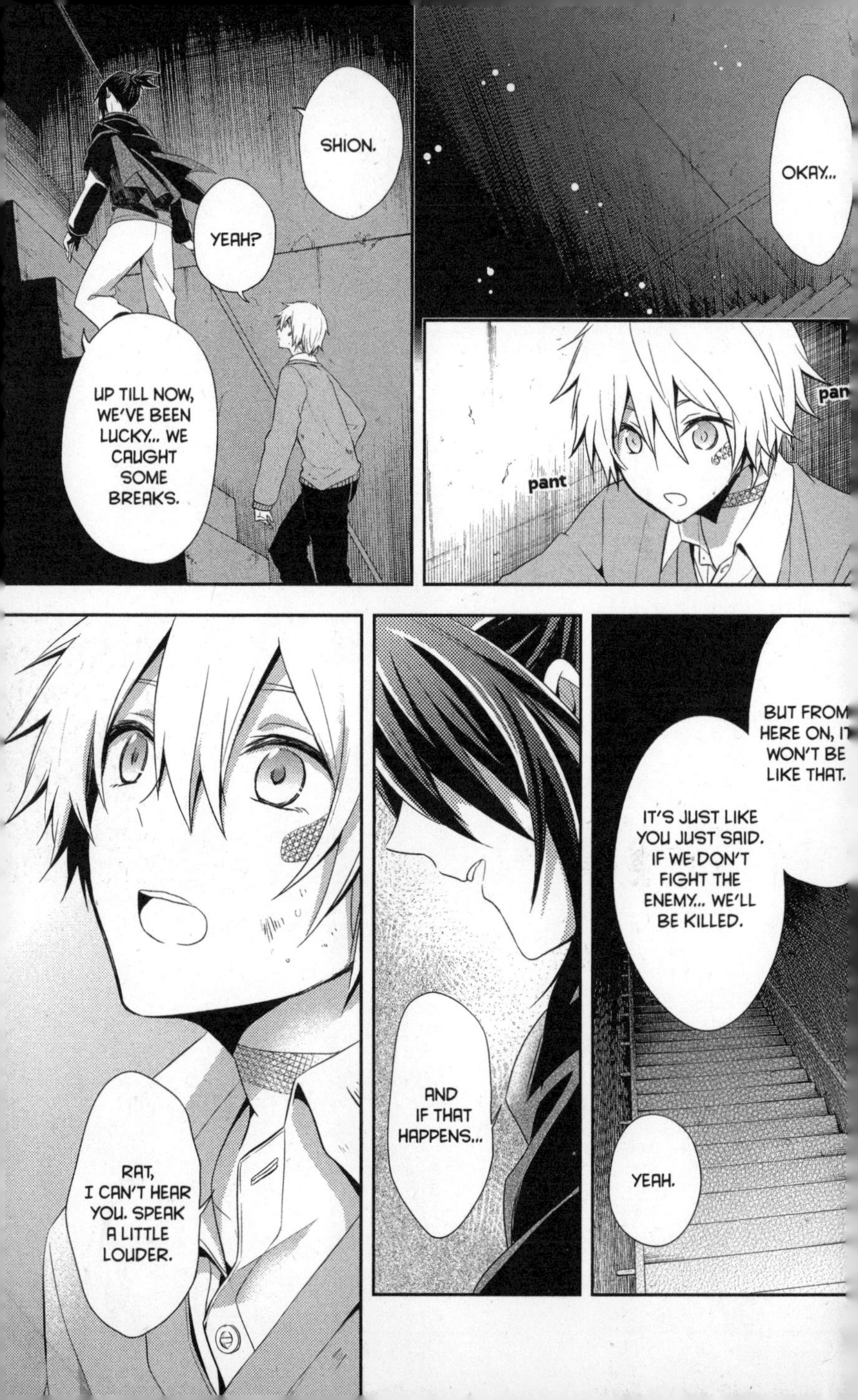

OKAY...
pan
pant
SHION.
YEAH?
UP TILL NOW, WE'VE BEEN LUCKY... WE CAUGHT SOME BREAKS.
BUT FROM HERE ON, IT WON'T BE LIKE THAT.
IT'S JUST LIKE YOU JUST SAID. IF WE DON'T FIGHT THE ENEMY... WE'LL BE KILLED.
YEAH.
AND IF THAT HAPPENS...
RAT, I CAN'T HEAR YOU. SPEAK A LITTLE LOUDER.

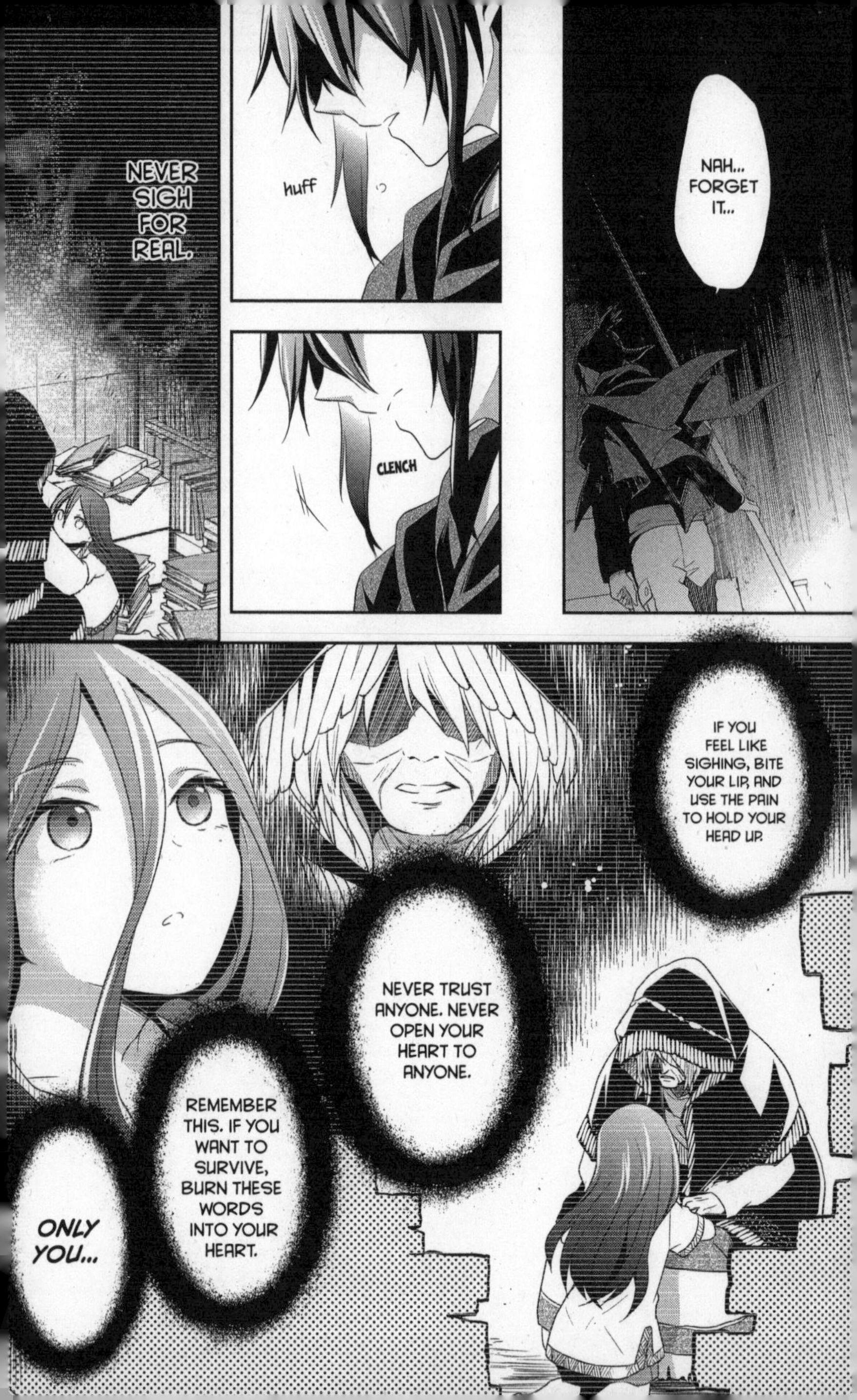
NAH... FORGET IT...
huff
CLENCH
NEVER SIGH FOR REAL.
IF YOU FEEL LIKE SIGHING, BITE YOUR LIP, AND USE THE PAIN TO HOLD YOUR HEAD UP.
NEVER TRUST ANYONE. NEVER OPEN YOUR HEART TO ANYONE.
REMEMBER THIS. IF YOU WANT TO SURVIVE, BURN THESE WORDS INTO YOUR HEART.
ONLY YOU...

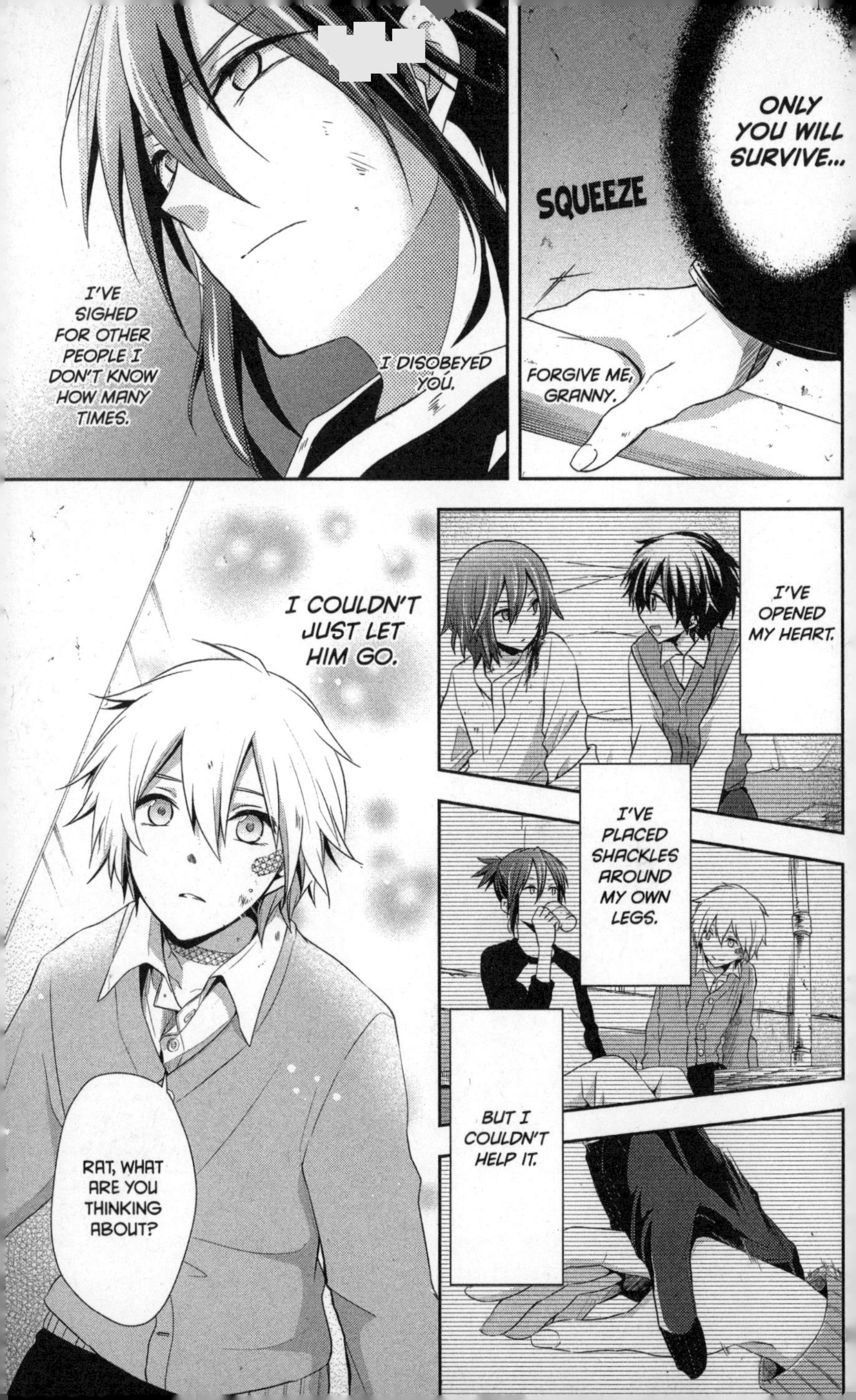
ONLY YOU WILL SURVIVE...
SQUEEZE
FORGIVE ME, GRANNY.
I DISOBEYED YOU.
I'VE SIGHED FOR OTHER PEOPLE I DON'T KNOW HOW MANY TIMES.
I'VE OPENED MY HEART.
I'VE PLACED SHACKLES AROUND MY OWN LEGS.
BUT I COULDN'T HELP IT.
I COULDN'T JUST LET HIM GO.
RAT, WHAT ARE YOU THINKING ABOUT?

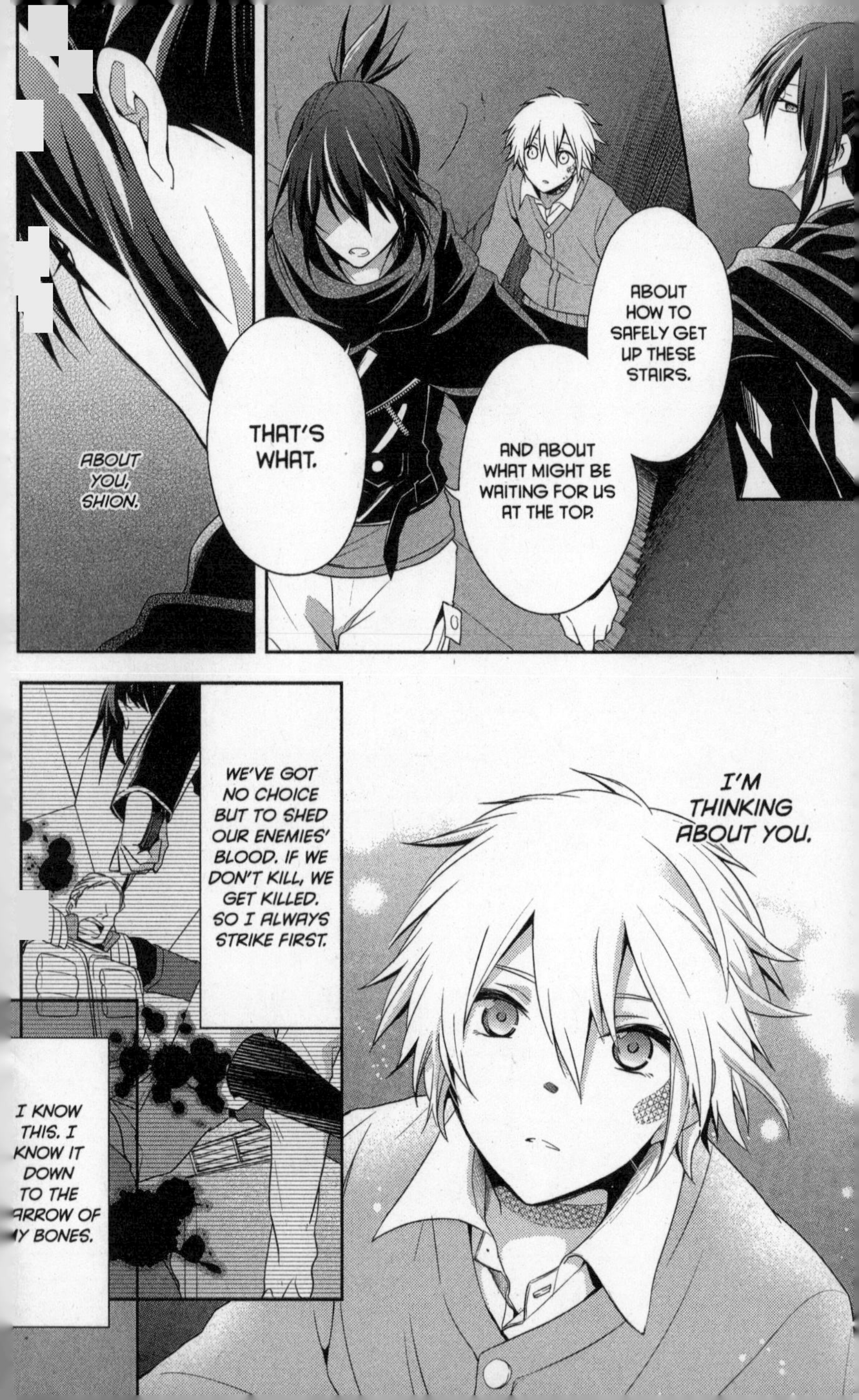
ABOUT HOW TO SAFELY GET UP THESE STAIRS.
AND ABOUT WHAT MIGHT BE WAITING FOR US AT THE TOP.
THAT'S WHAT.
ABOUT YOU, SHION.
I'M THINKING ABOUT YOU.
WE'VE GOT NO CHOICE BUT TO SHED OUR ENEMIES' BLOOD. IF WE DON'T KILL, WE GET KILLED. SO I ALWAYS STRIKE FIRST.
I KNOW THIS. I KNOW IT DOWN TO THE ARROW OF Y BONES.

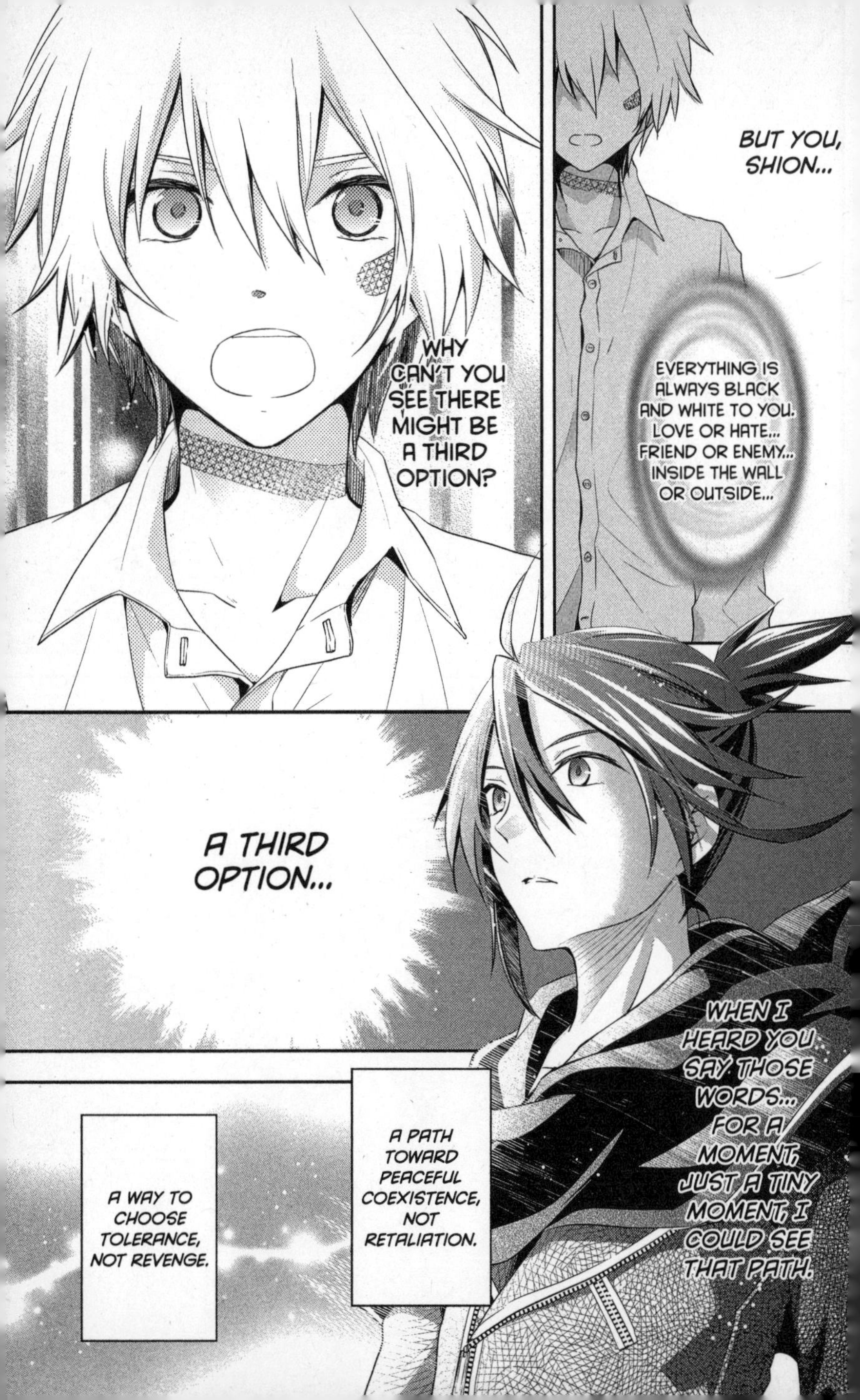
BUT YOU, SHION...
EVERYTHING IS ALWAYS BLACK AND WHITE TO YOU. LOVE OR HATE... FRIEND OR ENEMY... INSIDE THE WALL OR OUTSIDE...
WHY CAN'T YOU SEE THERE MIGHT BE A THIRD OPTION?
WHEN I HEARD YOU SAY THOSE WORDS... FOR A MOMENT, JUST A TINY MOMENT, I COULD SEE THAT PATH.
A THIRD OPTION...
A PATH TOWARD PEACEFUL COEXISTENCE, NOT RETALIATION.
A WAY TO CHOOSE TOLERANCE, NOT REVENGE.

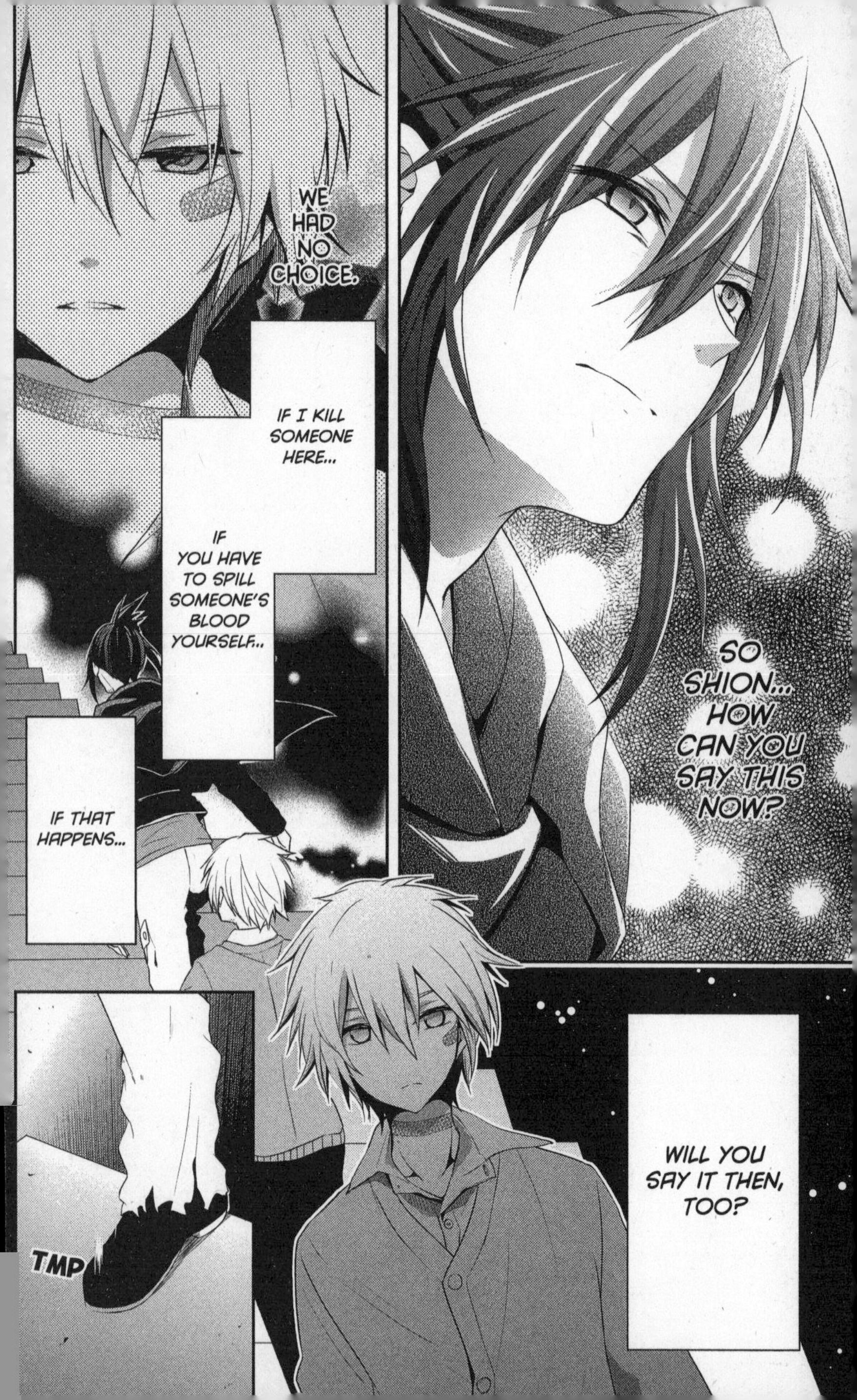
SO SHION... HOW CAN YOU SAY THIS NOW?
WE HAD NO CHOICE.
IF I KILL SOMEONE HERE...
IF YOU HAVE TO SPILL SOMEONE'S BLOOD YOURSELF...
IF THAT HAPPENS...
WILL YOU SAY IT THEN, TOO?
TMP

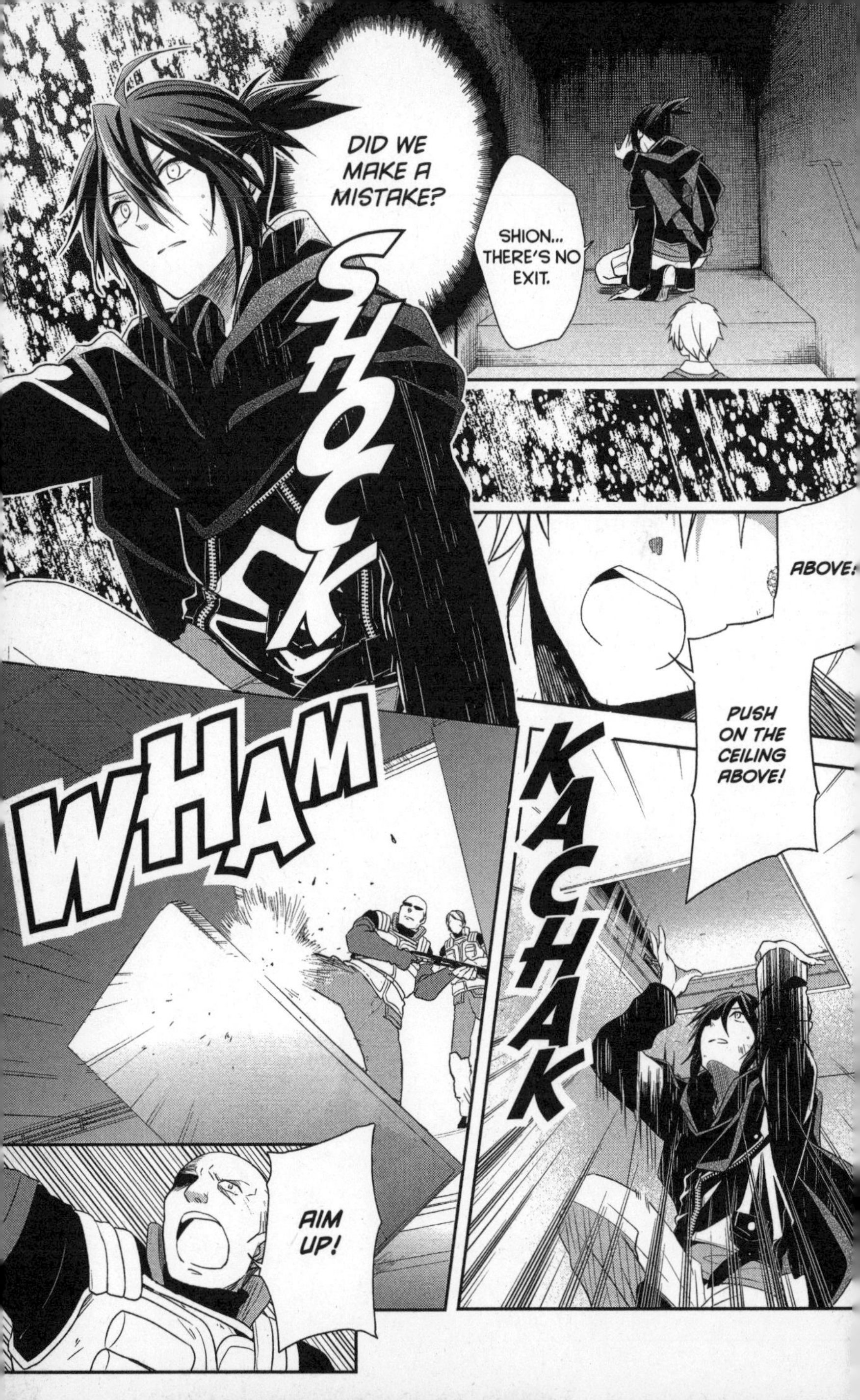

SHION... THERE'S NO EXIT.
ABOVE!
DID WE MAKE A MISTAKE?
SHOCK
PUSH ON THE CEILING ABOVE!
KACHAK
WHAM
AIM UP!

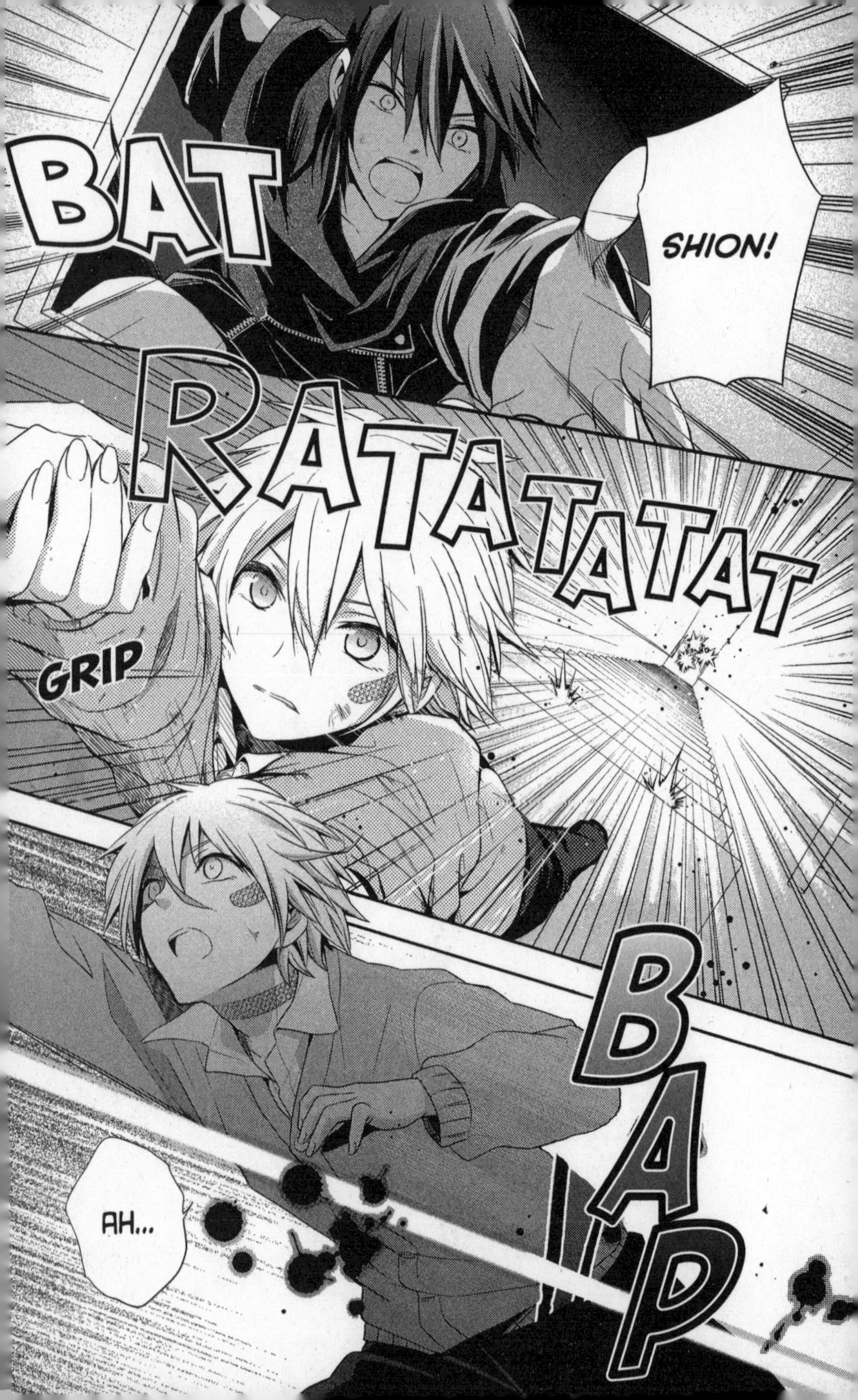
SHION!
BAT
RATATATATAT
GRIP
BAP
AH...

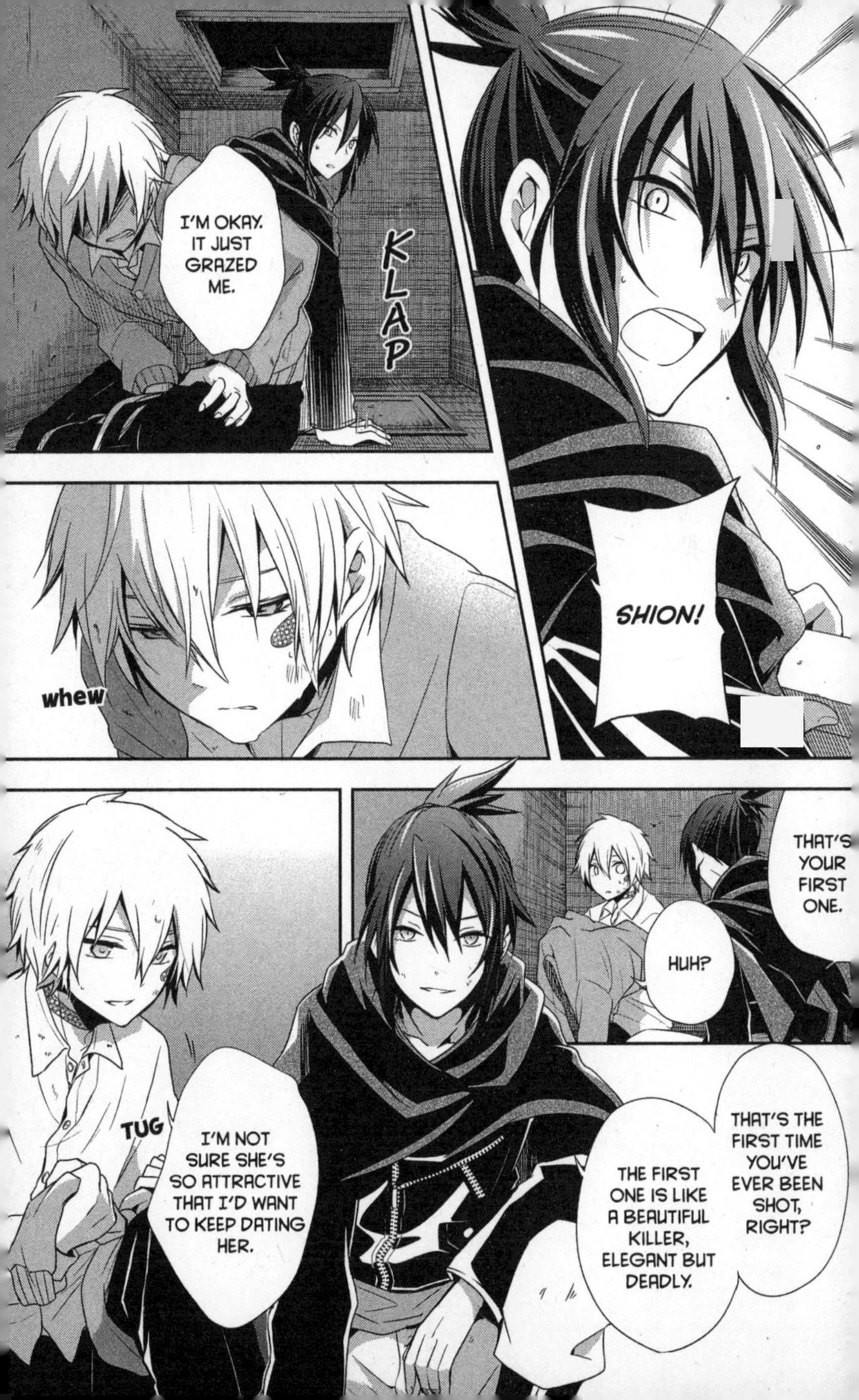
SHION!
I'M OKAY. IT JUST GRAZED ME.
KLAP
whew
THAT'S YOUR FIRST ONE.
HUH?
THAT'S THE FIRST TIME YOU'VE EVER BEEN SHOT, RIGHT?
THE FIRST ONE IS LIKE A BEAUTIFUL KILLER, ELEGANT BUT DEADLY.
TUG
I'M NOT SURE SHE'S SO ATTRACTIVE THAT I'D WANT TO KEEP DATING HER.

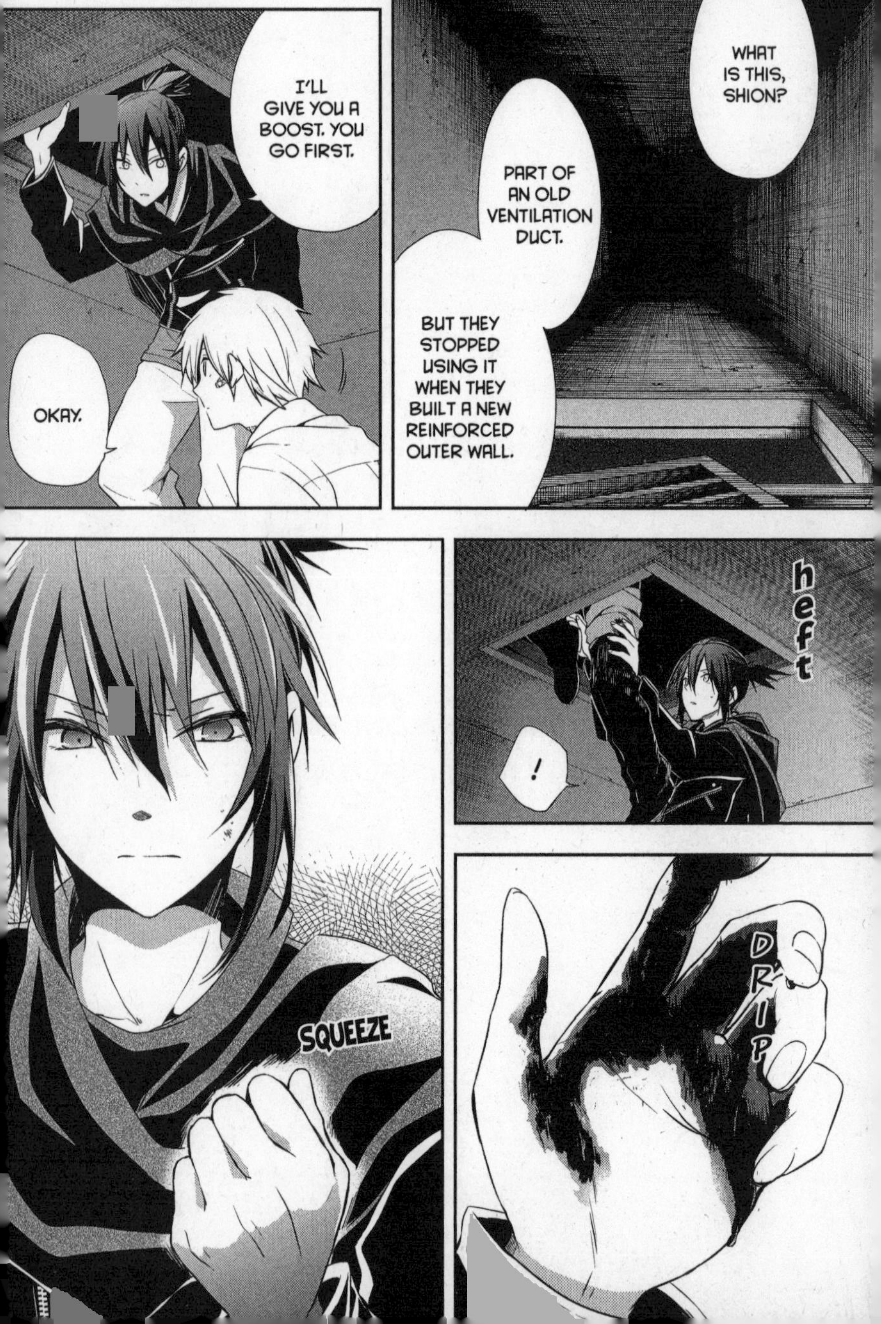
WHAT IS THIS, SHION?
PART OF AN OLD VENTILATION DUCT.
BUT THEY STOPPED USING IT WHEN THEY BUILT A NEW REINFORCED OUTER WALL.
I'LL GIVE YOU A BOOST. YOU GO FIRST.
OKAY.
heft
!
DRIP
SQUEEZE

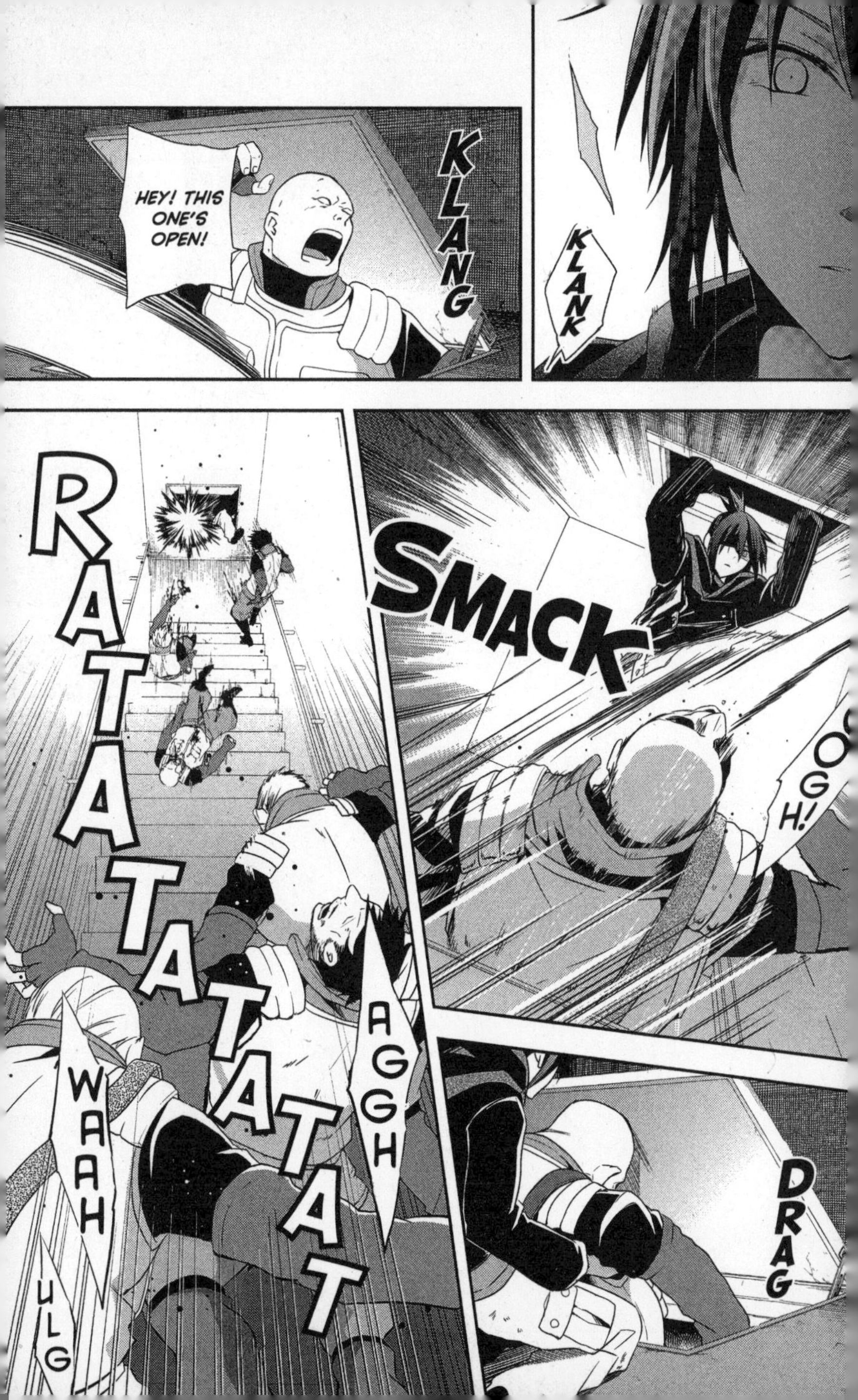
KLANK
KLANG
HEY! THIS ONE'S OPEN!
SMACK
OOGH!
DRAG
RATATATATAT
AGGH
WAAAH
ULG

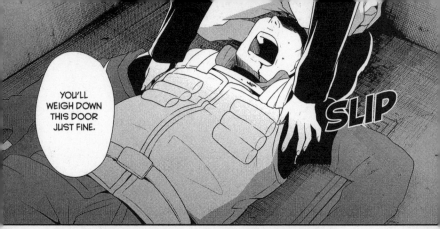

YOU'LL WEIGH DOWN THIS DOOR JUST FINE.

SLIP

CLIMB

SKIT SKIT

WHAT ARE YOU DOING, RAT? HURRY UP!

NOT SO FAST. I'VE GOT TO TAKE WHAT I CAN.

RUSTLE

RUSTLE

IT'S LIKE A RAT'S NEST IN HERE.

SKIT SKIT SKIT

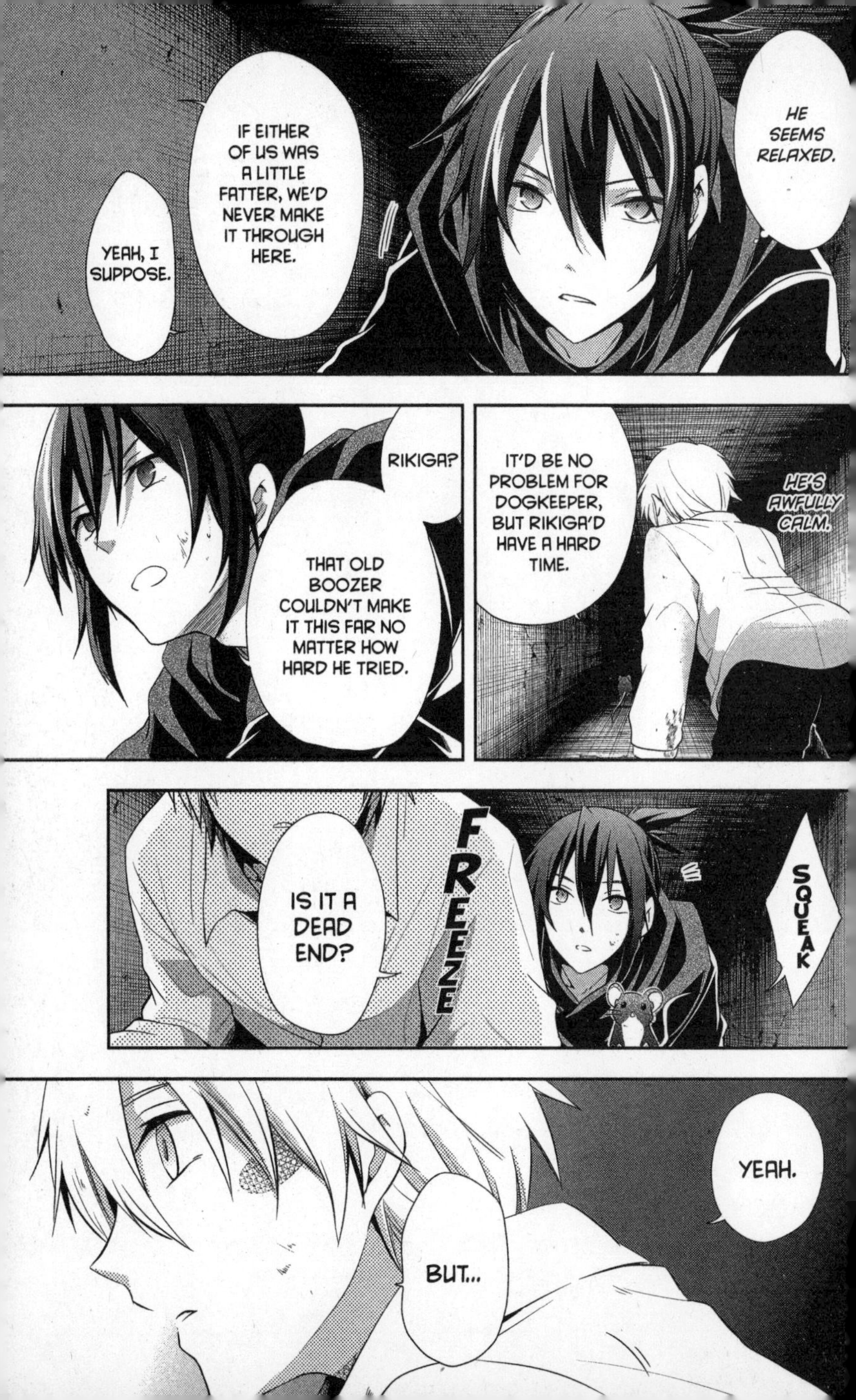
HE SEEMS RELAXED.
IF EITHER OF US WAS A LITTLE FATTER, WE'D NEVER MAKE IT THROUGH HERE.
YEAH, I SUPPOSE.
HE'S AWFULLY CALM.
IT'D BE NO PROBLEM FOR DOGKEEPER, BUT RIKIGA'D HAVE A HARD TIME.
RIKIGA?
THAT OLD BOOZER COULDN'T MAKE IT THIS FAR NO MATTER HOW HARD HE TRIED.
SQUEAK
FREEZE
IS IT A DEAD END?
YEAH.
BUT...

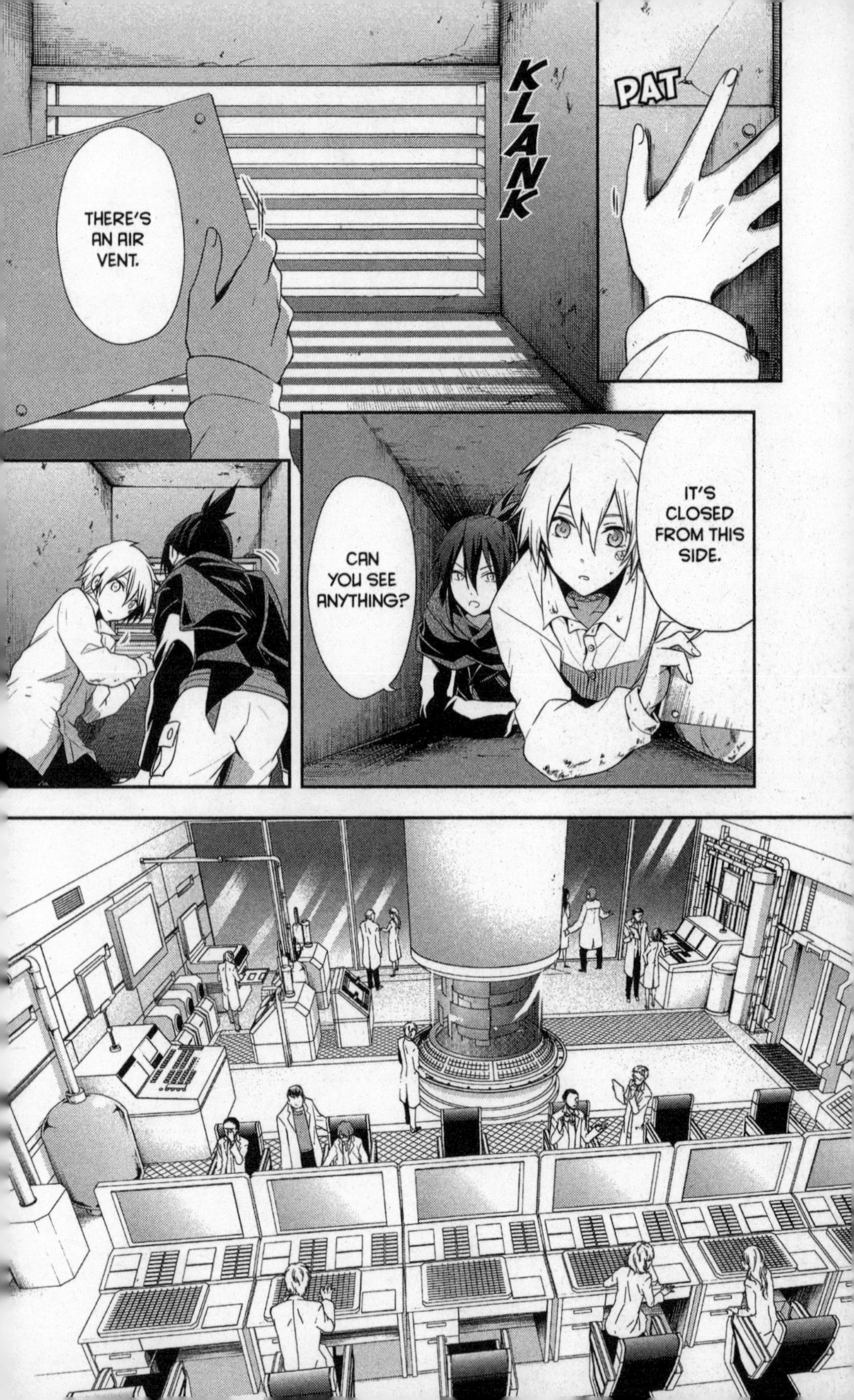
PAT
KLANK
THERE'S AN AIR VENT.
IT'S CLOSED FROM THIS SIDE.
CAN YOU SEE ANYTHING?

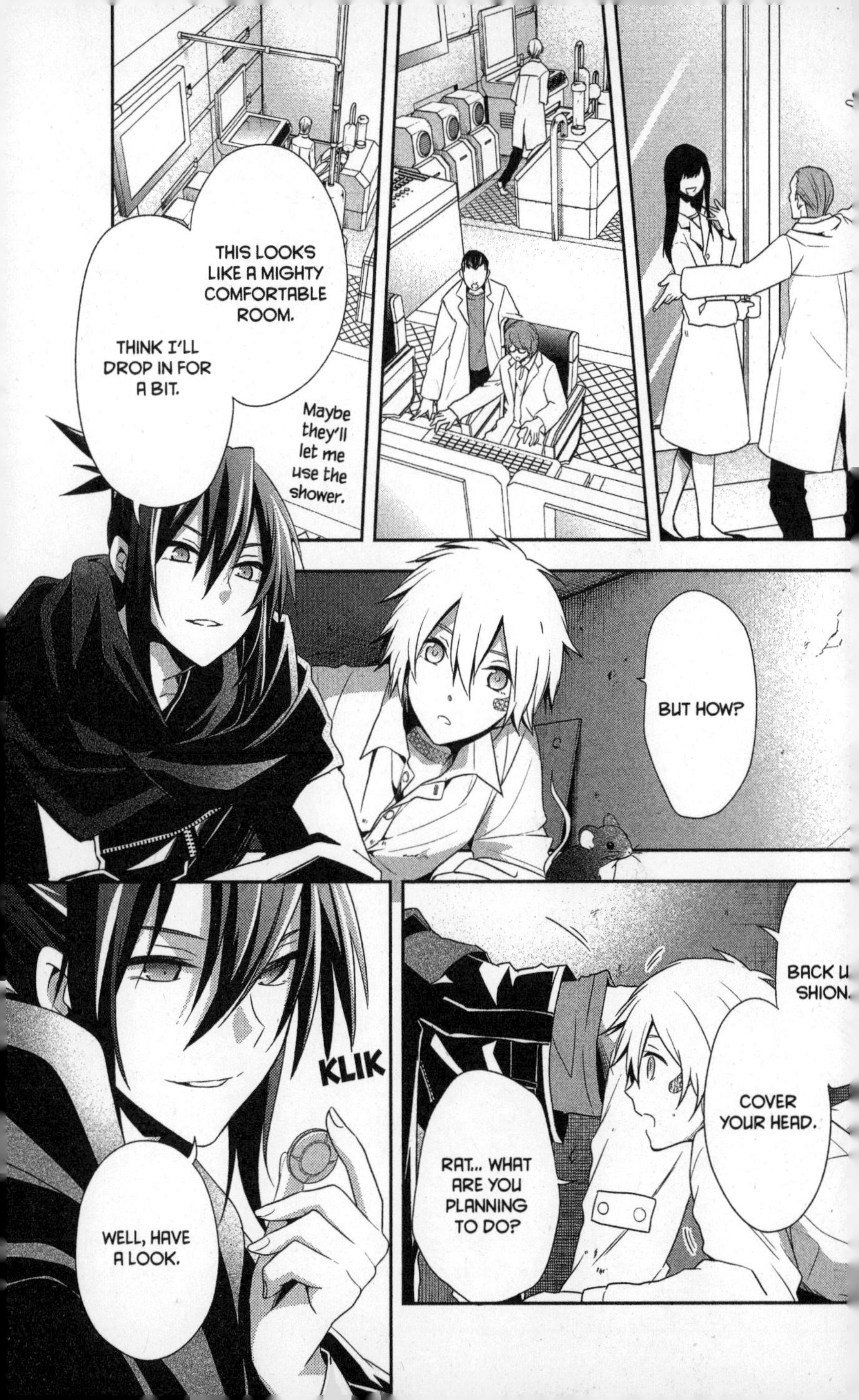
THIS LOOKS LIKE A MIGHTY COMFORTABLE ROOM.
THINK I'LL DROP IN FOR A BIT.
Maybe they'll let me use the shower.
BUT HOW?
BACK U SHION.
COVER YOUR HEAD.
RAT... WHAT ARE YOU PLANNING TO DO?
KLIK
WELL, HAVE A LOOK.

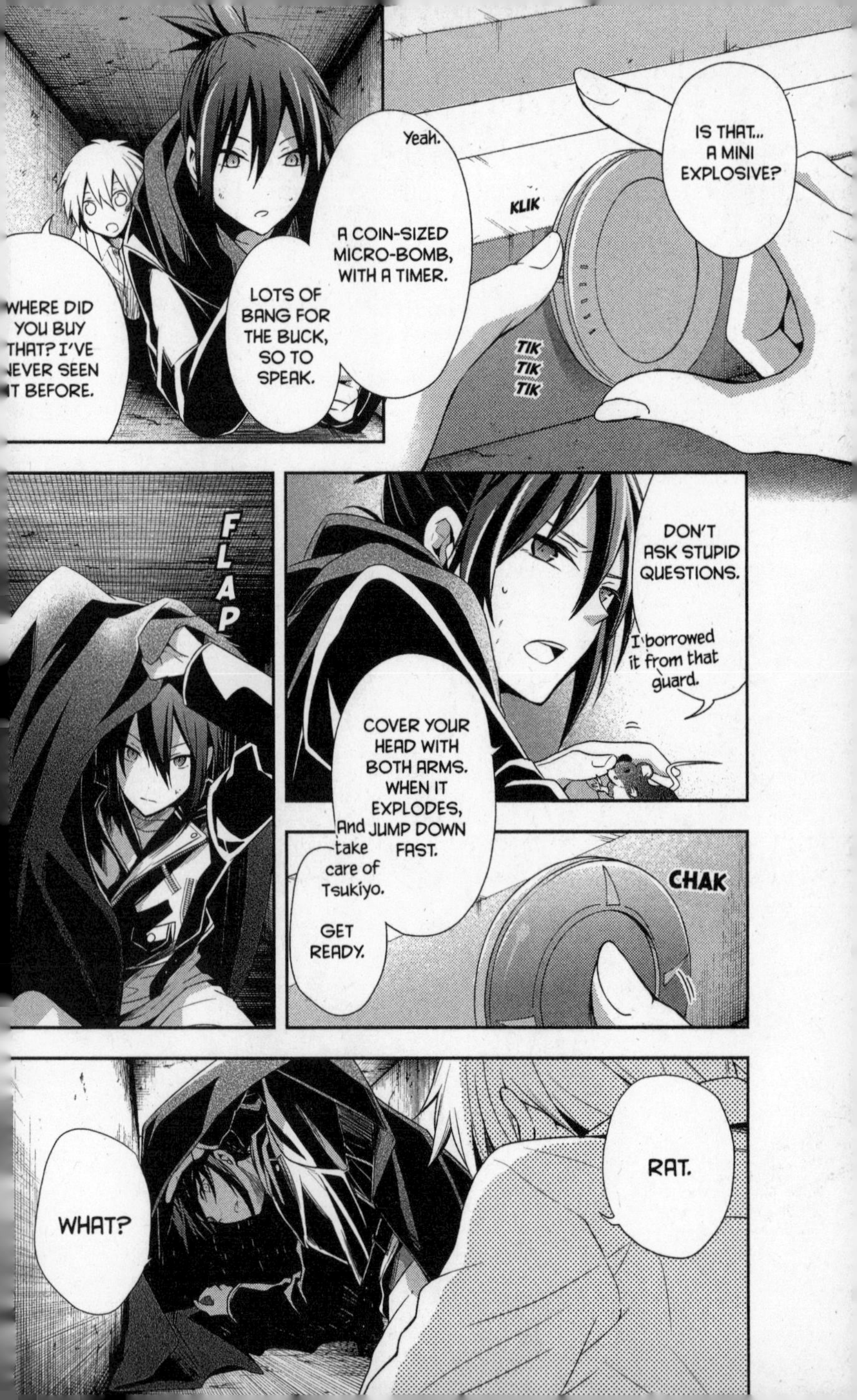
IS THAT... A MINI EXPLOSIVE?
KLIK
Yeah.
A COIN-SIZED MICRO-BOMB, WITH A TIMER.
TIK TIK TIK
LOTS OF BANG FOR THE BUCK, SO TO SPEAK.
WHERE DID YOU BUY THAT? I'VE NEVER SEEN IT BEFORE.
DON'T ASK STUPID QUESTIONS.
I borrowed it from that guard.
COVER YOUR HEAD WITH BOTH ARMS. WHEN IT EXPLODES, JUMP DOWN FAST.
CHAK
And take care of Tsukiyo.
GET READY.
FLAP
RAT.
WHAT?

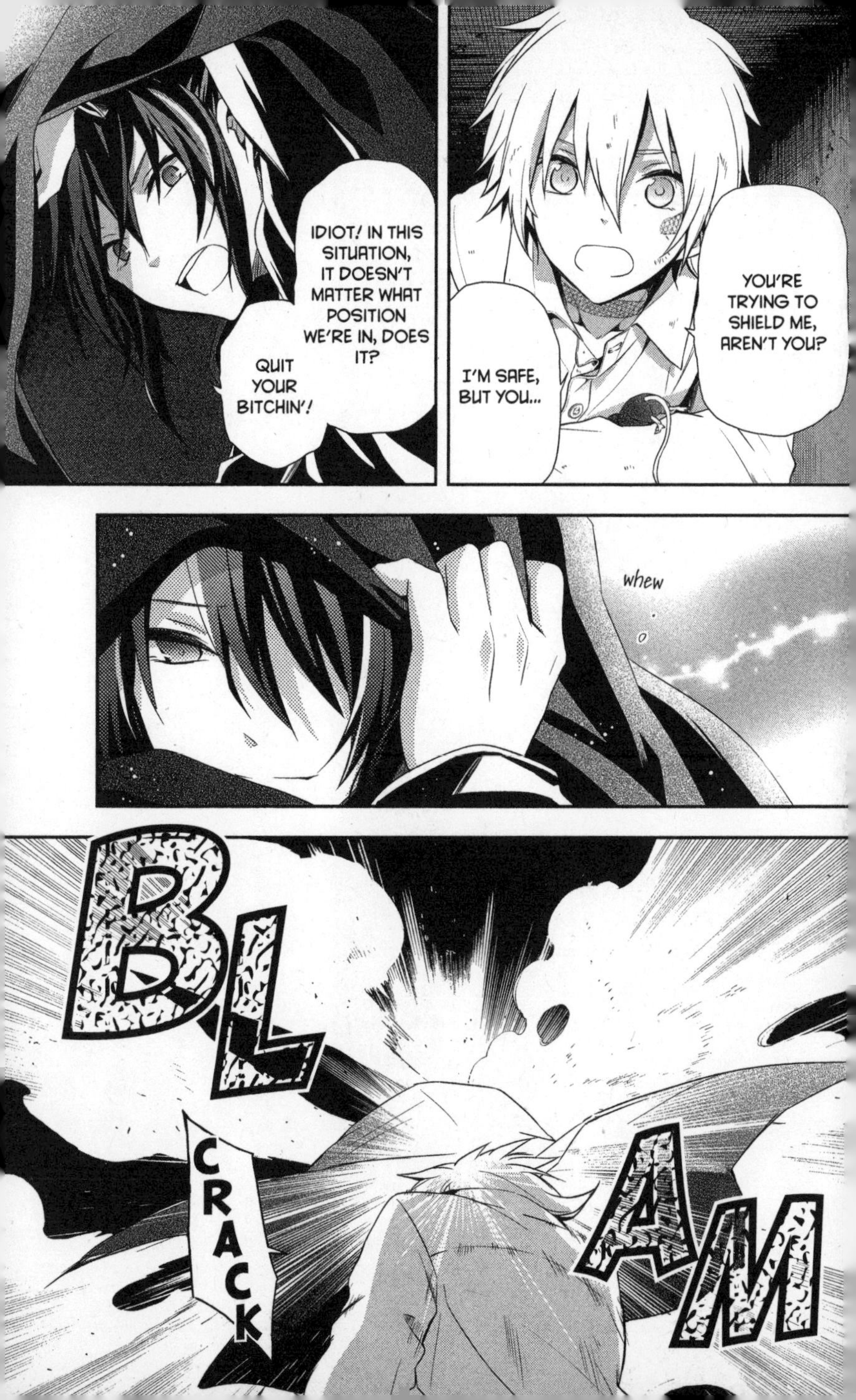
YOU'RE TRYING TO SHIELD ME, AREN'T YOU?
I'M SAFE, BUT YOU...
IDIOT! IN THIS SITUATION, IT DOESN'T MATTER WHAT POSITION WE'RE IN, DOES IT?
QUIT YOUR BITCHIN'!
whew
BLAM
CRACK

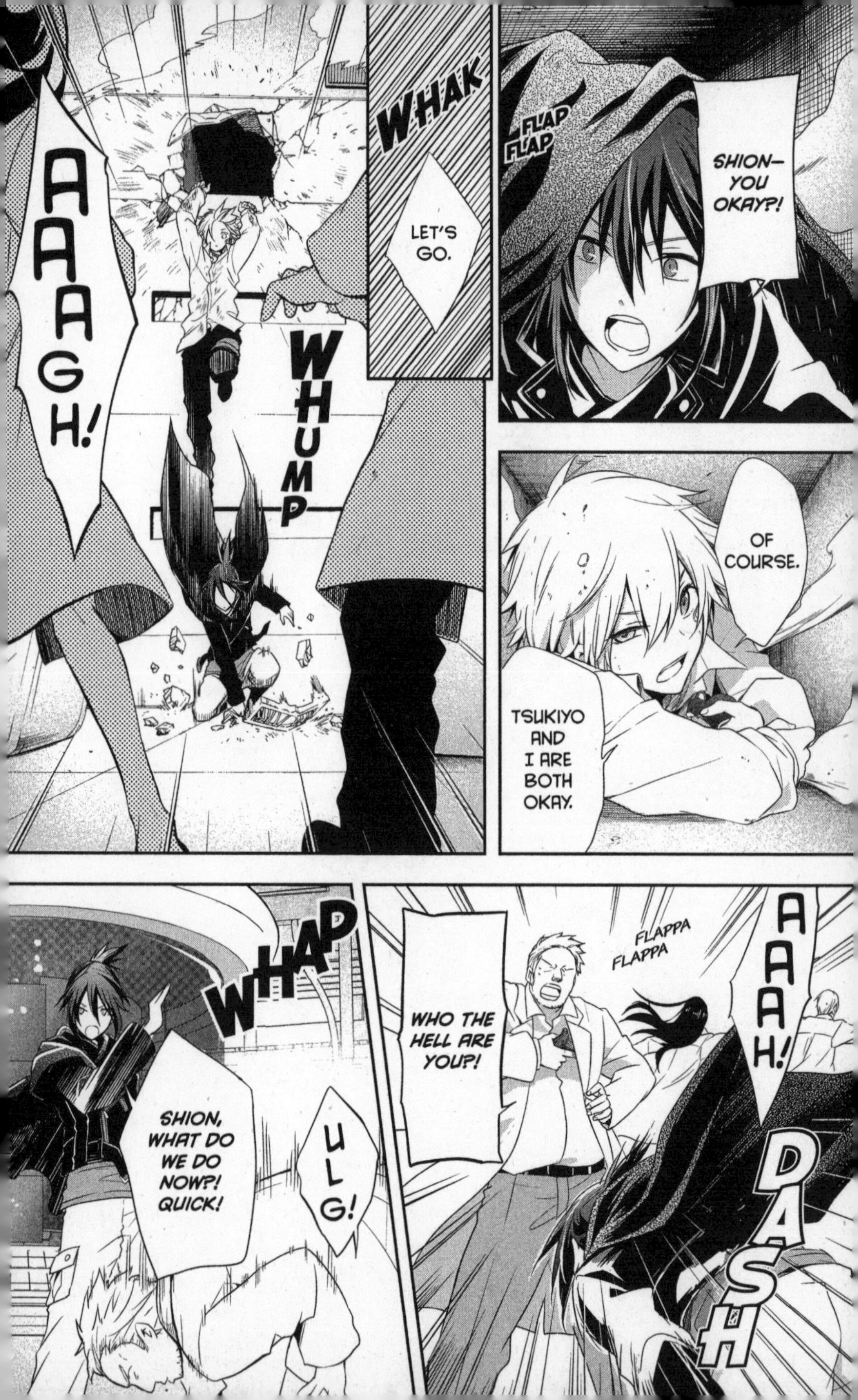
FLAP FLAP
SHION—YOU OKAY?!
OF COURSE.
TSUKIYO AND I ARE BOTH OKAY.
WHAK
LET'S GO.
AAAAGH!
WHUMP
AAAAH!
FLAPPA FLAPPA
WHO THE HELL ARE YOU?!
DASH
WHAP
ULG!
SHION, WHAT DO WE DO NOW?! QUICK!

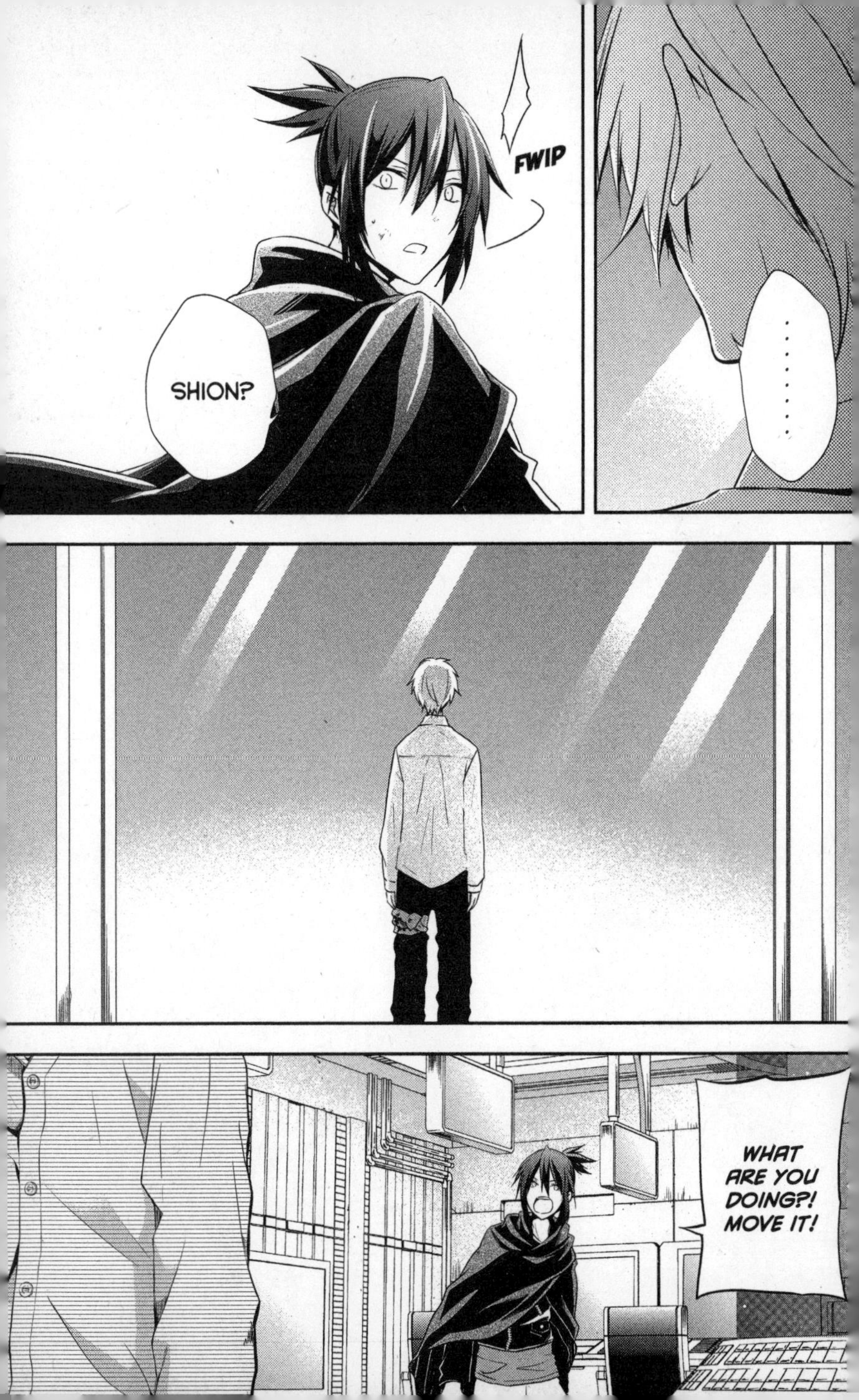
......
FWIP
SHION?
WHAT ARE YOU DOING?! MOVE IT!

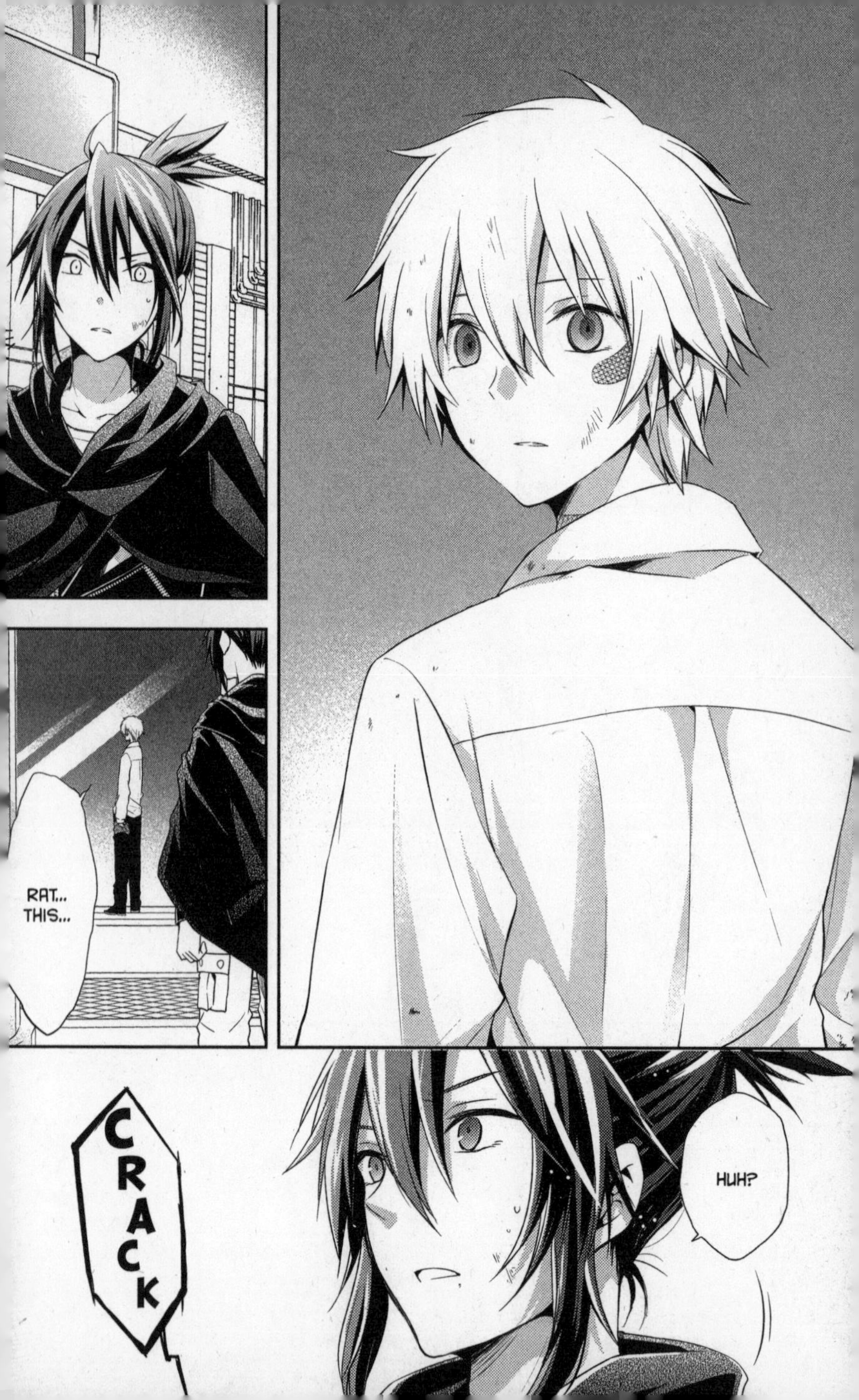
RAT... THIS...
HUH?
CRACK

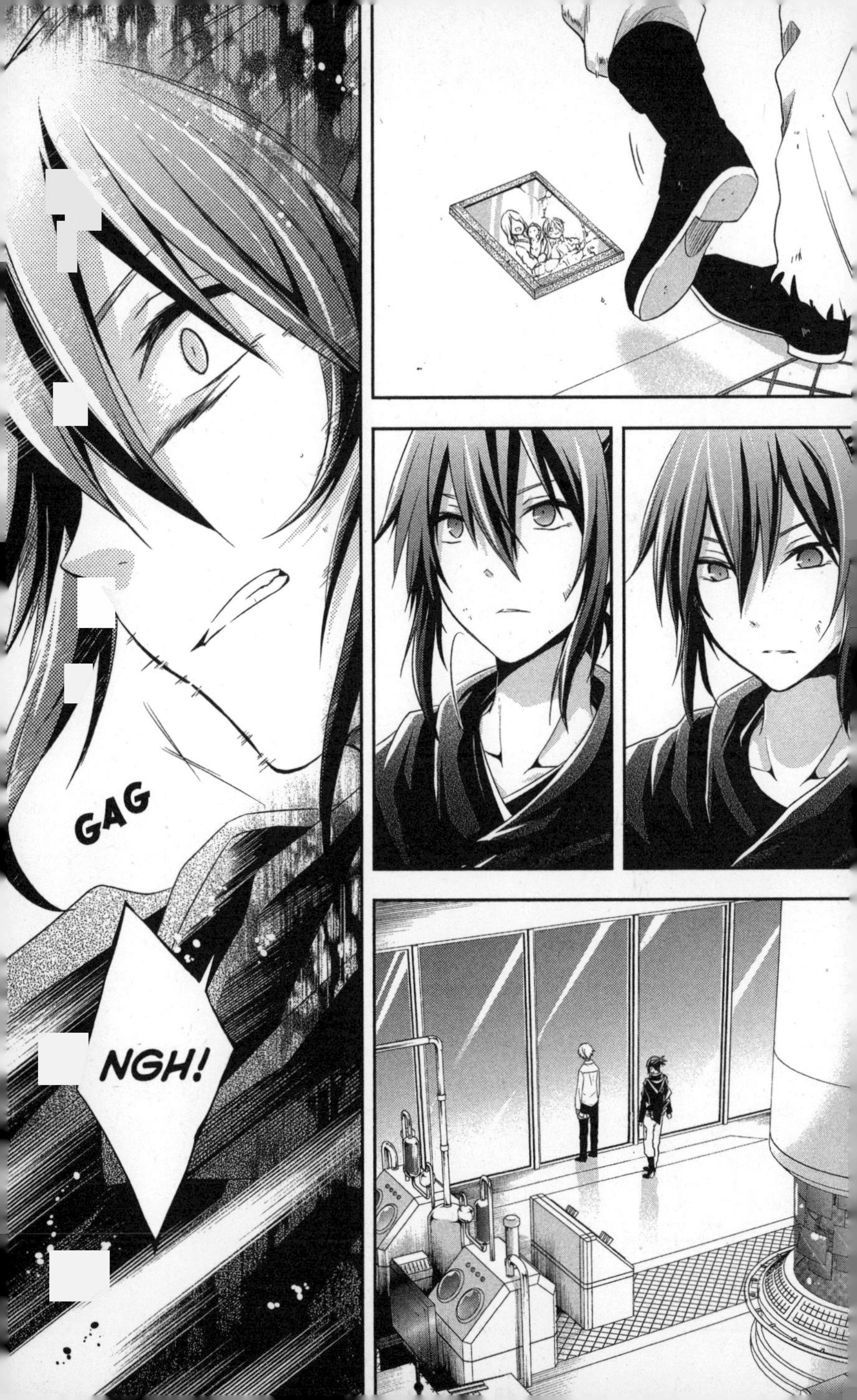
GAG
NGH!

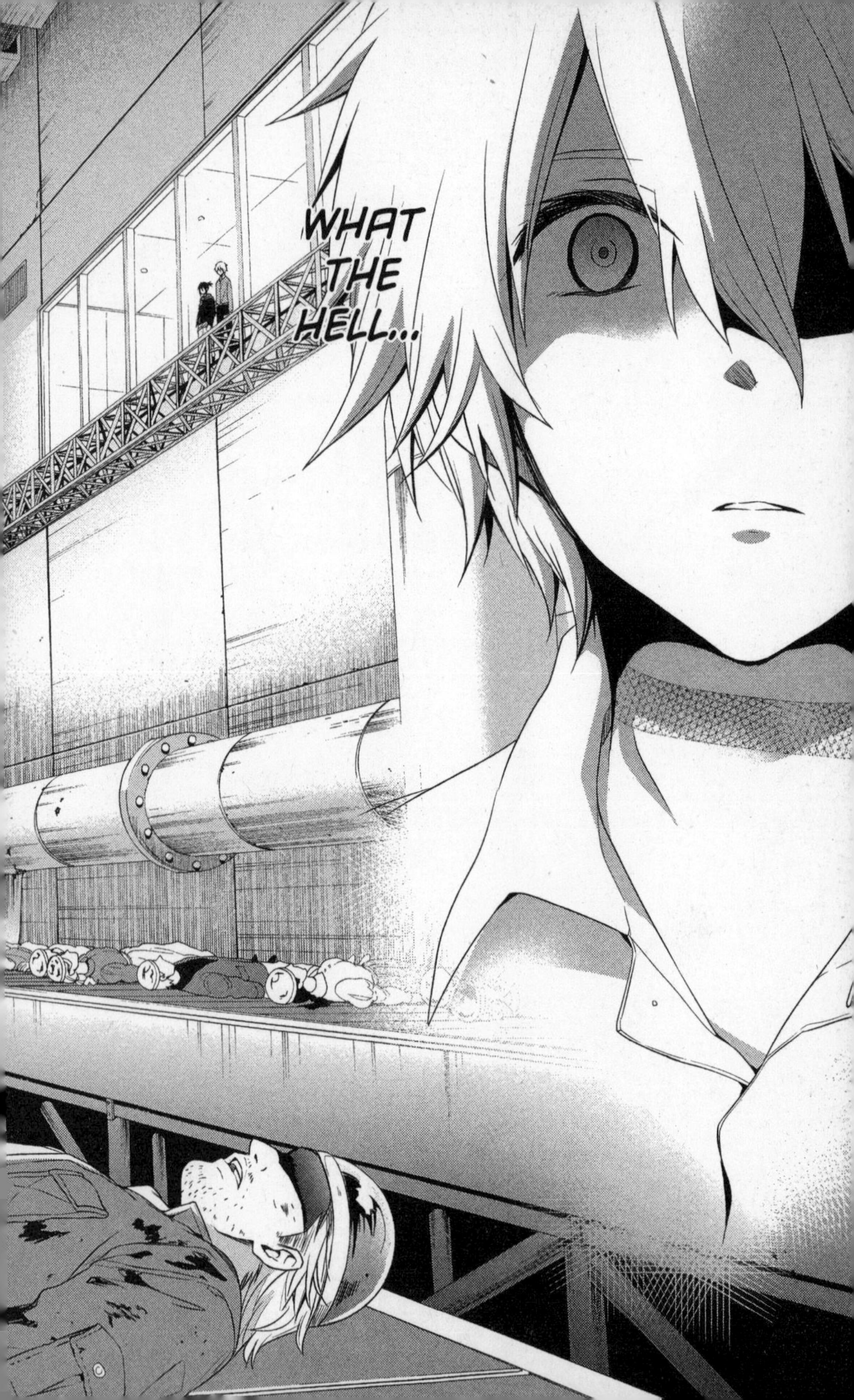
WHAT THE HELL...

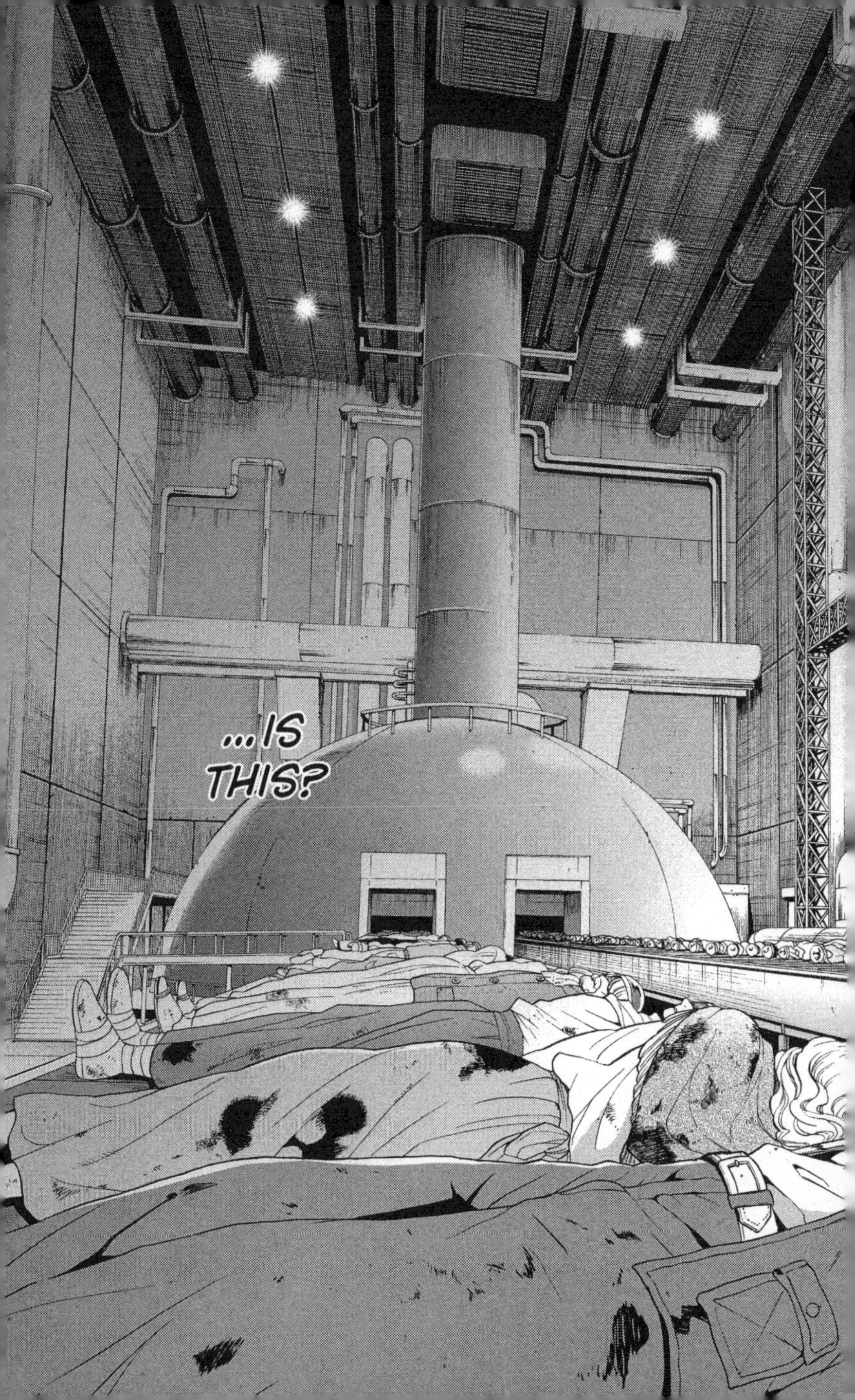
...IS THIS?

NO.6

Chapter 26: Are You Sad?

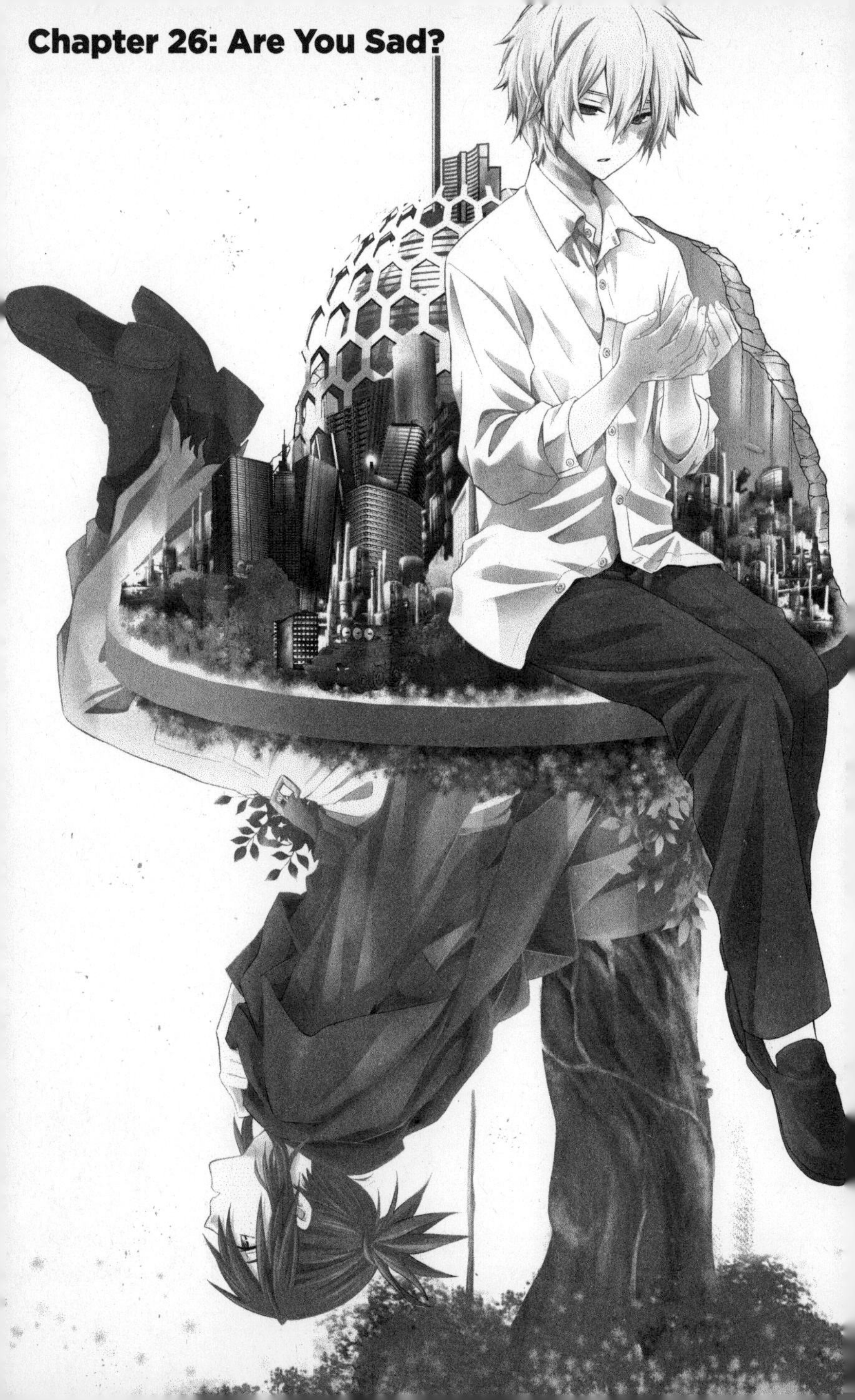

NO.6

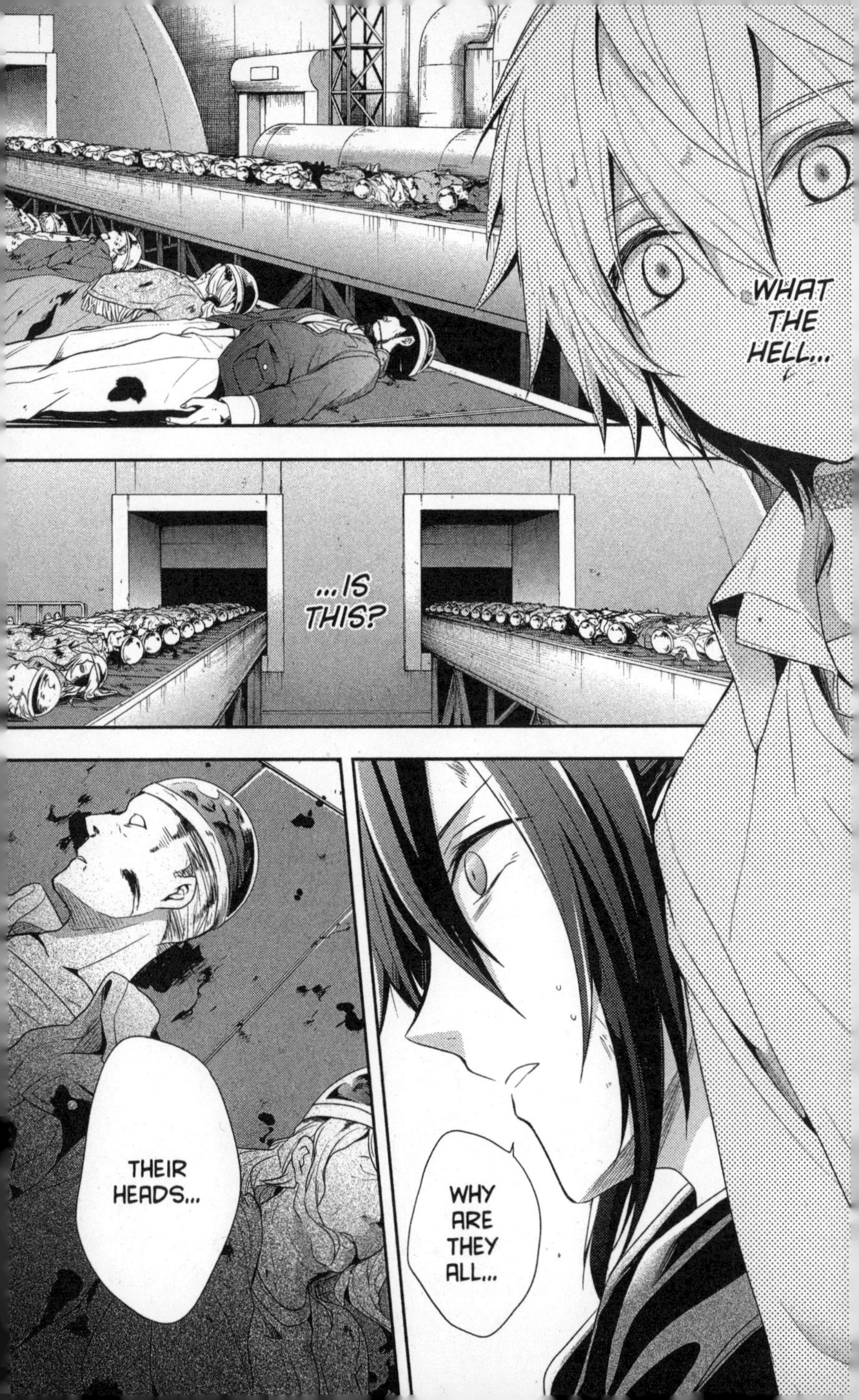
WHAT THE HELL...
...IS THIS?
WHY ARE THEY ALL...
THEIR HEADS...

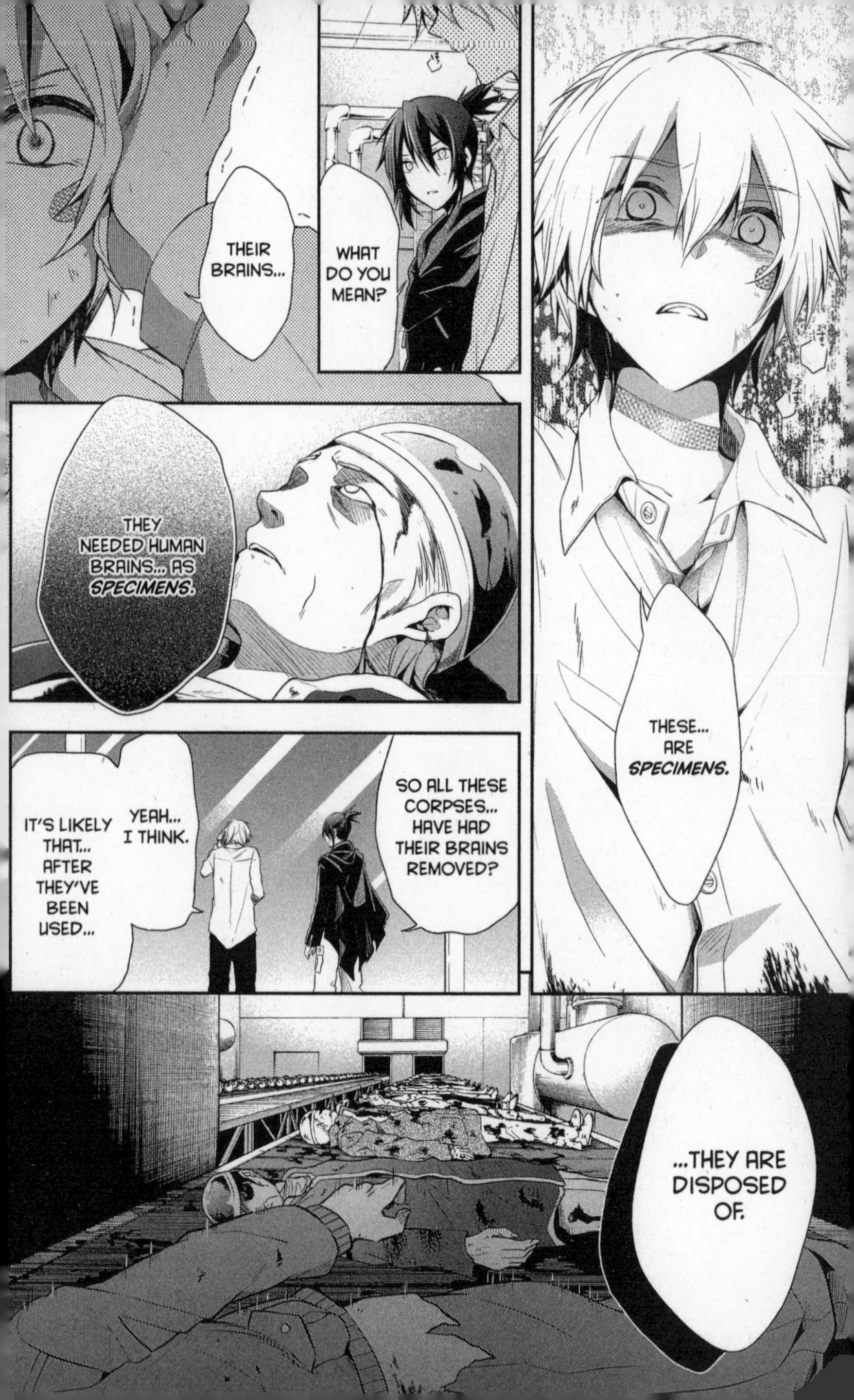
THESE... ARE *SPECIMENS.*
WHAT DO YOU MEAN?
THEIR BRAINS...
THEY NEEDED HUMAN BRAINS... AS *SPECIMENS.*
SO ALL THESE CORPSES... HAVE HAD THEIR BRAINS REMOVED?
YEAH... I THINK.
IT'S LIKELY THAT... AFTER THEY'VE BEEN USED...
...THEY ARE DISPOSED OF.

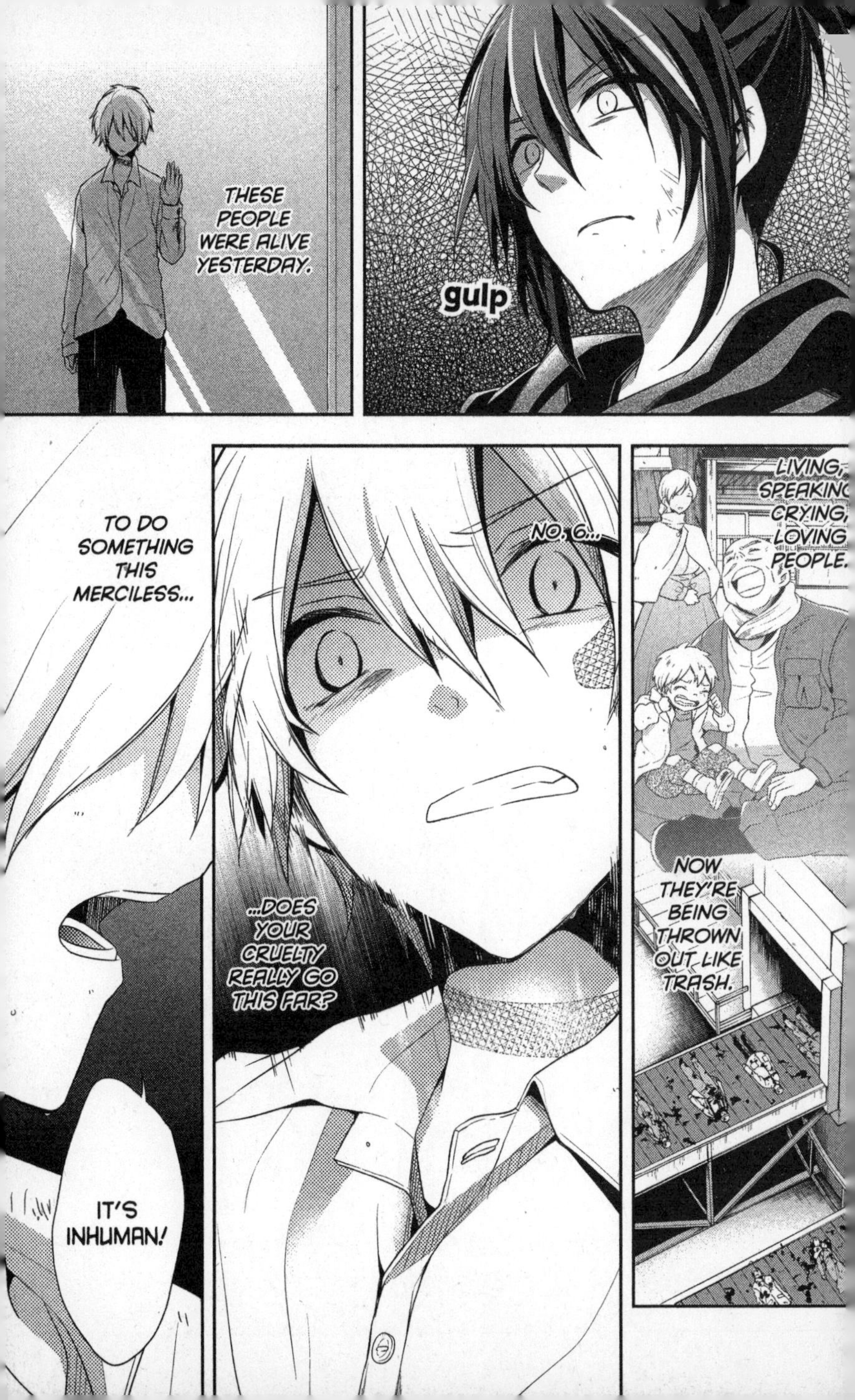
gulp
THESE PEOPLE WERE ALIVE YESTERDAY.
LIVING, SPEAKING, CRYING, LOVING PEOPLE.
NOW THEY'RE BEING THROWN OUT LIKE TRASH.
NO. 6...
...DOES YOUR CRUELTY REALLY GO THIS FAR?
TO DO SOMETHING THIS MERCILESS...
IT'S INHUMAN!

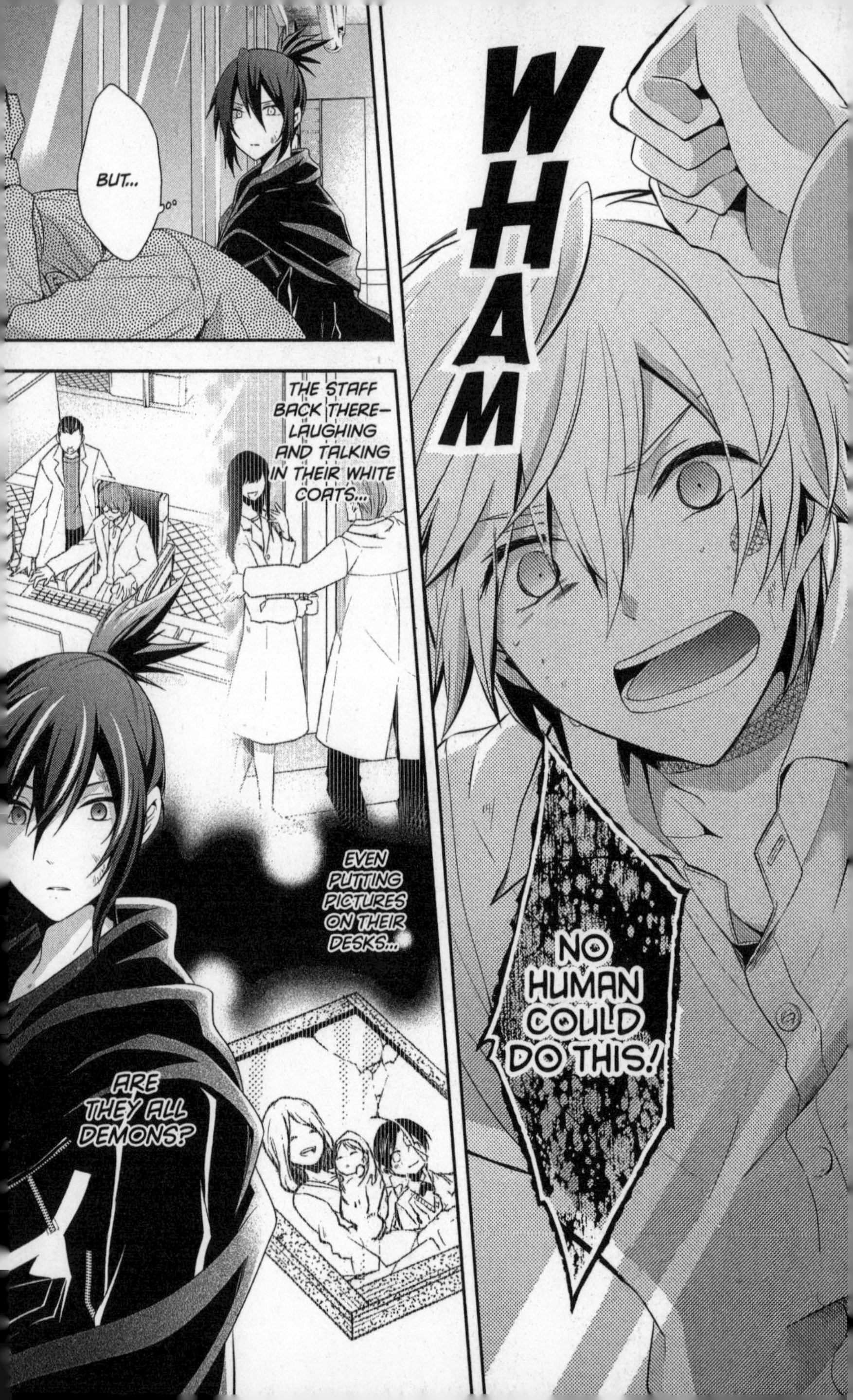
WHAM
NO HUMAN COULD DO THIS!
BUT...
THE STAFF BACK THERE— LAUGHING AND TALKING IN THEIR WHITE COATS...
EVEN PUTTING PICTURES ON THEIR DESKS...
ARE THEY ALL DEMONS?

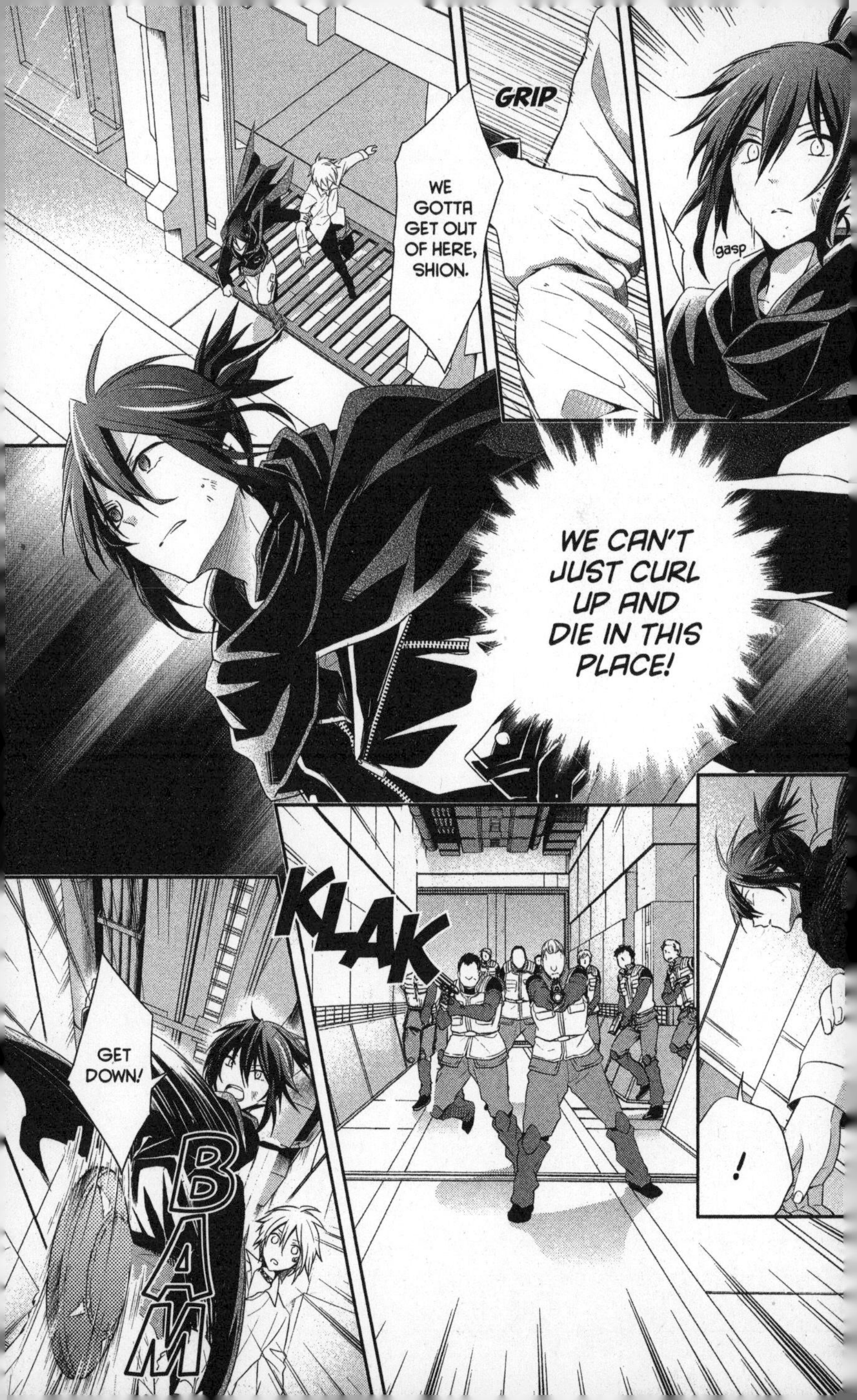
gasp
GRIP
WE GOTTA GET OUT OF HERE, SHION.
WE CAN'T JUST CURL UP AND DIE IN THIS PLACE!
!
KLAK
GET DOWN!
BAM

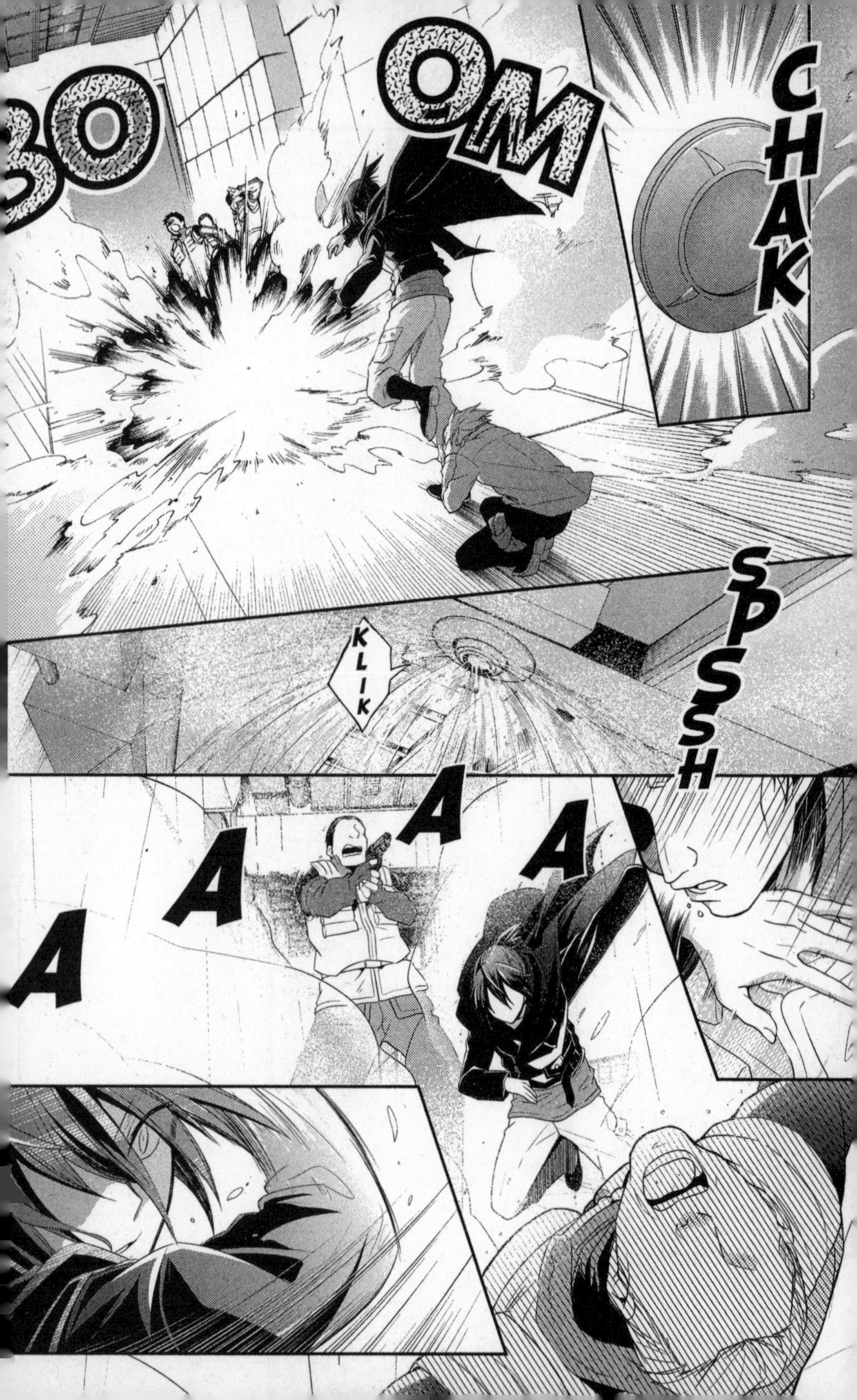
CHAK
BOOM
SPSSH
KLIK
A A A A A

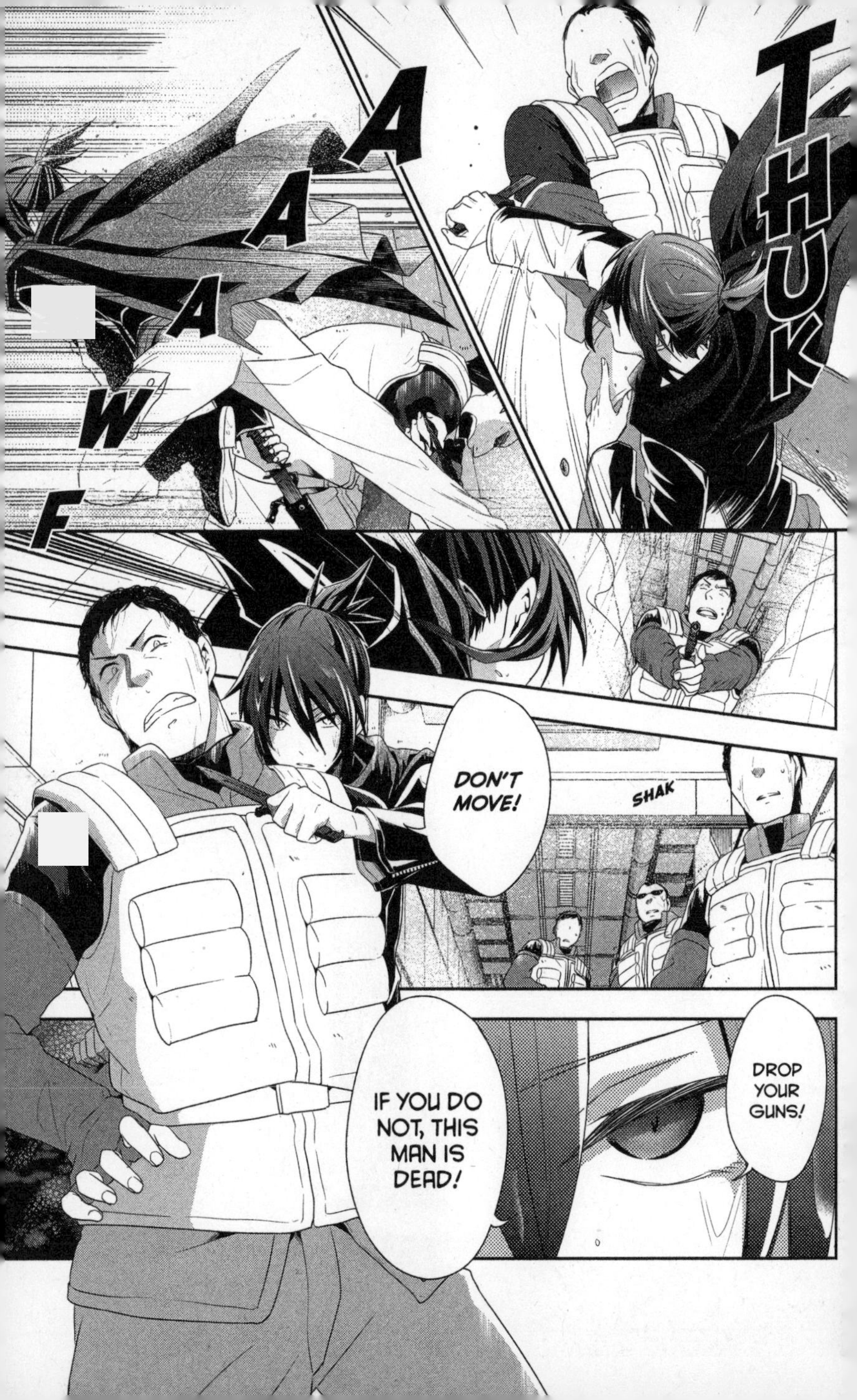
THUK
FWAAAA
SHAK
DON'T MOVE!
DROP YOUR GUNS!
IF YOU DO NOT, THIS MAN IS DEAD!

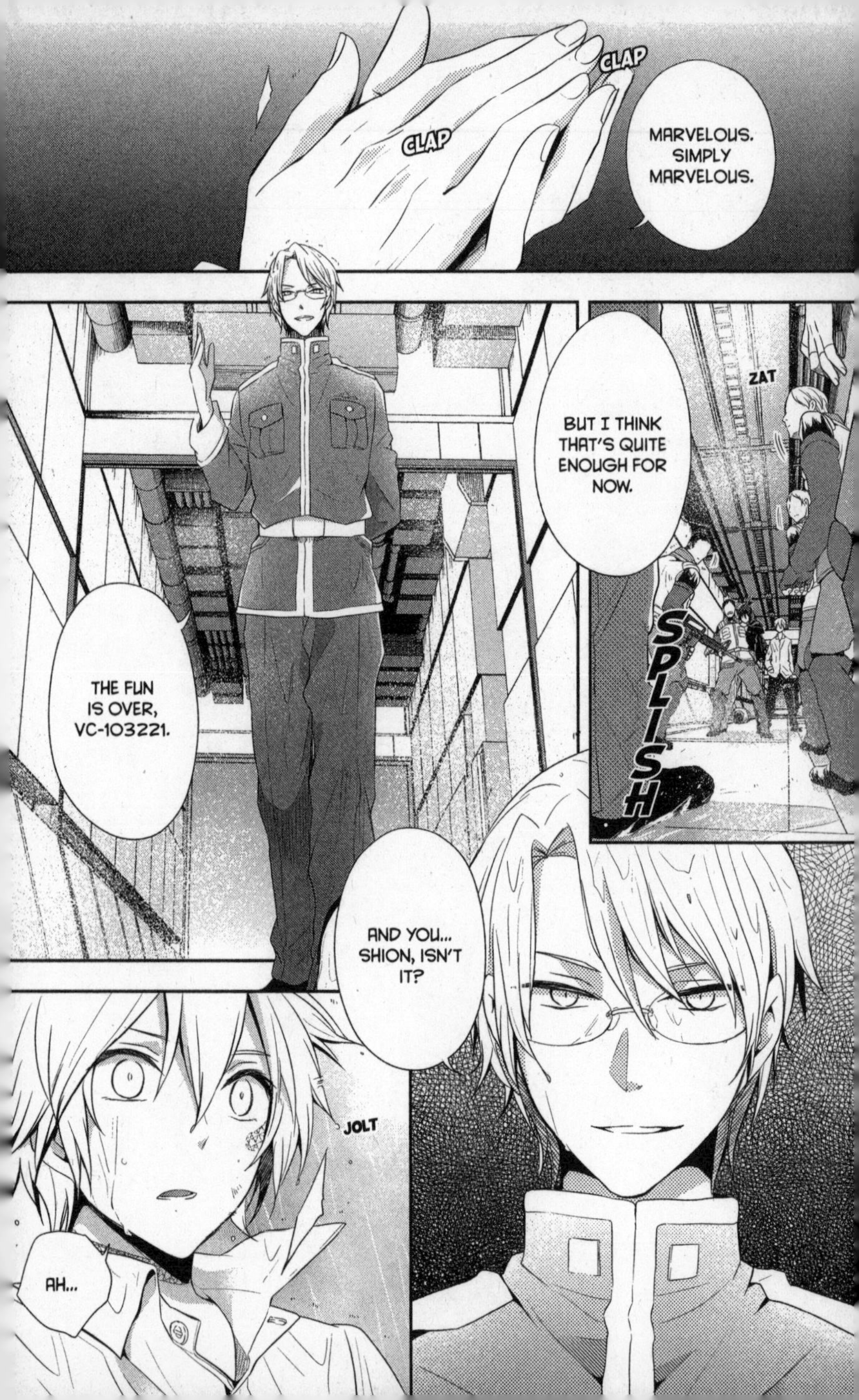
CLAP
MARVELOUS. SIMPLY MARVELOUS.
CLAP
ZAT
BUT I THINK THAT'S QUITE ENOUGH FOR NOW.
SPLISH
THE FUN IS OVER, VC-103221.
AND YOU... SHION, ISN'T IT?
JOLT
AH...

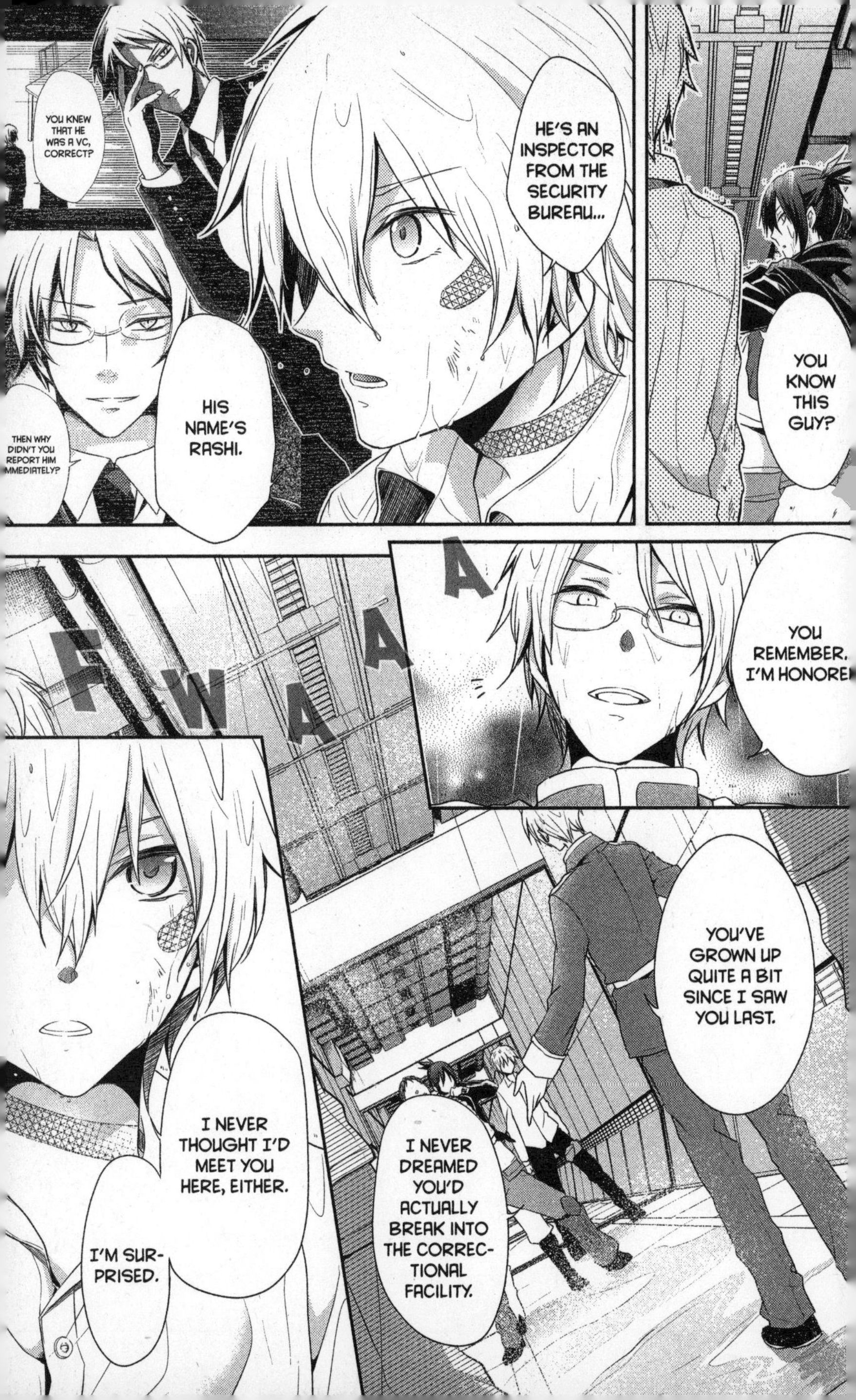
YOU KNOW THIS GUY?
HE'S AN INSPECTOR FROM THE SECURITY BUREAU...
HIS NAME'S RASHI.
YOU KNEW THAT HE WAS A VC, CORRECT?
THEN WHY DIDN'T YOU REPORT HIM MMEDIATELY?
YOU REMEMBER. I'M HONORE
FWAAA
YOU'VE GROWN UP QUITE A BIT SINCE I SAW YOU LAST.
I NEVER DREAMED YOU'D ACTUALLY BREAK INTO THE CORREC-TIONAL FACILITY.
I NEVER THOUGHT I'D MEET YOU HERE, EITHER.
I'M SUR-PRISED.

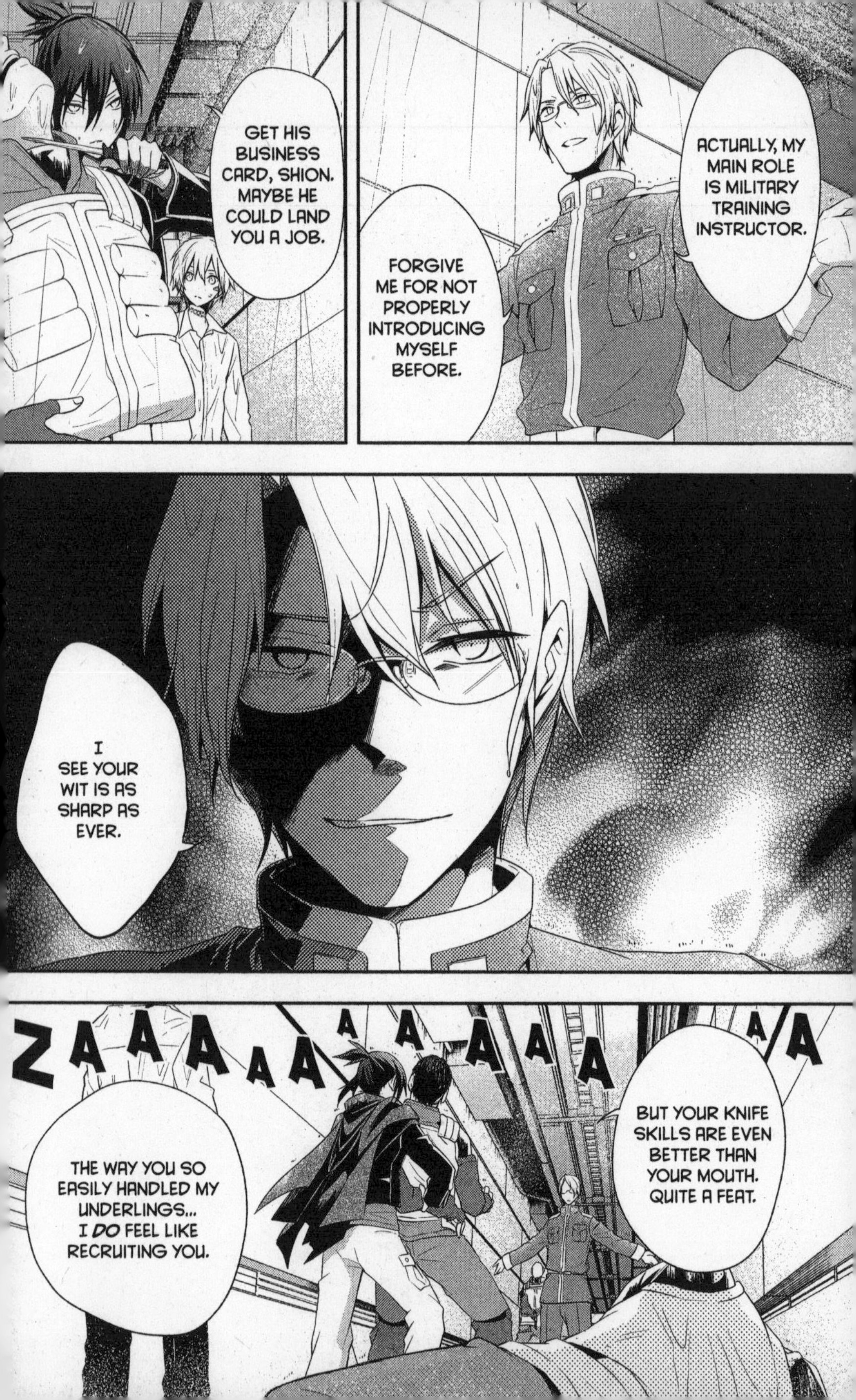
ACTUALLY, MY MAIN ROLE IS MILITARY TRAINING INSTRUCTOR.
FORGIVE ME FOR NOT PROPERLY INTRODUCING MYSELF BEFORE.
GET HIS BUSINESS CARD, SHION. MAYBE HE COULD LAND YOU A JOB.
I SEE YOUR WIT IS AS SHARP AS EVER.
ZAAAAAAAAAAAAA
BUT YOUR KNIFE SKILLS ARE EVEN BETTER THAN YOUR MOUTH. QUITE A FEAT.
THE WAY YOU SO EASILY HANDLED MY UNDERLINGS... I *DO* FEEL LIKE RECRUITING YOU.

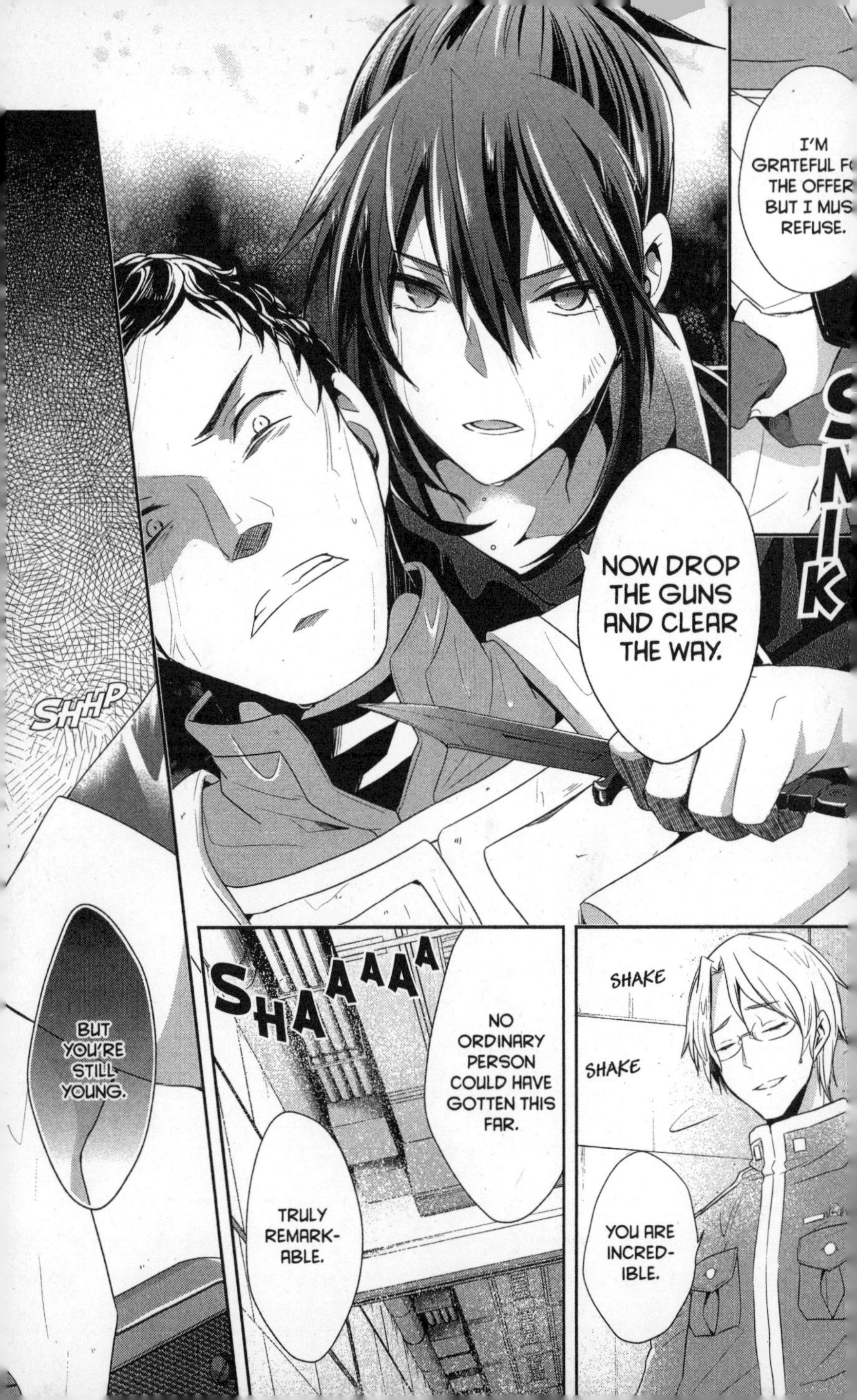
I'M GRATEFUL F
THE OFFER
BUT I MUS
REFUSE.
SNIK
NOW DROP THE GUNS AND CLEAR THE WAY.
SHHP
SHAKE
SHAKE
YOU ARE INCREDIBLE.
SHAAAAA
NO ORDINARY PERSON COULD HAVE GOTTEN THIS FAR.
TRULY REMARKABLE.
BUT YOU'RE STILL YOUNG.

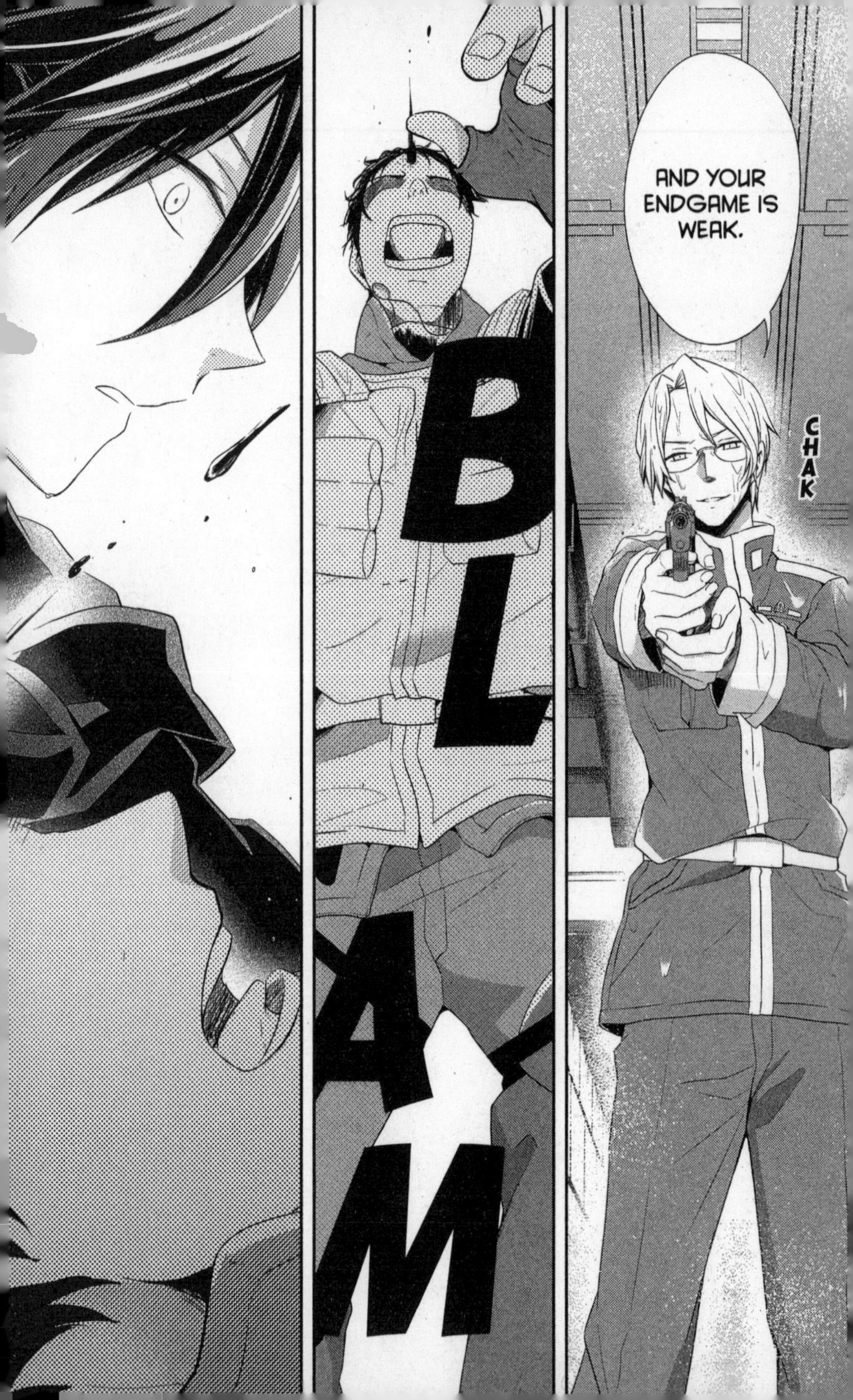
AND YOUR ENDGAME IS WEAK.
CHAK
BLAM

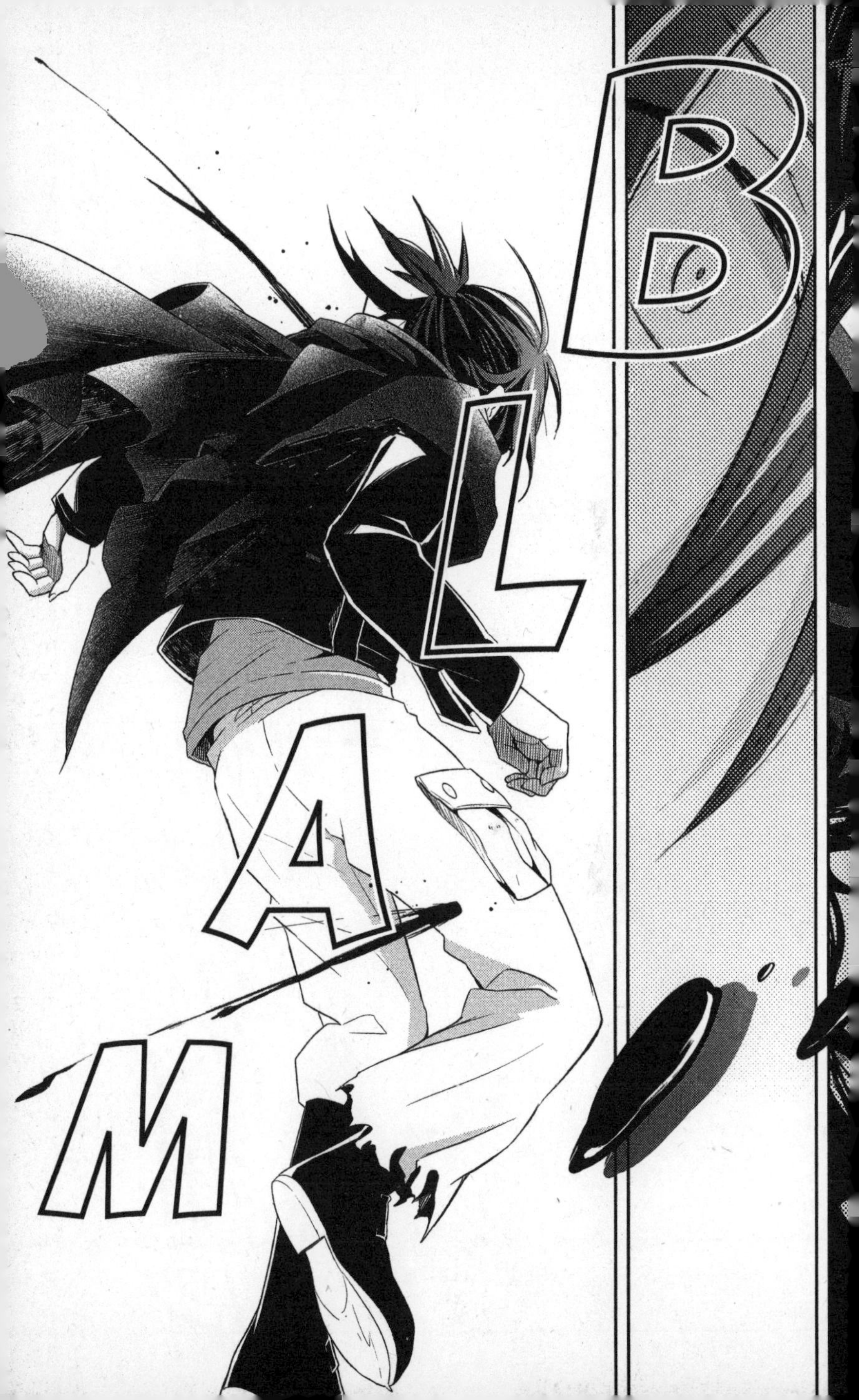
BLAM

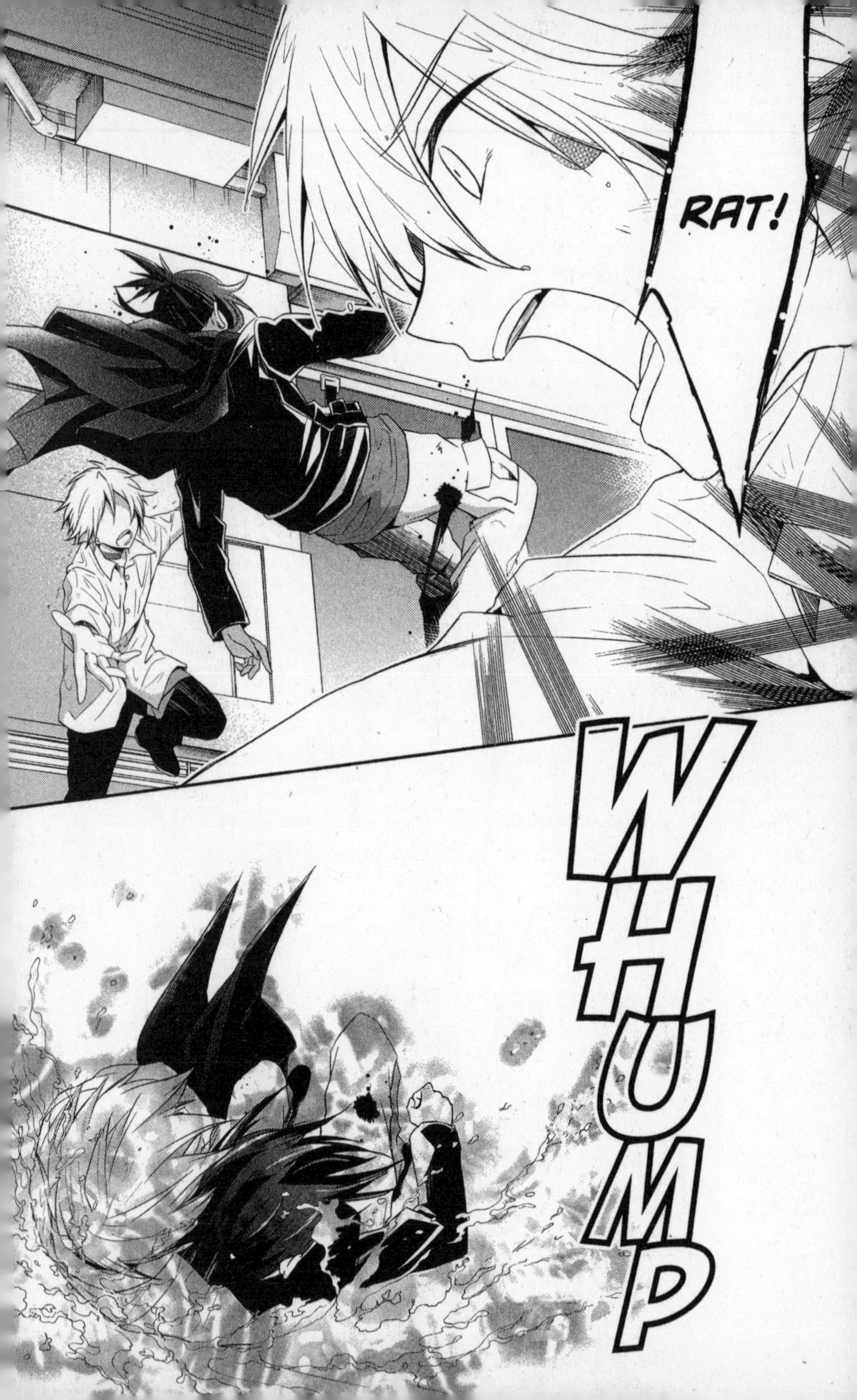
RAT!
WHUMP

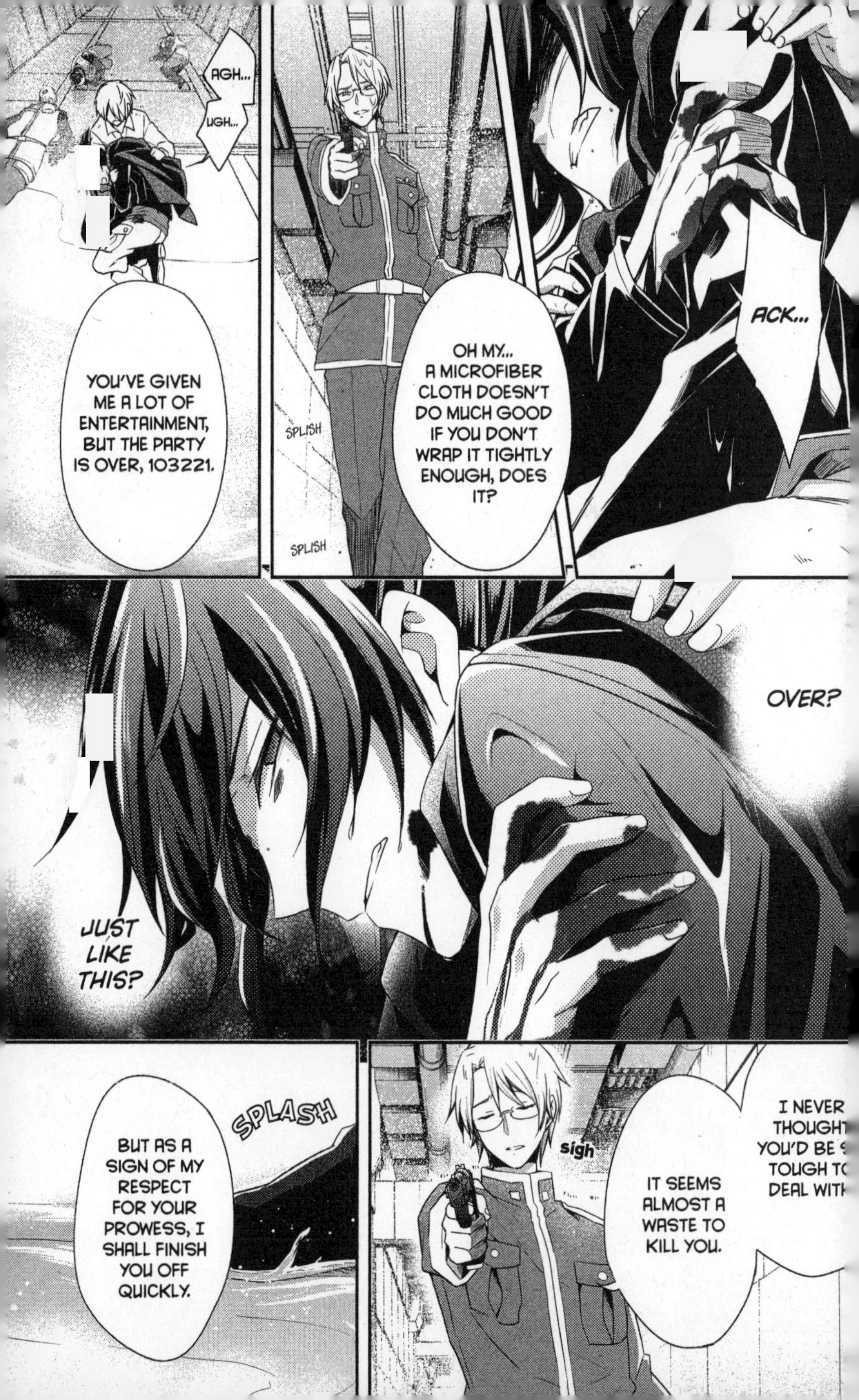
ACK...
OH MY... A MICROFIBER CLOTH DOESN'T DO MUCH GOOD IF YOU DON'T WRAP IT TIGHTLY ENOUGH, DOES IT?
SPLISH
SPLISH
AGH...
UGH...
YOU'VE GIVEN ME A LOT OF ENTERTAINMENT, BUT THE PARTY IS OVER, 103221.
OVER?
JUST LIKE THIS?
I NEVER THOUGHT YOU'D BE TOUGH DEAL WITH
sigh
IT SEEMS ALMOST A WASTE TO KILL YOU.
SPLASH
BUT AS A SIGN OF MY RESPECT FOR YOUR PROWESS, I SHALL FINISH YOU OFF QUICKLY.

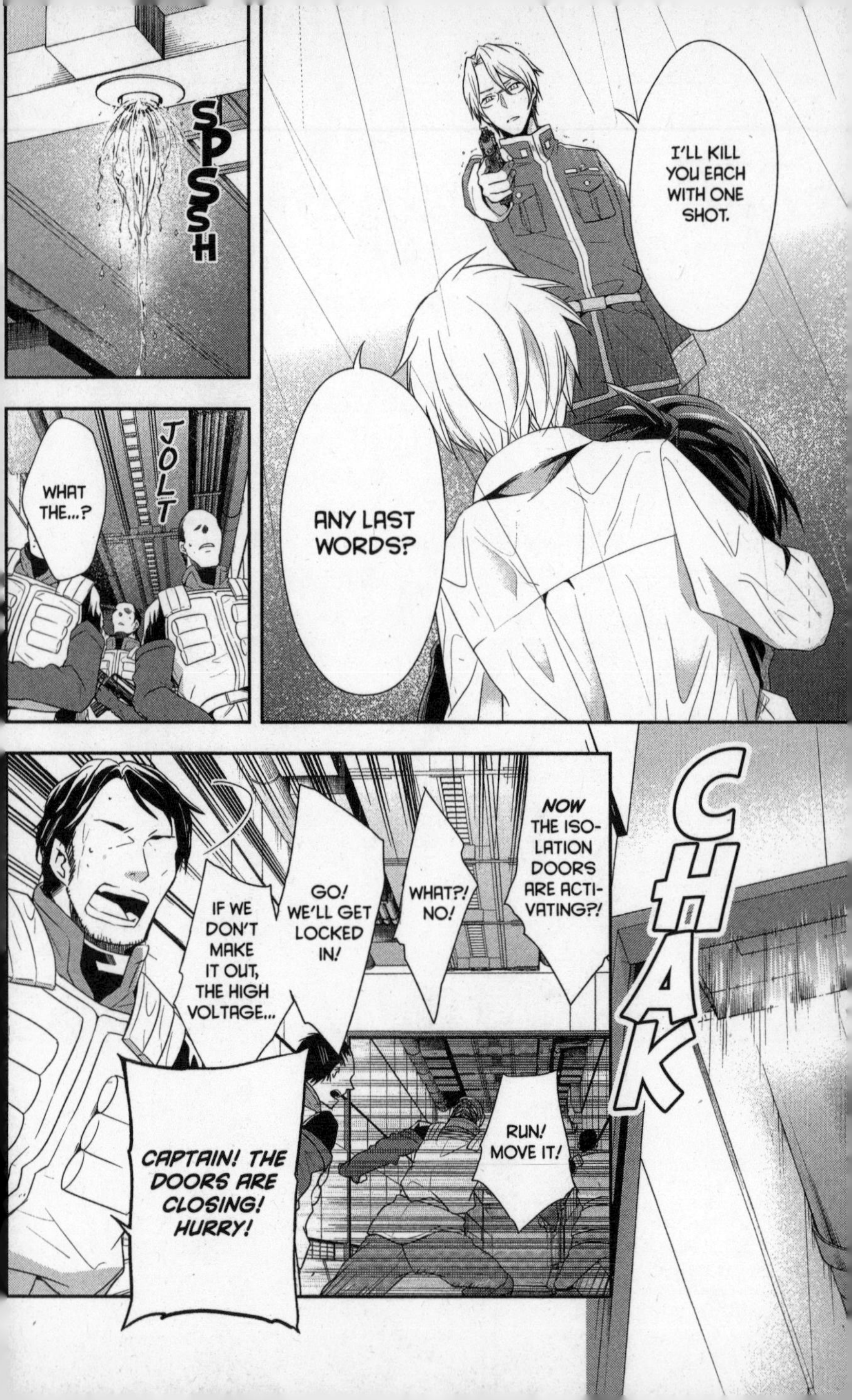
I'LL KILL YOU EACH WITH ONE SHOT.
ANY LAST WORDS?
SPSSH
JOLT
WHAT THE...?
CHAK
NOW THE ISO-LATION DOORS ARE ACTI-VATING?!
WHAT?! NO!
GO! WE'LL GET LOCKED IN!
IF WE DON'T MAKE IT OUT, THE HIGH VOLTAGE...
RUN! MOVE IT!
CAPTAIN! THE DOORS ARE CLOSING! HURRY!

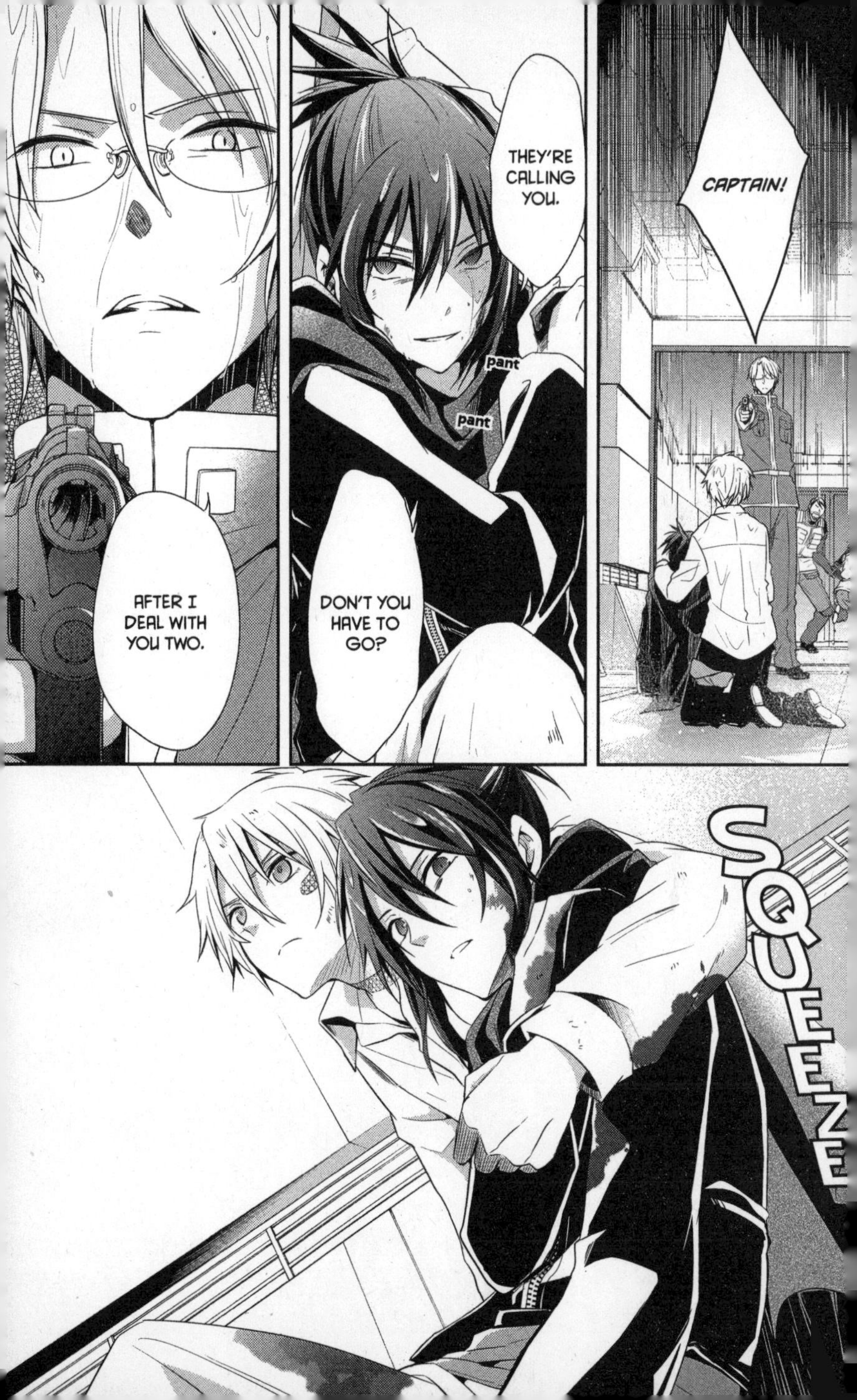
CAPTAIN!
THEY'RE CALLING YOU.
pant
pant
DON'T YOU HAVE TO GO?
AFTER I DEAL WITH YOU TWO.
SQUEEZE

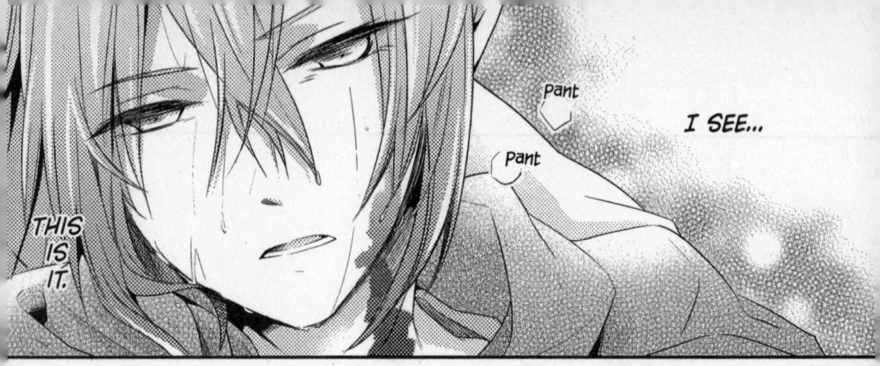
I SEE...
pant
pant
THIS IS IT.
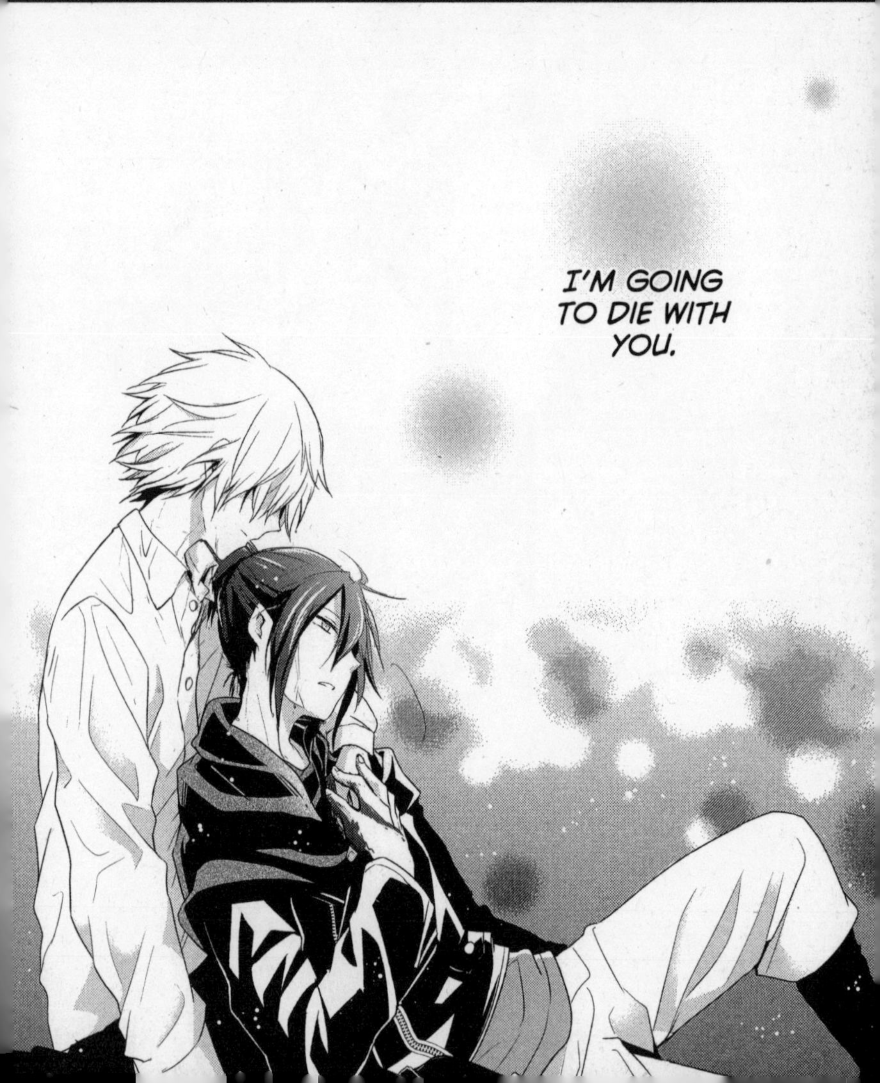
I'M GOING TO DIE WITH YOU.

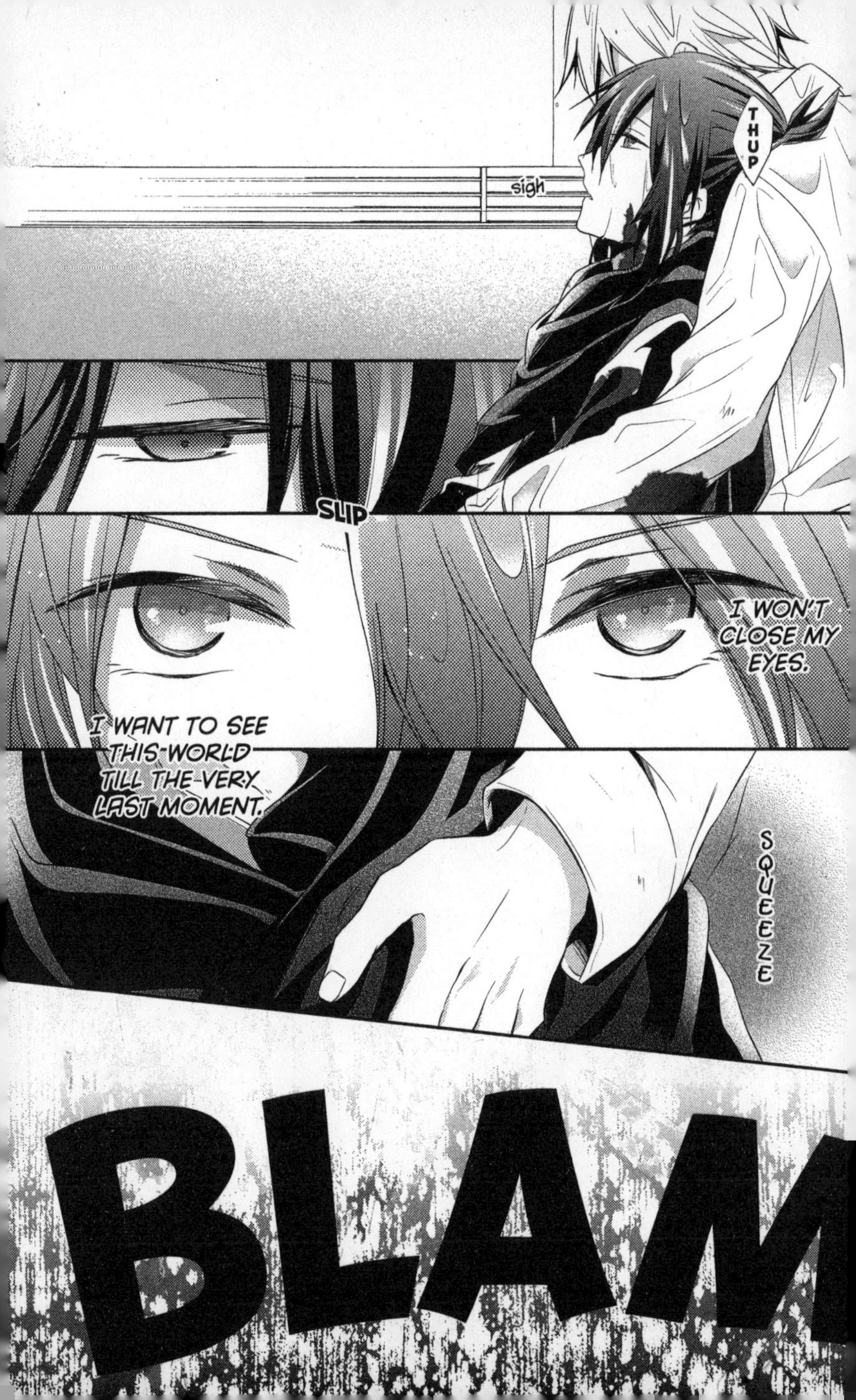
THUP
sigh
SLIP
I WON'T CLOSE MY EYES.
I WANT TO SEE THIS WORLD TILL THE VERY LAST MOMENT.
SQUEEZE
BLAM

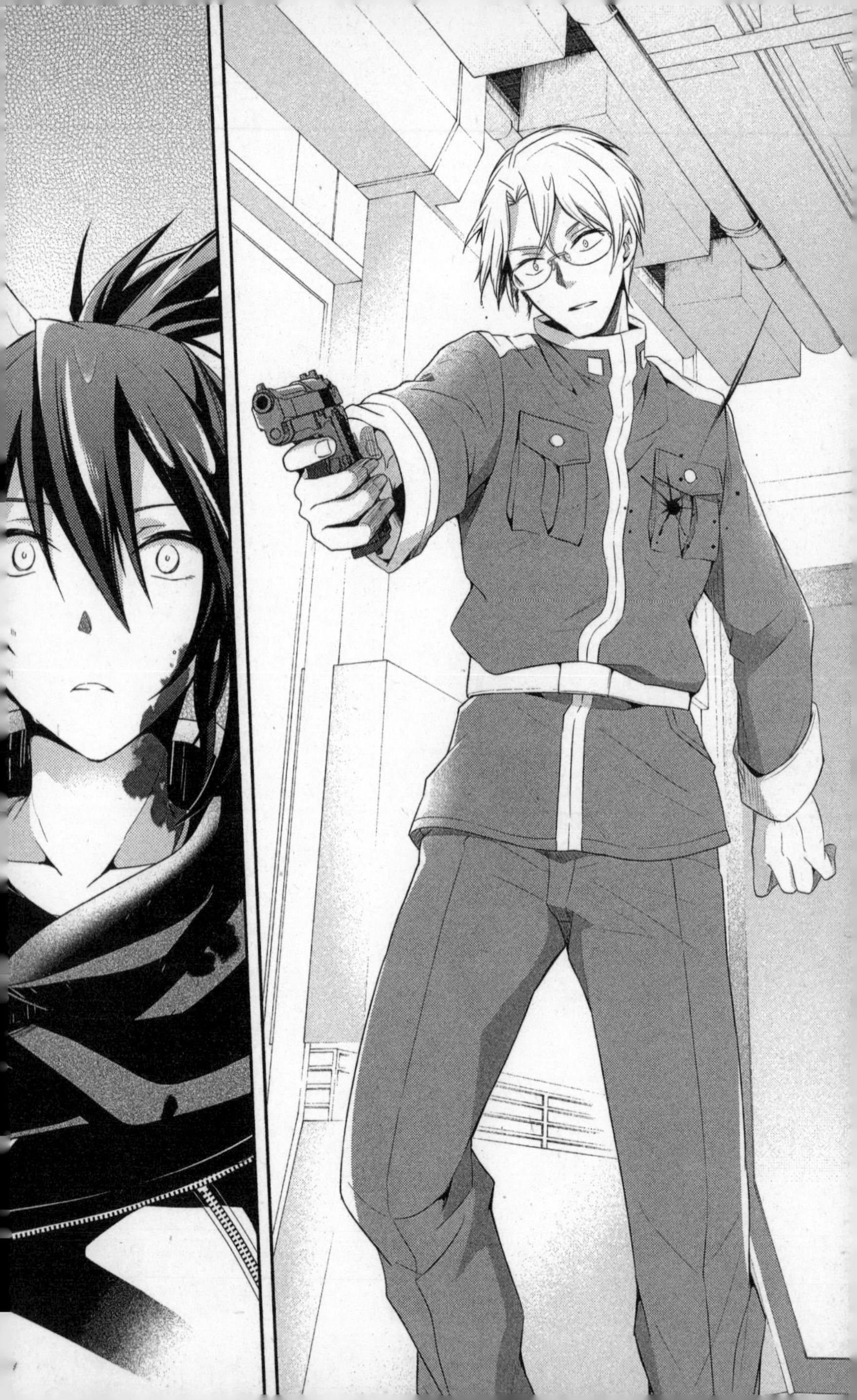

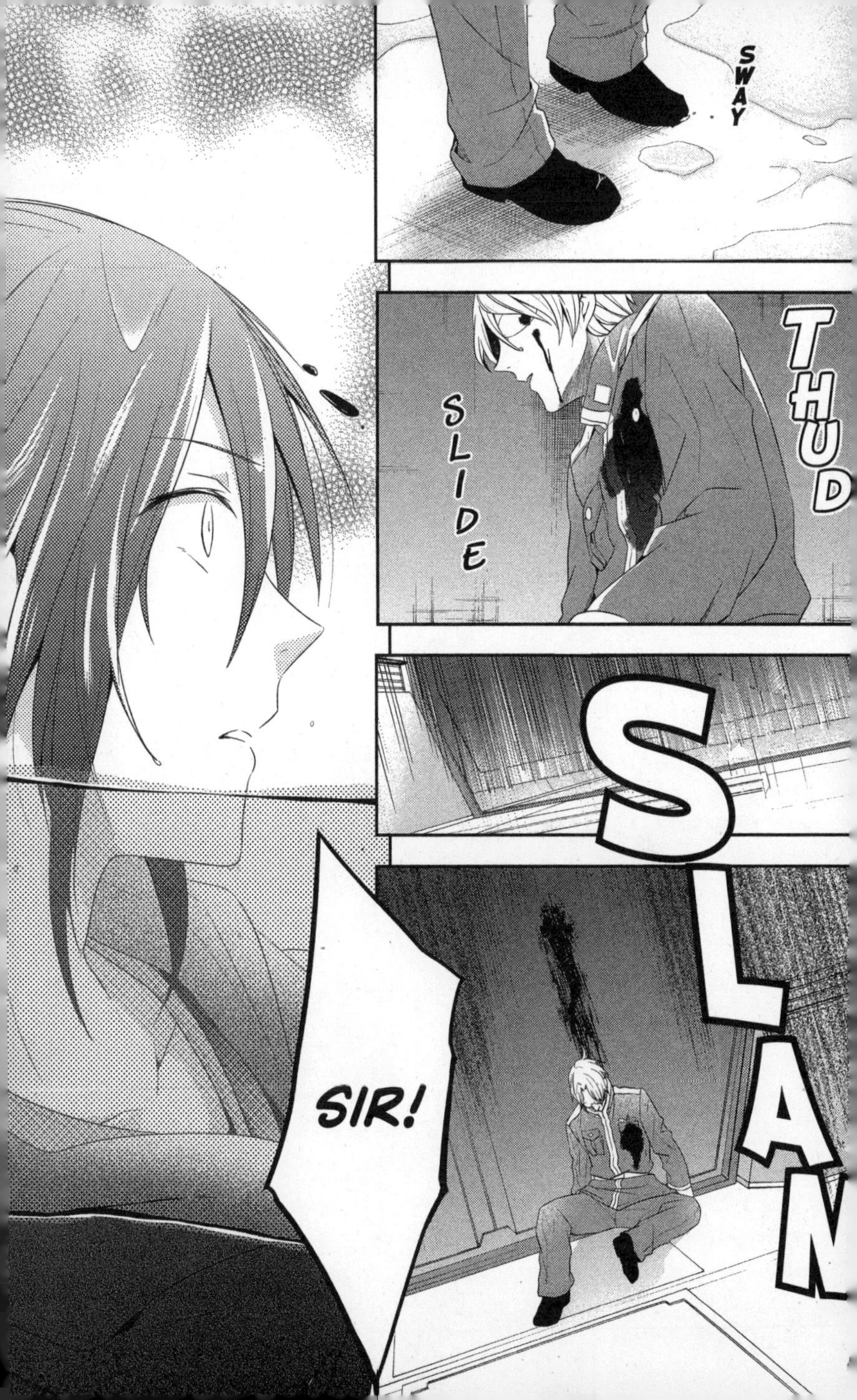
SWAY
THUD
SLIDE
SLAM
SIR!

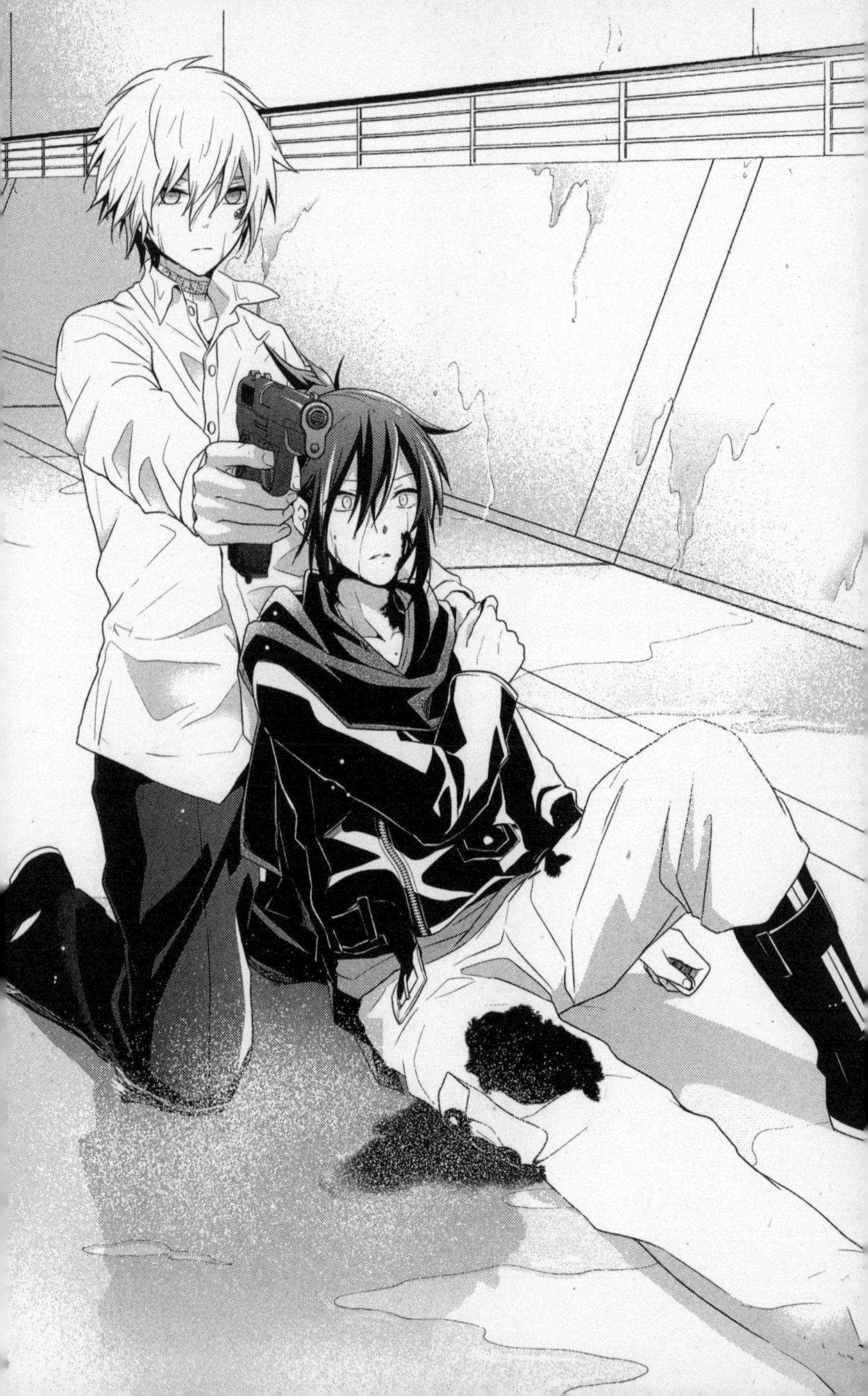

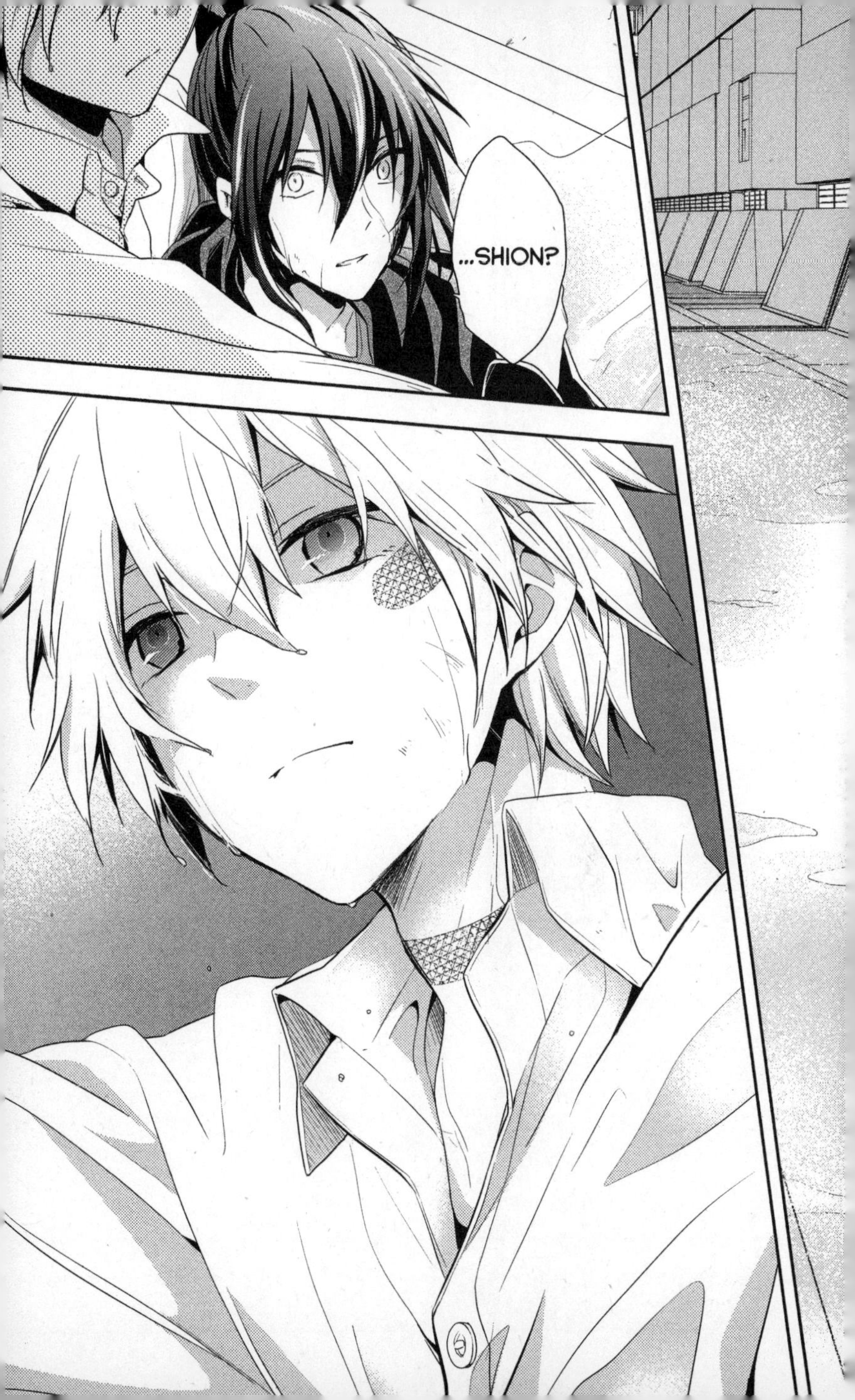
...SHION?

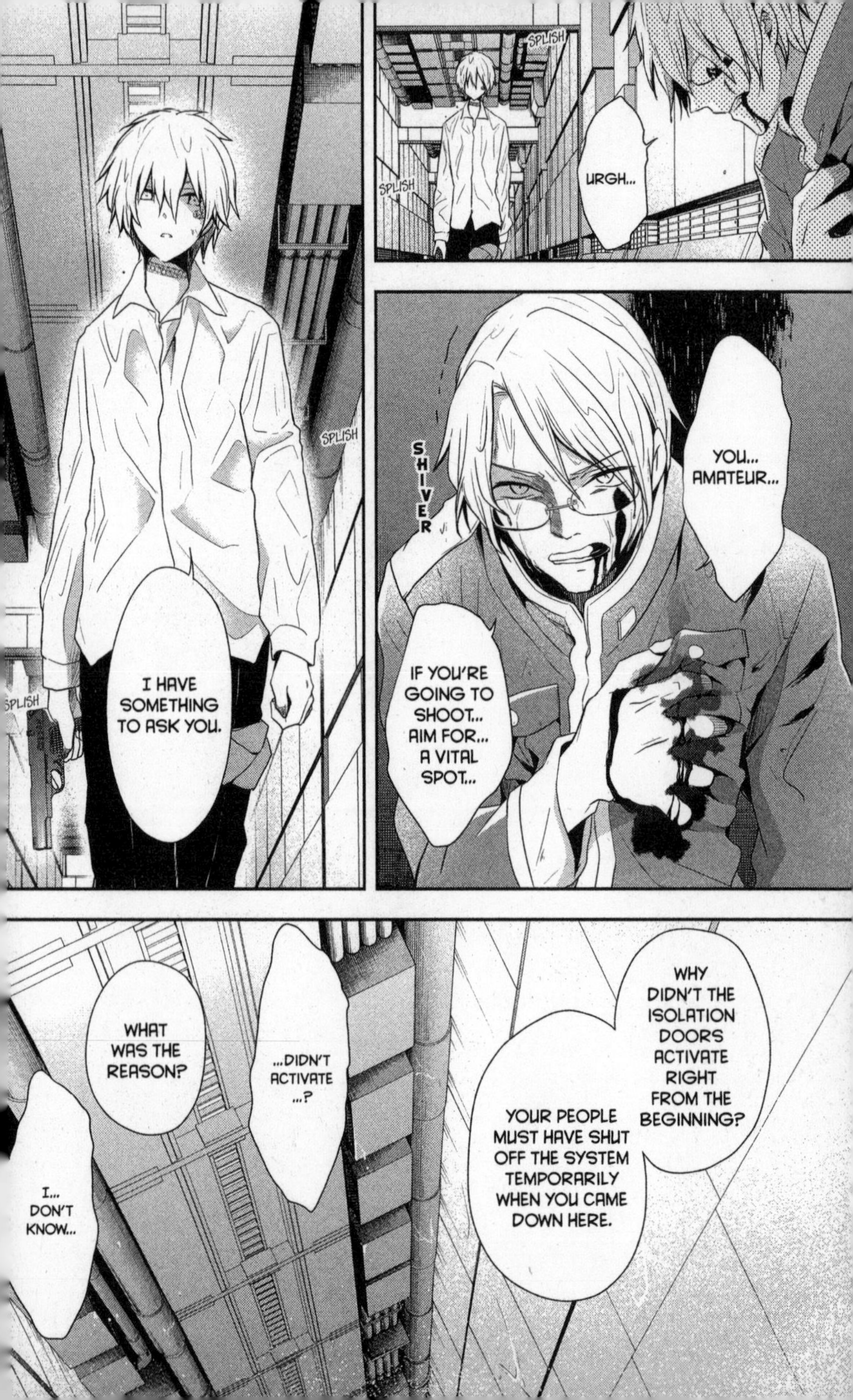
URGH...
SPLISH
SPLISH
SHIVER
YOU... AMATEUR...
IF YOU'RE GOING TO SHOOT... AIM FOR... A VITAL SPOT...
SPLISH
I HAVE SOMETHING TO ASK YOU.
SPLISH
WHY DIDN'T THE ISOLATION DOORS ACTIVATE RIGHT FROM THE BEGINNING?
YOUR PEOPLE MUST HAVE SHUT OFF THE SYSTEM TEMPORARILY WHEN YOU CAME DOWN HERE.
...DIDN'T ACTIVATE ...?
WHAT WAS THE REASON?
I... DON'T KNOW...

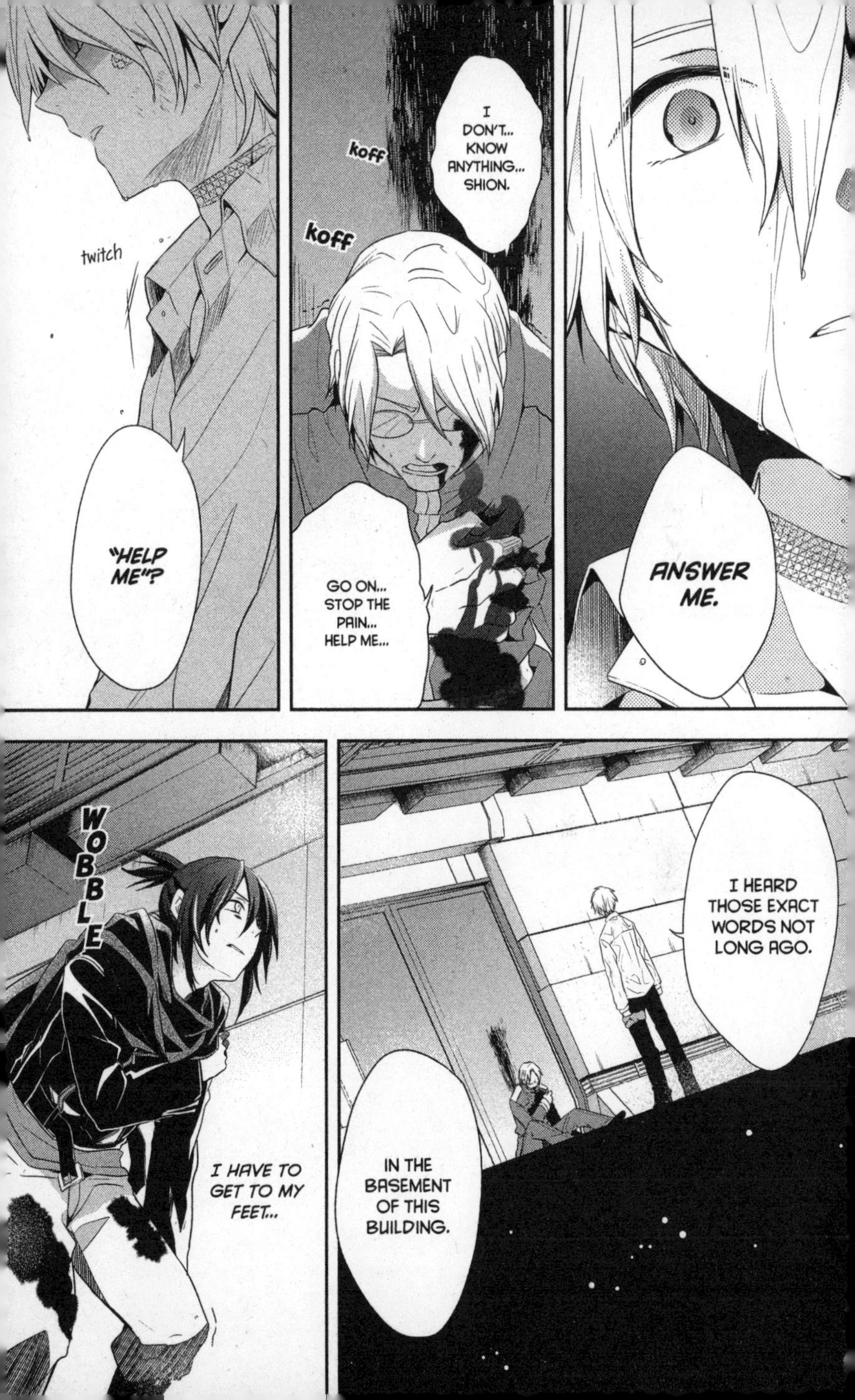
ANSWER ME.
I DON'T... KNOW ANYTHING... SHION.
koff
koff
GO ON... STOP THE PAIN... HELP ME...
twitch
"HELP ME"?
I HEARD THOSE EXACT WORDS NOT LONG AGO.
IN THE BASEMENT OF THIS BUILDING.
WOBBLE
I HAVE TO GET TO MY FEET...

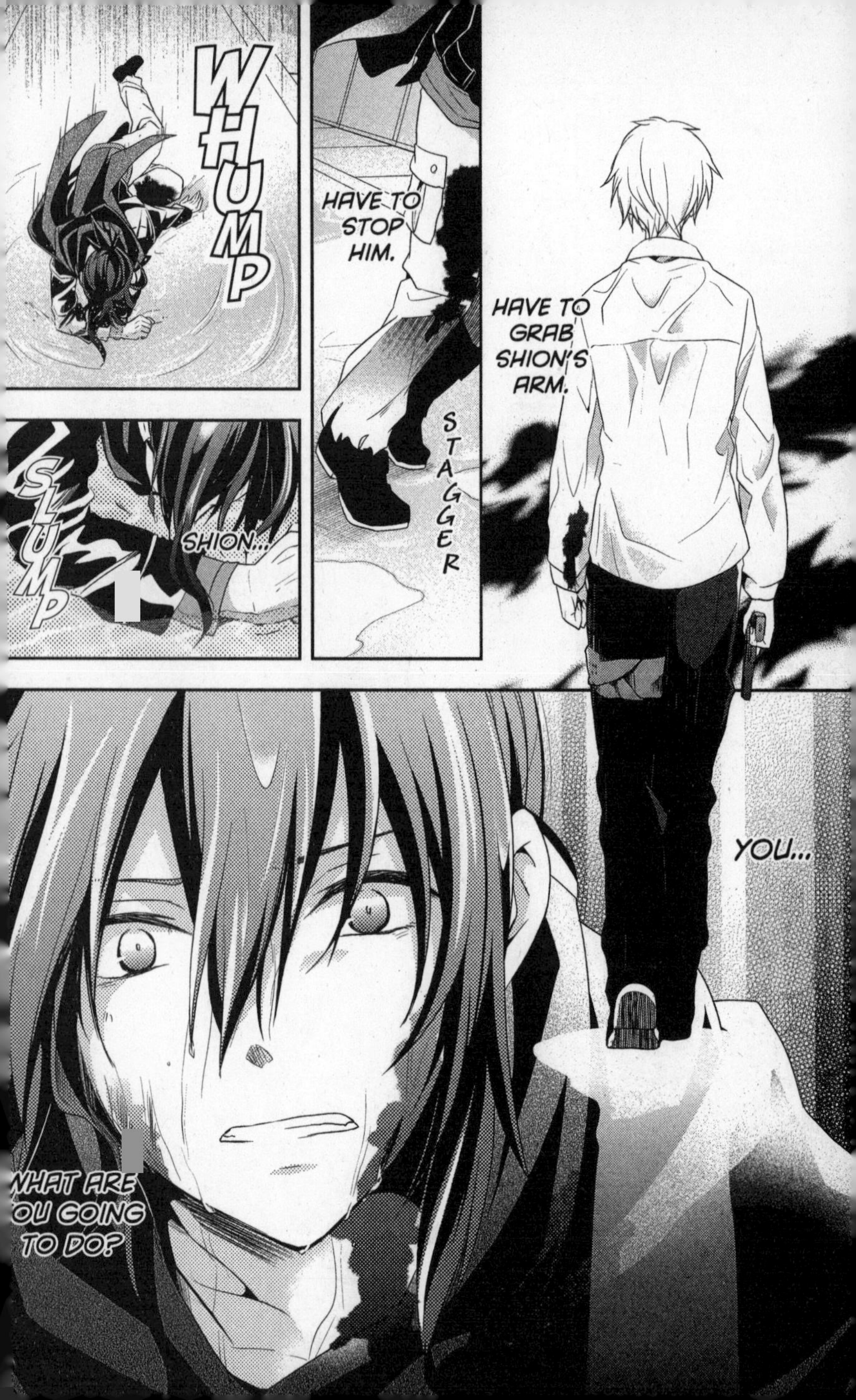
HAVE TO GRAB SHION'S ARM.
HAVE TO STOP HIM.
STAGGER
WHUMP
SLUMP
SHION...
YOU...
WHAT ARE OU GOING TO DO?

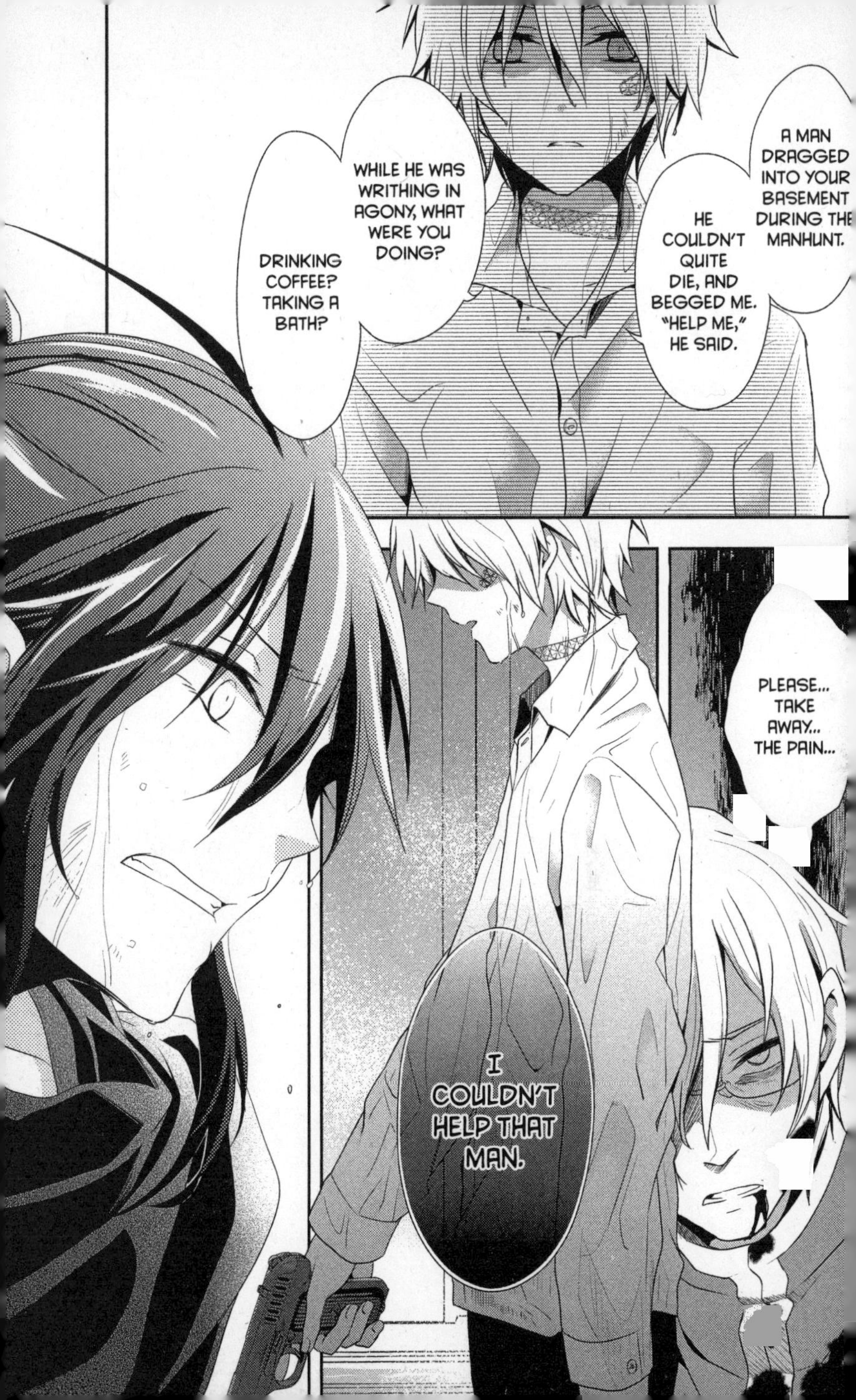
A MAN DRAGGED INTO YOUR BASEMENT DURING THE MANHUNT.
HE COULDN'T QUITE DIE, AND BEGGED ME. "HELP ME," HE SAID.
WHILE HE WAS WRITHING IN AGONY, WHAT WERE YOU DOING?
DRINKING COFFEE? TAKING A BATH?
PLEASE... TAKE AWAY... THE PAIN...
I COULDN'T HELP THAT MAN.

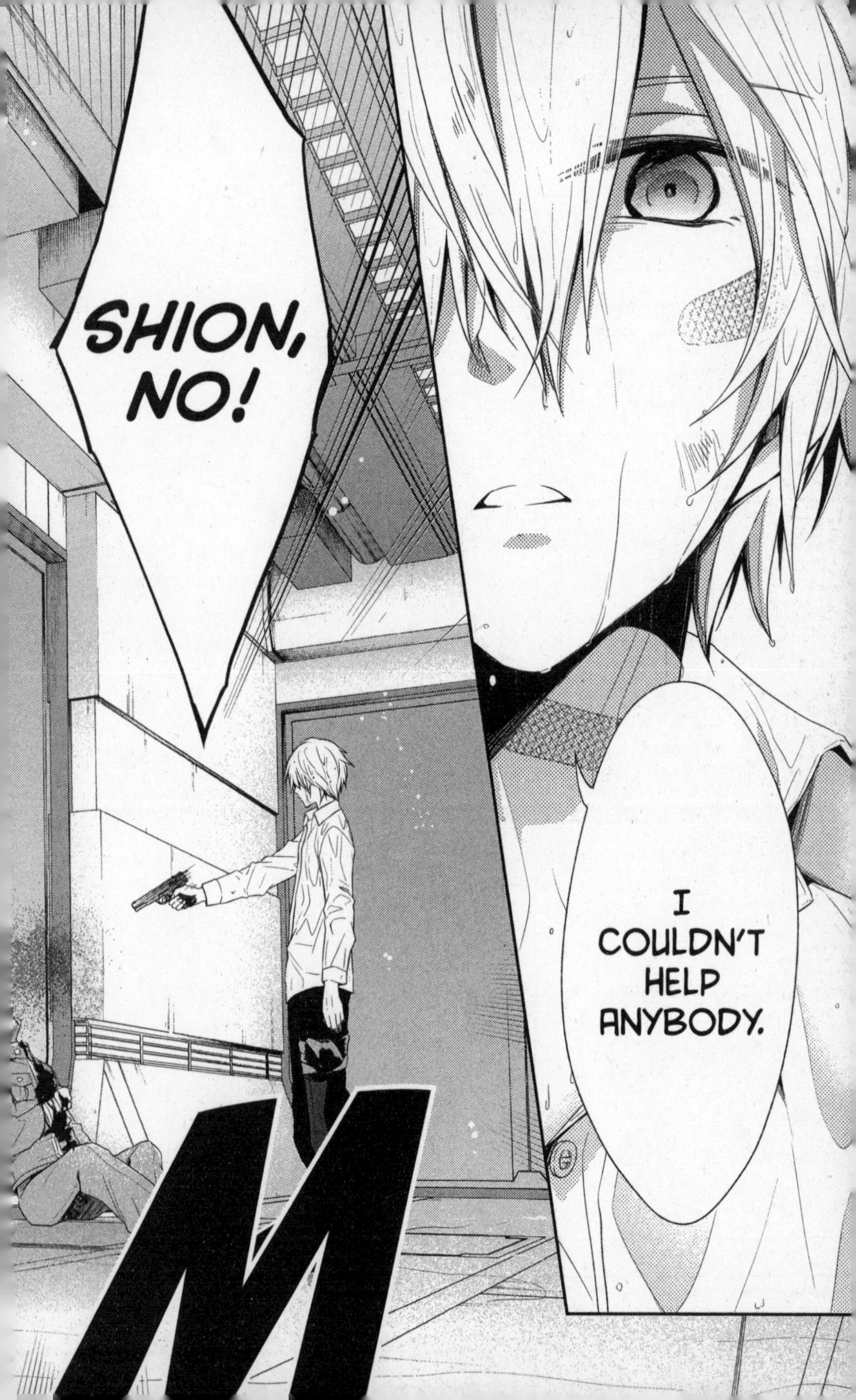
I COULDN'T HELP ANYBODY.
SHION, NO!
M

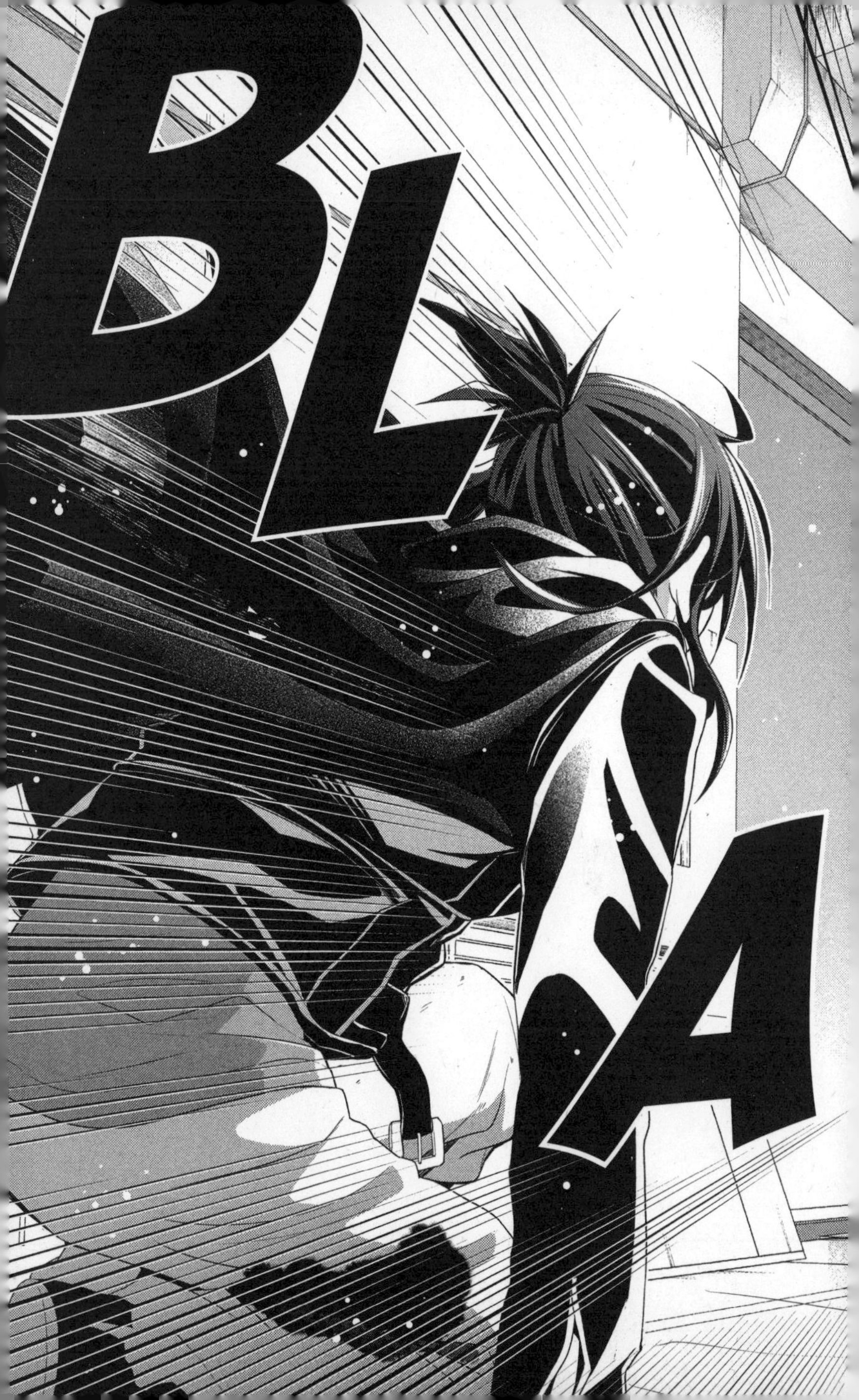
BLA

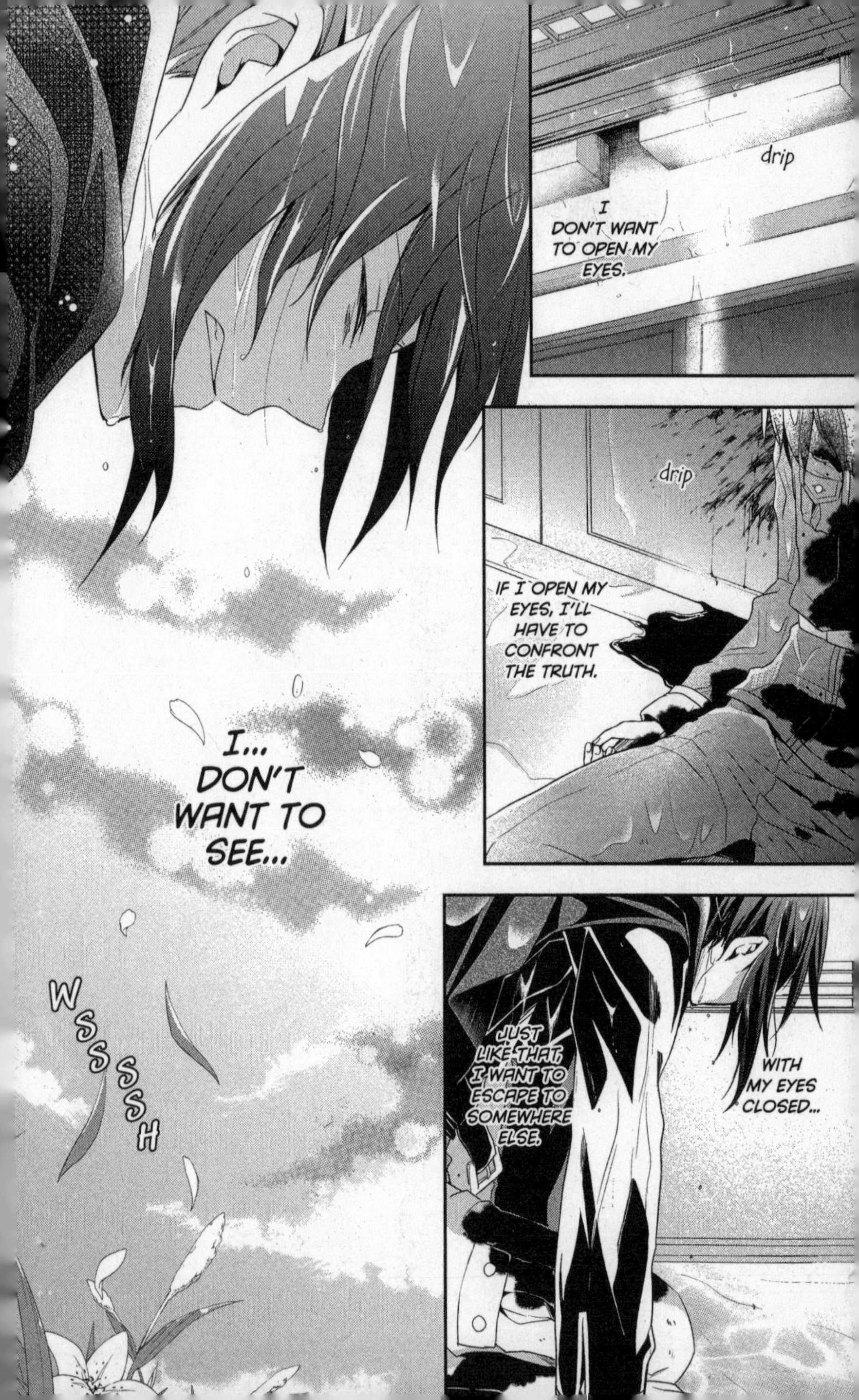
drip
I DON'T WANT TO OPEN MY EYES.
drip
IF I OPEN MY EYES, I'LL HAVE TO CONFRONT THE TRUTH.
WITH MY EYES CLOSED...
JUST LIKE THAT, I WANT TO ESCAPE TO SOMEWHERE ELSE.
I... DON'T WANT TO SEE...
WSSSSH

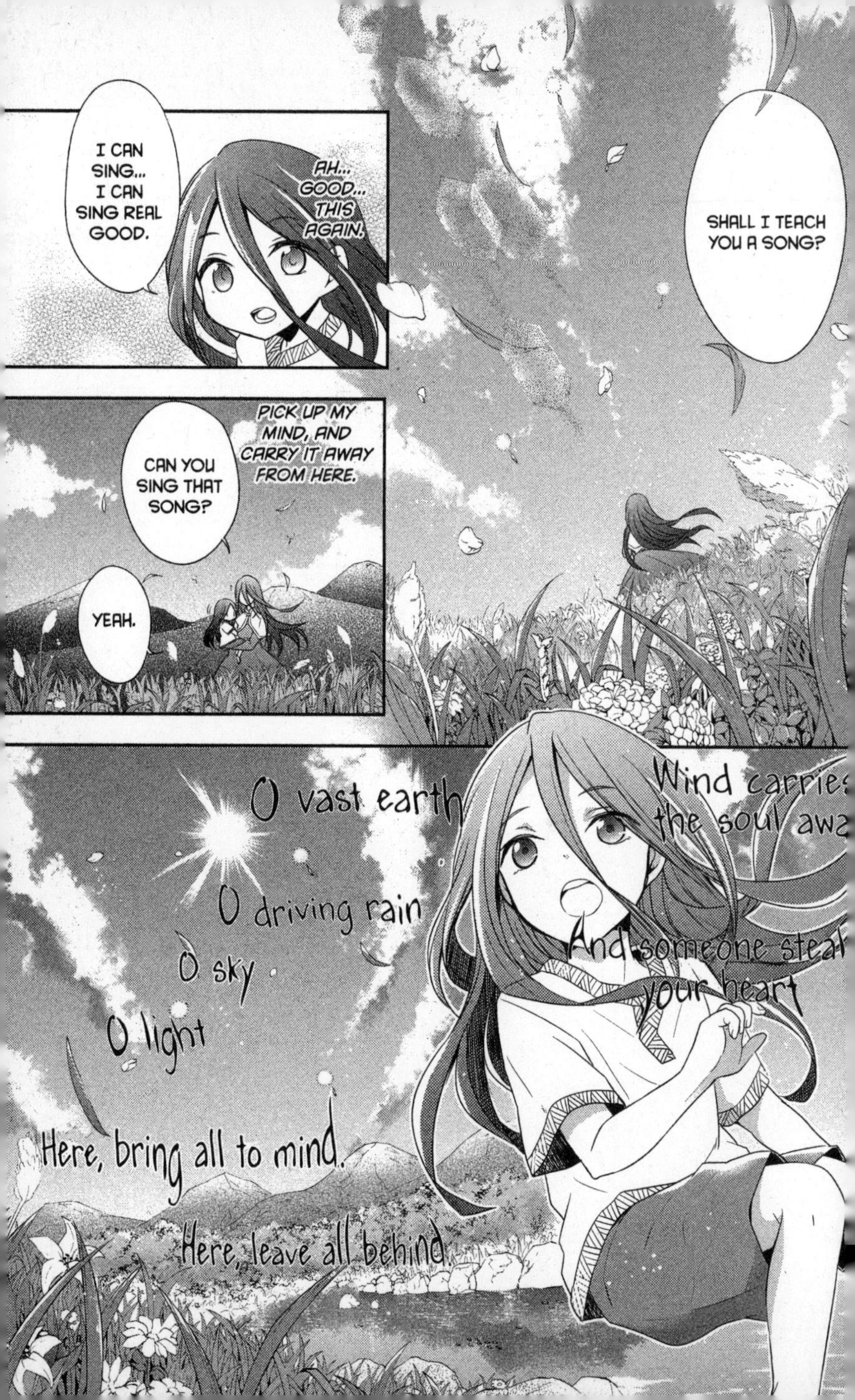
SHALL I TEACH YOU A SONG?
I CAN SING... I CAN SING REAL GOOD.
AH... GOOD... THIS AGAIN.
PICK UP MY MIND, AND CARRY IT AWAY FROM HERE.
CAN YOU SING THAT SONG?
YEAH.
Wind carries the soul awa
And someone steal your heart
O vast earth
O driving rain
O sky
O light
Here, bring all to mind.
Here, leave all behind.

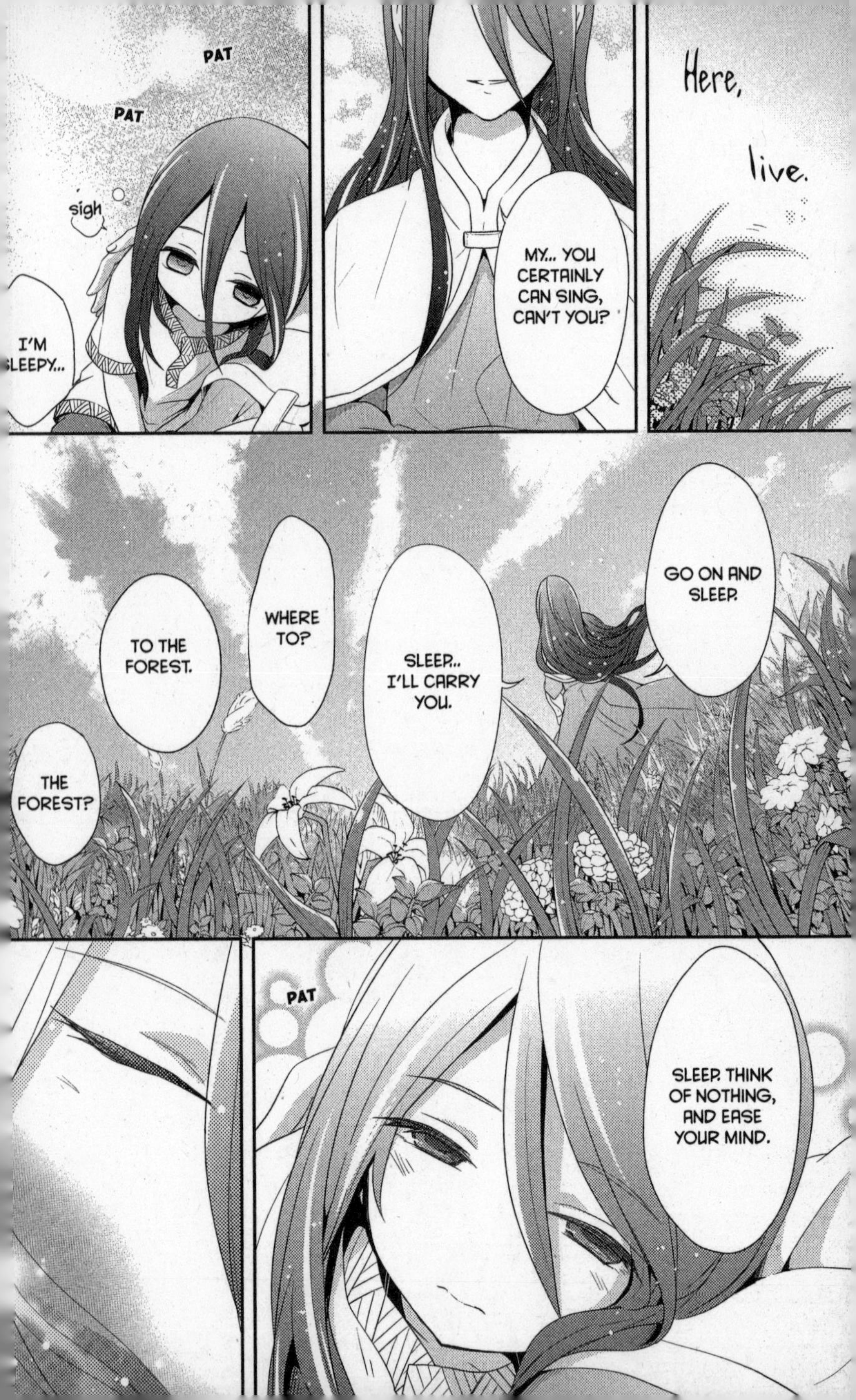
Here,
live.
MY... YOU CERTAINLY CAN SING, CAN'T YOU?
PAT
PAT
sigh
I'M LEEPY...
GO ON AND SLEEP.
SLEEP.. I'LL CARRY YOU.
WHERE TO?
TO THE FOREST.
THE FOREST?
SLEEP. THINK OF NOTHING, AND EASE YOUR MIND.
PAT

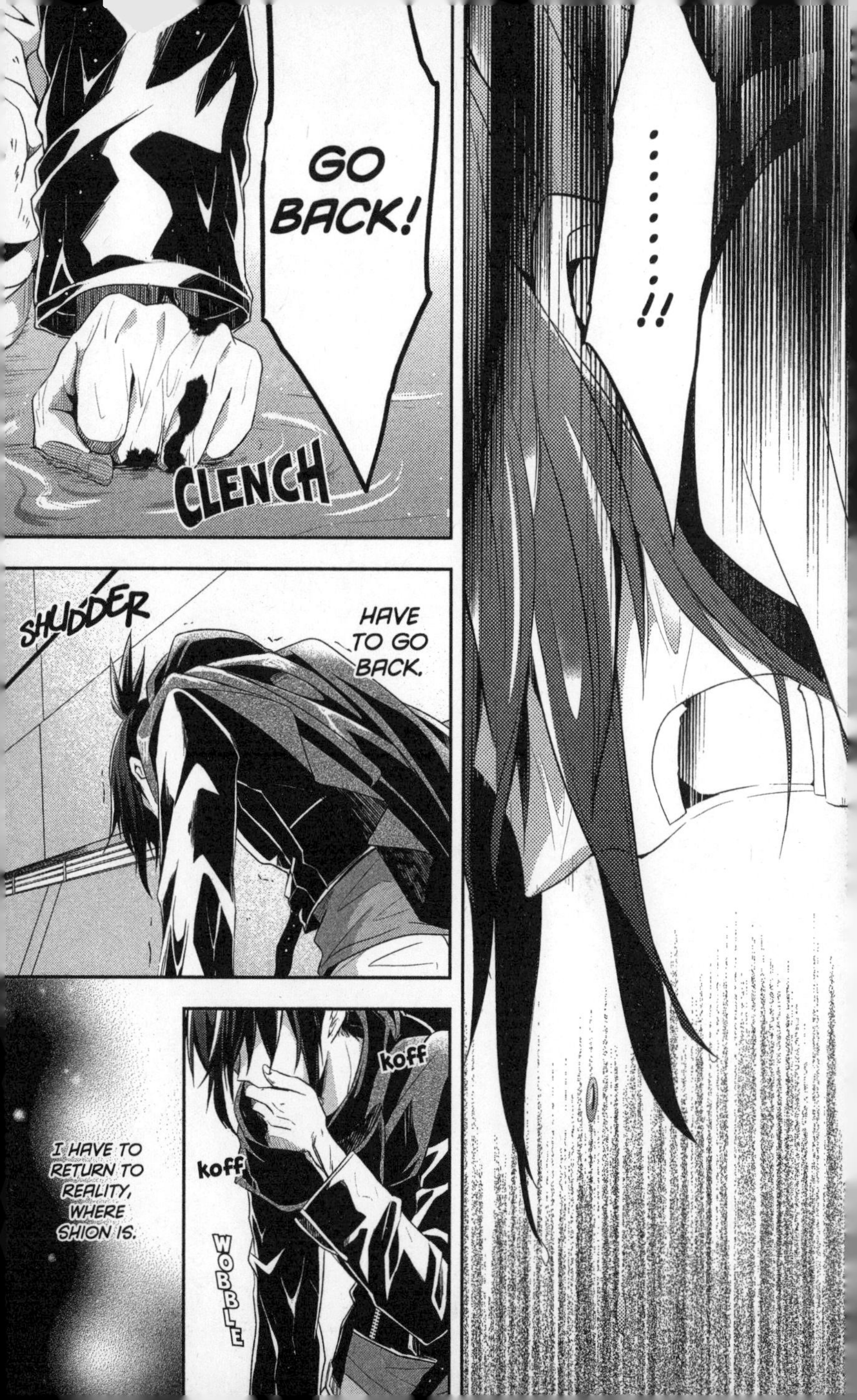
......!!
GO BACK!
CLENCH
HAVE TO GO BACK.
SHUDDER
koff
I HAVE TO RETURN TO REALITY, WHERE SHION IS.
koff
WOBBLE

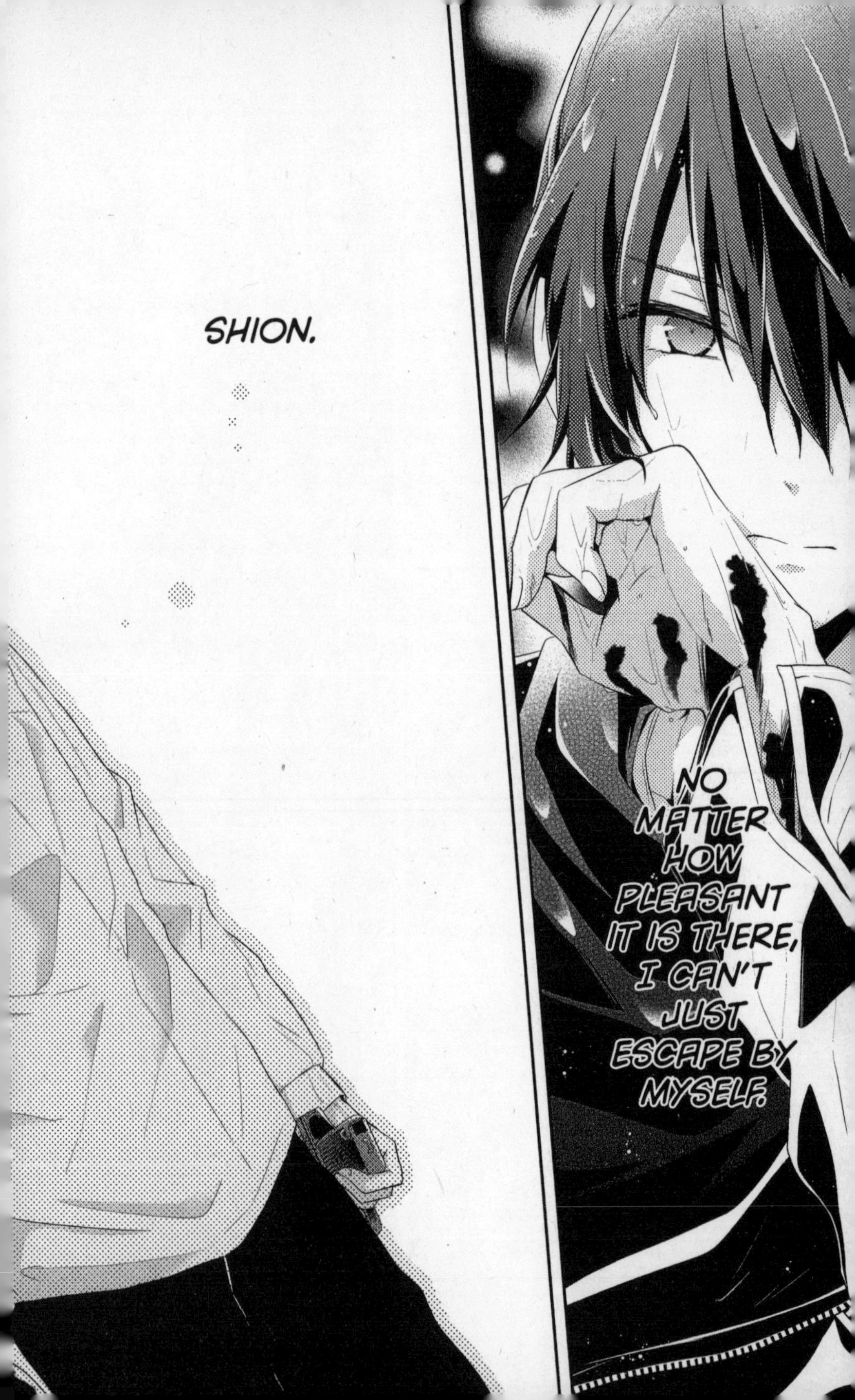
NO MATTER HOW PLEASANT IT IS THERE, I CAN'T JUST ESCAPE BY MYSELF.
SHION.

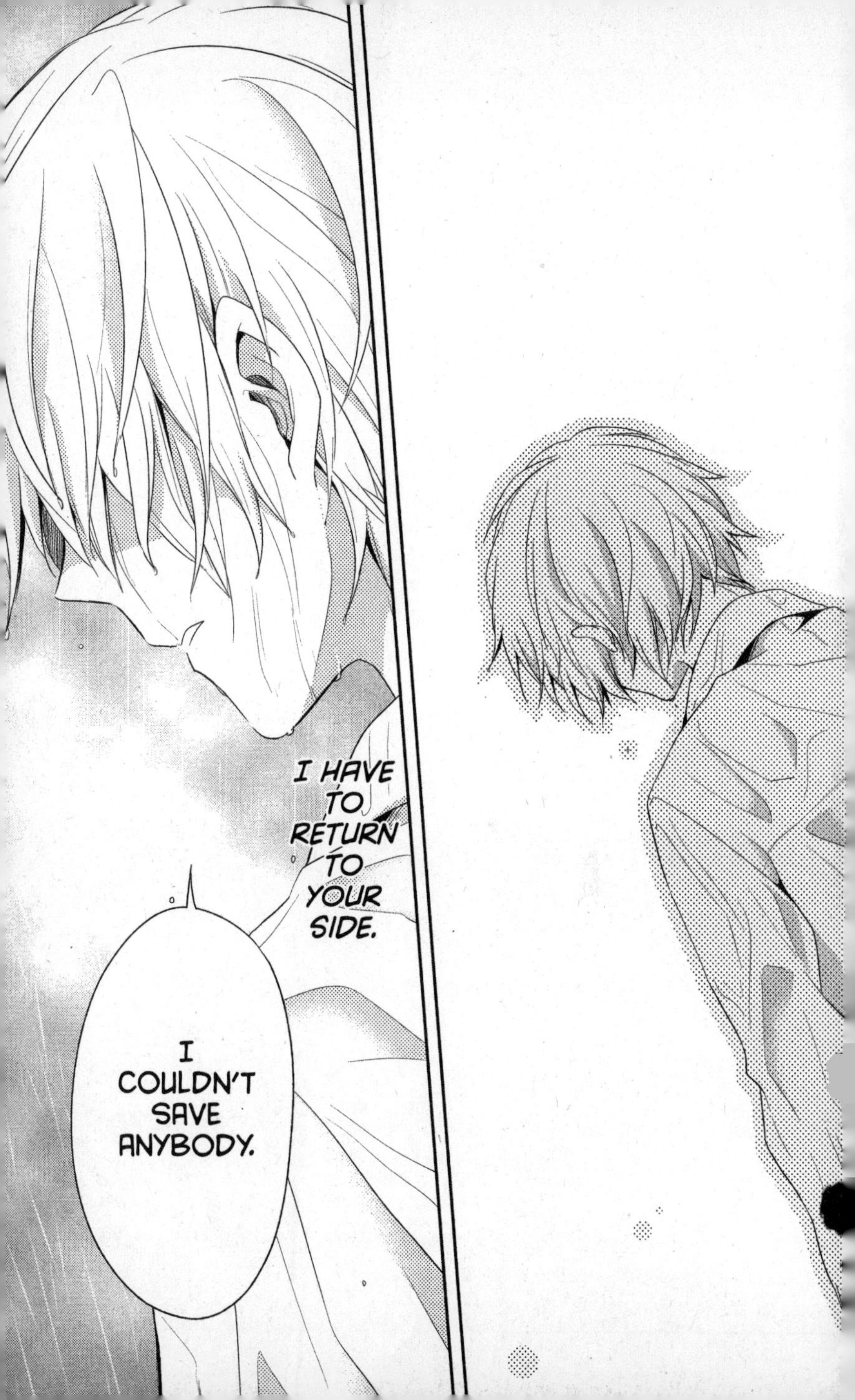
I HAVE TO RETURN TO YOUR SIDE.
I COULDN'T SAVE ANYBODY.

NO.6

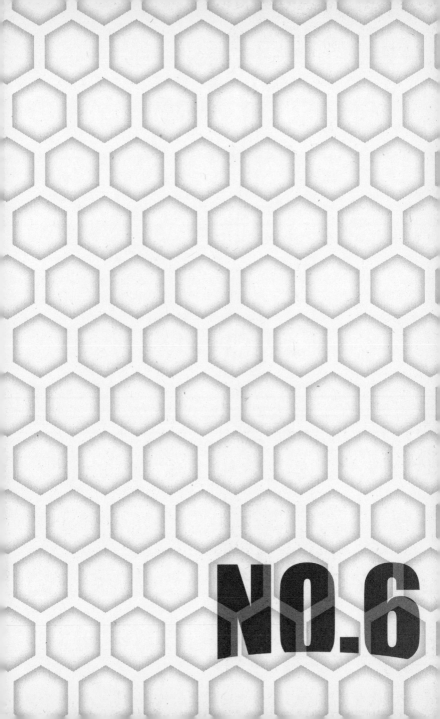

Chapter 27: False Delight

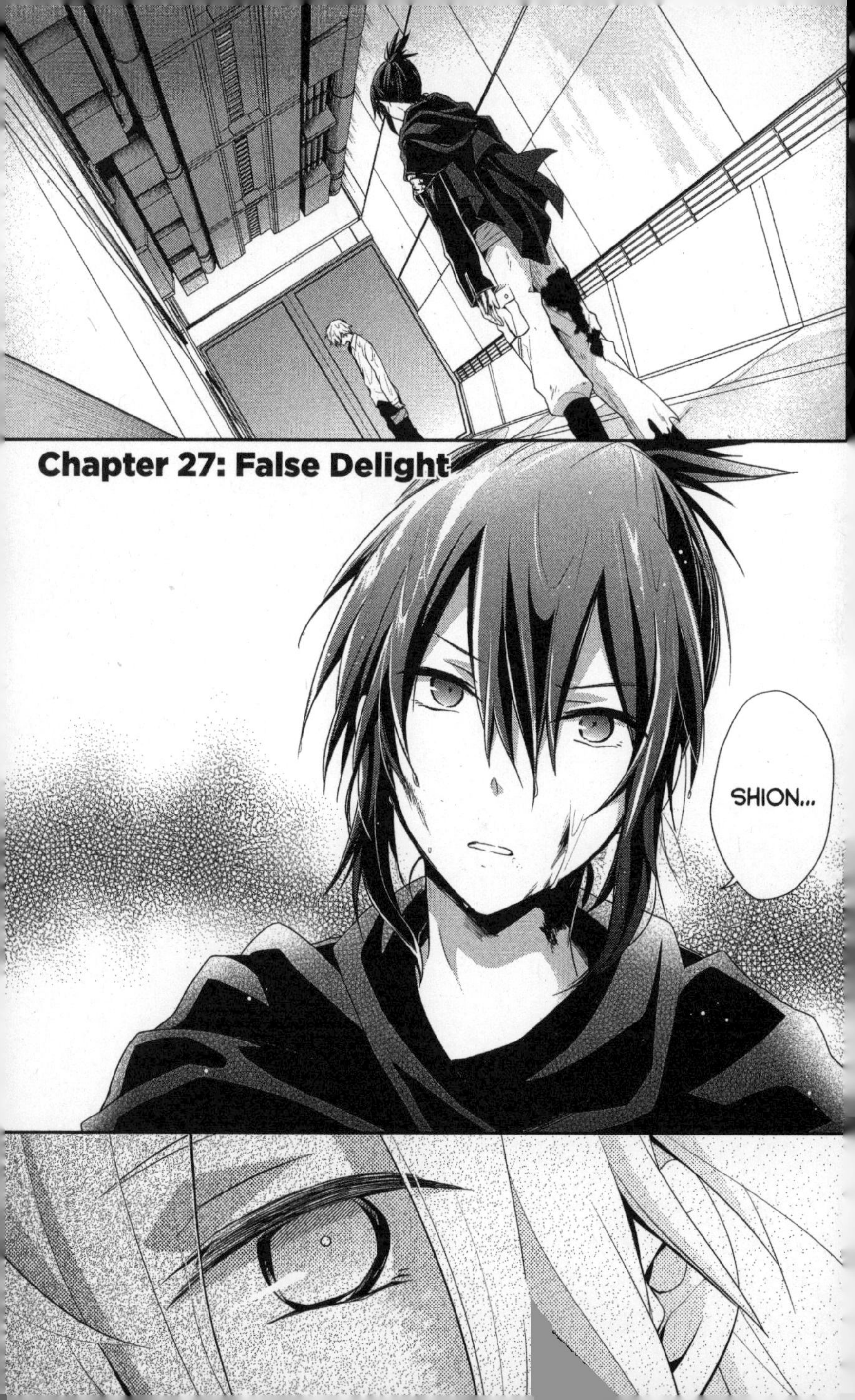
SHION...

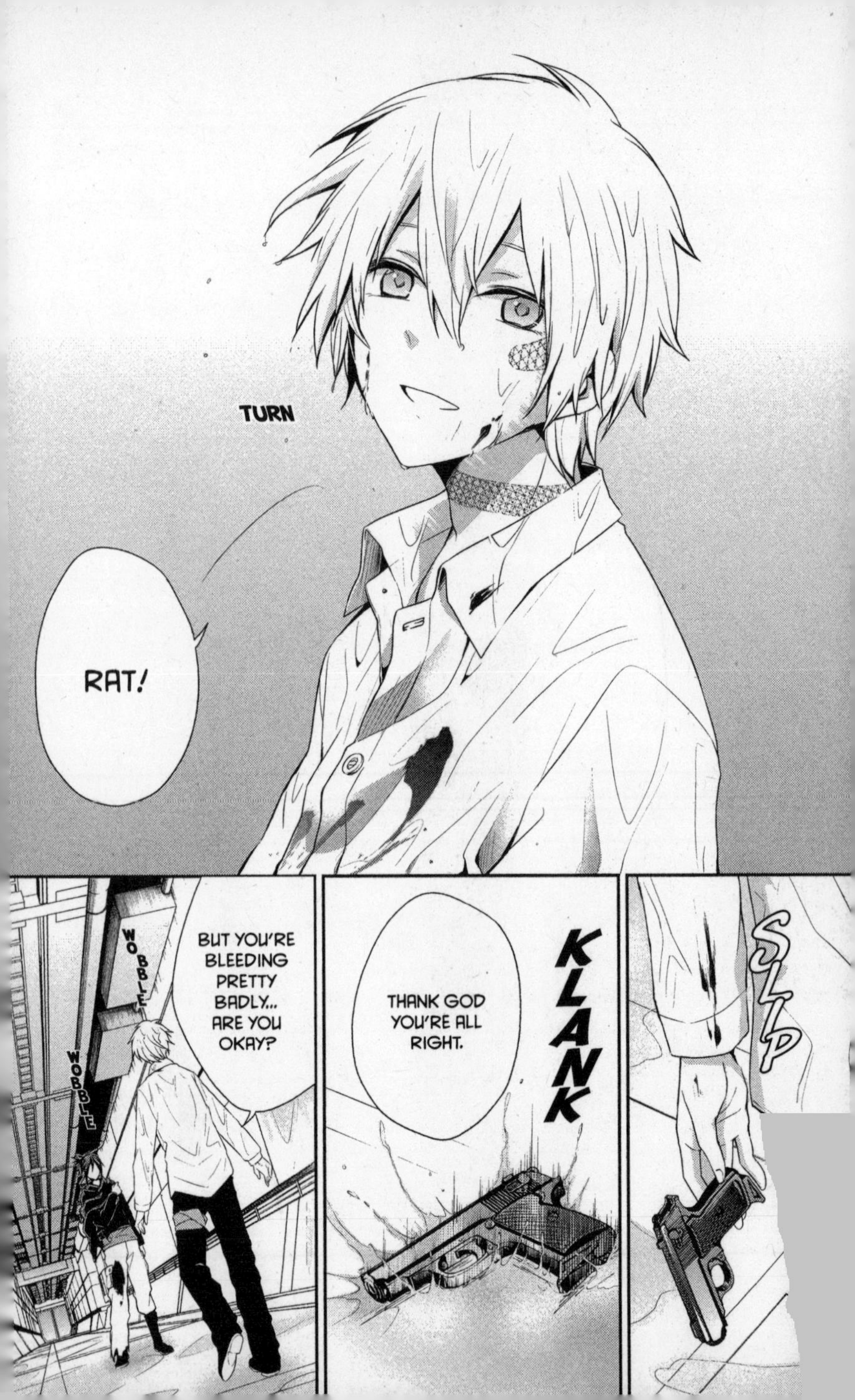
TURN
RAT!
SLIP
KLANK
THANK GOD YOU'RE ALL RIGHT.
BUT YOU'RE BLEEDING PRETTY BADLY... ARE YOU OKAY?
WOBBLE
WOBBLE

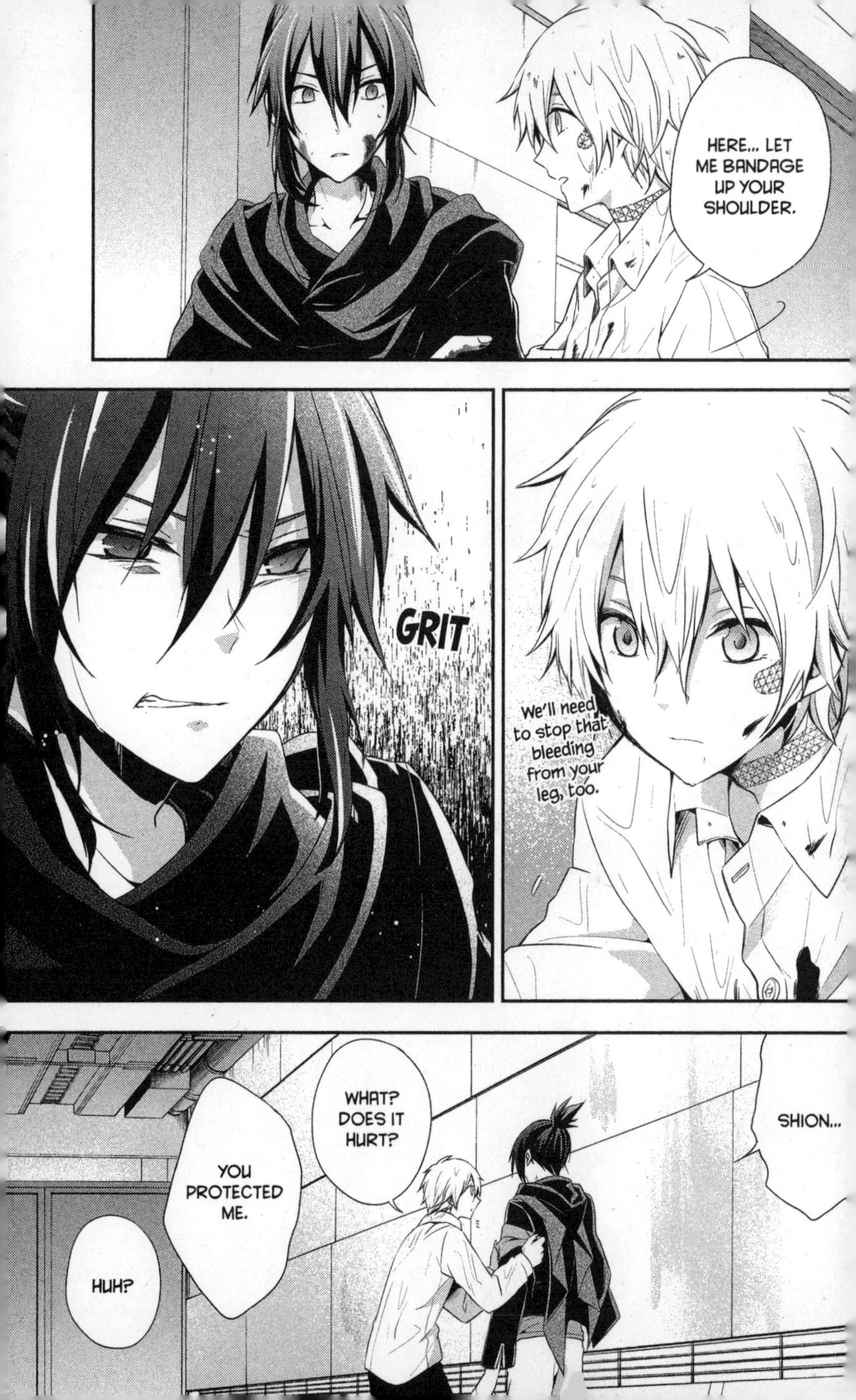
HERE... LET ME BANDAGE UP YOUR SHOULDER.
We'll need to stop that bleeding from your leg, too.
GRIT
SHION...
WHAT? DOES IT HURT?
YOU PROTECTED ME.
HUH?

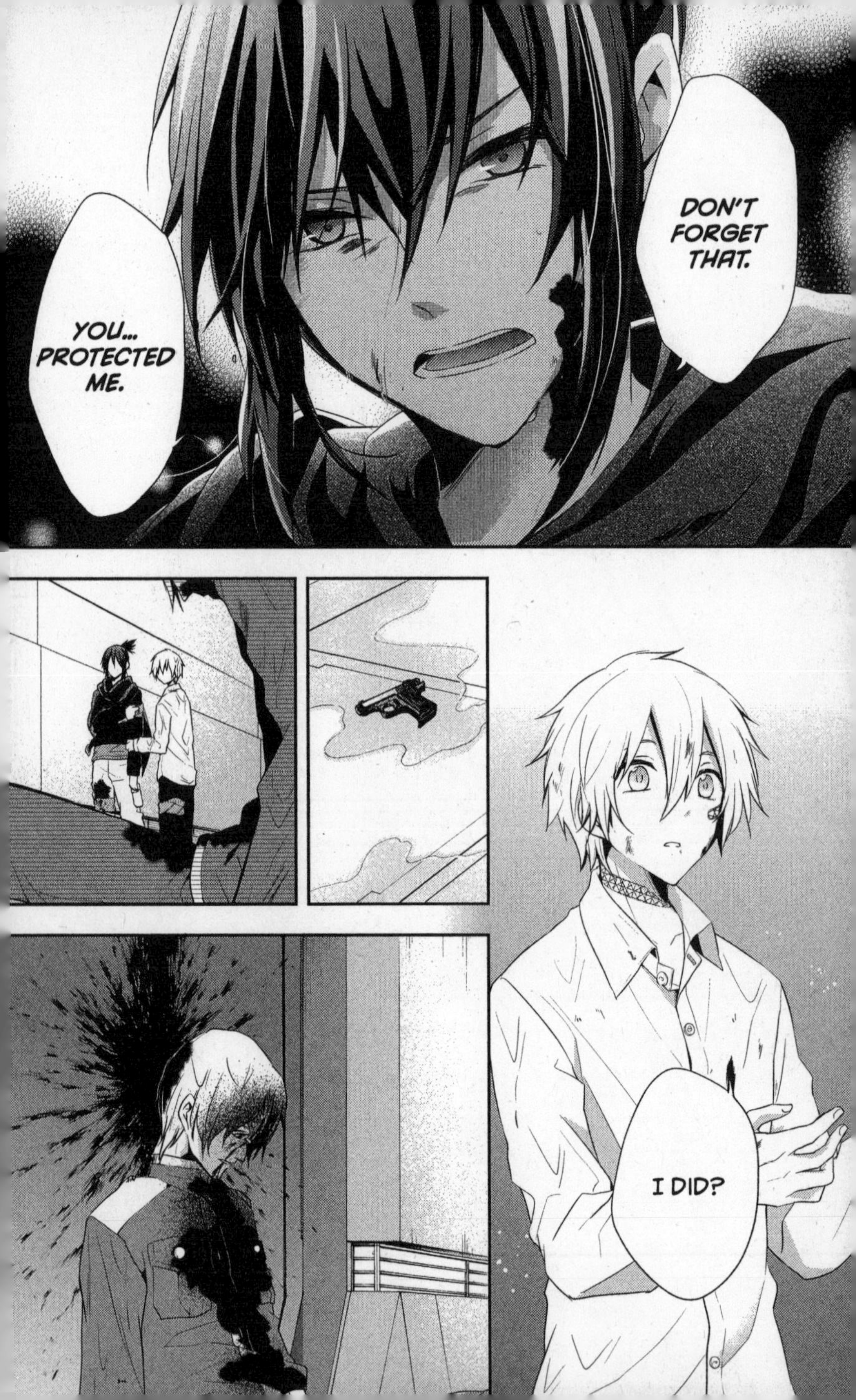
DON'T FORGET THAT.
YOU... PROTECTED ME.
I DID?

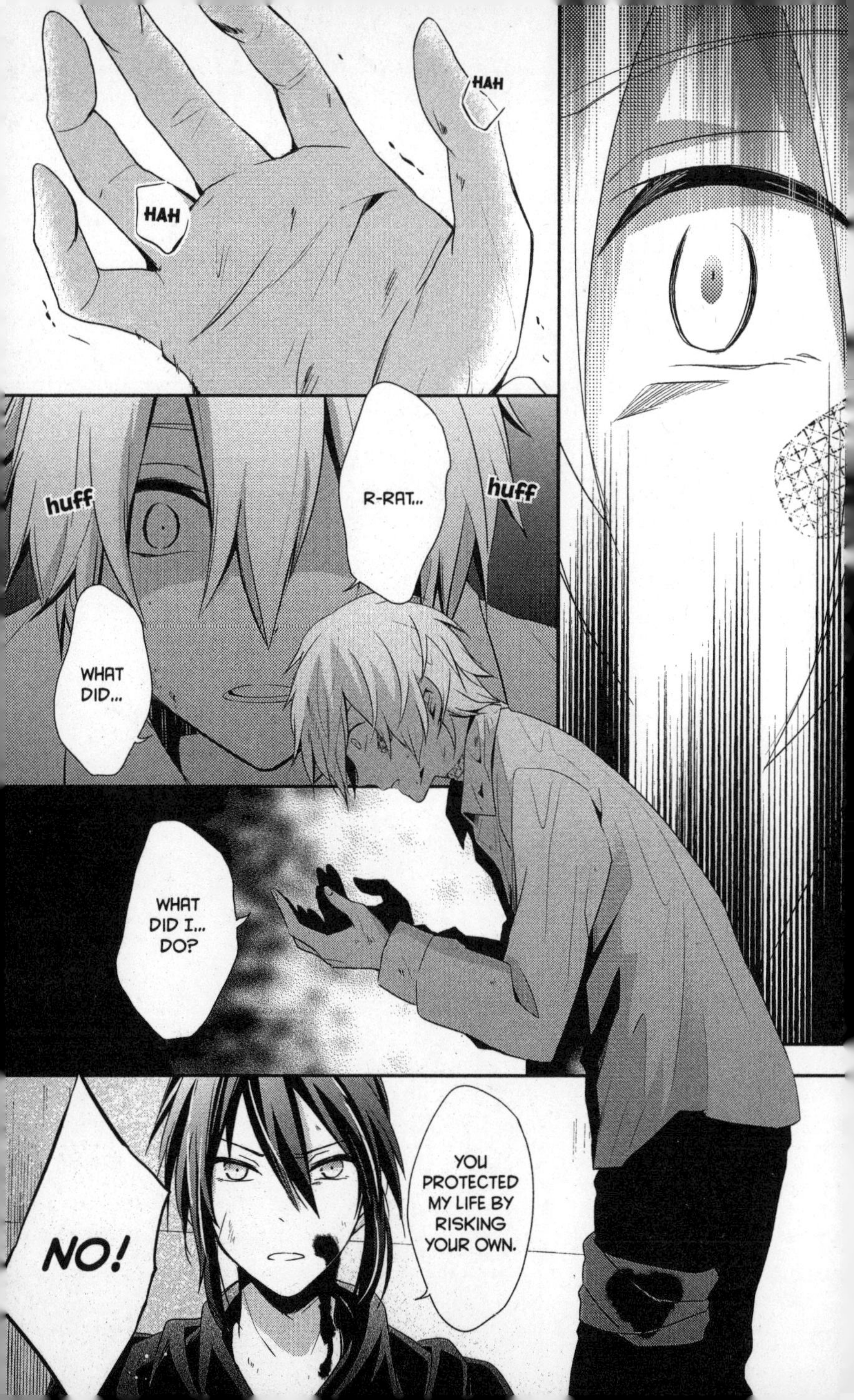
HAH
HAH
huff
R-RAT...
huff
WHAT DID...
WHAT DID I... DO?
YOU PROTECTED MY LIFE BY RISKING YOUR OWN.
NO!

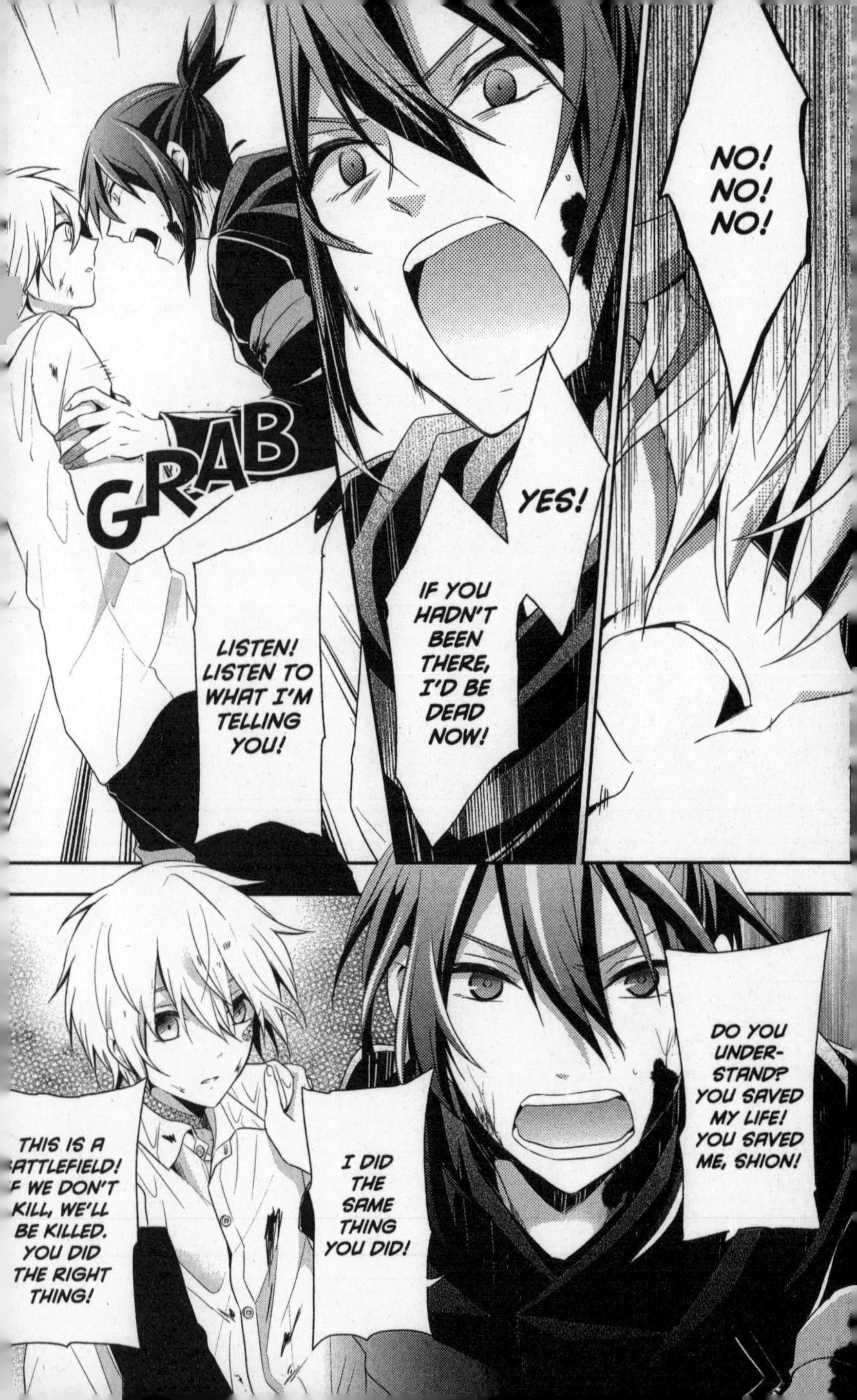
NO! NO! NO!
YES!
IF YOU HADN'T BEEN THERE, I'D BE DEAD NOW!
GRAB
LISTEN! LISTEN TO WHAT I'M TELLING YOU!
DO YOU UNDER-STAND? YOU SAVED MY LIFE! YOU SAVED ME, SHION!
I DID THE SAME THING YOU DID!
THIS IS A ATTLEFIELD! F WE DON'T KILL, WE'LL BE KILLED. YOU DID THE RIGHT THING!

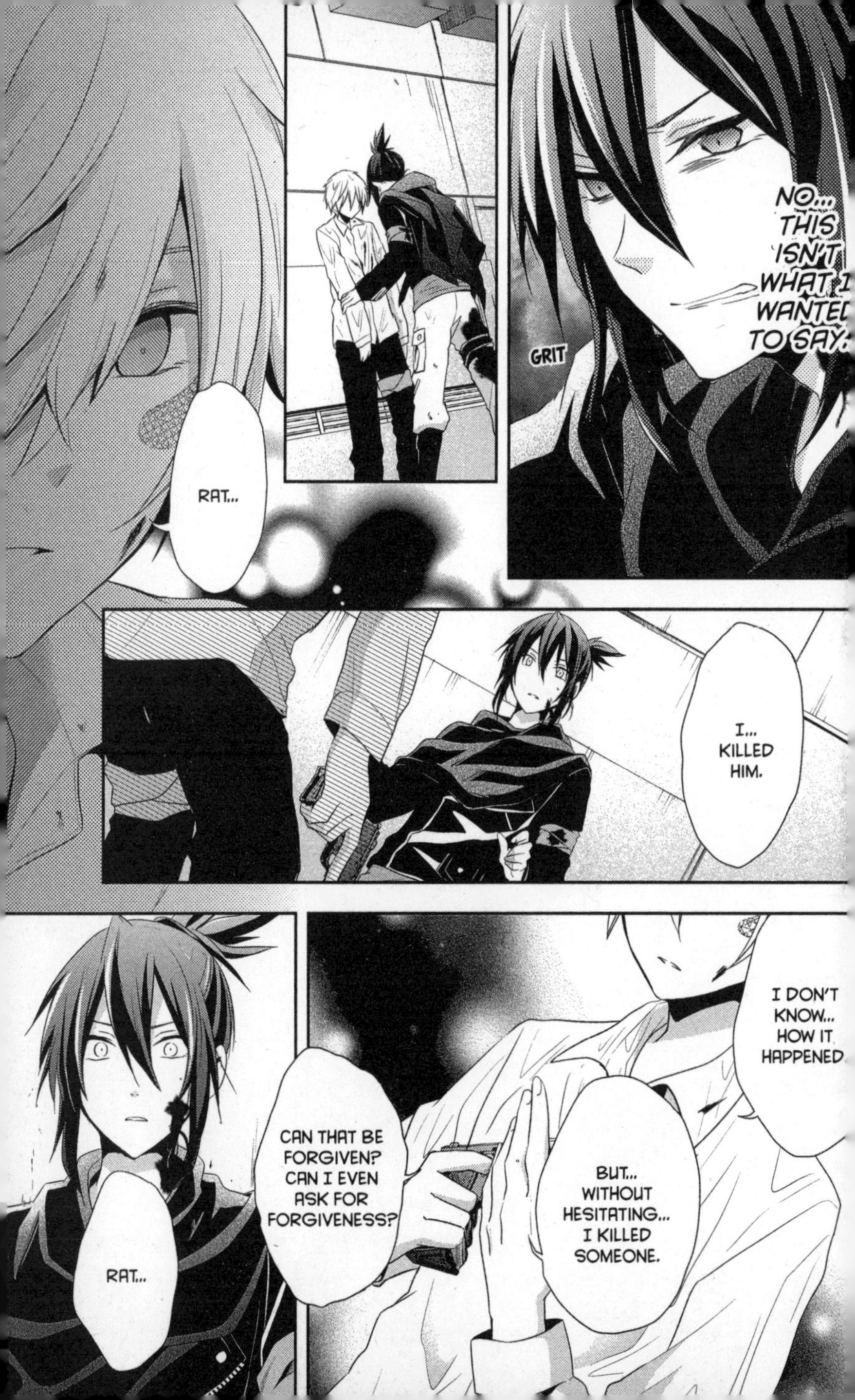

NO... THIS ISN'T WHAT I WANTED TO SAY...
GRIT
RAT...
I... KILLED HIM.
I DON'T KNOW... HOW IT HAPPENED.
BUT... WITHOUT HESITATING... I KILLED SOMEONE.
CAN THAT BE FORGIVEN? CAN I EVEN ASK FOR FORGIVENESS?
RAT...

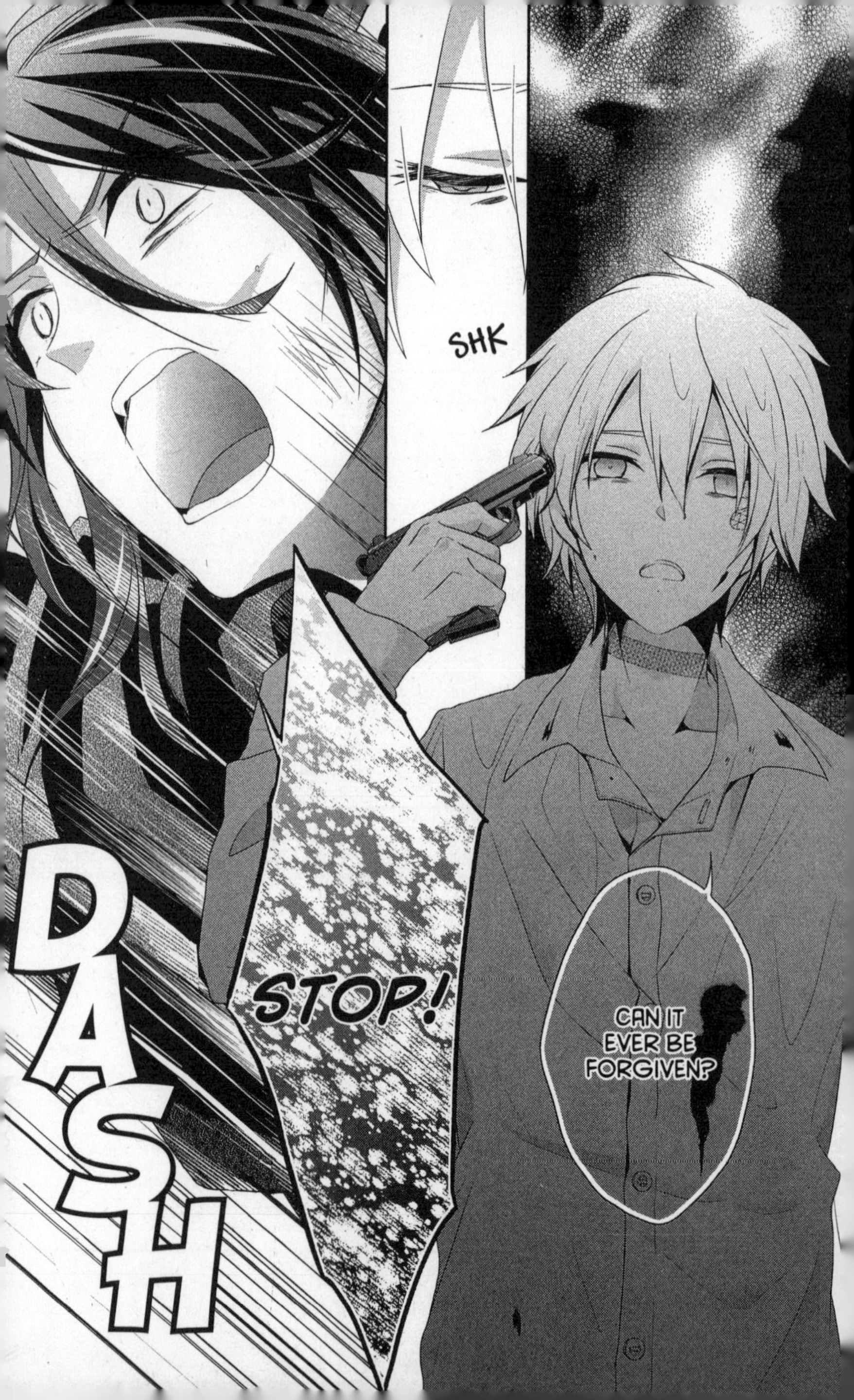
SHK
CAN IT EVER BE FORGIVEN?
STOP!
DASH

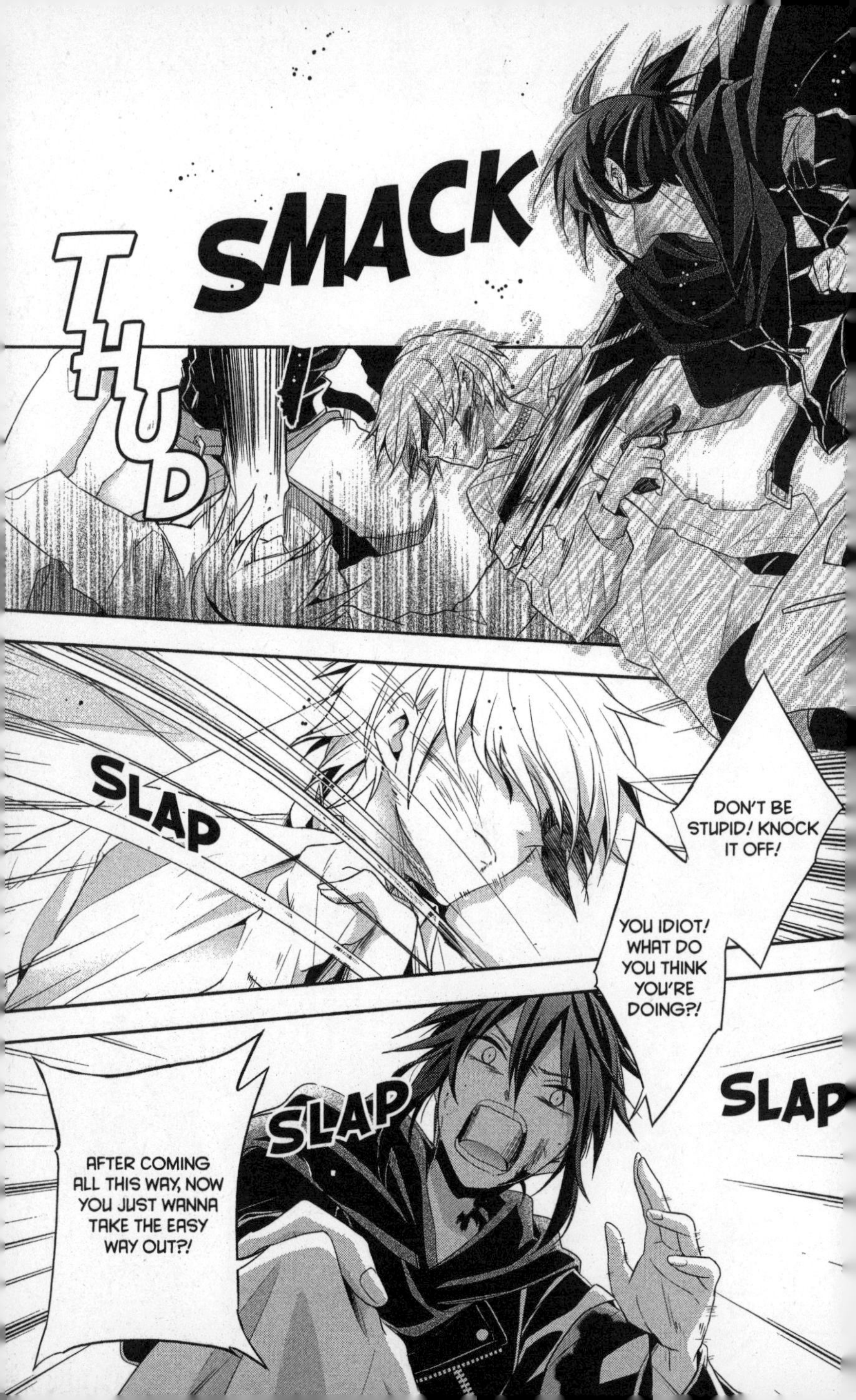
SMACK
THUD
DON'T BE STUPID! KNOCK IT OFF!
SLAP
YOU IDIOT! WHAT DO YOU THINK YOU'RE DOING?!
SLAP
SLAP
AFTER COMING ALL THIS WAY, NOW YOU JUST WANNA TAKE THE EASY WAY OUT?!

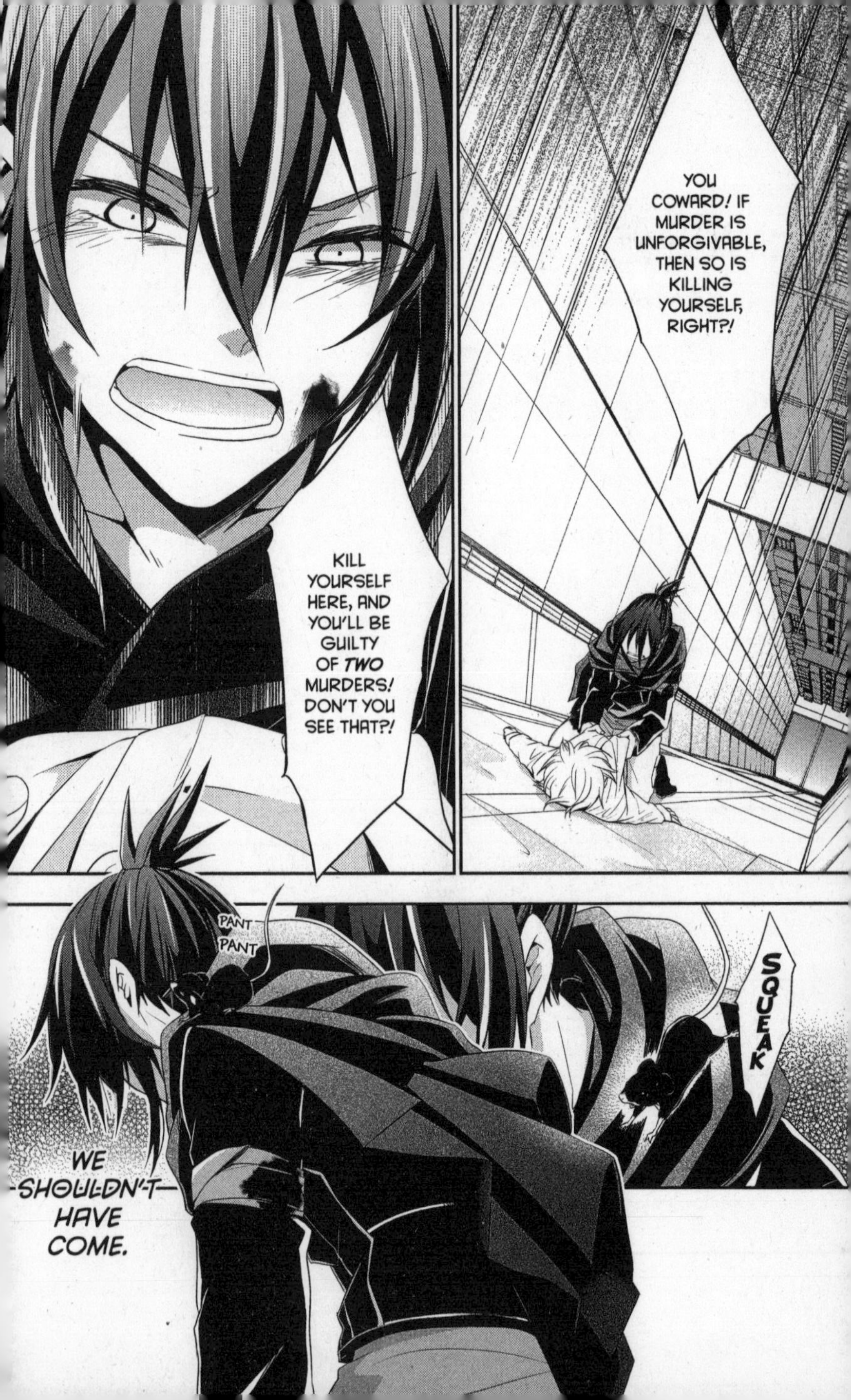
YOU COWARD! IF MURDER IS UNFORGIVABLE, THEN SO IS KILLING YOURSELF, RIGHT?!
KILL YOURSELF HERE, AND YOU'LL BE GUILTY OF *TWO* MURDERS! DON'T YOU SEE THAT?!
SQUEAK
PANT PANT
WE SHOULDN'T HAVE COME.

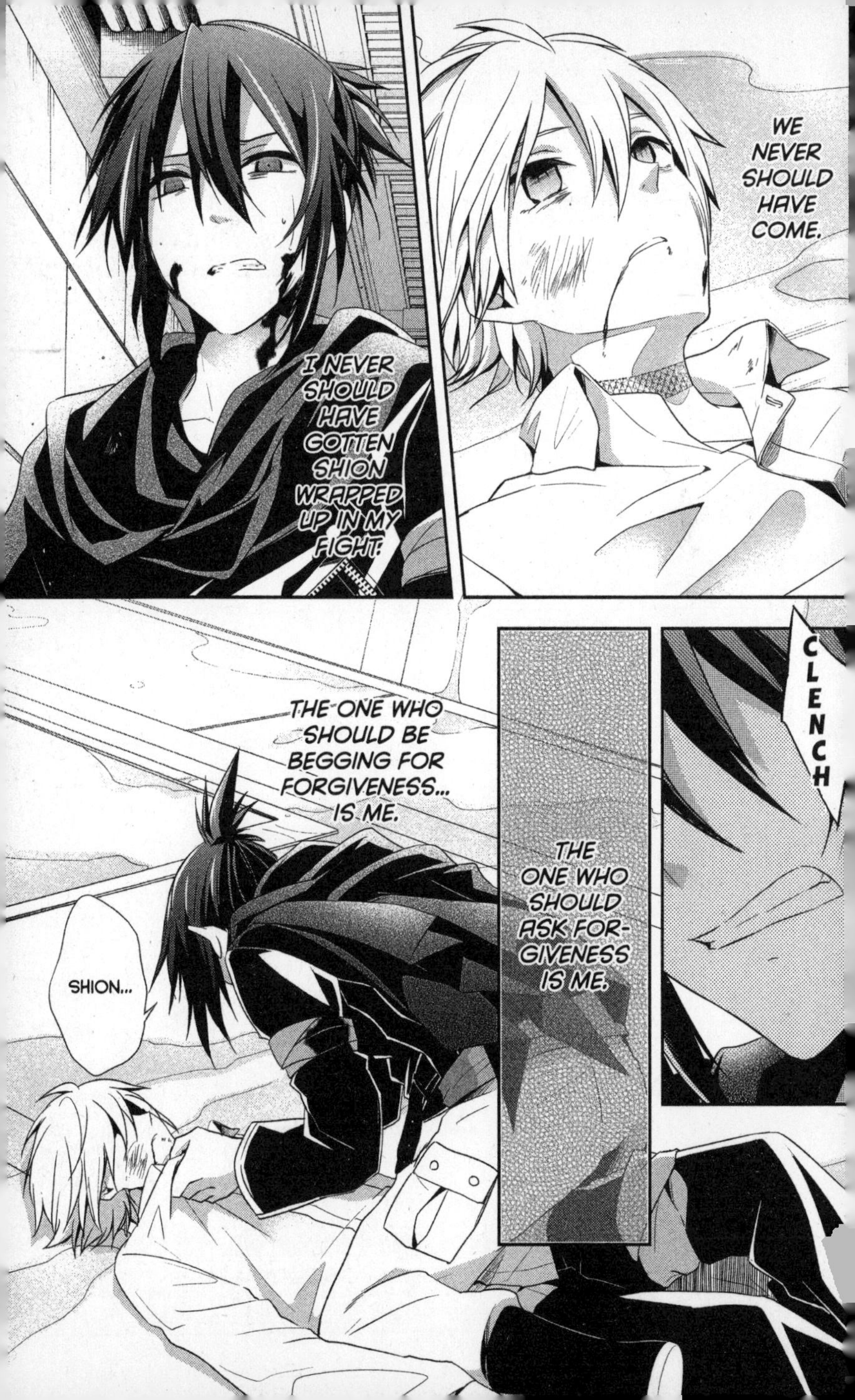
WE NEVER SHOULD HAVE COME.
I NEVER SHOULD HAVE GOTTEN SHION WRAPPED UP IN MY FIGHT.
CLENCH
THE ONE WHO SHOULD ASK FOR-GIVENESS IS ME.
THE ONE WHO SHOULD BE BEGGING FOR FORGIVENESS... IS ME.
SHION...

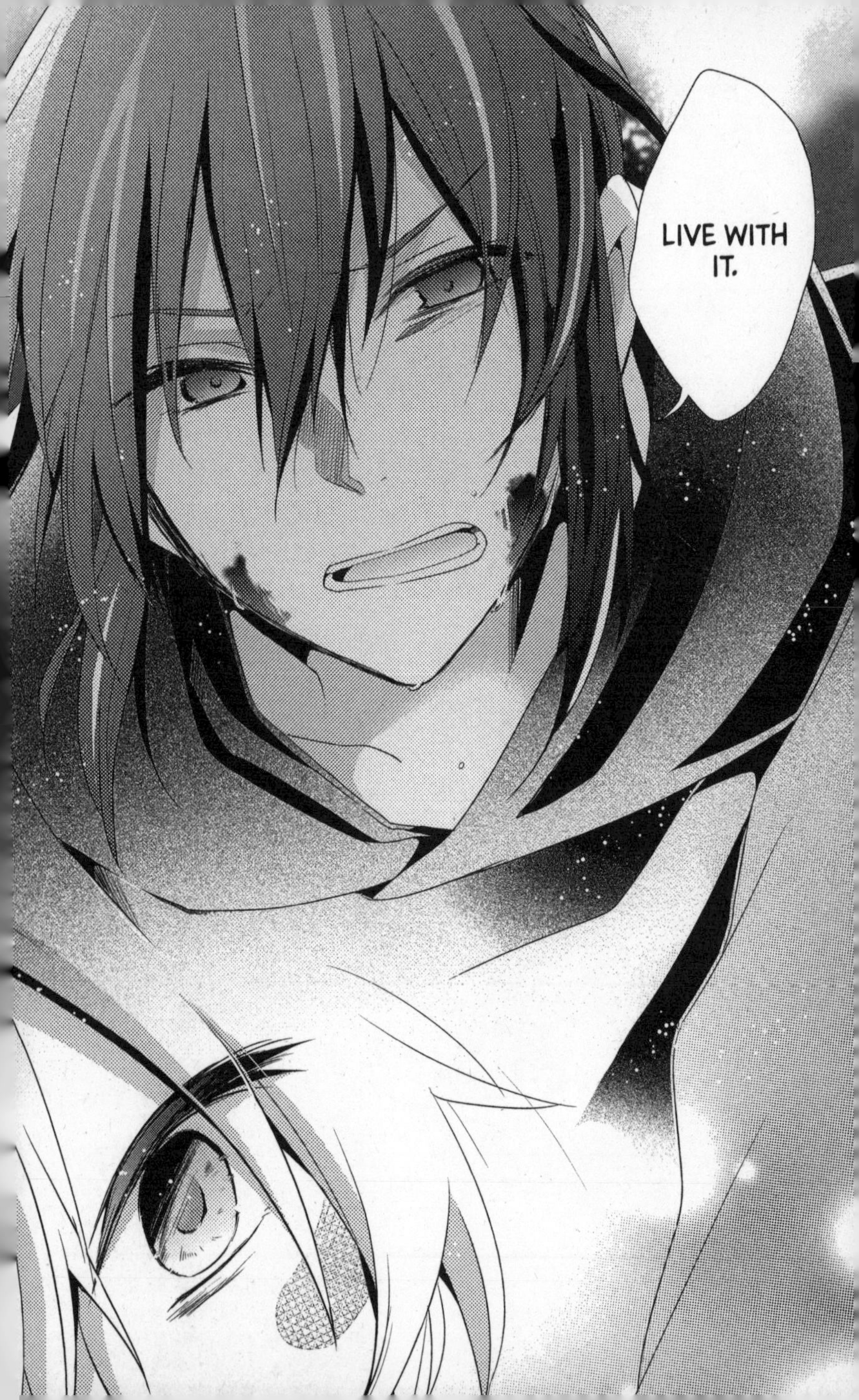
LIVE WITH IT.

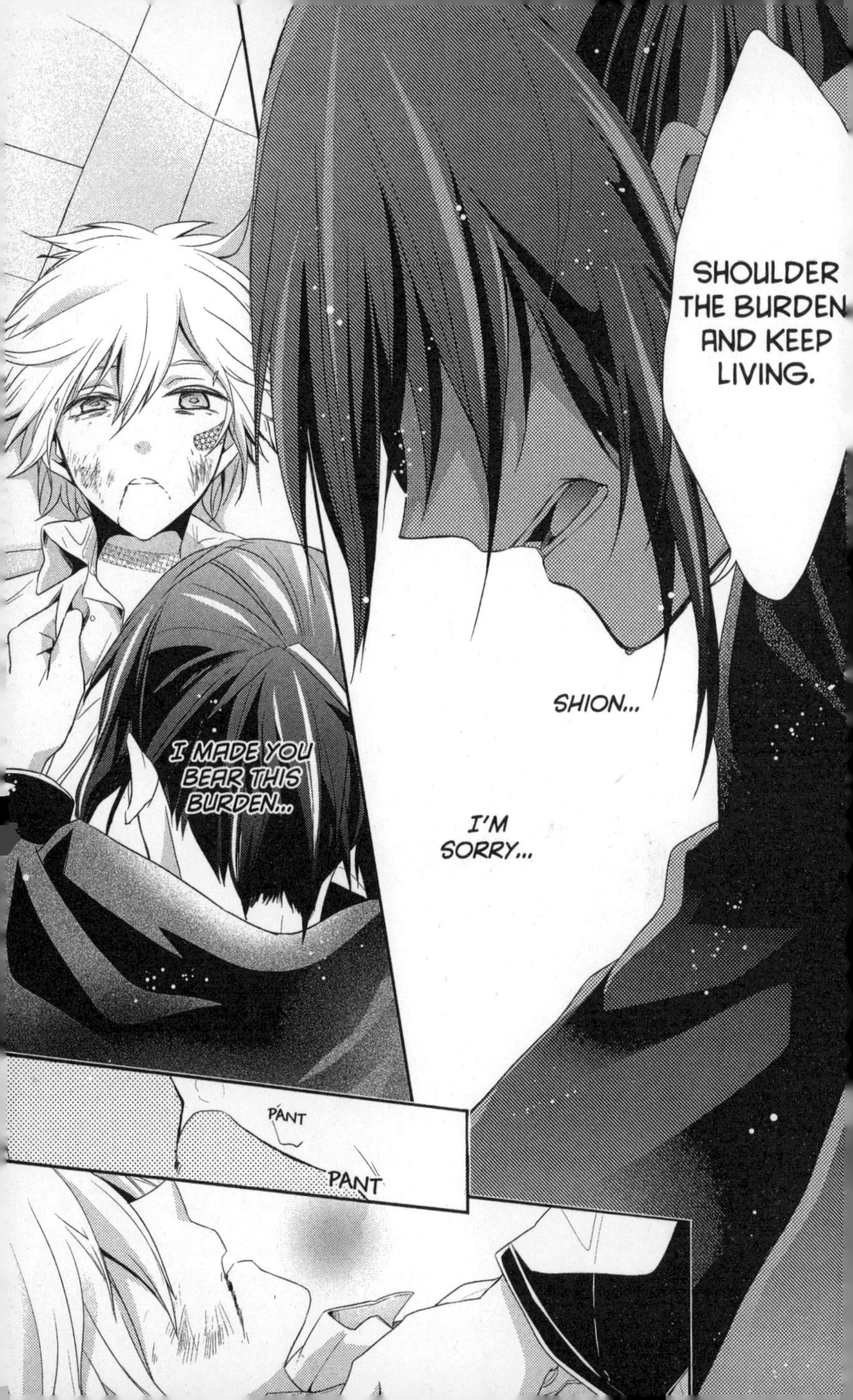
SHOULDER THE BURDEN AND KEEP LIVING.
SHION...
I'M SORRY...
I MADE YOU BEAR THIS BURDEN...
PANT
PANT

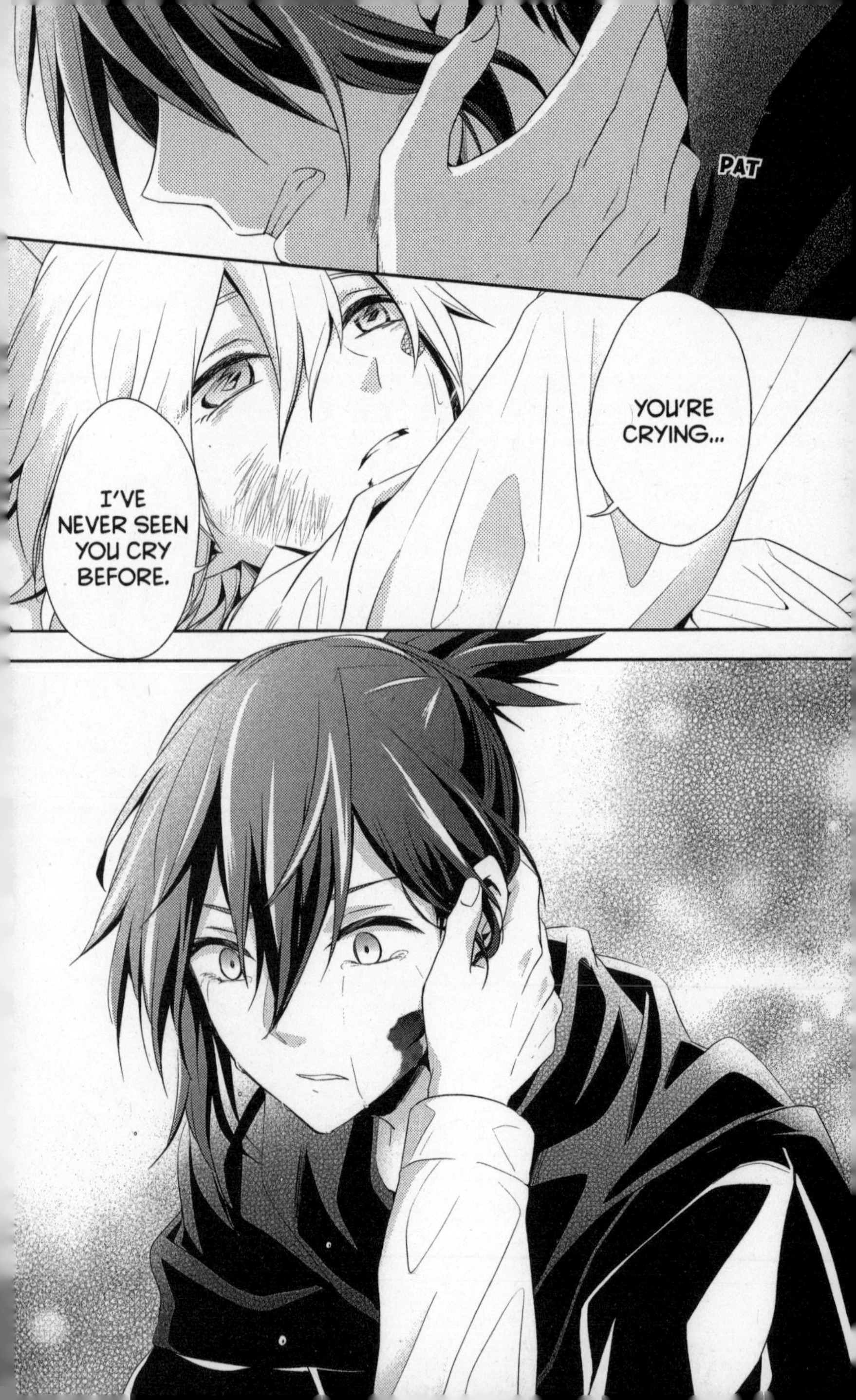
PAT
YOU'RE CRYING...
I'VE NEVER SEEN YOU CRY BEFORE.

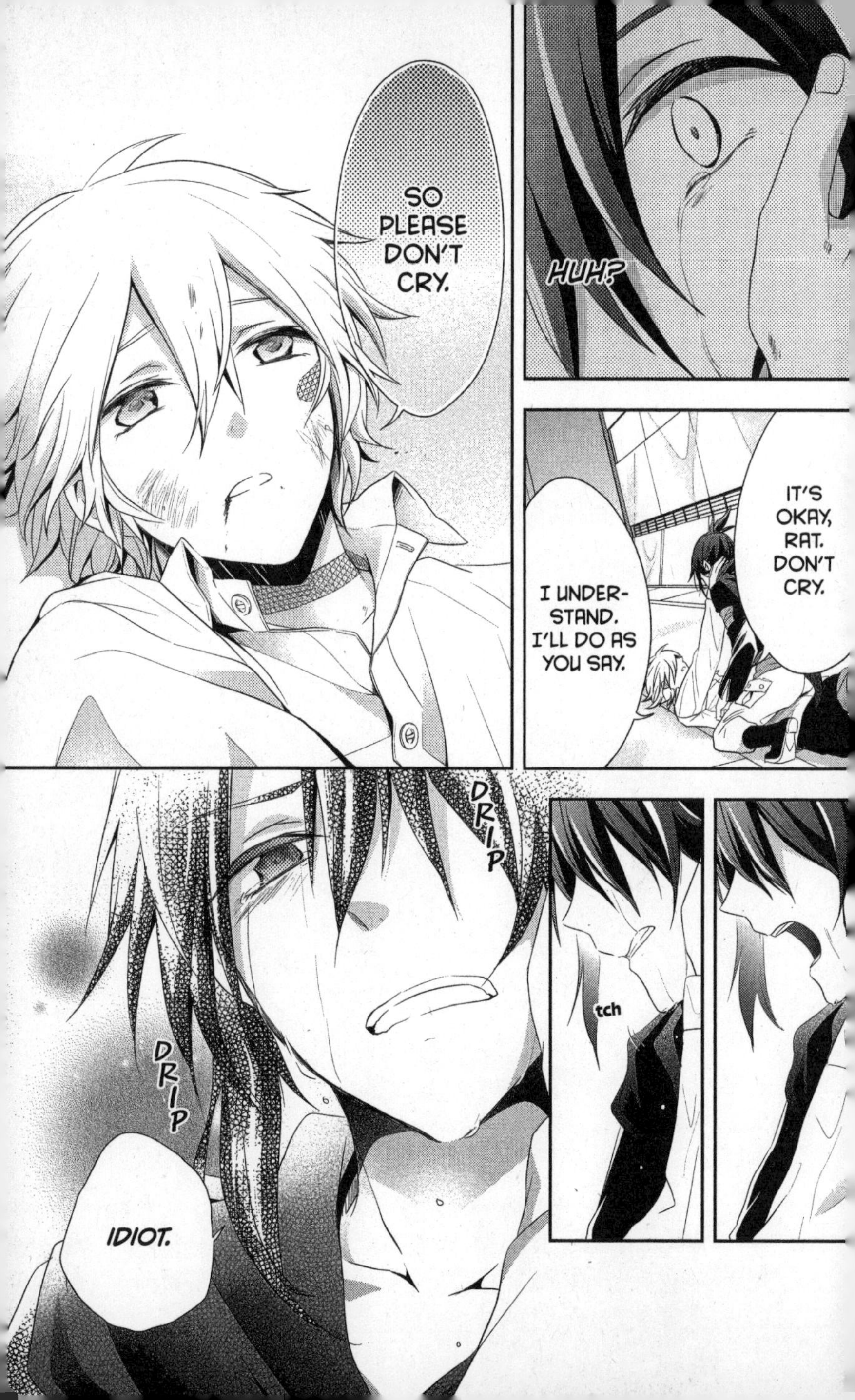
HUH?
IT'S OKAY, RAT. DON'T CRY.
I UNDERSTAND. I'LL DO AS YOU SAY.
SO PLEASE DON'T CRY.
tch
DRIP DRIP
DRIP DRIP
IDIOT.

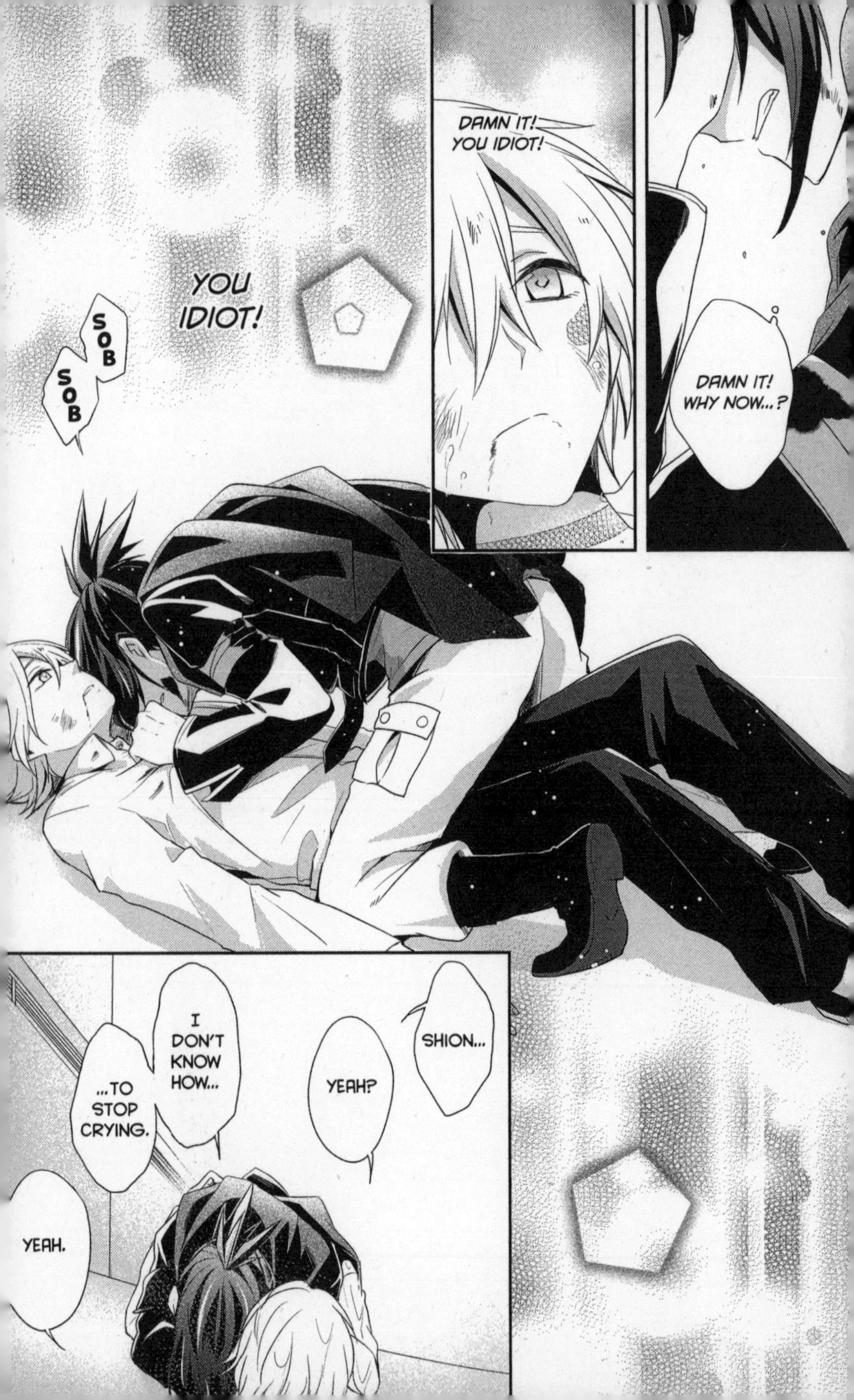
DAMN IT! WHY NOW...?
DAMN IT! YOU IDIOT!
YOU IDIOT!
SOB SOB
SHION...
YEAH?
I DON'T KNOW HOW...
...TO STOP CRYING.
YEAH.

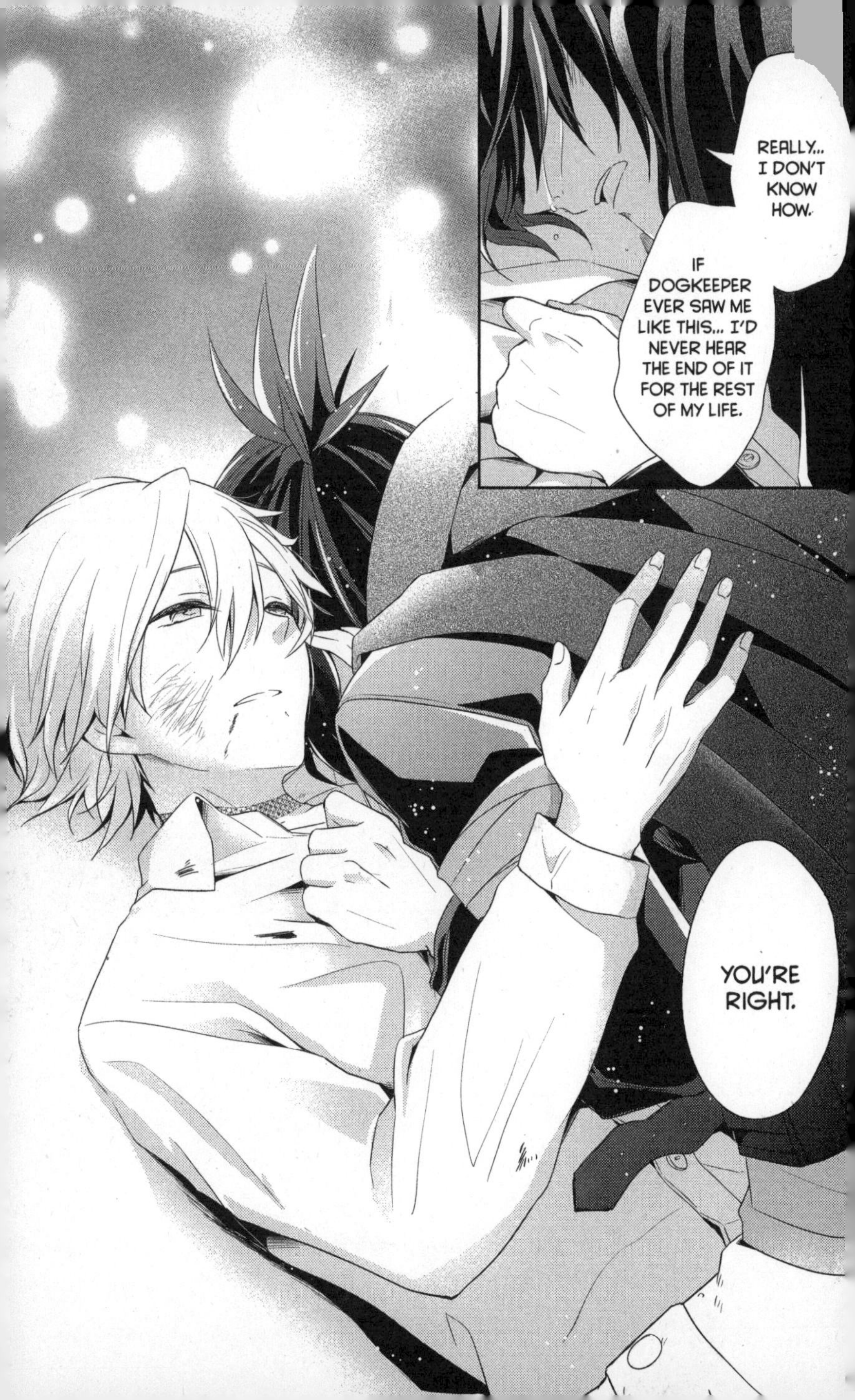
REALLY... I DON'T KNOW HOW.
IF DOGKEEPER EVER SAW ME LIKE THIS... I'D NEVER HEAR THE END OF IT FOR THE REST OF MY LIFE.
YOU'RE RIGHT.

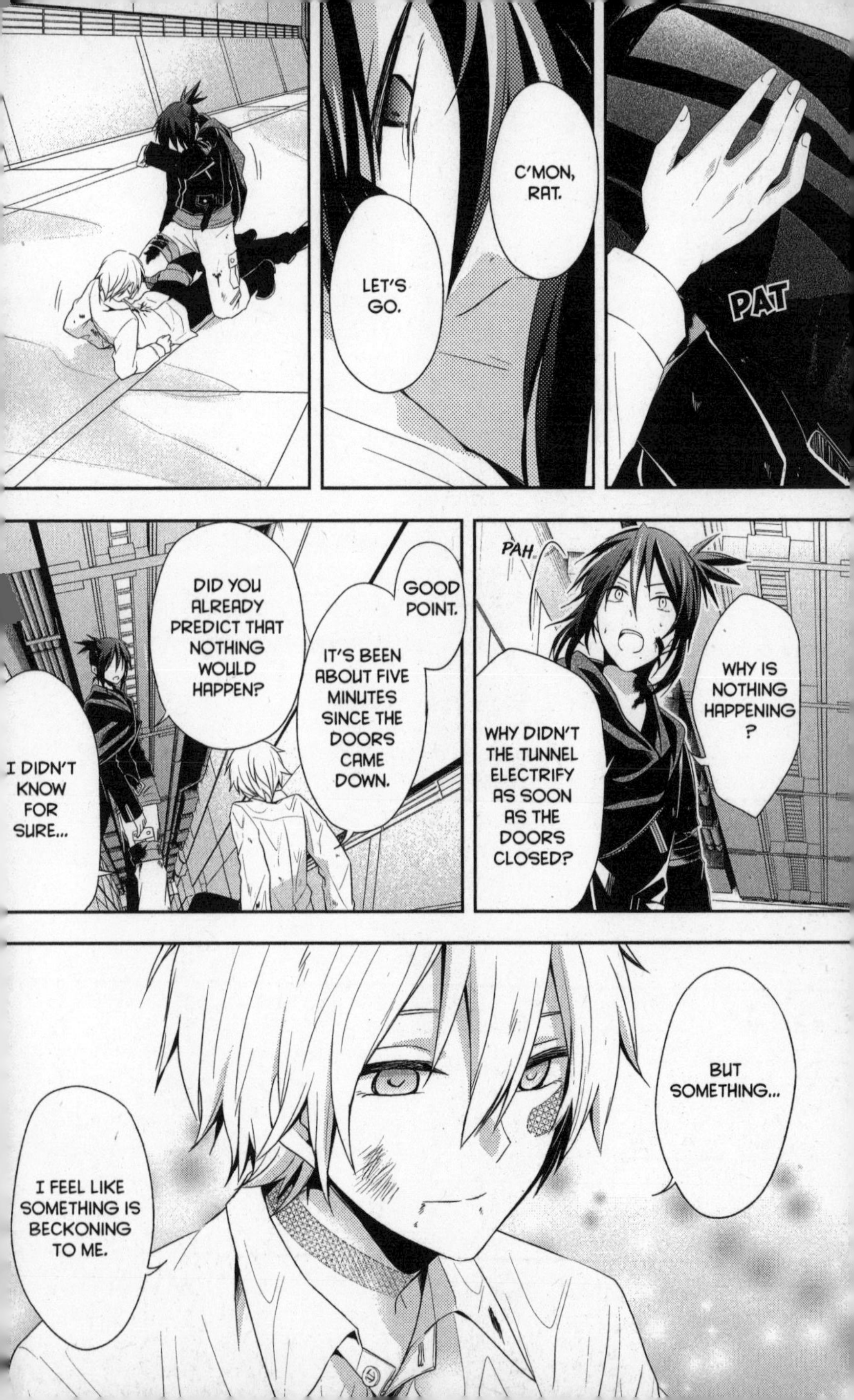
PAT
C'MON, RAT.
LET'S GO.
PAH
WHY IS NOTHING HAPPENING?
WHY DIDN'T THE TUNNEL ELECTRIFY AS SOON AS THE DOORS CLOSED?
GOOD POINT.
IT'S BEEN ABOUT FIVE MINUTES SINCE THE DOORS CAME DOWN.
DID YOU ALREADY PREDICT THAT NOTHING WOULD HAPPEN?
I DIDN'T KNOW FOR SURE...
BUT SOMETHING...
I FEEL LIKE SOMETHING IS BECKONING TO ME.

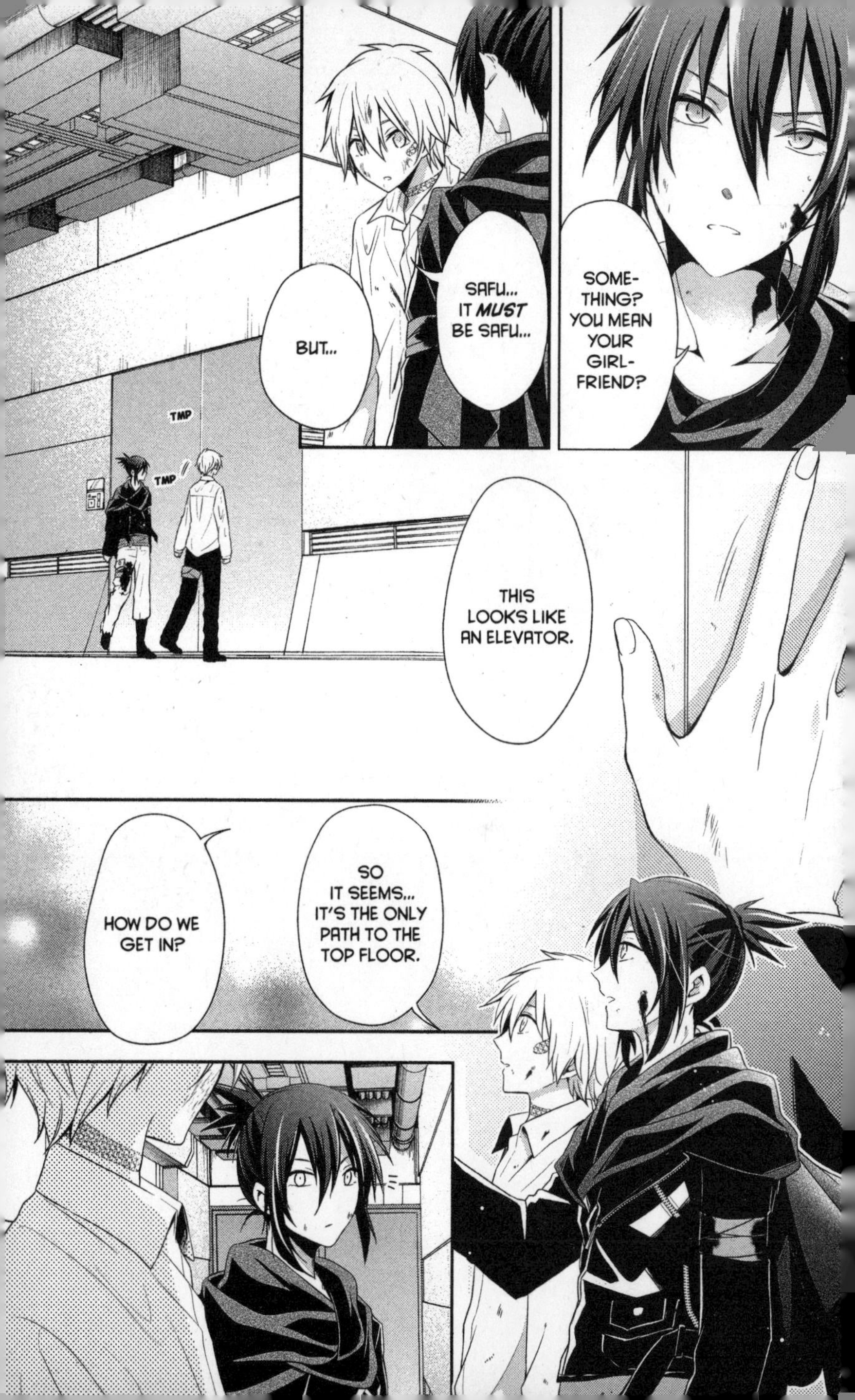
SOME-THING? YOU MEAN YOUR GIRL-FRIEND?
SAFU... IT *MUST* BE SAFU...
BUT...
THIS LOOKS LIKE AN ELEVATOR.
TMP
TMP
SO IT SEEMS... IT'S THE ONLY PATH TO THE TOP FLOOR.
HOW DO WE GET IN?

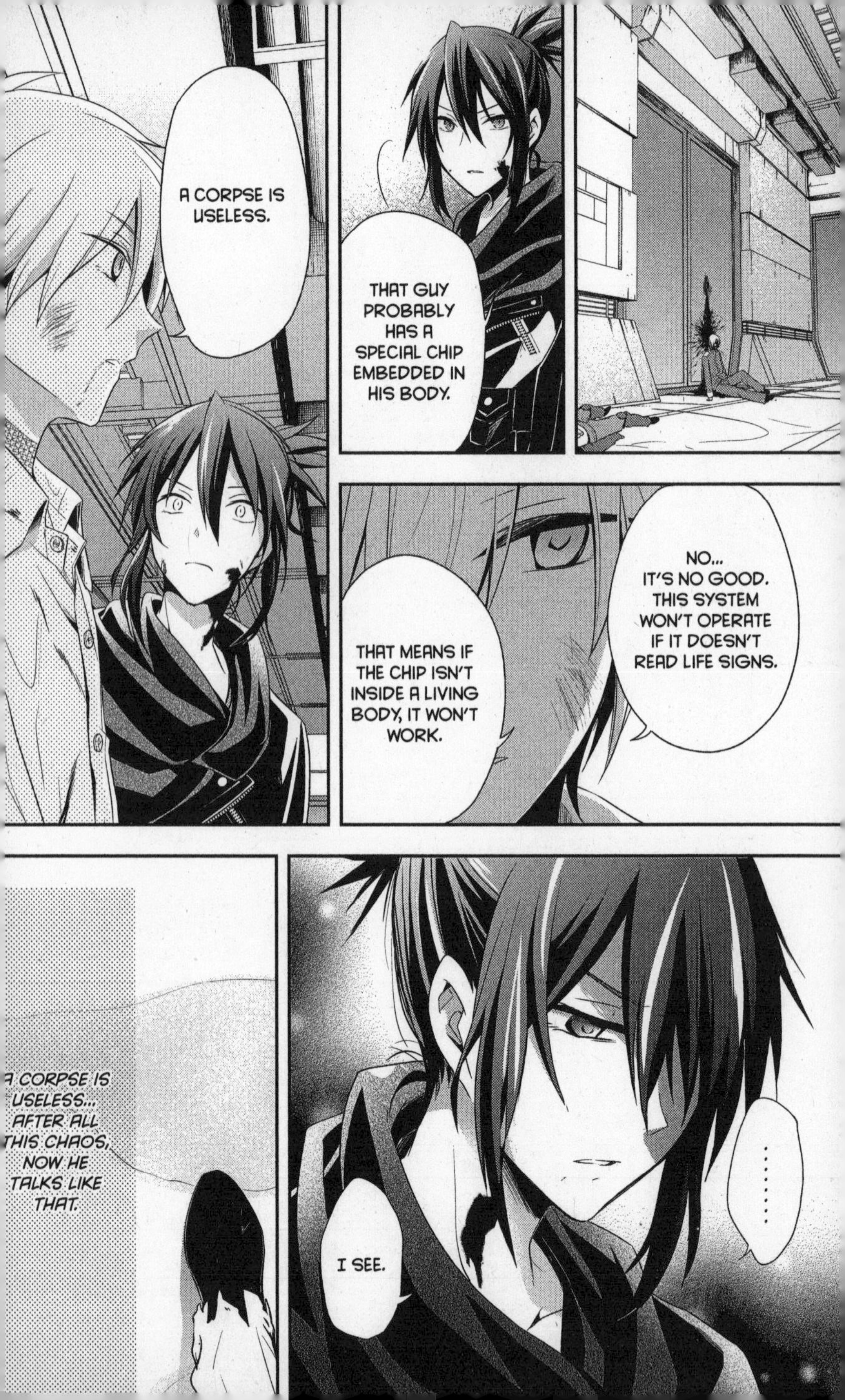
THAT GUY PROBABLY HAS A SPECIAL CHIP EMBEDDED IN HIS BODY.
NO... IT'S NO GOOD. THIS SYSTEM WON'T OPERATE IF IT DOESN'T READ LIFE SIGNS.
THAT MEANS IF THE CHIP ISN'T INSIDE A LIVING BODY, IT WON'T WORK.
A CORPSE IS USELESS.
......
I SEE.
A CORPSE IS USELESS... AFTER ALL THIS CHAOS, NOW HE TALKS LIKE THAT.

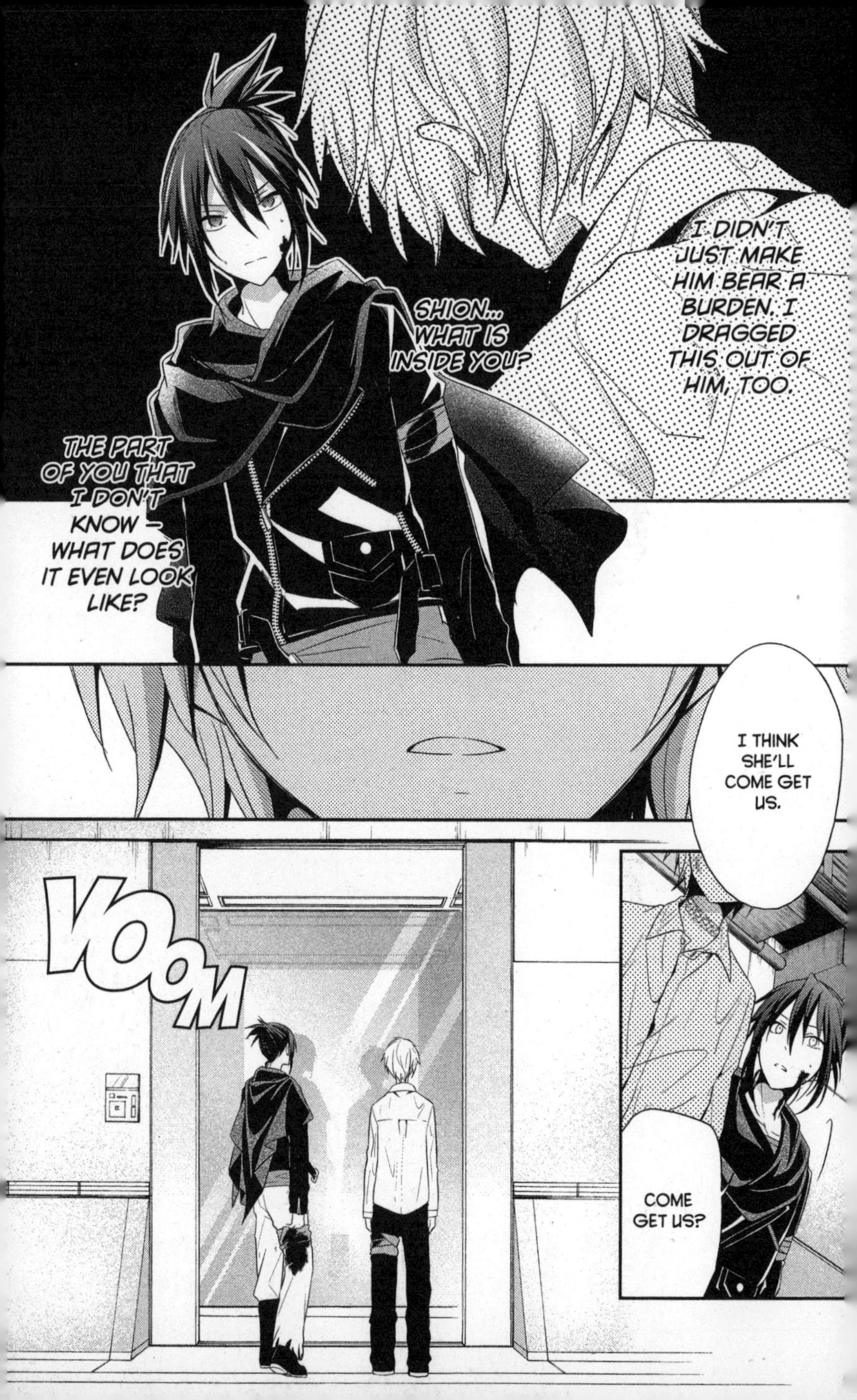
I DIDN'T JUST MAKE HIM BEAR A BURDEN. I DRAGGED THIS OUT OF HIM, TOO.
SHION... WHAT IS INSIDE YOU?
THE PART OF YOU THAT I DON'T KNOW – WHAT DOES IT EVEN LOOK LIKE?
I THINK SHE'LL COME GET US.
COME GET US?
VOOM

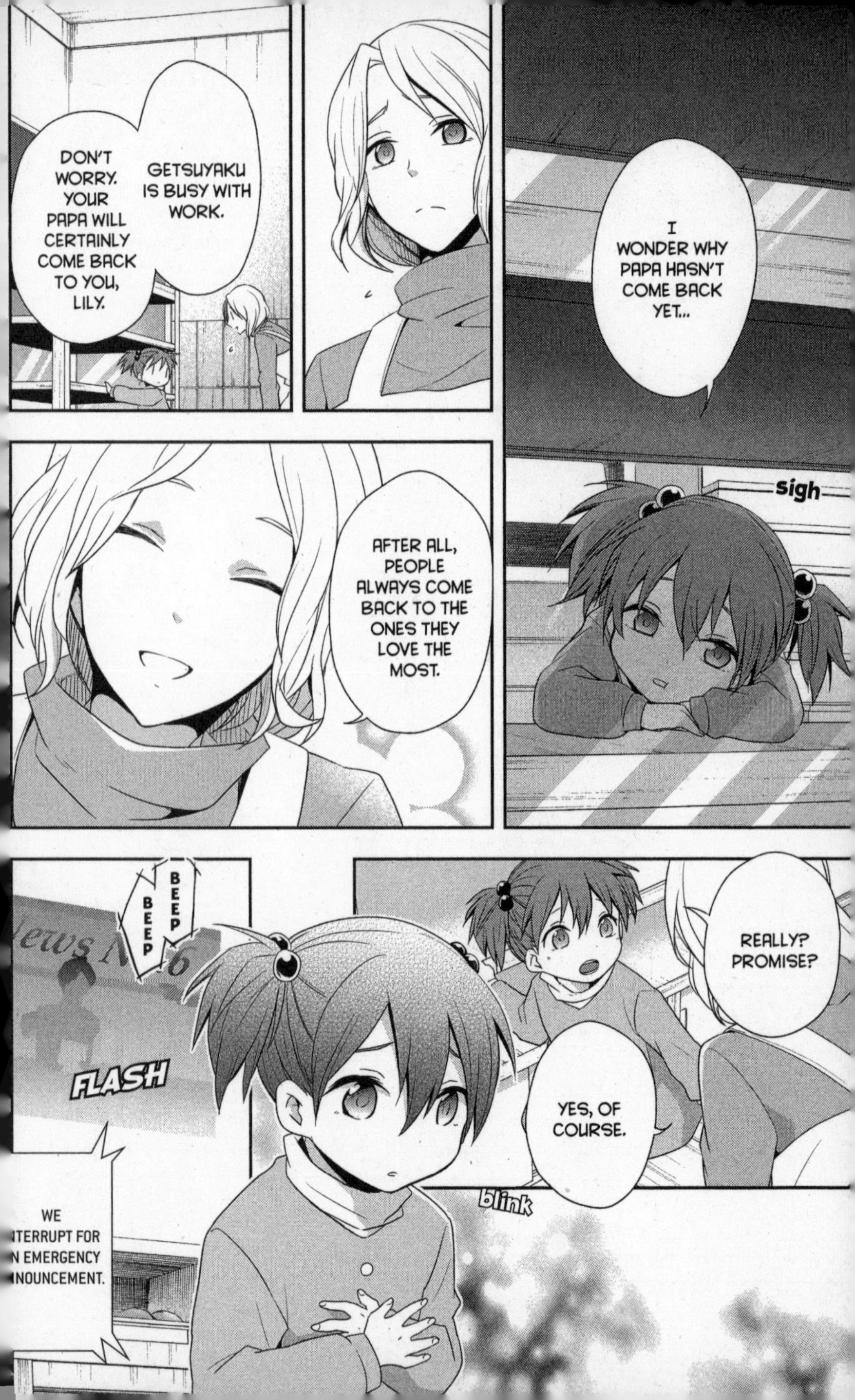
I WONDER WHY PAPA HASN'T COME BACK YET...
GETSUYAKU IS BUSY WITH WORK.
DON'T WORRY. YOUR PAPA WILL CERTAINLY COME BACK TO YOU, LILY.
sigh
AFTER ALL, PEOPLE ALWAYS COME BACK TO THE ONES THEY LOVE THE MOST.
REALLY? PROMISE?
YES, OF COURSE.
blink
BEEP BEEP
FLASH
WE TERRUPT FOR N EMERGENCY NOUNCEMENT.

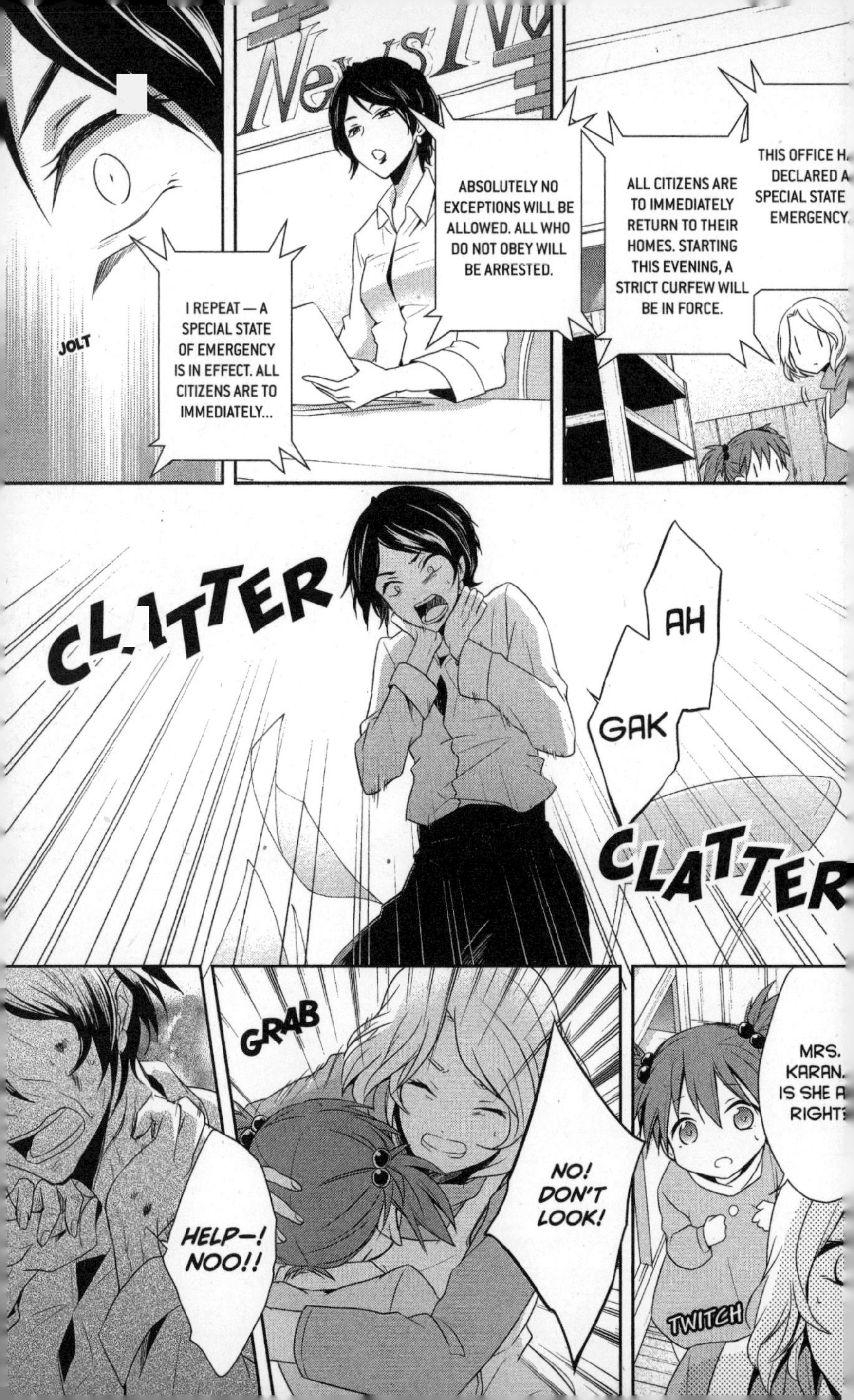
THIS OFFICE HA DECLARED A SPECIAL STATE EMERGENCY.
ALL CITIZENS ARE TO IMMEDIATELY RETURN TO THEIR HOMES. STARTING THIS EVENING, A STRICT CURFEW WILL BE IN FORCE.
ABSOLUTELY NO EXCEPTIONS WILL BE ALLOWED. ALL WHO DO NOT OBEY WILL BE ARRESTED.
I REPEAT — A SPECIAL STATE OF EMERGENCY IS IN EFFECT. ALL CITIZENS ARE TO IMMEDIATELY...
JOLT
AH
GAK
CLATTER
CLATTER
MRS. KARAN. IS SHE A RIGHT?
TWITCH
NO! DON'T LOOK!
GRAB
HELP—! NOO!!

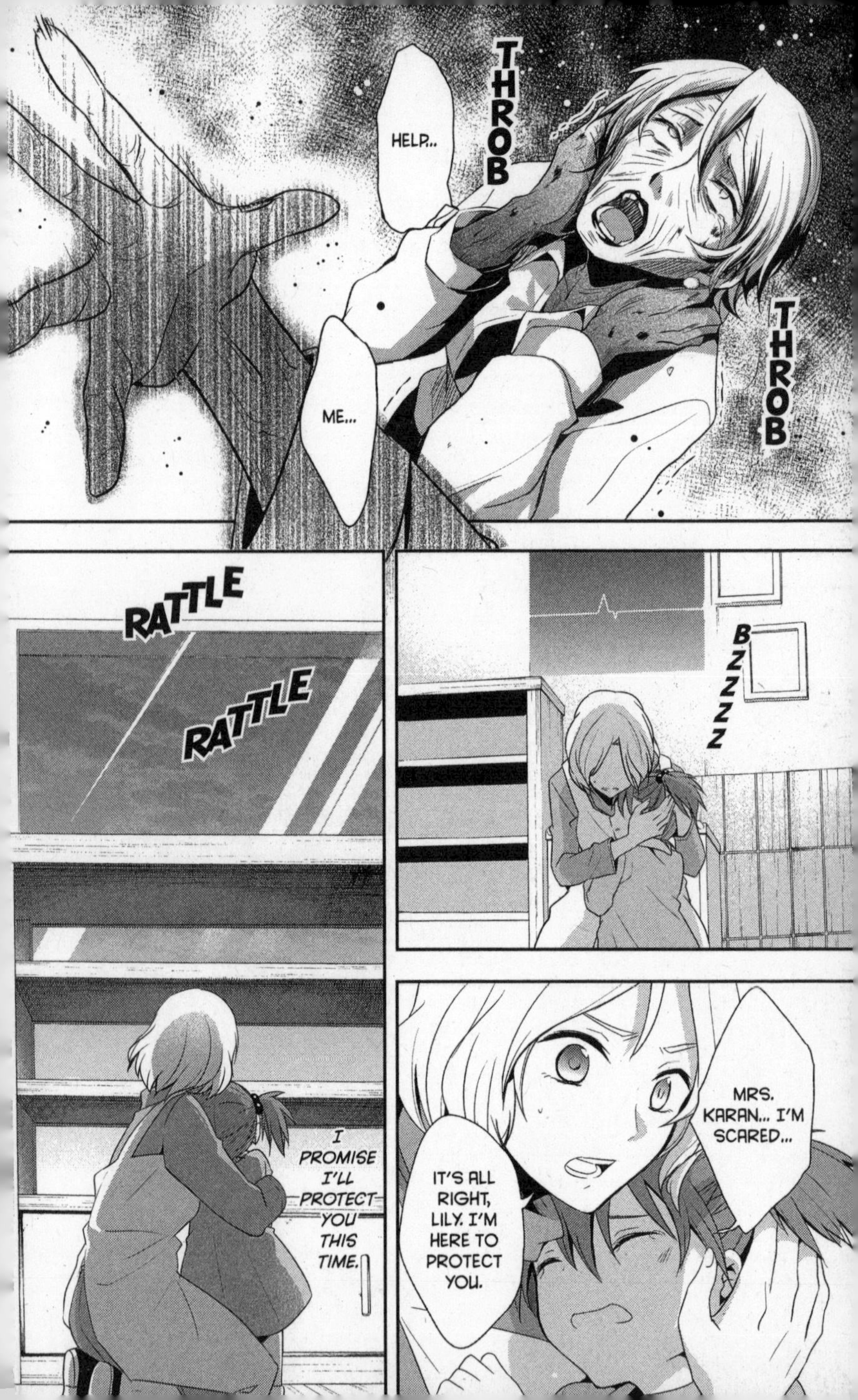
THROB
HELP...
THROB
ME...
BZZZZZ
RATTLE
RATTLE
MRS. KARAN... I'M SCARED...
IT'S ALL RIGHT, LILY. I'M HERE TO PROTECT YOU.
I PROMISE I'LL PROTECT YOU THIS TIME.

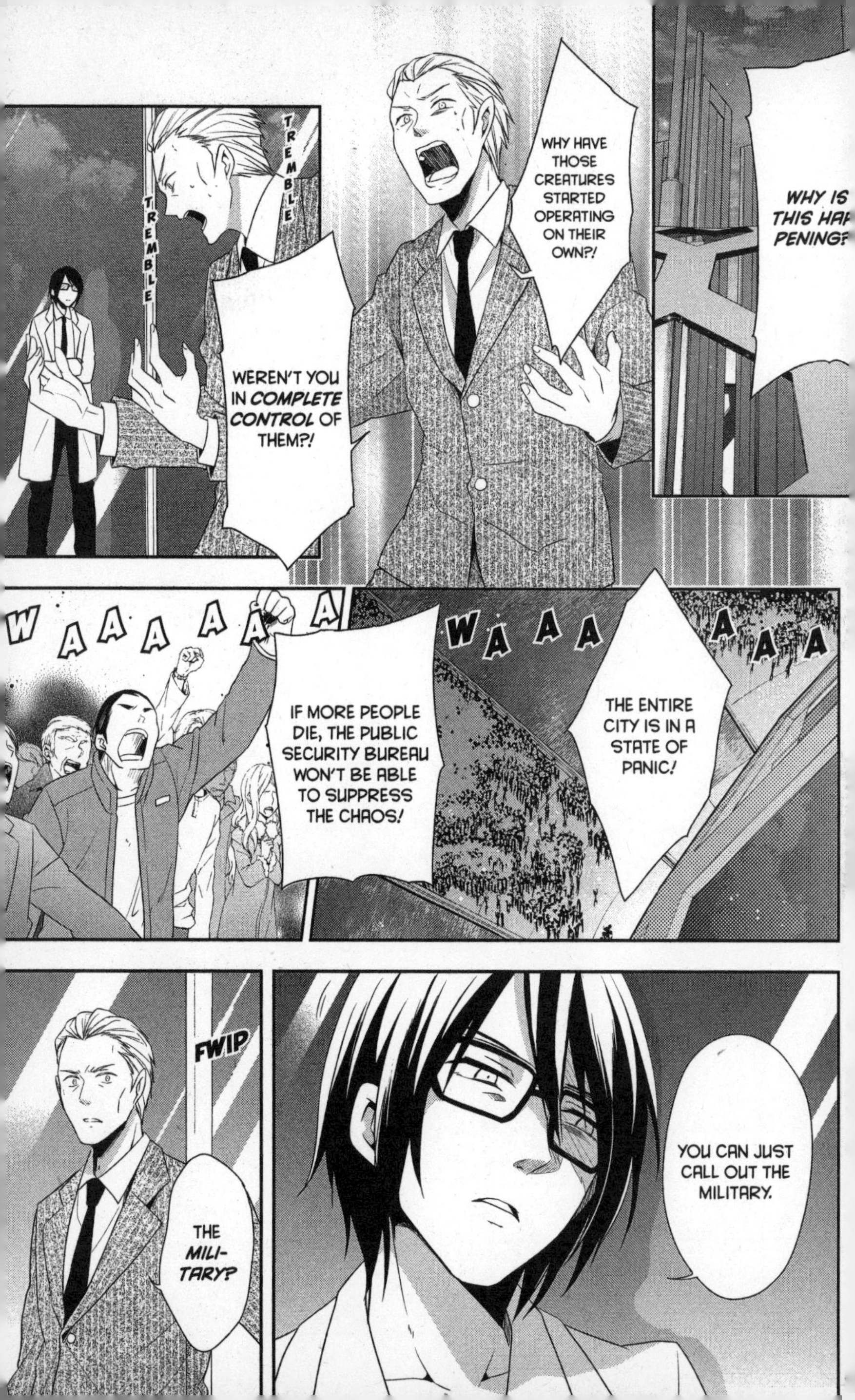
WHY IS THIS HAP PENING?
WHY HAVE THOSE CREATURES STARTED OPERATING ON THEIR OWN?!
TREMBLE
TREMBLE
WEREN'T YOU IN *COMPLETE CONTROL* OF THEM?!
WAAAAAA
THE ENTIRE CITY IS IN A STATE OF PANIC!
WAAAAAA
IF MORE PEOPLE DIE, THE PUBLIC SECURITY BUREAU WON'T BE ABLE TO SUPPRESS THE CHAOS!
YOU CAN JUST CALL OUT THE MILITARY.
FWIP
THE *MILI-TARY?*

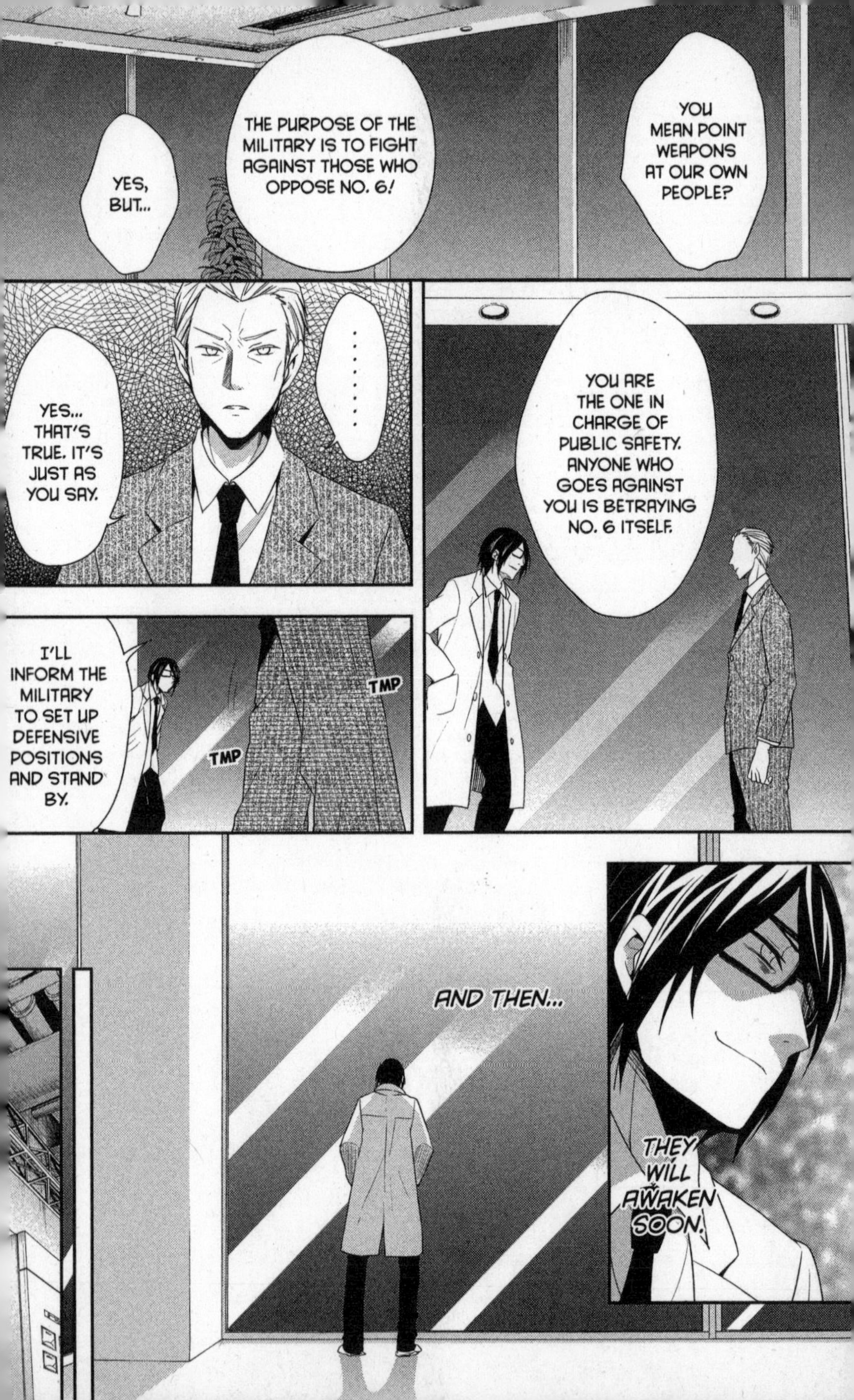
YOU MEAN POINT WEAPONS AT OUR OWN PEOPLE?
THE PURPOSE OF THE MILITARY IS TO FIGHT AGAINST THOSE WHO OPPOSE NO. 6!
YES, BUT...
YOU ARE THE ONE IN CHARGE OF PUBLIC SAFETY. ANYONE WHO GOES AGAINST YOU IS BETRAYING NO. 6 ITSELF.
......
YES... THAT'S TRUE. IT'S JUST AS YOU SAY.
TMP
TMP
I'LL INFORM THE MILITARY TO SET UP DEFENSIVE POSITIONS AND STAND BY.
AND THEN...
THEY WILL AWAKEN SOON.

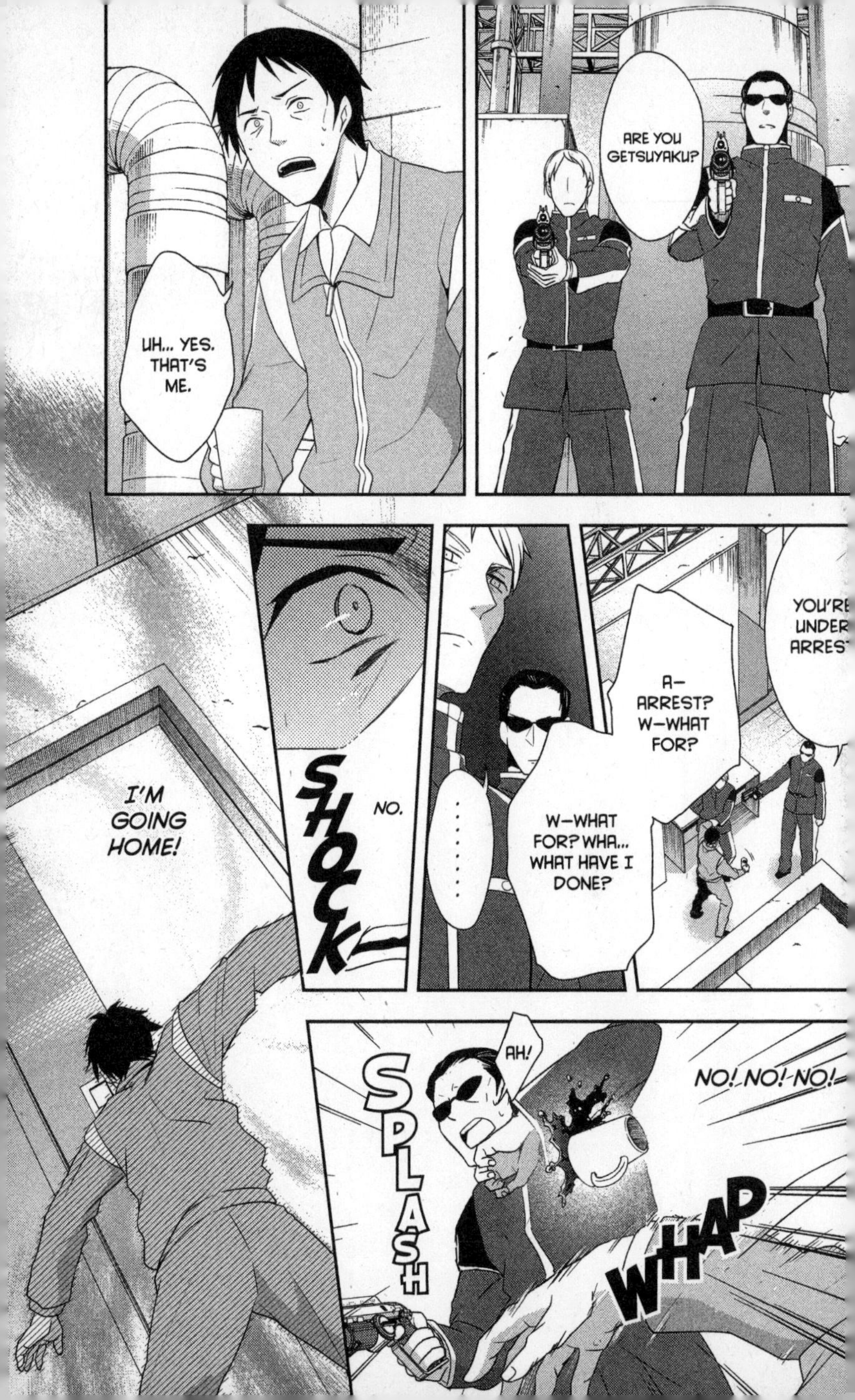
ARE YOU GETSUYAKU?
UH... YES. THAT'S ME.
YOU'RE UNDER ARREST
A— ARREST? W—WHAT FOR?
W—WHAT FOR? WHA... WHAT HAVE I DONE?
......
NO.
SHOCK
NO! NO! NO!
AH!
SPLASH
WHAP
I'M GOING HOME!

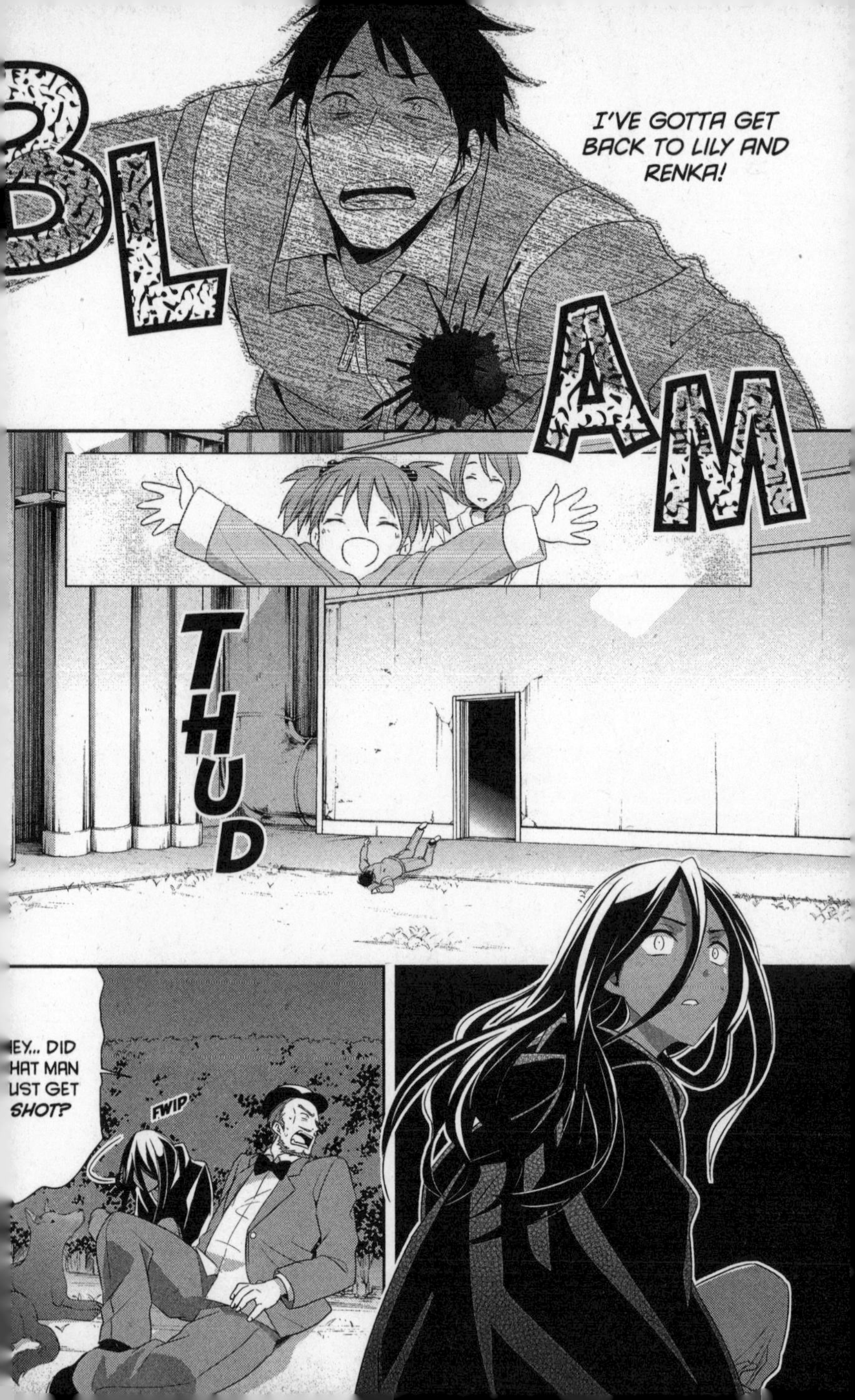
I'VE GOTTA GET BACK TO LILY AND RENKA!
BLAM
THUD
FWIP
HEY... DID THAT MAN JUST GET SHOT?

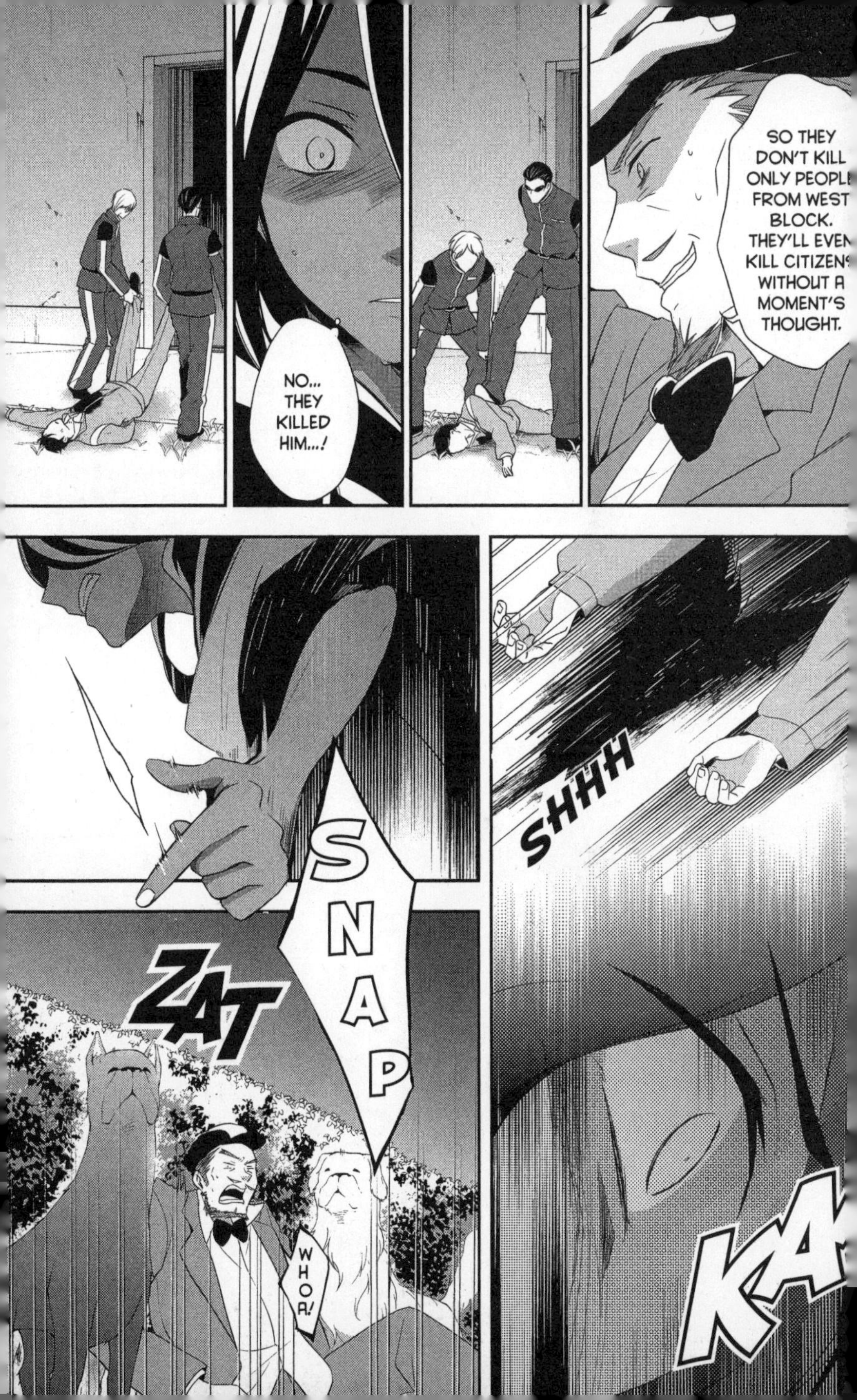
SO THEY DON'T KILL ONLY PEOPLE FROM WEST BLOCK. THEY'LL EVEN KILL CITIZENS WITHOUT A MOMENT'S THOUGHT.
NO... THEY KILLED HIM...!
SHHH
KA
SNAP
ZAT
WHOA!

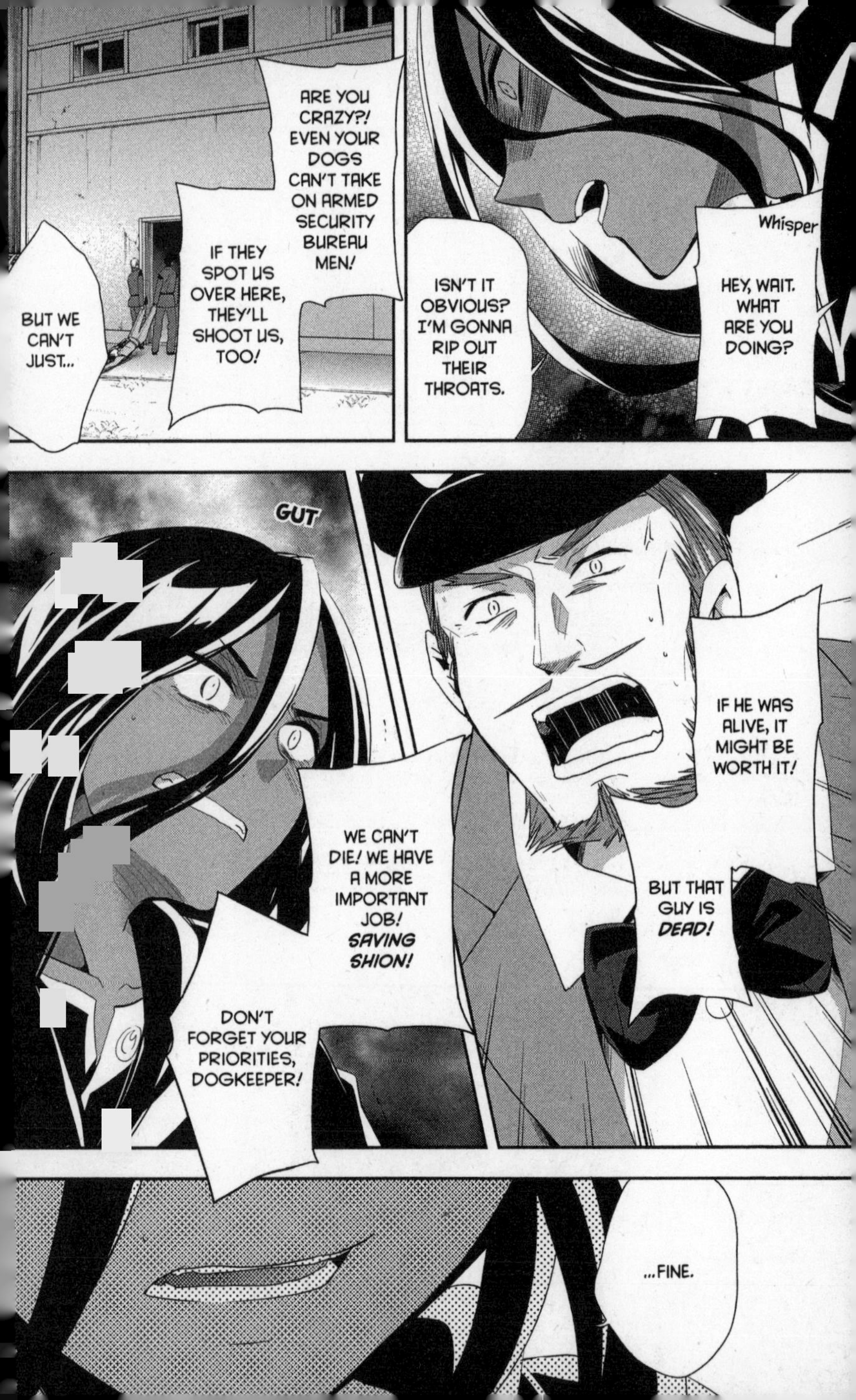
Whisper
HEY, WAIT. WHAT ARE YOU DOING?
ISN'T IT OBVIOUS? I'M GONNA RIP OUT THEIR THROATS.
ARE YOU CRAZY?! EVEN YOUR DOGS CAN'T TAKE ON ARMED SECURITY BUREAU MEN!
IF THEY SPOT US OVER HERE, THEY'LL SHOOT US, TOO!
BUT WE CAN'T JUST...
IF HE WAS ALIVE, IT MIGHT BE WORTH IT!
BUT THAT GUY IS *DEAD!*
GUT
WE CAN'T DIE! WE HAVE A MORE IMPORTANT JOB! *SAVING SHION!*
DON'T FORGET YOUR PRIORITIES, DOGKEEPER!
...FINE.

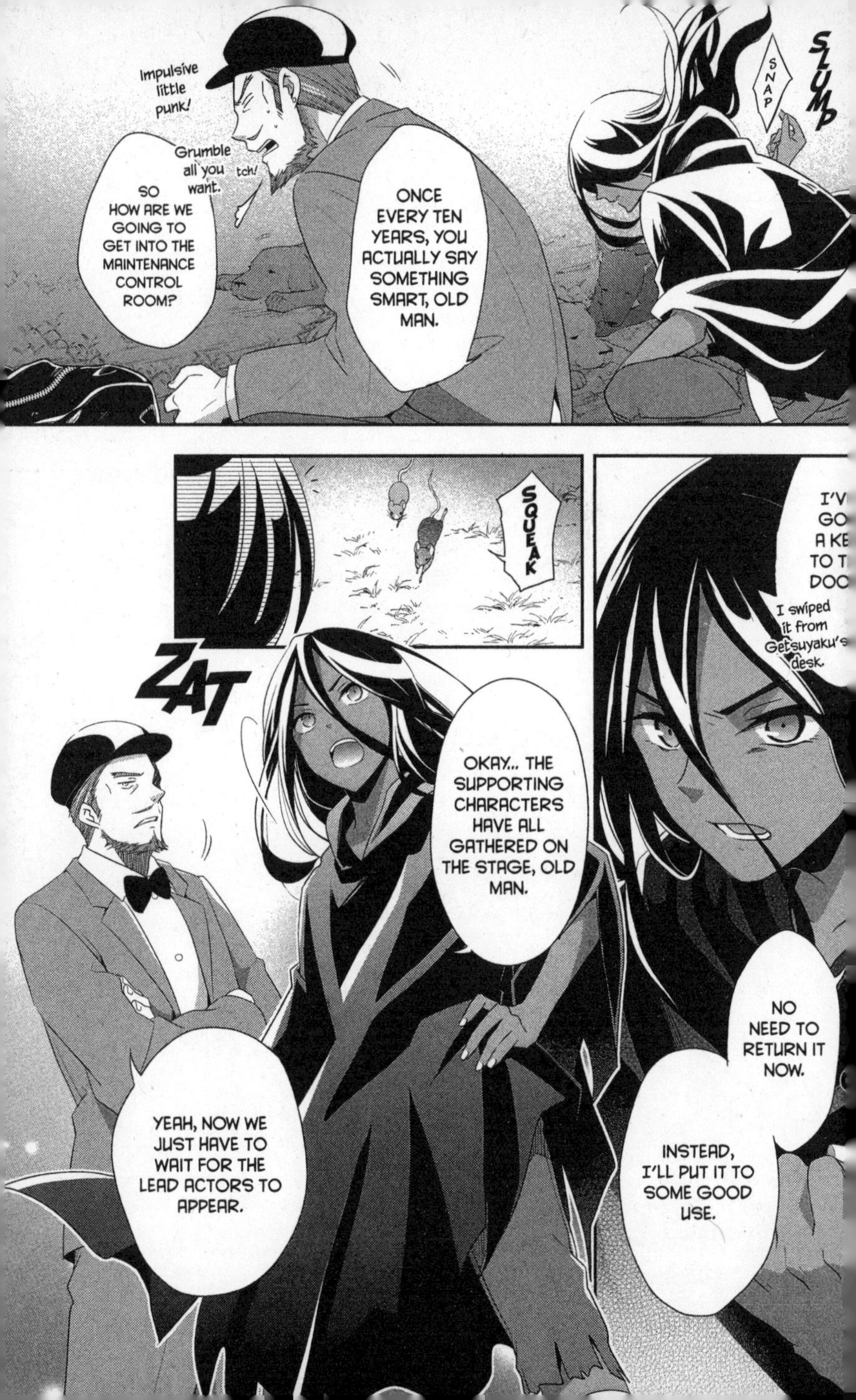
SLUMP
SNAP
ONCE EVERY TEN YEARS, YOU ACTUALLY SAY SOMETHING SMART, OLD MAN.
Impulsive little punk!
Grumble all you want.
tch!
SO HOW ARE WE GOING TO GET INTO THE MAINTENANCE CONTROL ROOM?
I'V GO A KE TO T DOO
I swiped it from Getsuyaku's desk.
NO NEED TO RETURN IT NOW.
INSTEAD, I'LL PUT IT TO SOME GOOD USE.
SQUEAK
ZAT
OKAY... THE SUPPORTING CHARACTERS HAVE ALL GATHERED ON THE STAGE, OLD MAN.
YEAH, NOW WE JUST HAVE TO WAIT FOR THE LEAD ACTORS TO APPEAR.

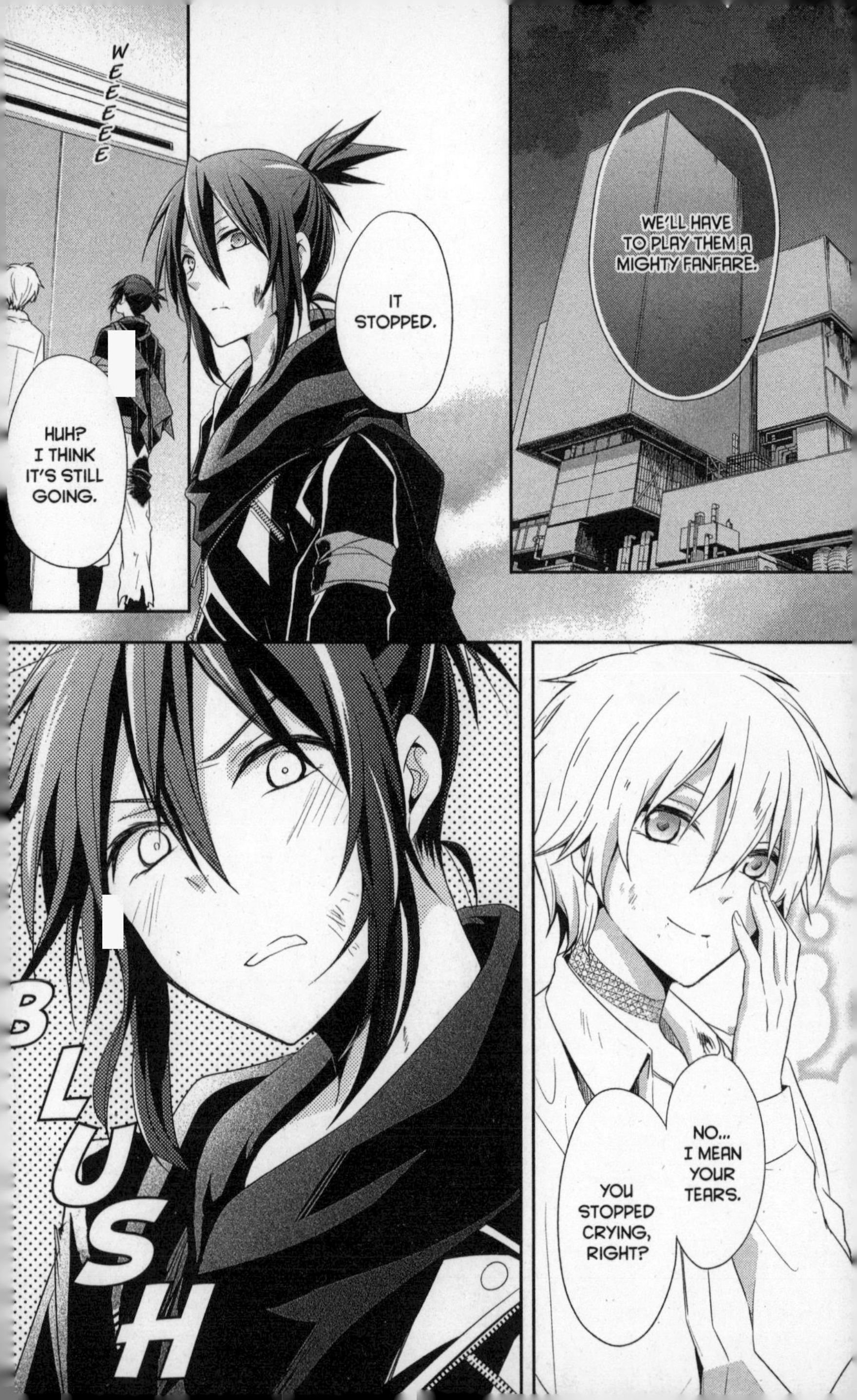
WE'LL HAVE TO PLAY THEM A MIGHTY FANFARE.
WEEEEEE
IT STOPPED.
HUH? I THINK IT'S STILL GOING.
NO... I MEAN YOUR TEARS.
YOU STOPPED CRYING, RIGHT?
BLUSH

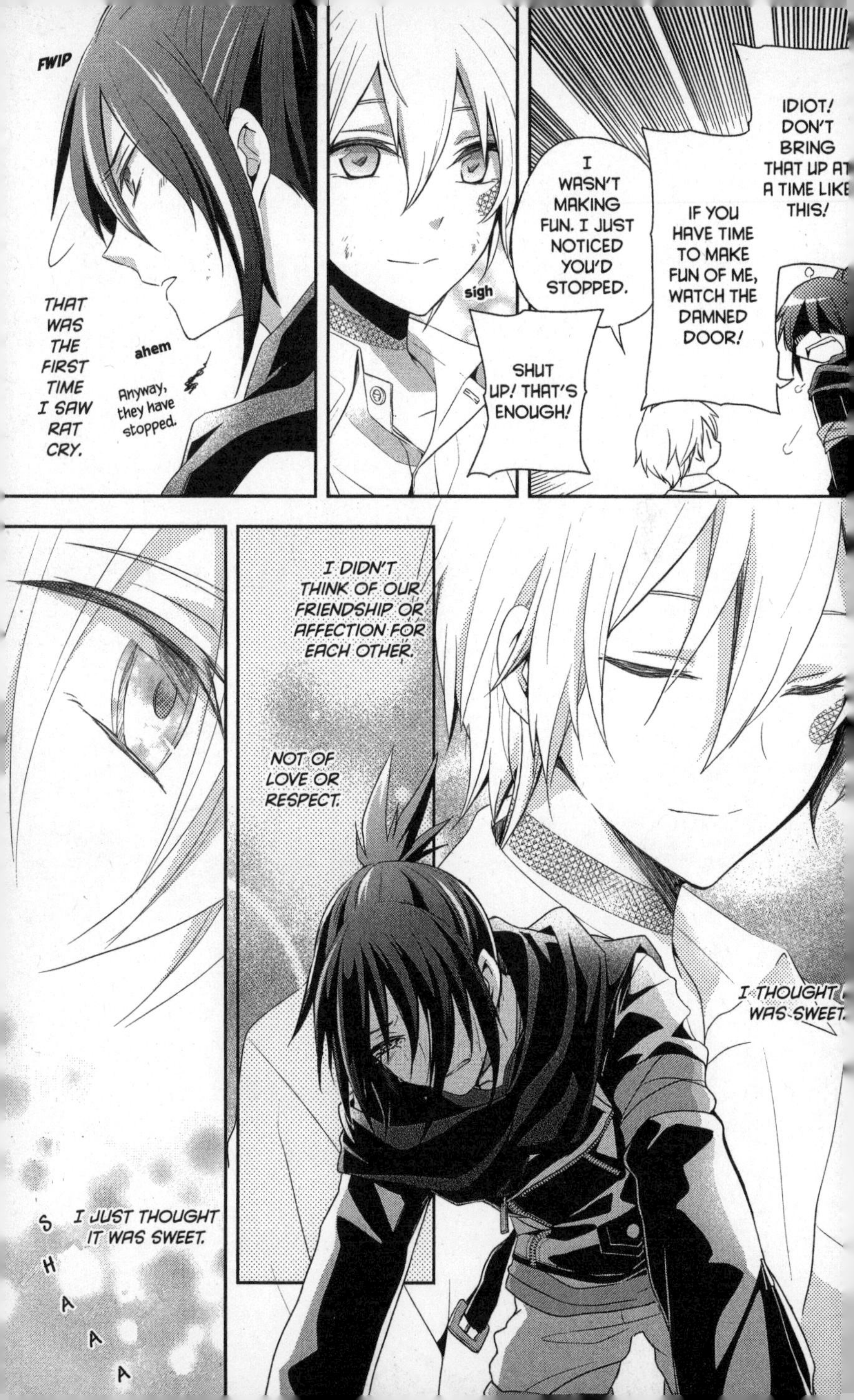
IDIOT! DON'T BRING THAT UP AT A TIME LIKE THIS!
IF YOU HAVE TIME TO MAKE FUN OF ME, WATCH THE DAMNED DOOR!
I WASN'T MAKING FUN. I JUST NOTICED YOU'D STOPPED.
SHUT UP! THAT'S ENOUGH!
sigh
FWIP
THAT WAS THE FIRST TIME I SAW RAT CRY.
ahem
Anyway, they have stopped.
I DIDN'T THINK OF OUR FRIENDSHIP OR AFFECTION FOR EACH OTHER.
NOT OF LOVE OR RESPECT.
I THOUGHT
WAS SWEET.
I JUST THOUGHT IT WAS SWEET.
SHAAAA

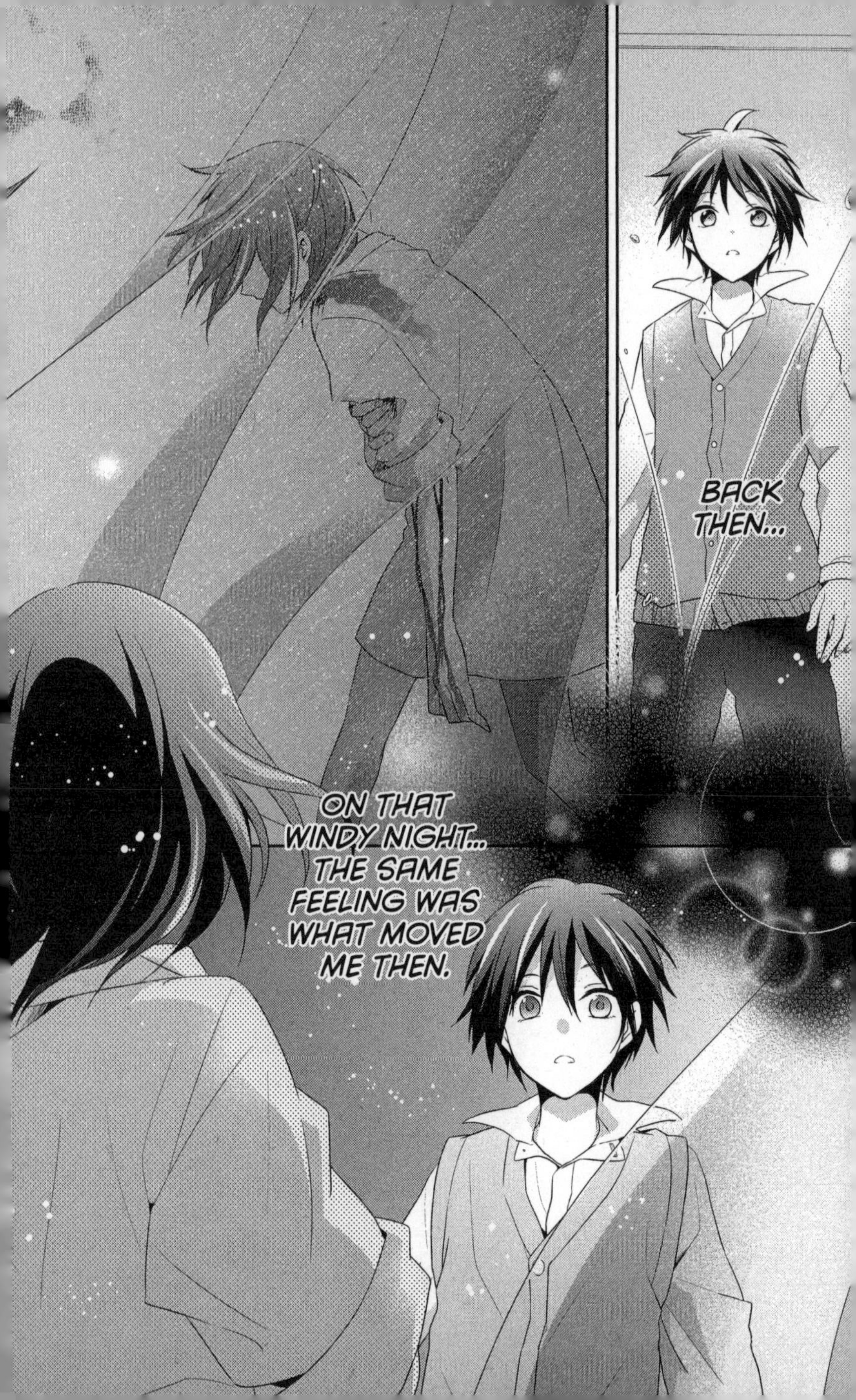
BACK THEN...
ON THAT WINDY NIGHT... THE SAME FEELING WAS WHAT MOVED ME THEN.

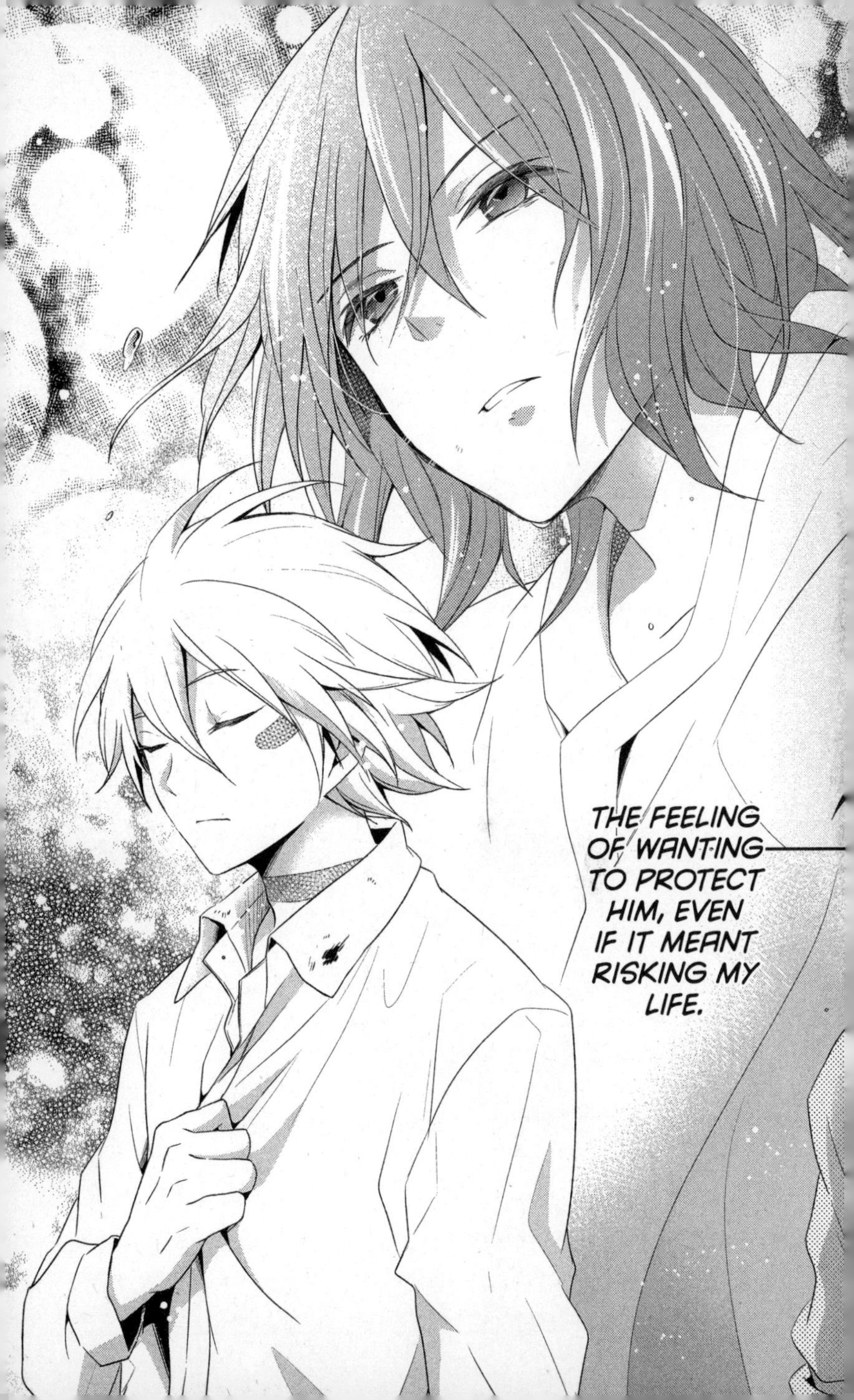
THE FEELING OF WANT-ING— TO PROTECT HIM, EVEN IF IT MEANT RISKING MY LIFE.

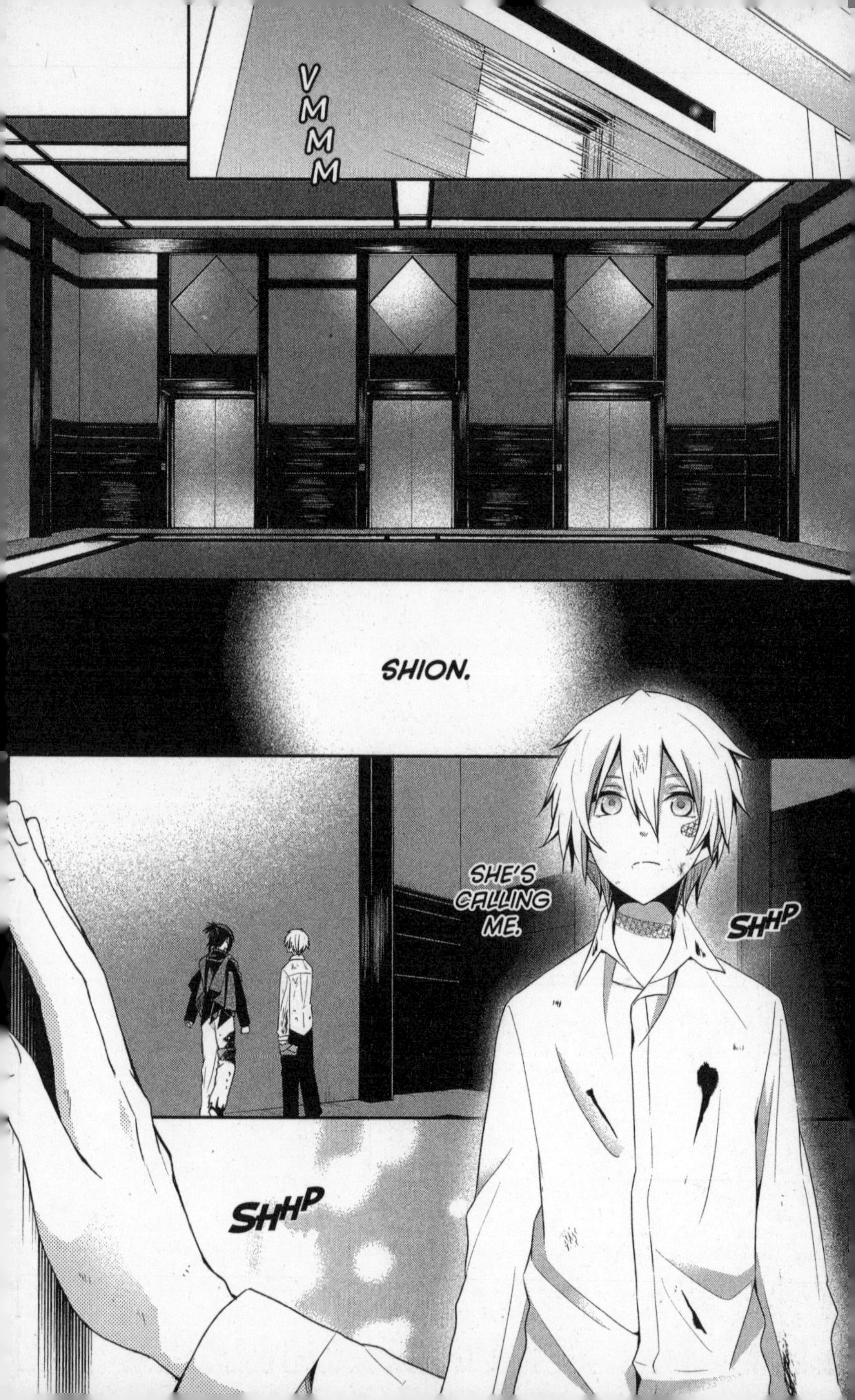
VMMM
SHION.
SHHP
SHE'S CALLING ME.
SHHP

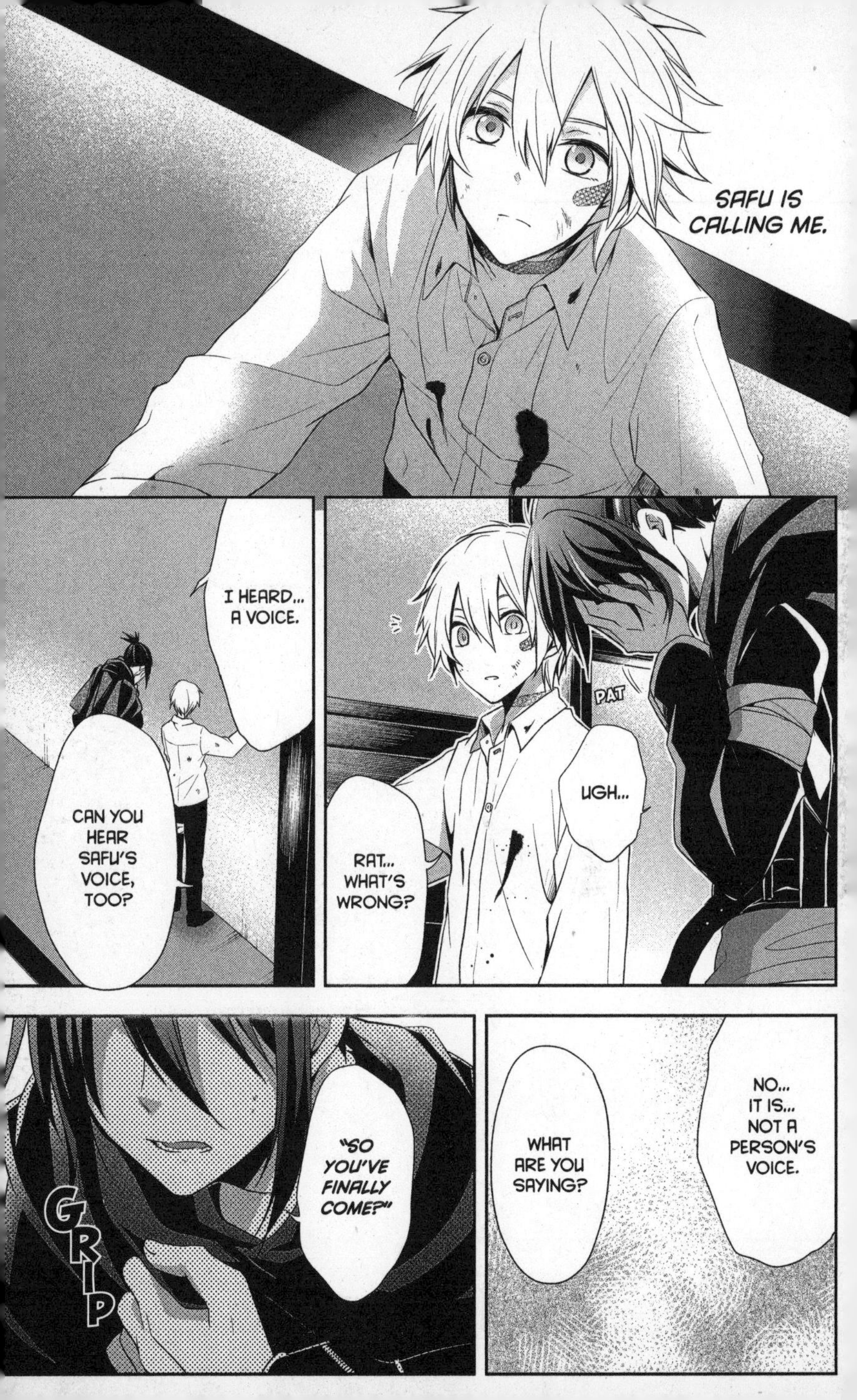
SAFU IS CALLING ME.
PAT
UGH...
RAT... WHAT'S WRONG?
I HEARD... A VOICE.
CAN YOU HEAR SAFU'S VOICE, TOO?
NO... IT IS... NOT A PERSON'S VOICE.
WHAT ARE YOU SAYING?
"SO YOU'VE FINALLY COME?"
GRIP

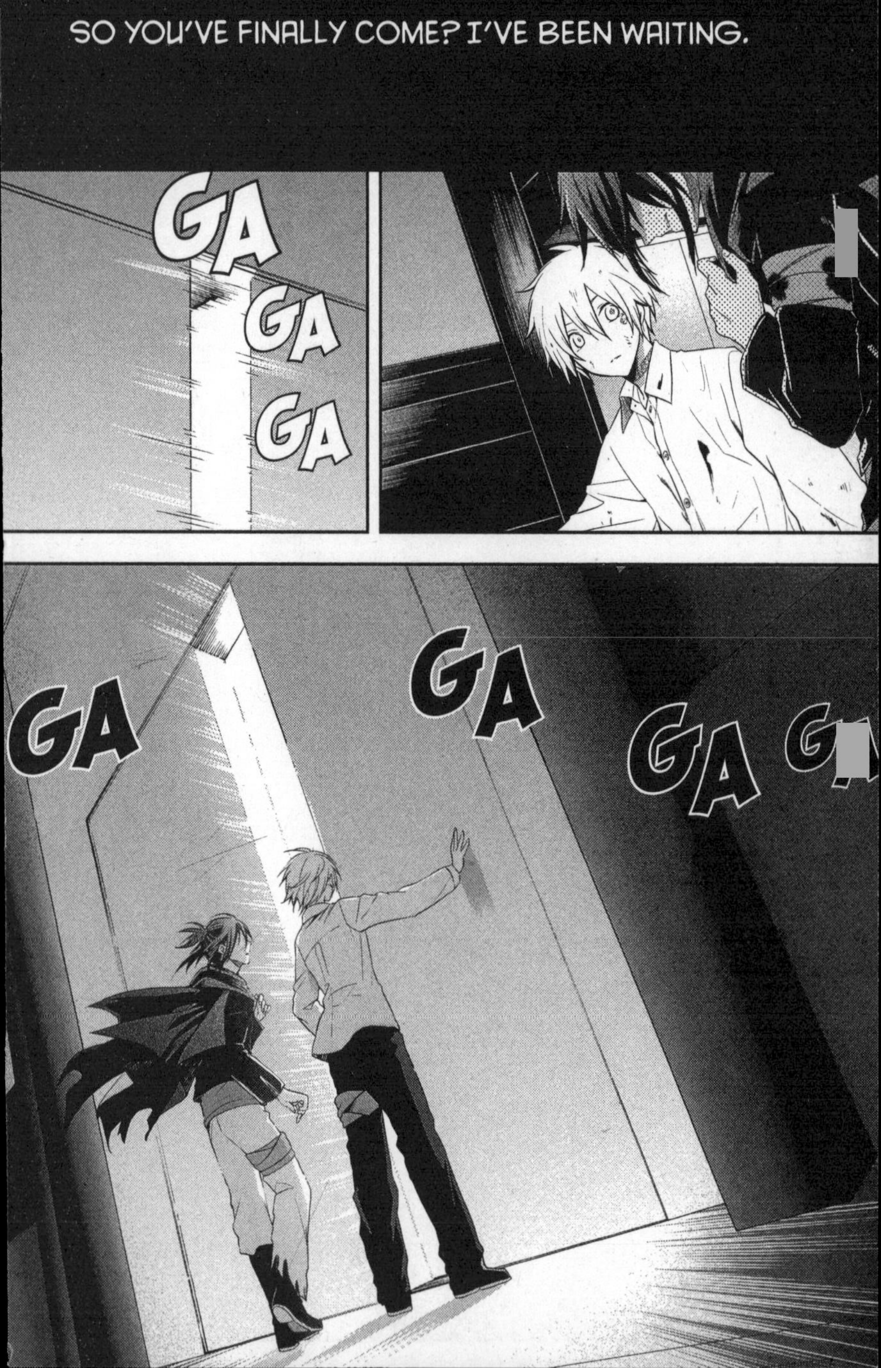
SO YOU'VE FINALLY COME? I'VE BEEN WAITING.
GA
GA
GA
GA
GA
GA
GA

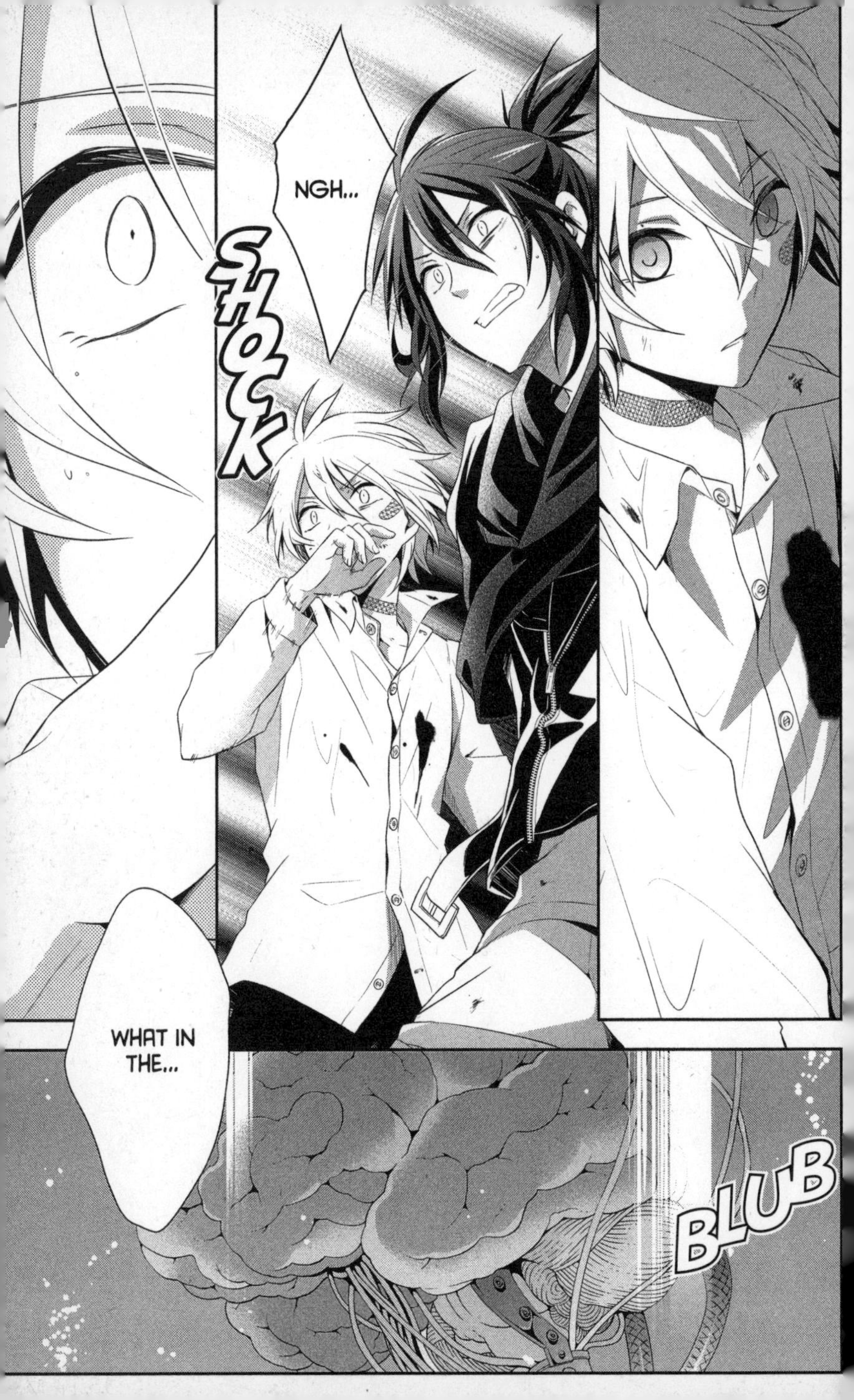
NGH...
SHOCK
WHAT IN THE...
BLUB

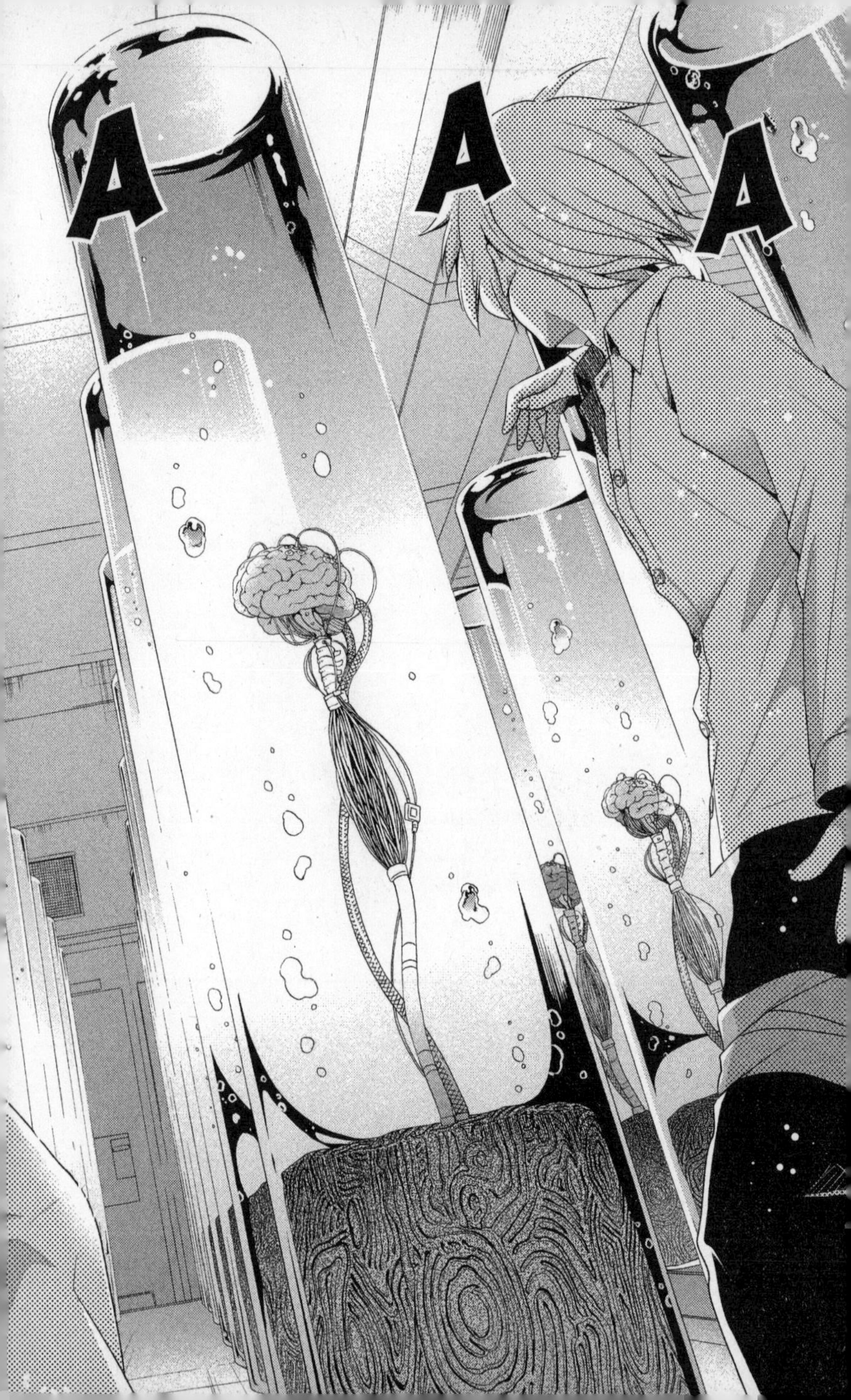
A
A
A

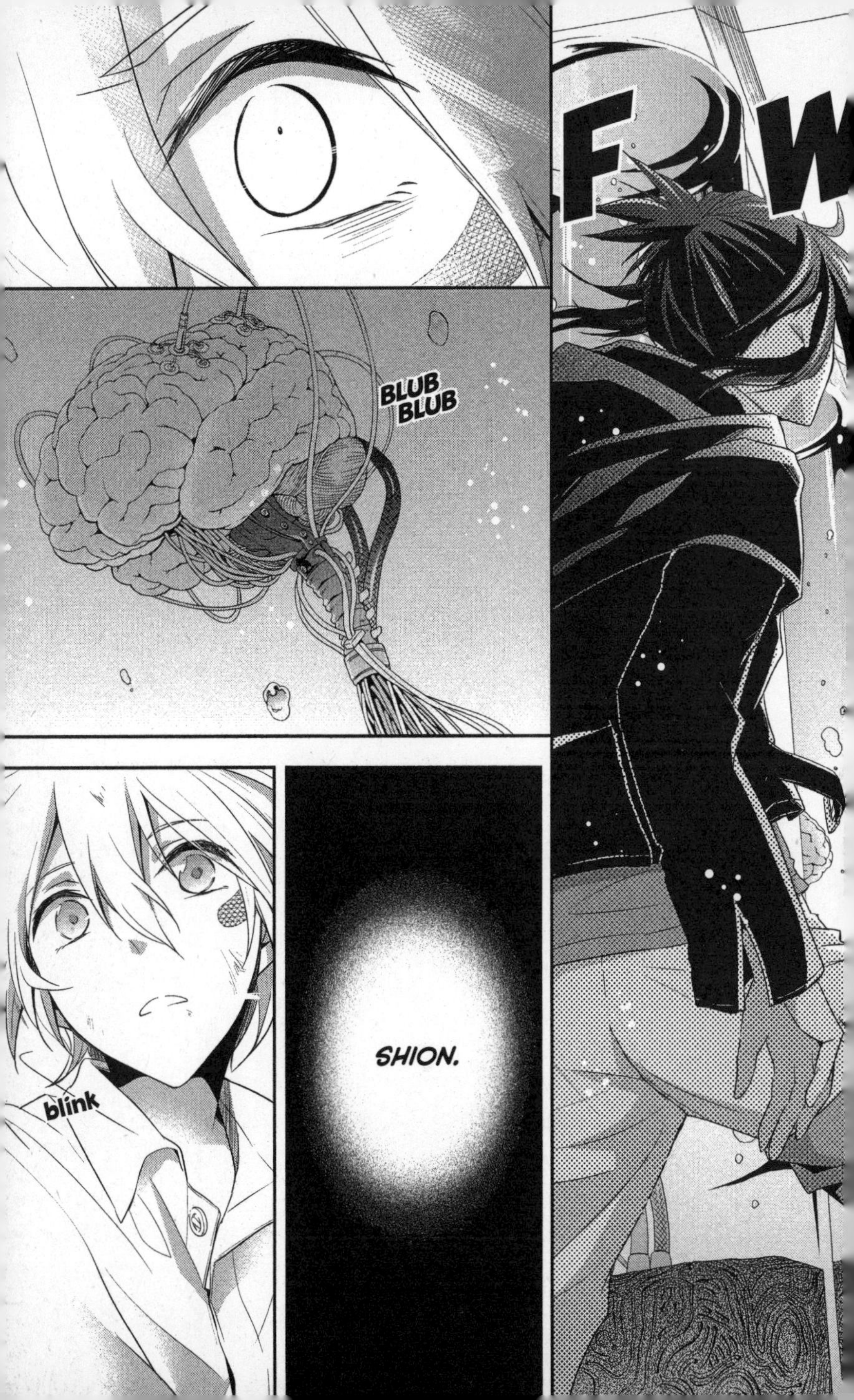
BLUB BLUB
SHION.
blink

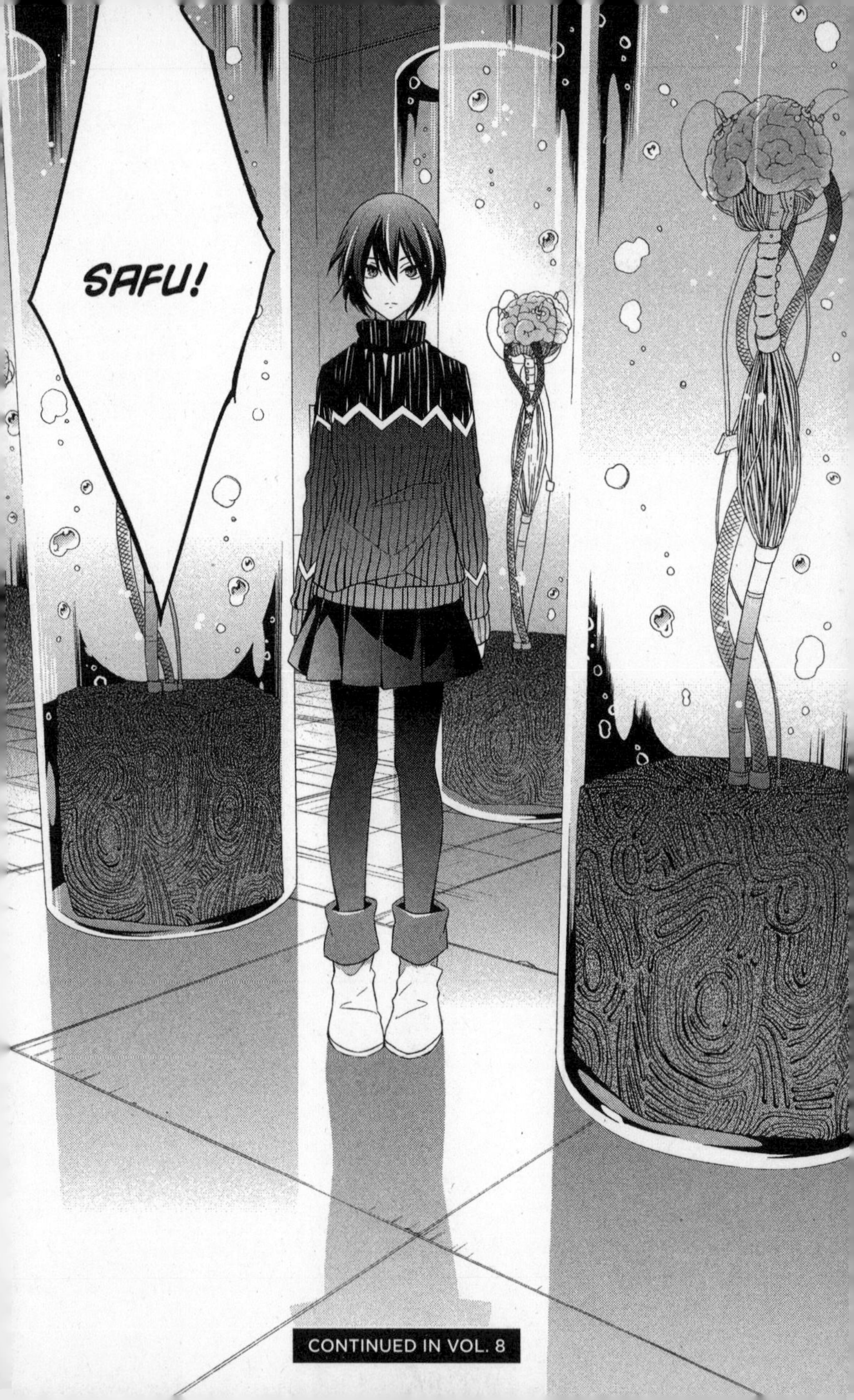
SAFU!

CONTINUED IN VOL. 8

NO.6

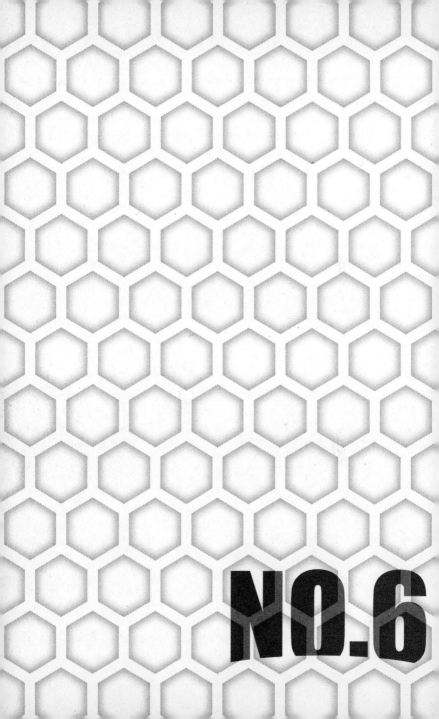

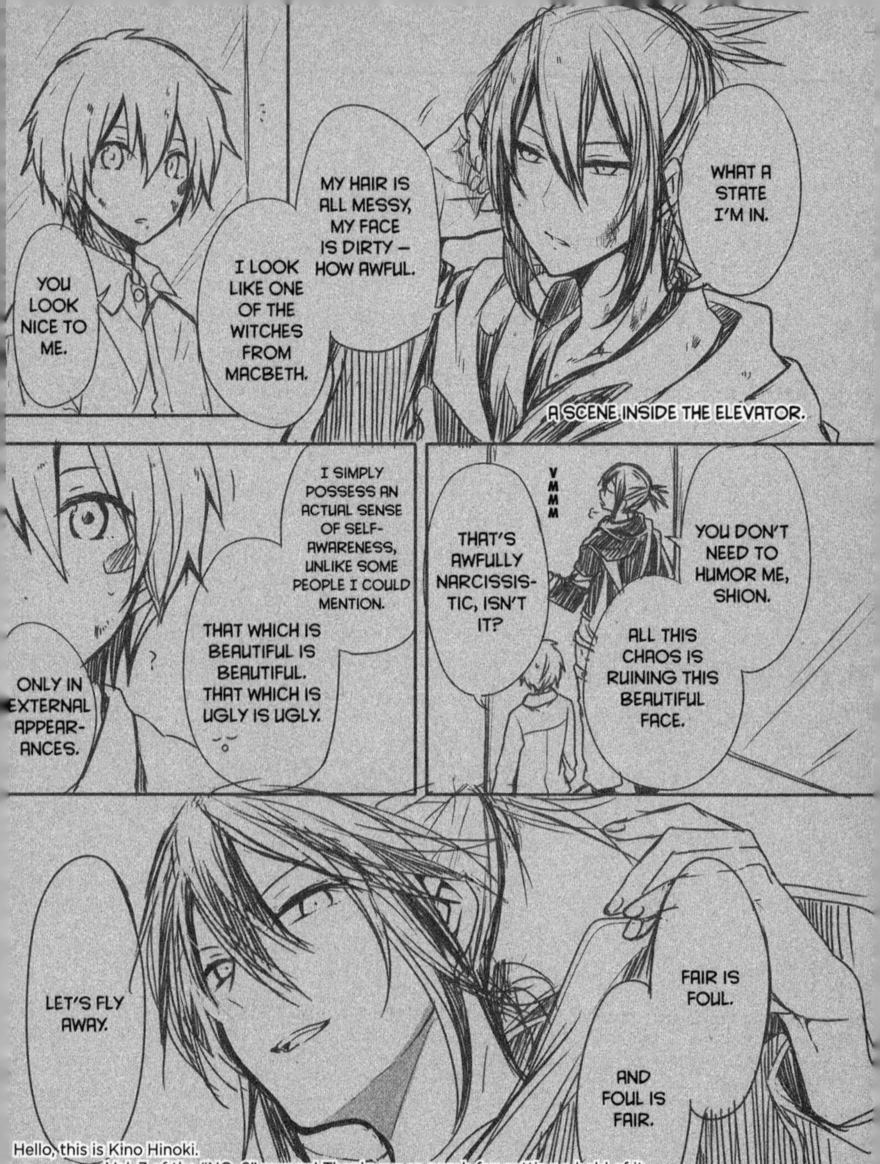
WHAT A STATE I'M IN.
MY HAIR IS ALL MESSY, MY FACE IS DIRTY — HOW AWFUL.
I LOOK LIKE ONE OF THE WITCHES FROM MACBETH.
YOU LOOK NICE TO ME.
A SCENE INSIDE THE ELEVATOR.
YOU DON'T NEED TO HUMOR ME, SHION.
ALL THIS CHAOS IS RUINING THIS BEAUTIFUL FACE.
VMMM
THAT'S AWFULLY NARCISSIS-TIC, ISN'T IT?
I SIMPLY POSSESS AN ACTUAL SENSE OF SELF-AWARENESS, UNLIKE SOME PEOPLE I COULD MENTION.
THAT WHICH IS BEAUTIFUL IS BEAUTIFUL. THAT WHICH IS UGLY IS UGLY.
ONLY IN EXTERNAL APPEAR-ANCES.
FAIR IS FOUL.
AND FOUL IS FAIR.
LET'S FLY AWAY.

Hello, this is Kino Hinoki.

Vol. 7 of the "NO. 6" manga! Thank you so much for getting a hold of it. This is from the original novel, volume 7, entitled "Are you sad?" When I first read it, I unconsciously closed the book, it was such a shock. The further I read, the more exciting the story got. I was so worried about what was coming next that I was too scared to read, yet I couldn't stop reading. The same feeling kept repeating itself. For me to try and recreate this shock in a new form... how could I do it?!

And also, volume 7 came out in a special edition! It includes a booklet with the first scene from the novel volume 8, with the part about Macbeth. It's also got a link to the manga volume 8, so please go out and read the booklet!*

We finally get to see Safu again. Can they escape the Correctional Facility? Can Shion stay Shion? I look forward to meeting you again in the next volume.

August, 2013 Hinoki Kino

*The story from this booklet is included in the back of this volume as a bonus.

SPECIAL THANKS!

Atsuko Asano

Everyone in the Kodansha
Aria Editorial Department

Everyone on the NO. 6 Team
Editor K
Toi8
Everyone on the anime staff
Everyone at NARTi:S
Ginkyo

* Production Cooperation
Honma
Megi
Matsugi

* Finishing
Tsunocchi

* 3D
Rinkan Kei

* Color Backgrounds
Mr. dominori

Family (Mom, Dad, siblings, Granny, the dog)

And everyone else who helped out

Also, all you readers!

Thank you all so very much!

TEACH US, PROFESSOR SHION!
THE CORRECTIONAL FACILITY'S DESIGN IS SO COMPLICATED, I DON'T UNDERSTAND.
smak smak
ISN'T IT, SHION?
PLEASE EXPLAIN.
LEAVE IT TO ME!
SINCE YOU'VE ASKED.
TOP FLOOR
SAFU
?
Elevator
RASHI
Research room
Conveyor
Operations system room
Hidden stairway
Entrance
Locker room
Caverns
Cleaning room
Garbage
IN A NUTSHELL, THAT'S IT!
WHEN THE ISOLATION DOORS CLOSE, A HIGH VOLTAGE CURRENT RUNS THROUGH.
Safu was on the top floor after all!!
YOU GUYS BARELY SUR-VIVED!
NO REAL PUNCH LINE HERE

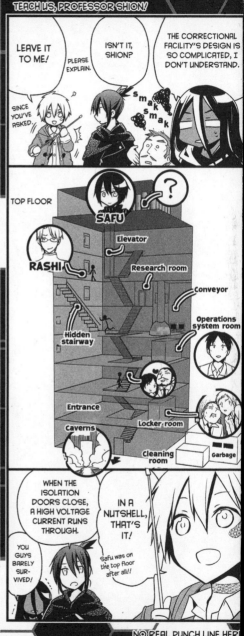

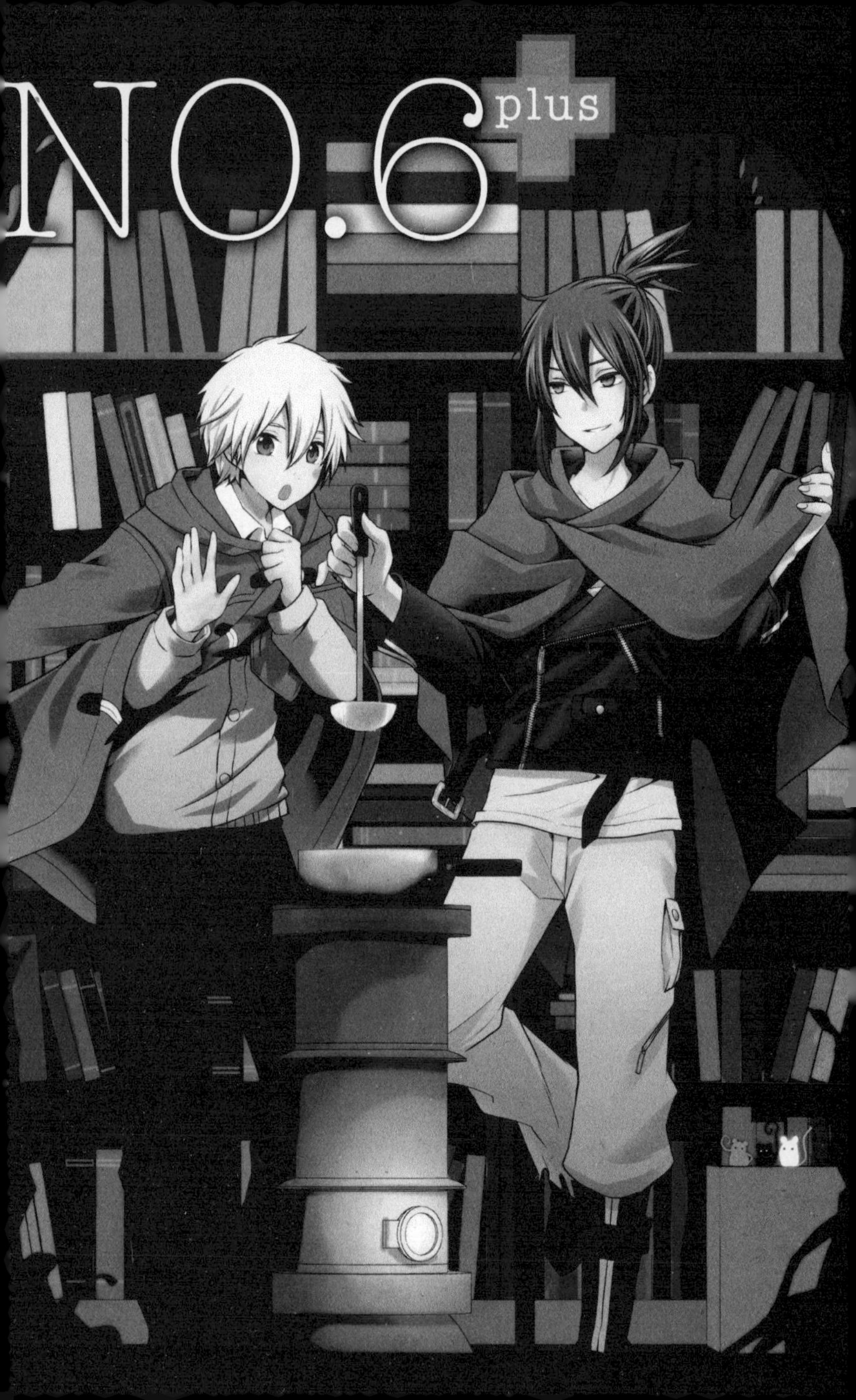
NO.6 plus

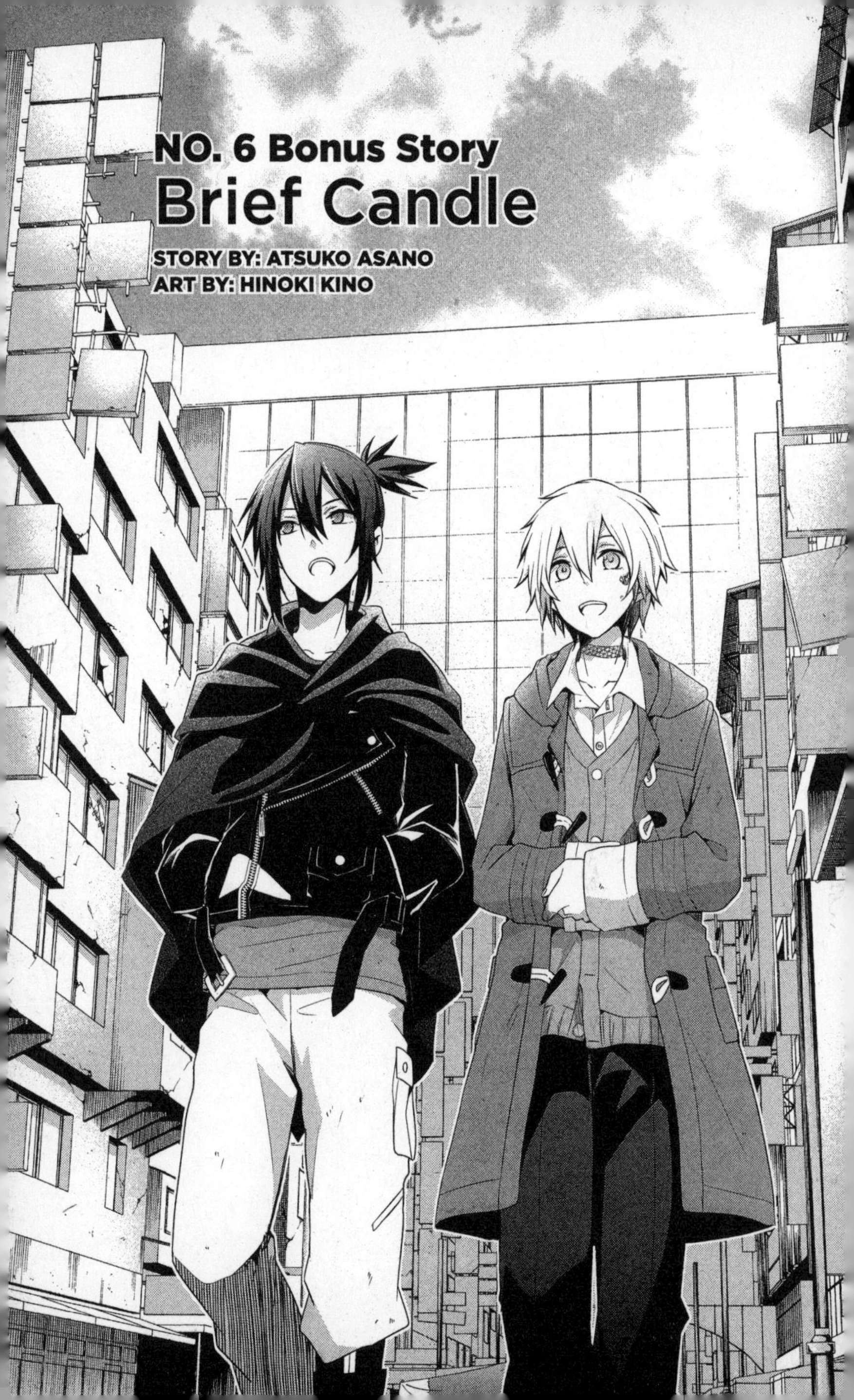
NO. 6 Bonus Story
Brief Candle
STORY BY: ATSUKO ASANO
ART BY: HINOKI KINO

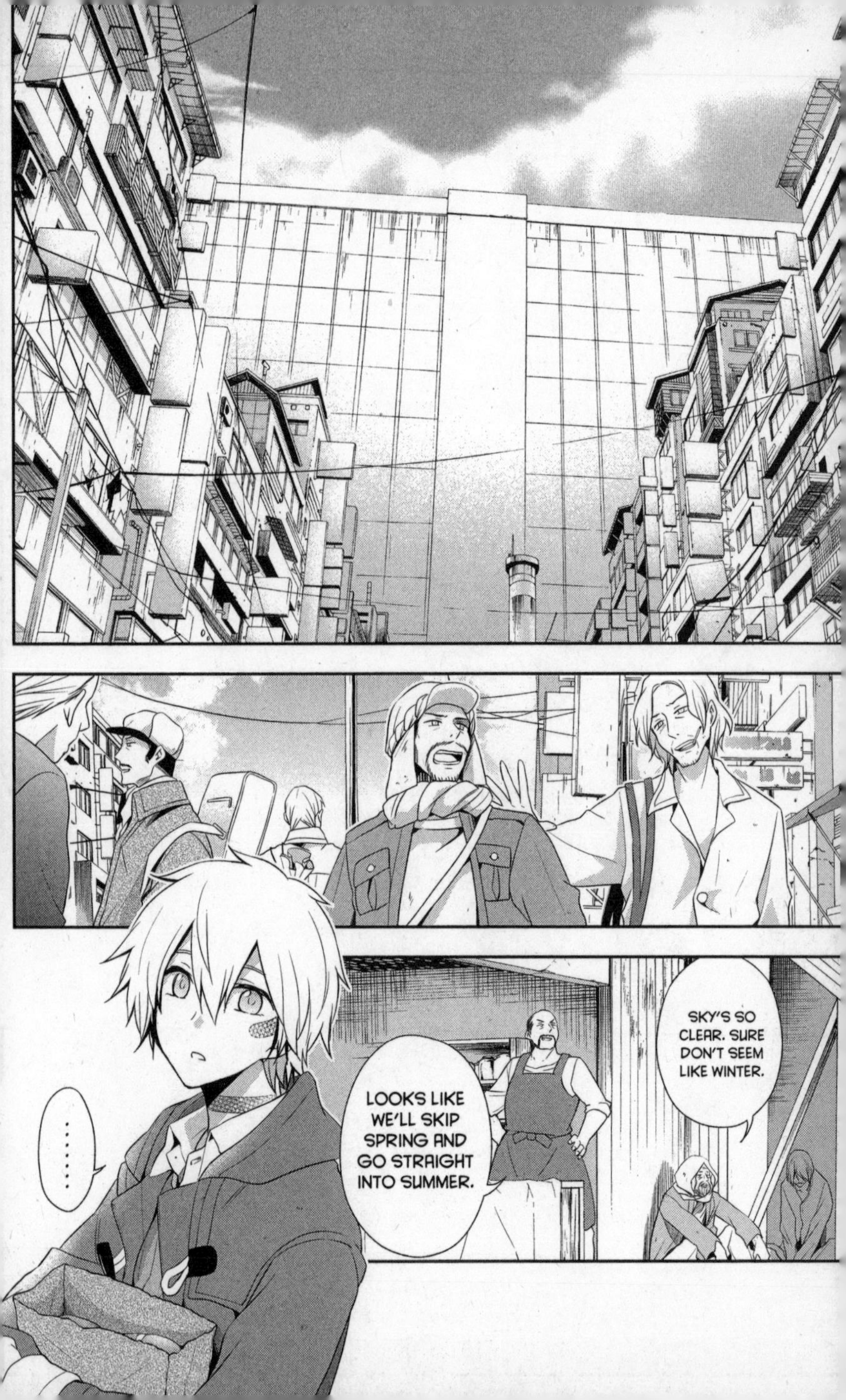
SKY'S SO CLEAR. SURE DON'T SEEM LIKE WINTER.
LOOKS LIKE WE'LL SKIP SPRING AND GO STRAIGHT INTO SUMMER.
......

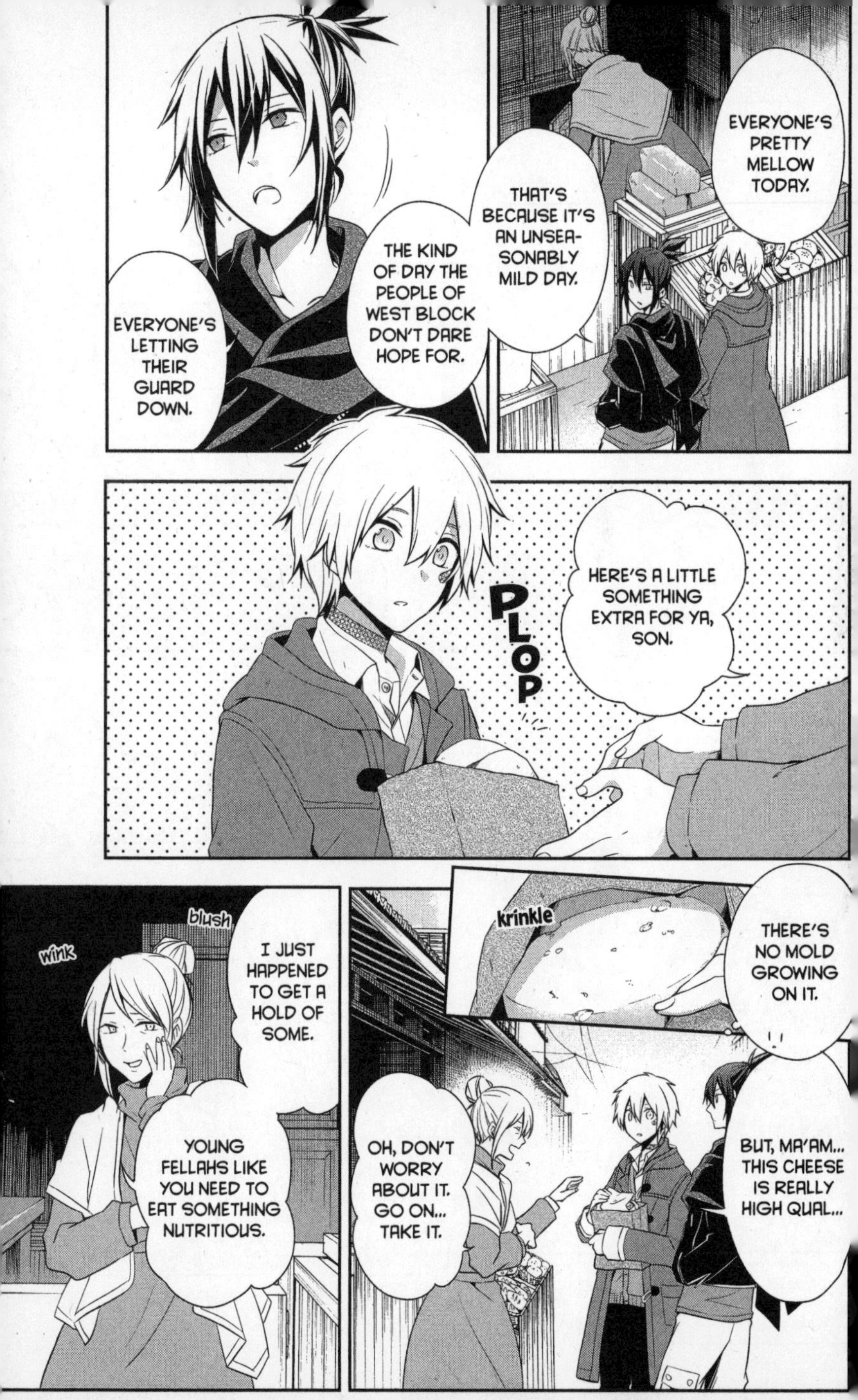
EVERYONE'S PRETTY MELLOW TODAY.
THAT'S BECAUSE IT'S AN UNSEA-SONABLY MILD DAY.
THE KIND OF DAY THE PEOPLE OF WEST BLOCK DON'T DARE HOPE FOR.
EVERYONE'S LETTING THEIR GUARD DOWN.
HERE'S A LITTLE SOMETHING EXTRA FOR YA, SON.
PLOP
krinkle
THERE'S NO MOLD GROWING ON IT.
BUT, MA'AM... THIS CHEESE IS REALLY HIGH QUAL...
OH, DON'T WORRY ABOUT IT. GO ON... TAKE IT.
blush
I JUST HAPPENED TO GET A HOLD OF SOME.
wink
YOUNG FELLAHS LIKE YOU NEED TO EAT SOMETHING NUTRITIOUS.

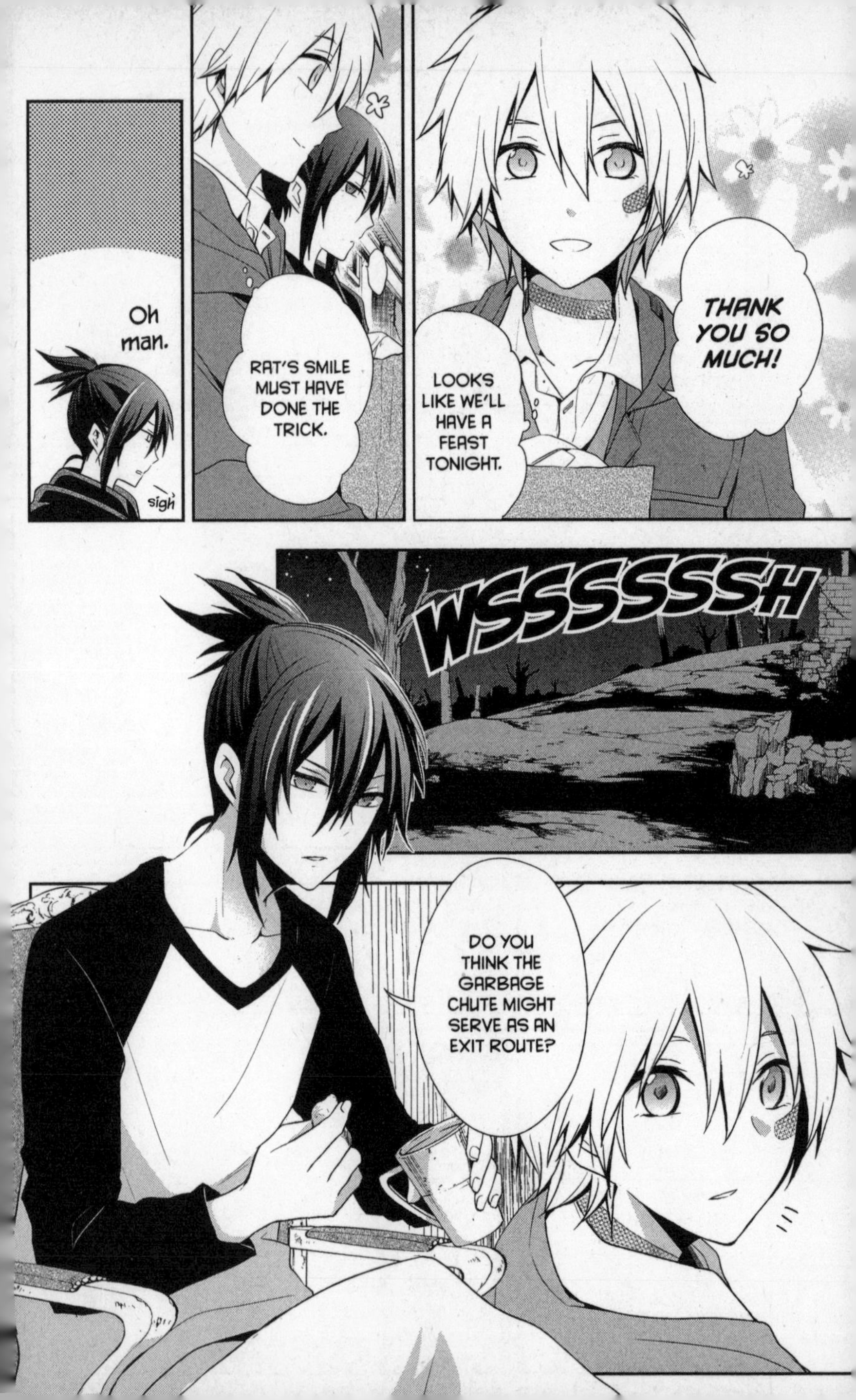
THANK YOU SO MUCH!
LOOKS LIKE WE'LL HAVE A FEAST TONIGHT.
RAT'S SMILE MUST HAVE DONE THE TRICK.
Oh man.
sigh
WSSSSSSH
DO YOU THINK THE GARBAGE CHUTE MIGHT SERVE AS AN EXIT ROUTE?

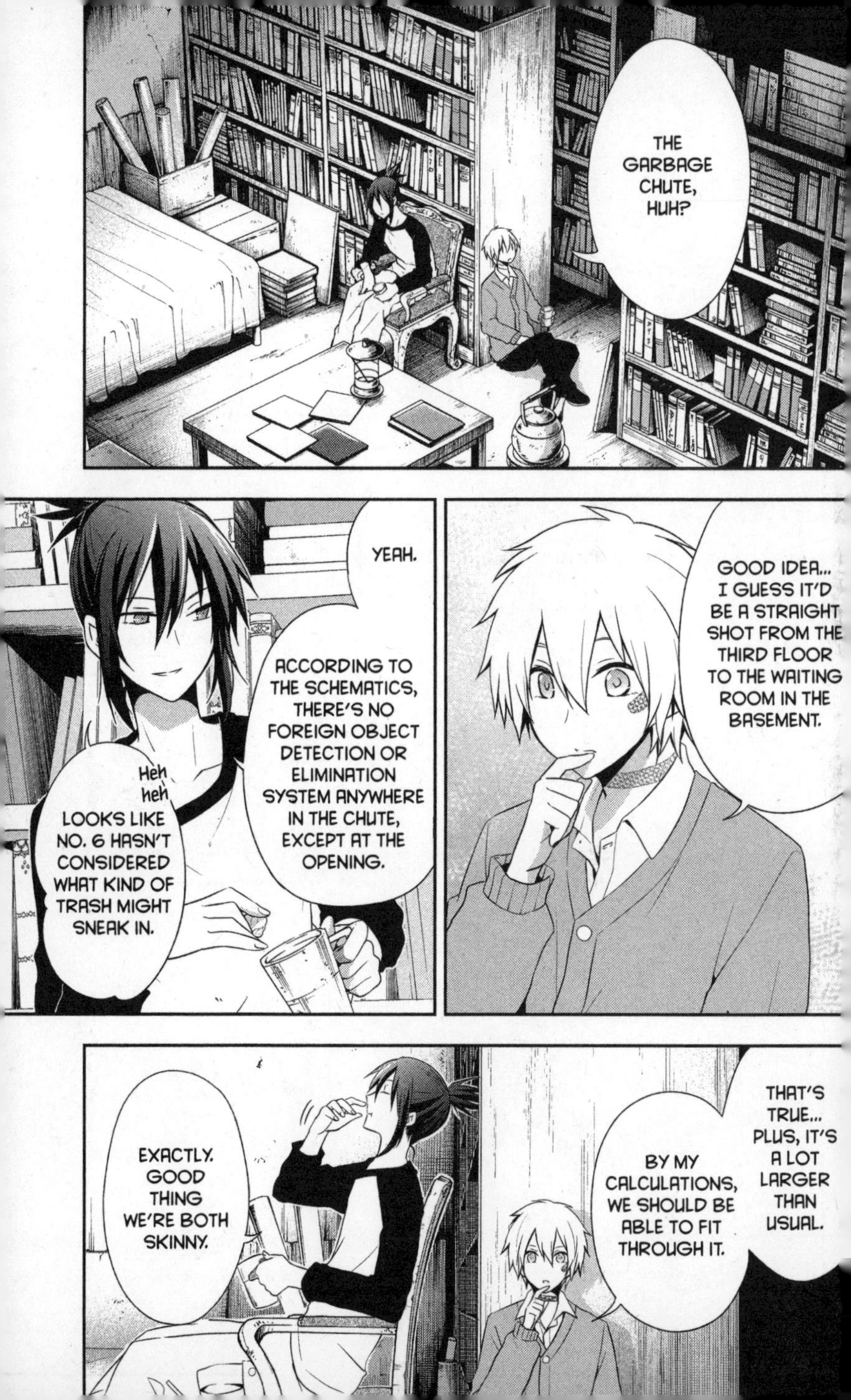
THE GARBAGE CHUTE, HUH?
GOOD IDEA... I GUESS IT'D BE A STRAIGHT SHOT FROM THE THIRD FLOOR TO THE WAITING ROOM IN THE BASEMENT.
YEAH.
ACCORDING TO THE SCHEMATICS, THERE'S NO FOREIGN OBJECT DETECTION OR ELIMINATION SYSTEM ANYWHERE IN THE CHUTE, EXCEPT AT THE OPENING.
Heh heh
LOOKS LIKE NO. 6 HASN'T CONSIDERED WHAT KIND OF TRASH MIGHT SNEAK IN.
THAT'S TRUE... PLUS, IT'S A LOT LARGER THAN USUAL.
BY MY CALCULATIONS, WE SHOULD BE ABLE TO FIT THROUGH IT.
EXACTLY. GOOD THING WE'RE BOTH SKINNY.

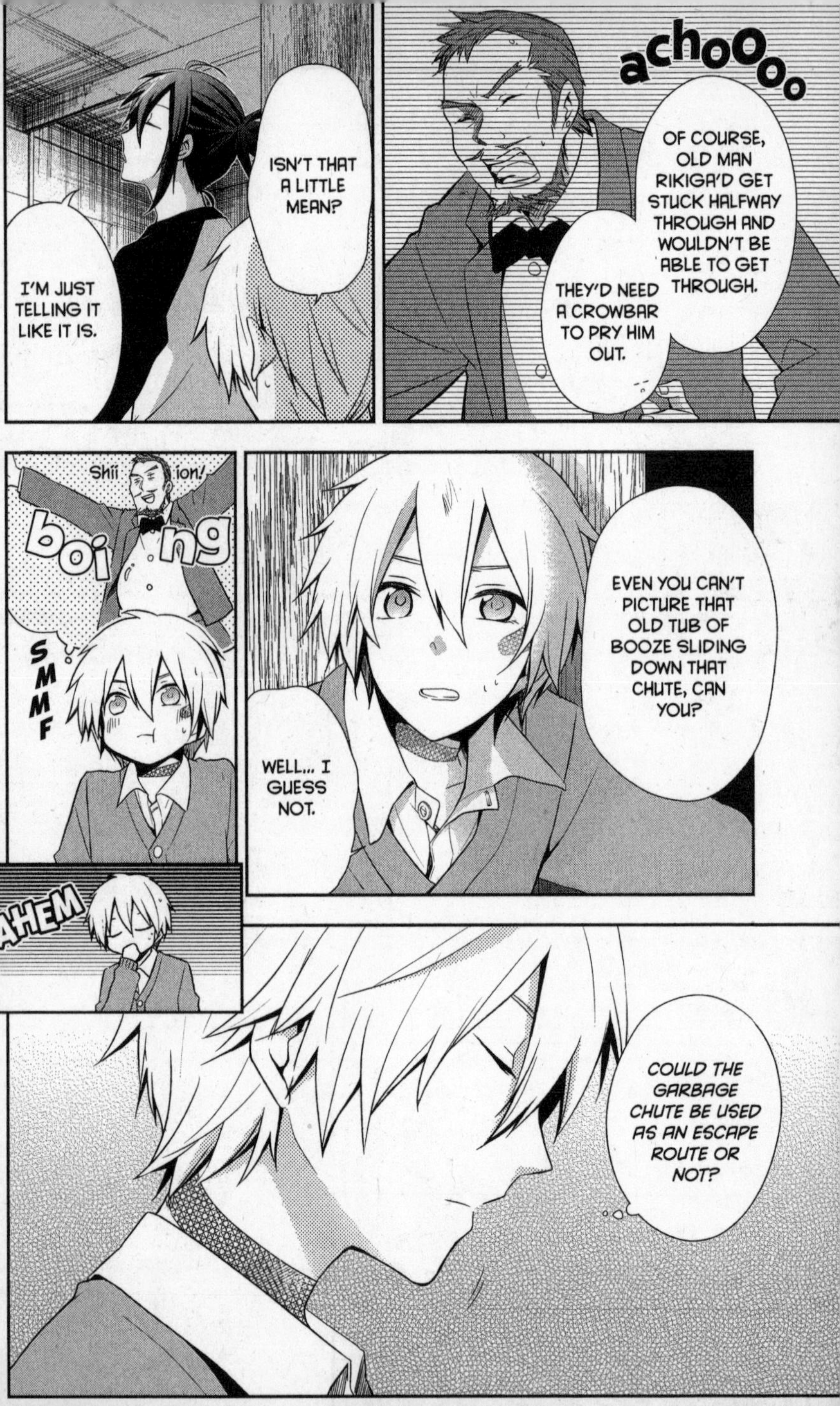
achoOooo
OF COURSE, OLD MAN RIKIGA'D GET STUCK HALFWAY THROUGH AND WOULDN'T BE ABLE TO GET THROUGH.
THEY'D NEED A CROWBAR TO PRY HIM OUT.
ISN'T THAT A LITTLE MEAN?
I'M JUST TELLING IT LIKE IT IS.
EVEN YOU CAN'T PICTURE THAT OLD TUB OF BOOZE SLIDING DOWN THAT CHUTE, CAN YOU?
WELL... I GUESS NOT.
Shii ion!
boing
SMMF
AHEM
COULD THE GARBAGE CHUTE BE USED AS AN ESCAPE ROUTE OR NOT?

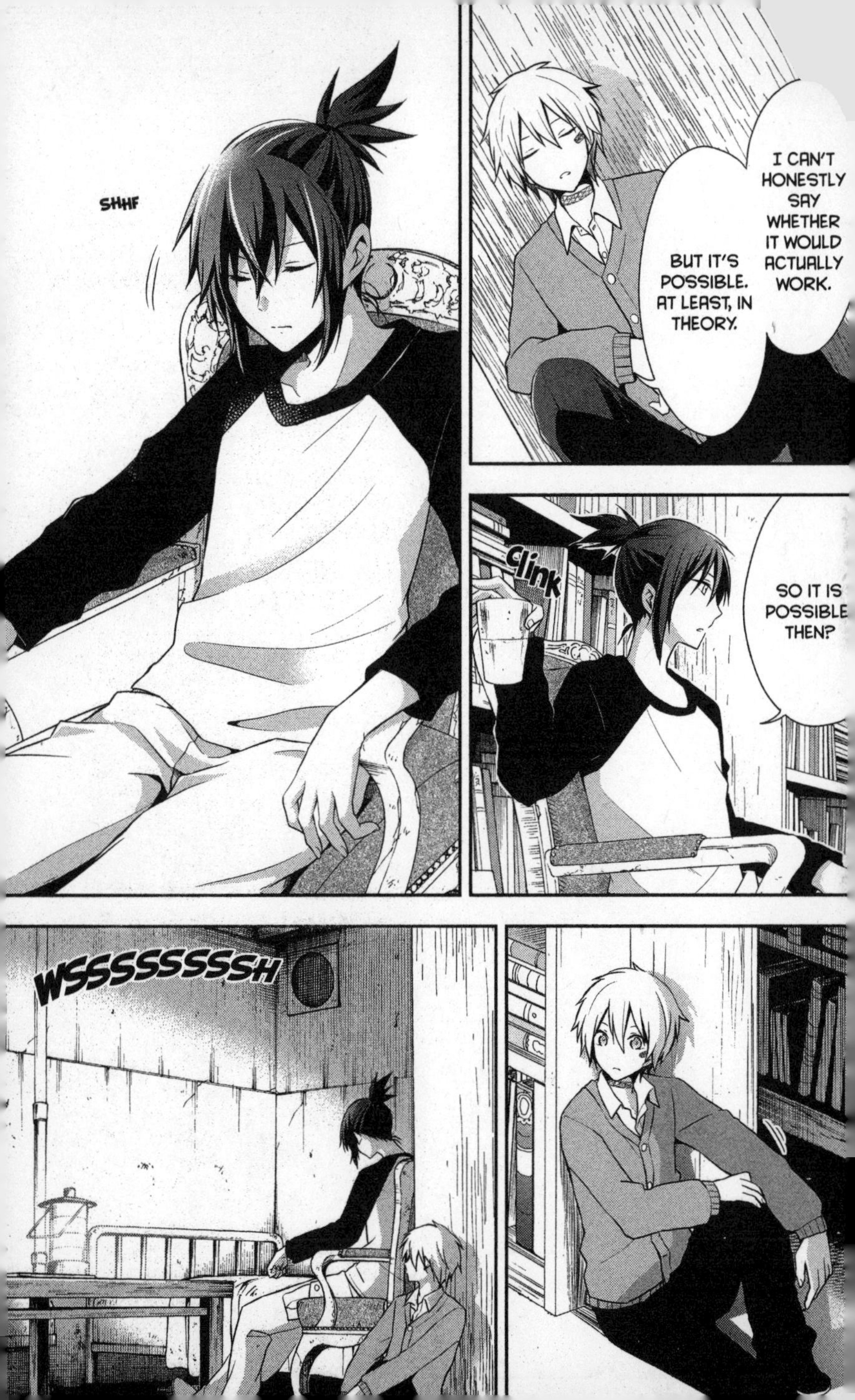
I CAN'T HONESTLY SAY WHETHER IT WOULD ACTUALLY WORK.
BUT IT'S POSSIBLE. AT LEAST, IN THEORY.
SO IT IS POSSIBLE THEN?
Clink
SHHF
WSSSSSSSSH

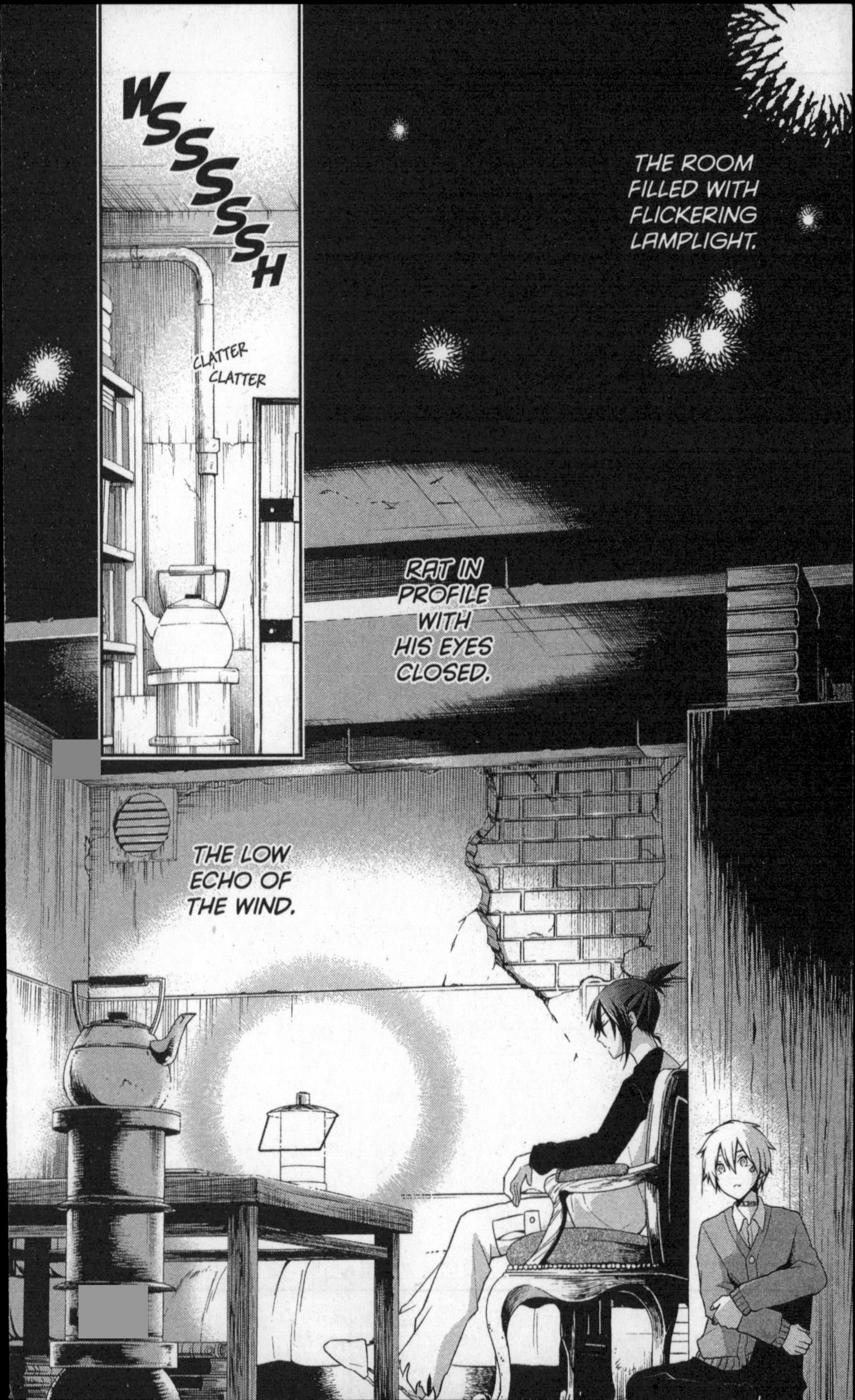
THE ROOM FILLED WITH FLICKERING LAMPLIGHT.
WSSSSSH
CLATTER CLATTER
RAT IN PROFILE WITH HIS EYES CLOSED.
THE LOW ECHO OF THE WIND.

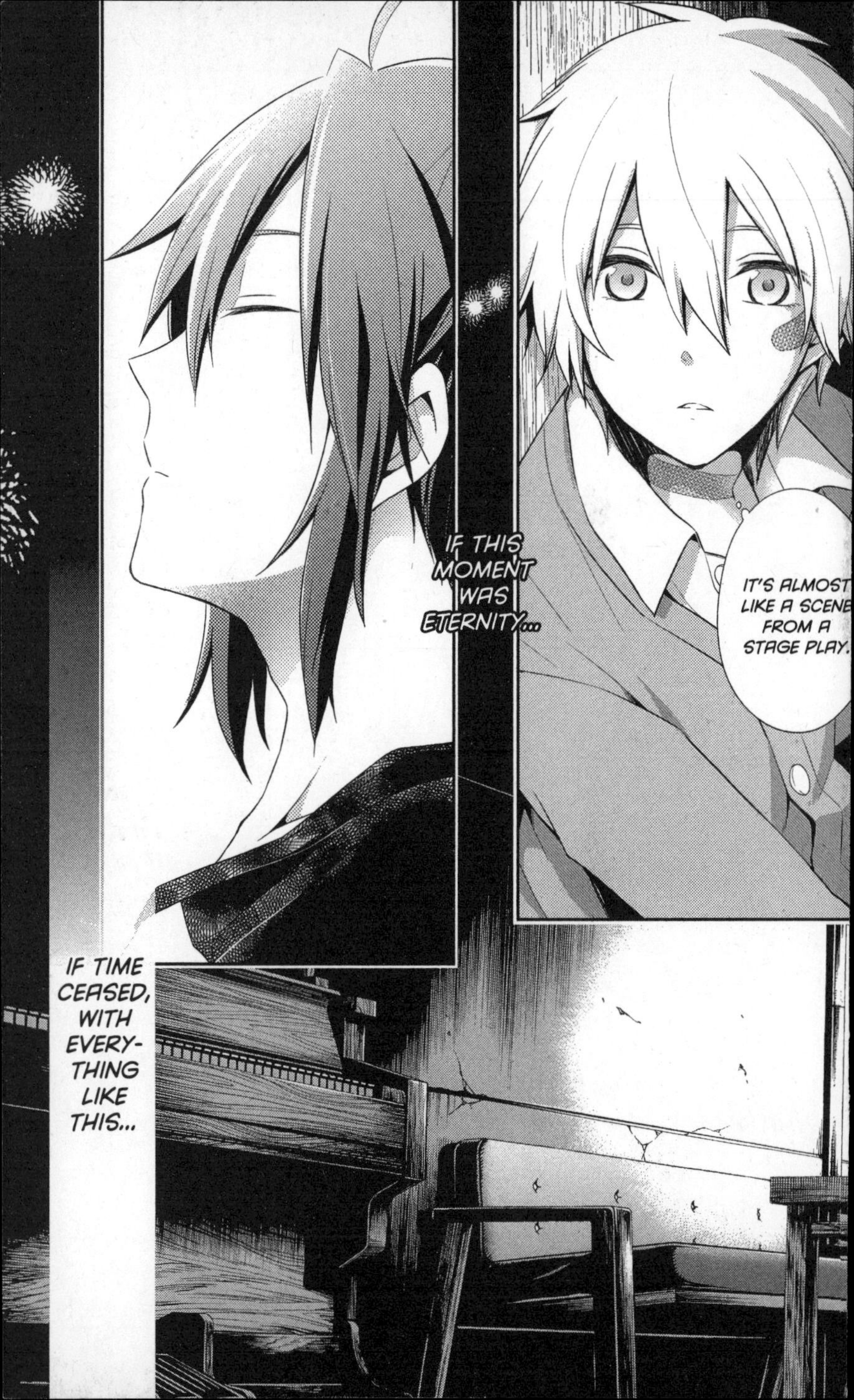
IT'S ALMOST LIKE A SCENE FROM A STAGE PLAY.
IF THIS MOMENT WAS ETERNITY...
IF TIME CEASED, WITH EVERY-THING LIKE THIS...

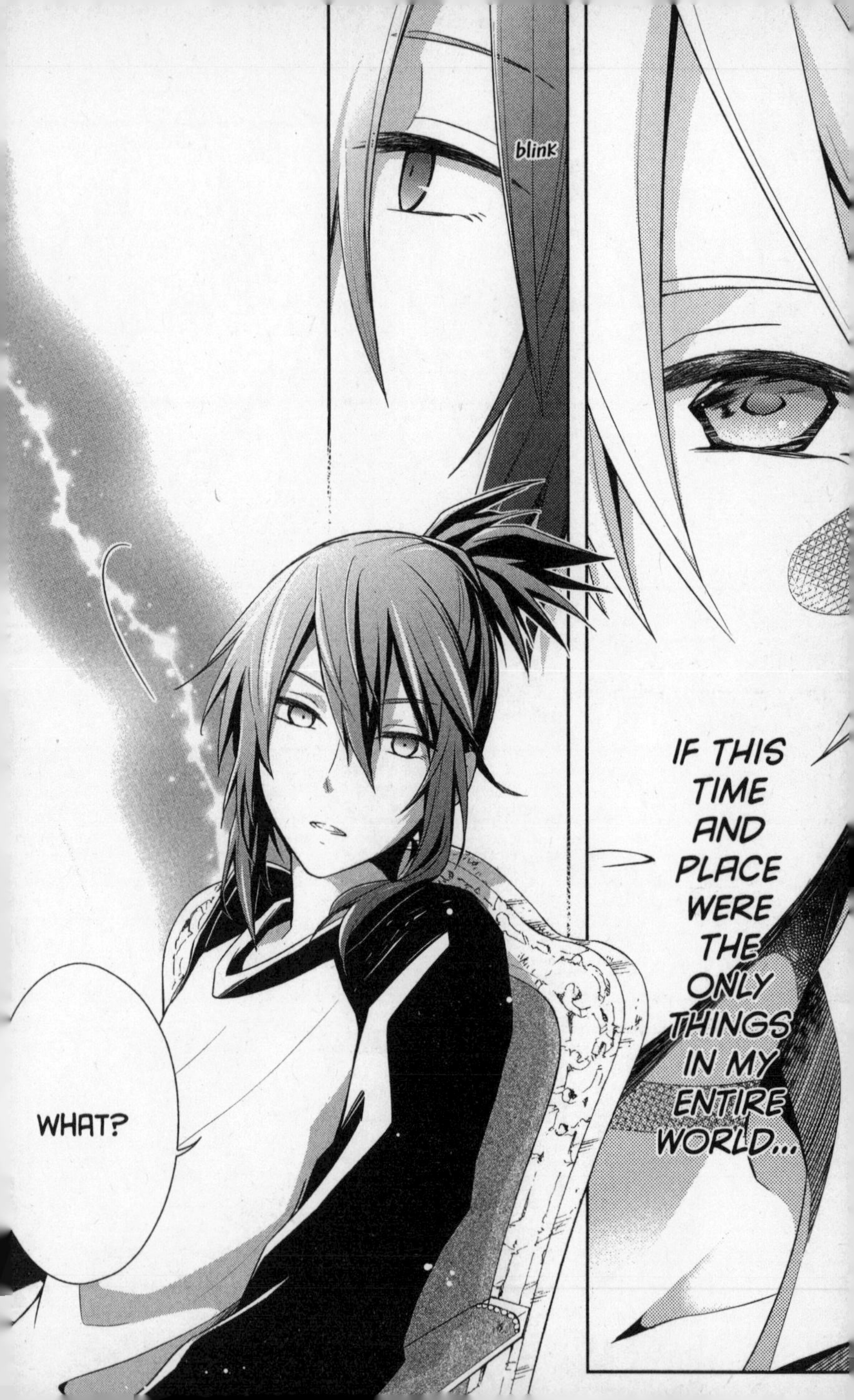
IF THIS TIME AND PLACE WERE THE ONLY THINGS IN MY ENTIRE WORLD...
blink
WHAT?

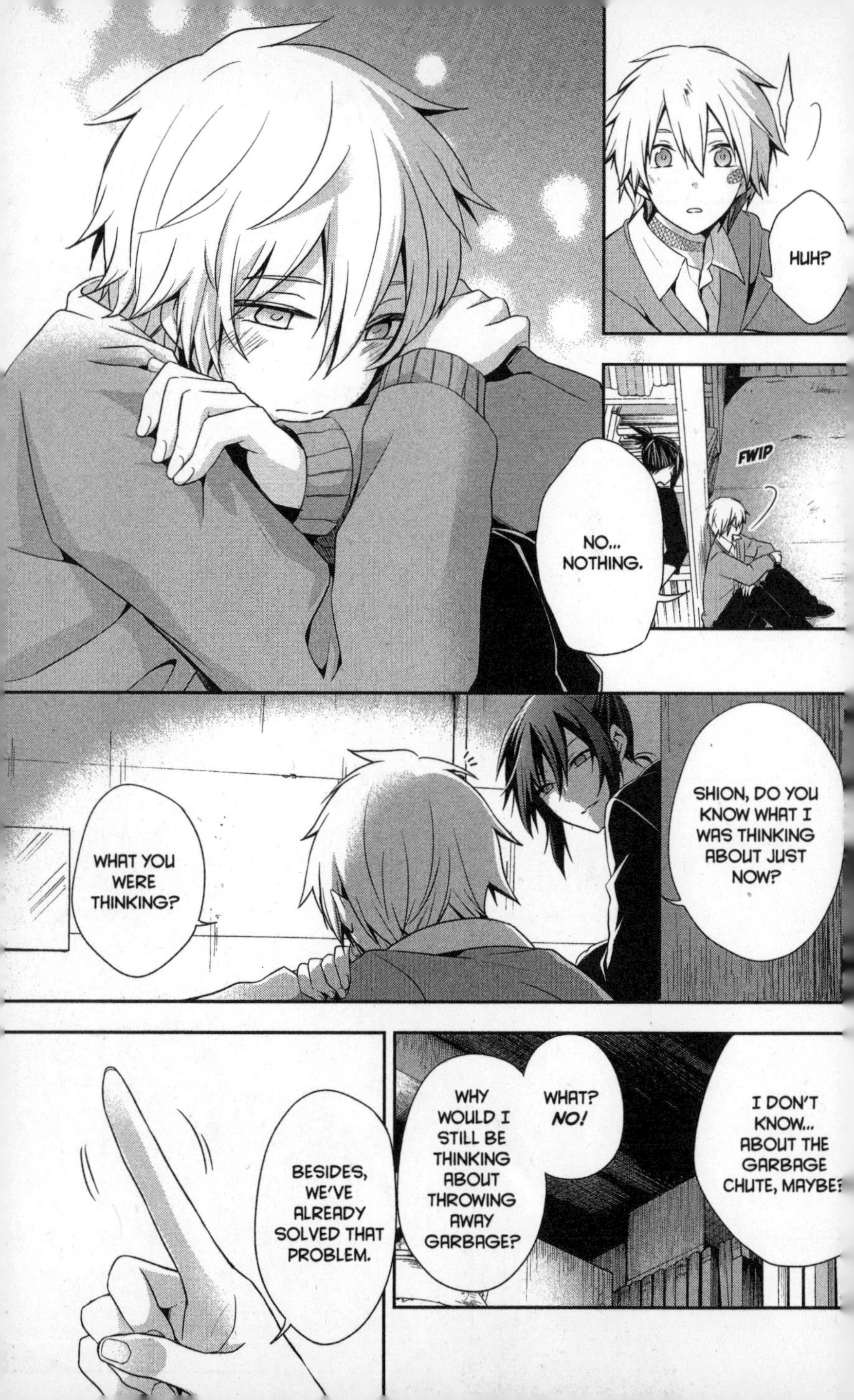
HUH?
FWIP
NO... NOTHING.
SHION, DO YOU KNOW WHAT I WAS THINKING ABOUT JUST NOW?
WHAT YOU WERE THINKING?
I DON'T KNOW... ABOUT THE GARBAGE CHUTE, MAYBE?
WHAT? *NO!*
WHY WOULD I STILL BE THINKING ABOUT THROWING AWAY GARBAGE?
BESIDES, WE'VE ALREADY SOLVED THAT PROBLEM.

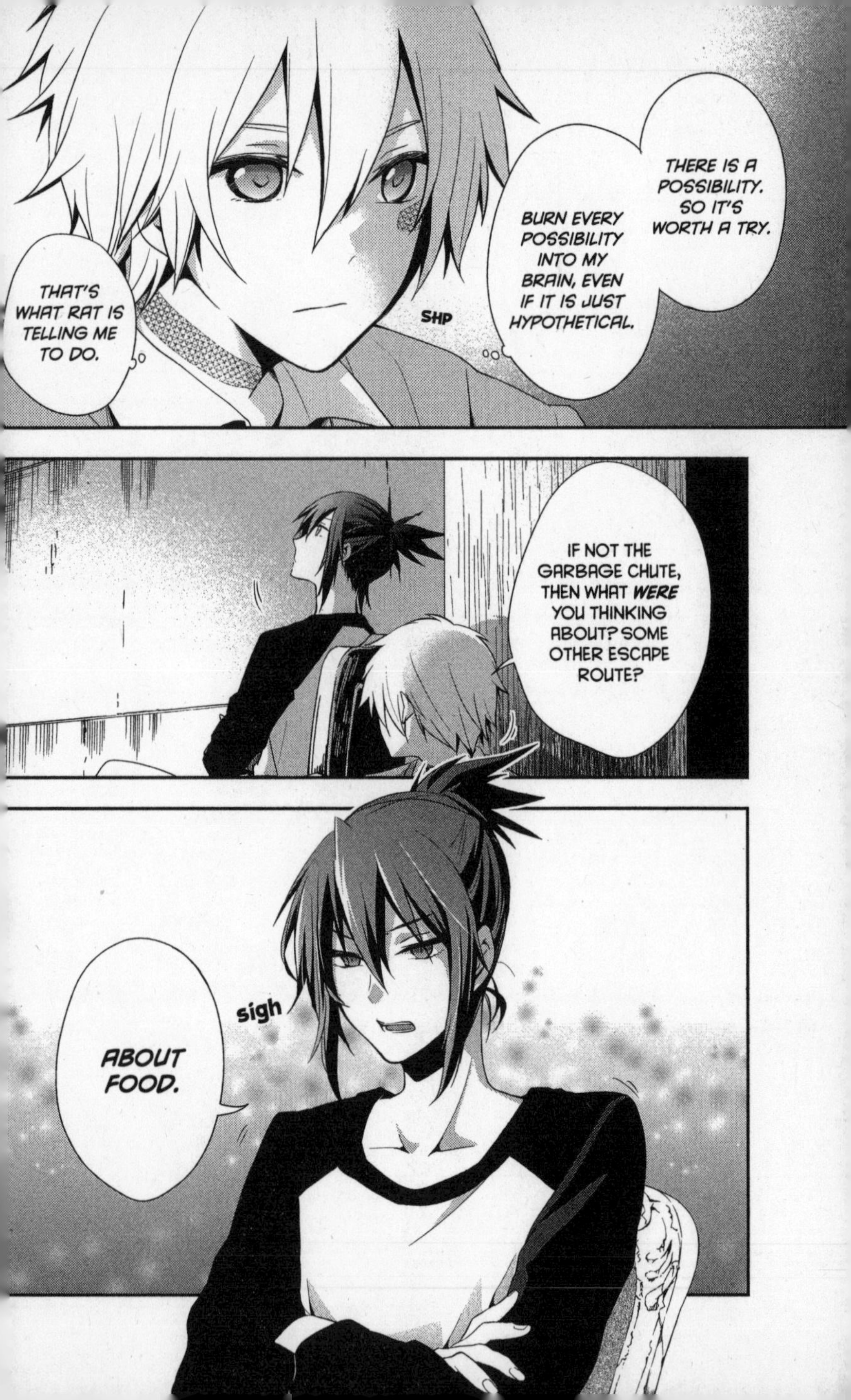
THERE IS A POSSIBILITY. SO IT'S WORTH A TRY.
BURN EVERY POSSIBILITY INTO MY BRAIN, EVEN IF IT IS JUST HYPOTHETICAL.
SHP
THAT'S WHAT RAT IS TELLING ME TO DO.
IF NOT THE GARBAGE CHUTE, THEN WHAT *WERE* YOU THINKING ABOUT? SOME OTHER ESCAPE ROUTE?
sigh
ABOUT FOOD.

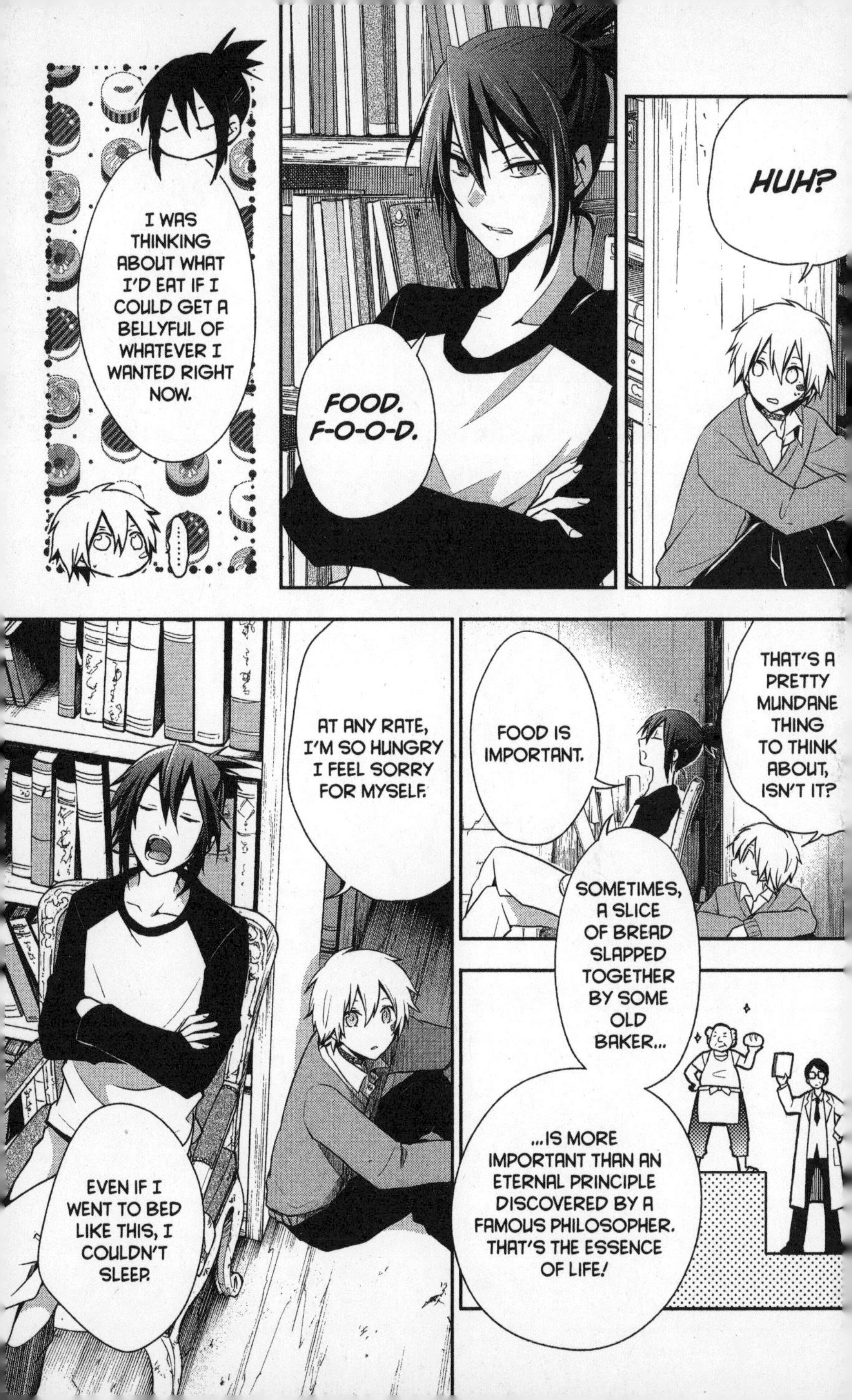
HUH?
FOOD. F-O-O-D.
I WAS THINKING ABOUT WHAT I'D EAT IF I COULD GET A BELLYFUL OF WHATEVER I WANTED RIGHT NOW.
...
THAT'S A PRETTY MUNDANE THING TO THINK ABOUT, ISN'T IT?
FOOD IS IMPORTANT.
SOMETIMES, A SLICE OF BREAD SLAPPED TOGETHER BY SOME OLD BAKER...
...IS MORE IMPORTANT THAN AN ETERNAL PRINCIPLE DISCOVERED BY A FAMOUS PHILOSOPHER. THAT'S THE ESSENCE OF LIFE!
AT ANY RATE, I'M SO HUNGRY I FEEL SORRY FOR MYSELF.
EVEN IF I WENT TO BED LIKE THIS, I COULDN'T SLEEP.

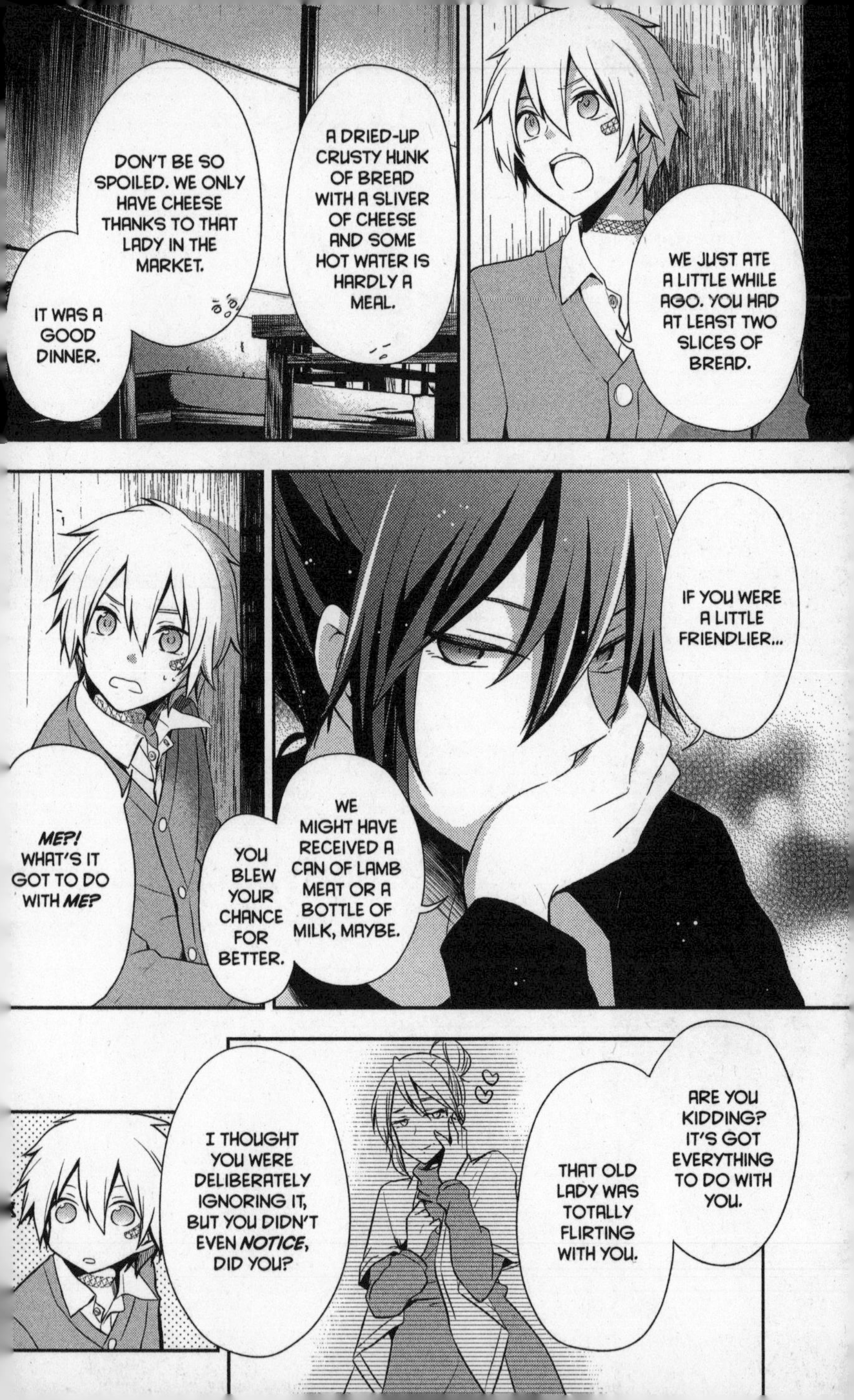
WE JUST ATE A LITTLE WHILE AGO. YOU HAD AT LEAST TWO SLICES OF BREAD.
A DRIED-UP CRUSTY HUNK OF BREAD WITH A SLIVER OF CHEESE AND SOME HOT WATER IS HARDLY A MEAL.
DON'T BE SO SPOILED. WE ONLY HAVE CHEESE THANKS TO THAT LADY IN THE MARKET.
IT WAS A GOOD DINNER.
IF YOU WERE A LITTLE FRIENDLIER...
WE MIGHT HAVE RECEIVED A CAN OF LAMB MEAT OR A BOTTLE OF MILK, MAYBE.
YOU BLEW YOUR CHANCE FOR BETTER.
ME?! WHAT'S IT GOT TO DO WITH *ME?*
ARE YOU KIDDING? IT'S GOT EVERYTHING TO DO WITH YOU.
THAT OLD LADY WAS TOTALLY FLIRTING WITH YOU.
I THOUGHT YOU WERE DELIBERATELY IGNORING IT, BUT YOU DIDN'T EVEN *NOTICE*, DID YOU?

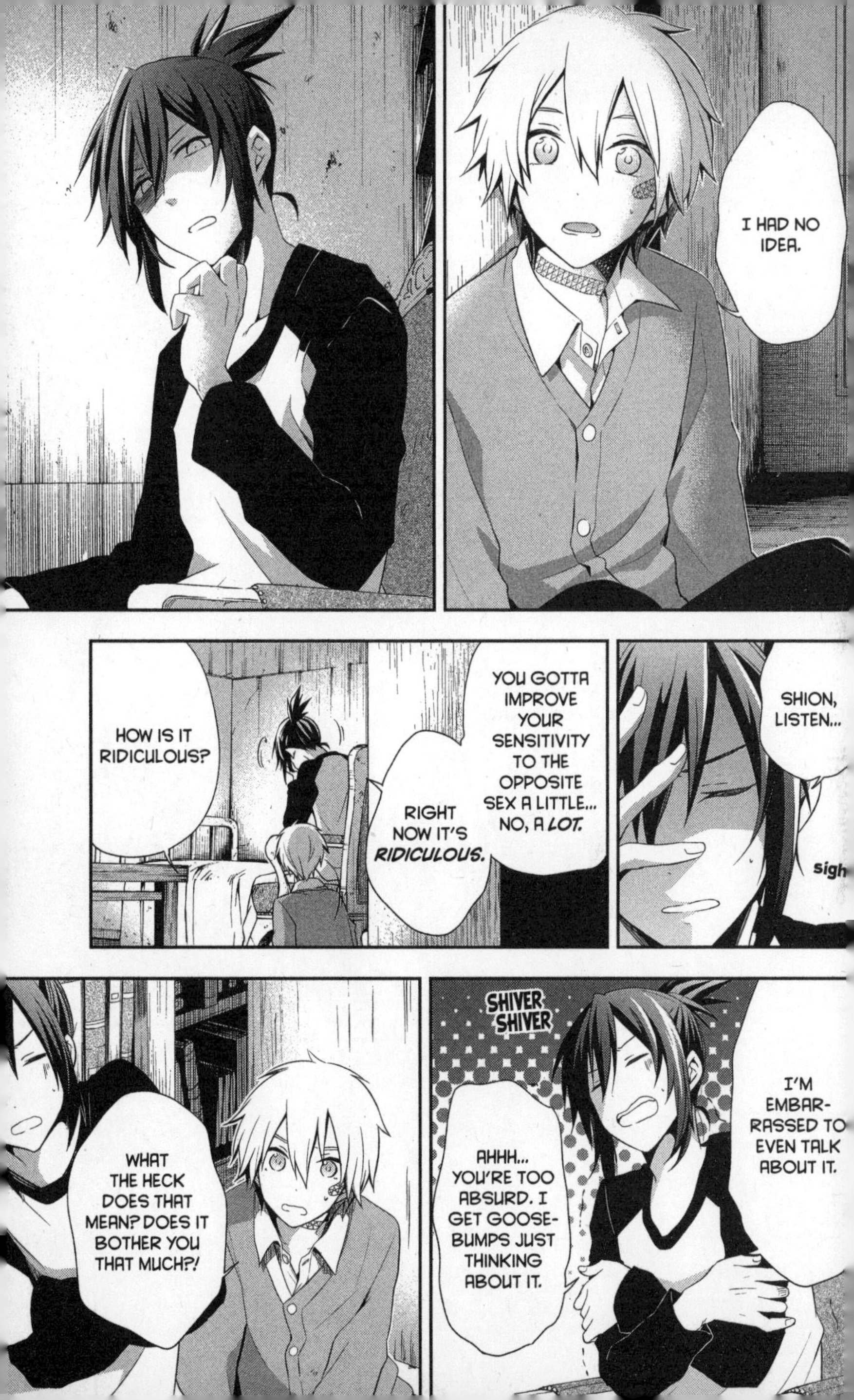
I HAD NO IDEA.
SHION, LISTEN...
sigh
YOU GOTTA IMPROVE YOUR SENSITIVITY TO THE OPPOSITE SEX A LITTLE... NO, A *LOT.*
RIGHT NOW IT'S *RIDICULOUS.*
HOW IS IT RIDICULOUS?
I'M EMBARRASSED TO EVEN TALK ABOUT IT.
SHIVER SHIVER
AHHH... YOU'RE TOO ABSURD. I GET GOOSEBUMPS JUST THINKING ABOUT IT.
WHAT THE HECK DOES THAT MEAN? DOES IT BOTHER YOU THAT MUCH?!

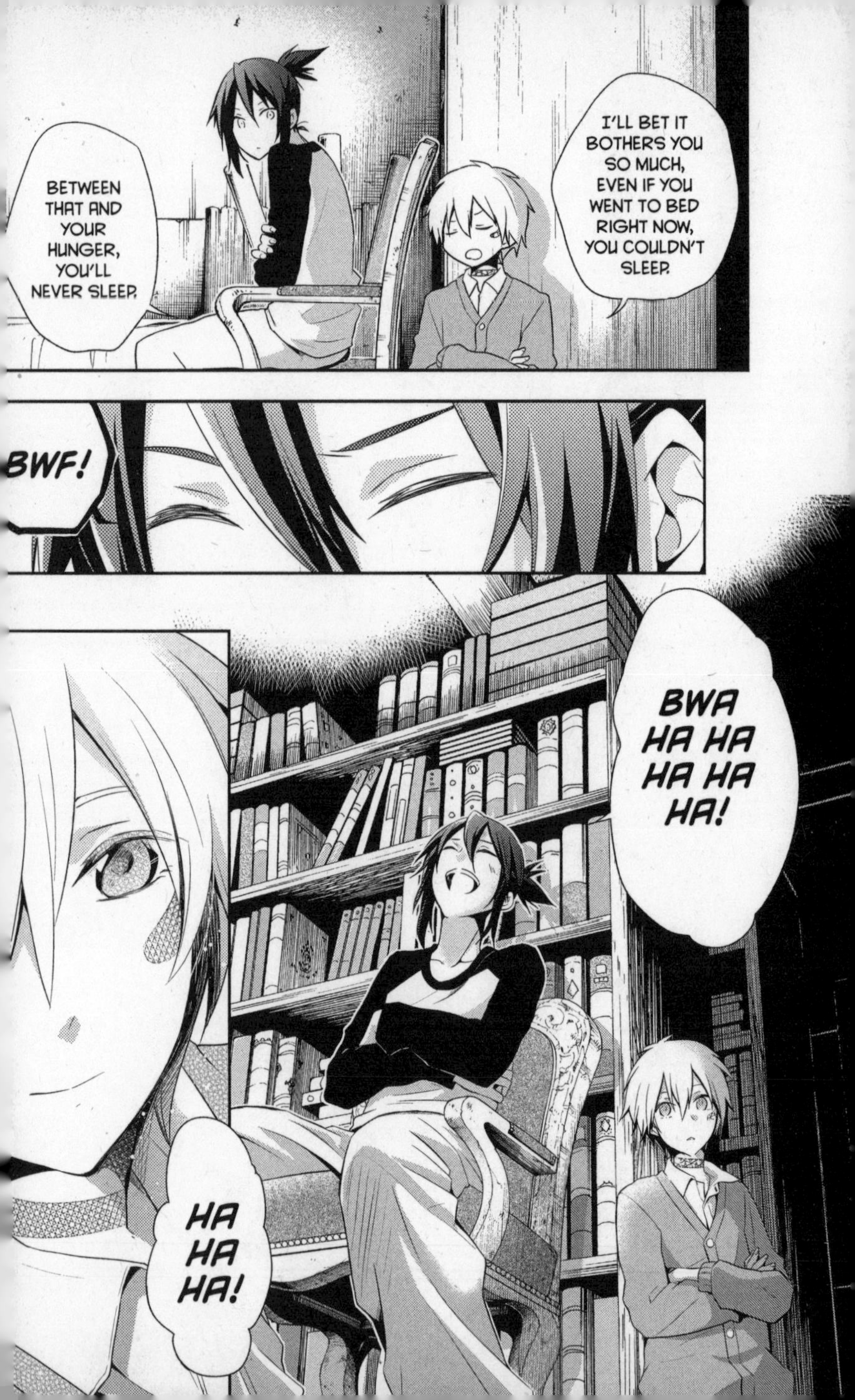
I'LL BET IT BOTHERS YOU SO MUCH, EVEN IF YOU WENT TO BED RIGHT NOW, YOU COULDN'T SLEEP.
BETWEEN THAT AND YOUR HUNGER, YOU'LL NEVER SLEEP.
BWF!
BWA HA HA HA HA HA!
HA HA HA!

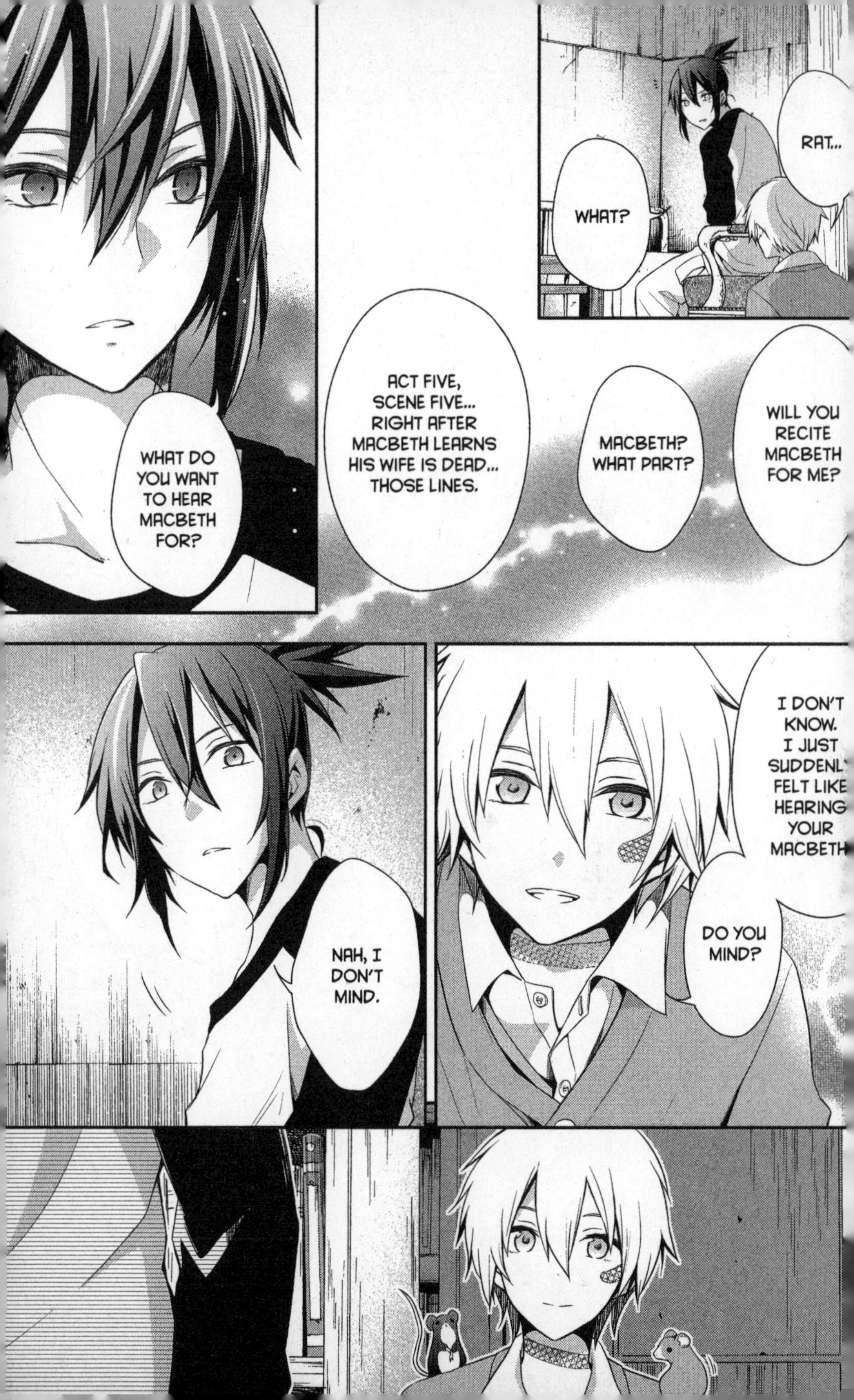
RAT...
WHAT?
WILL YOU RECITE MACBETH FOR ME?
MACBETH? WHAT PART?
ACT FIVE, SCENE FIVE... RIGHT AFTER MACBETH LEARNS HIS WIFE IS DEAD... THOSE LINES.
WHAT DO YOU WANT TO HEAR MACBETH FOR?
I DON'T KNOW. I JUST SUDDENLY FELT LIKE HEARING YOUR MACBETH
DO YOU MIND?
NAH, I DON'T MIND.

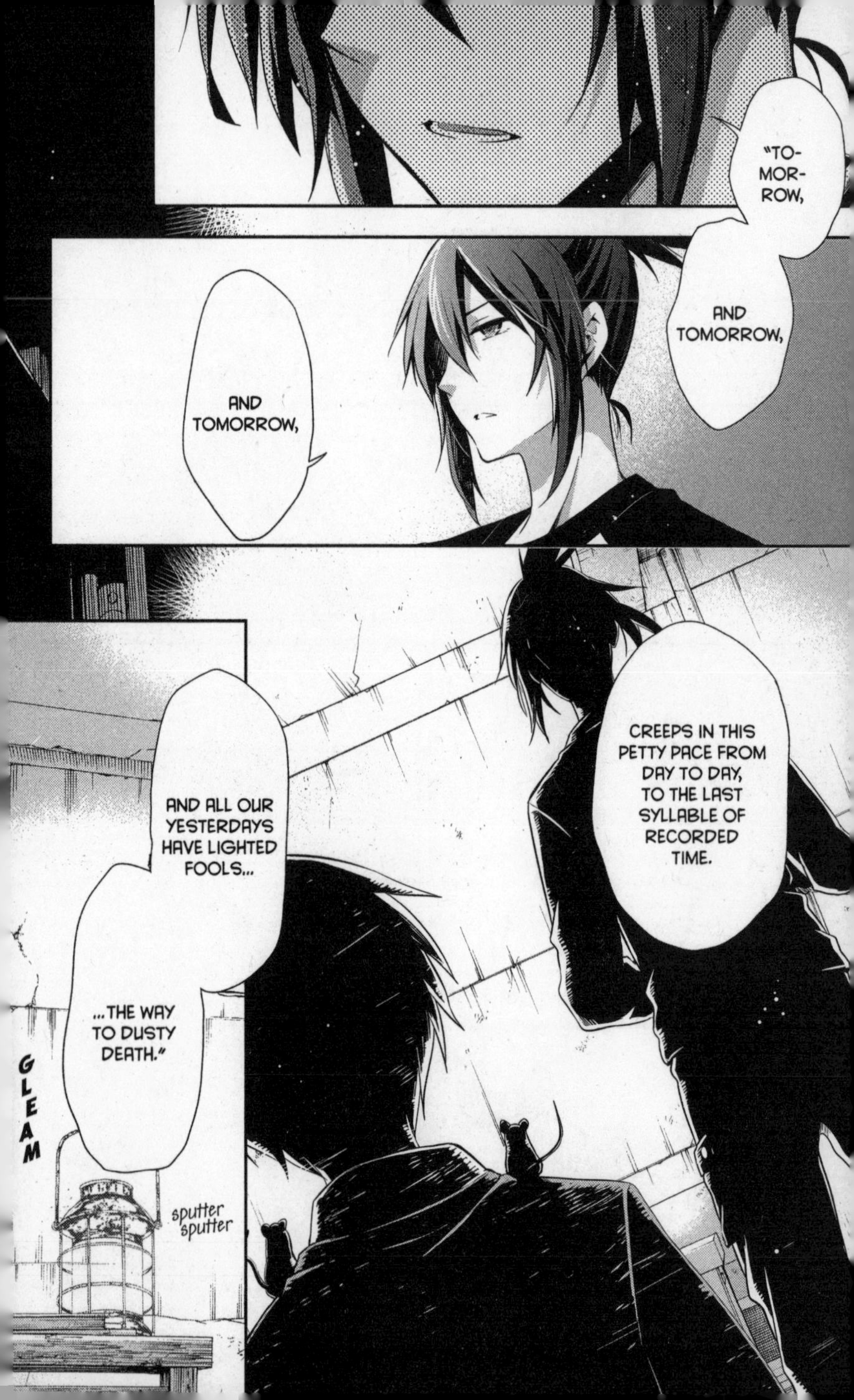
"TO-MOR-ROW,
AND TOMORROW,
AND TOMORROW,
CREEPS IN THIS PETTY PACE FROM DAY TO DAY, TO THE LAST SYLLABLE OF RECORDED TIME.
AND ALL OUR YESTERDAYS HAVE LIGHTED FOOLS...
...THE WAY TO DUSTY DEATH."
GLEAM
sputter sputter

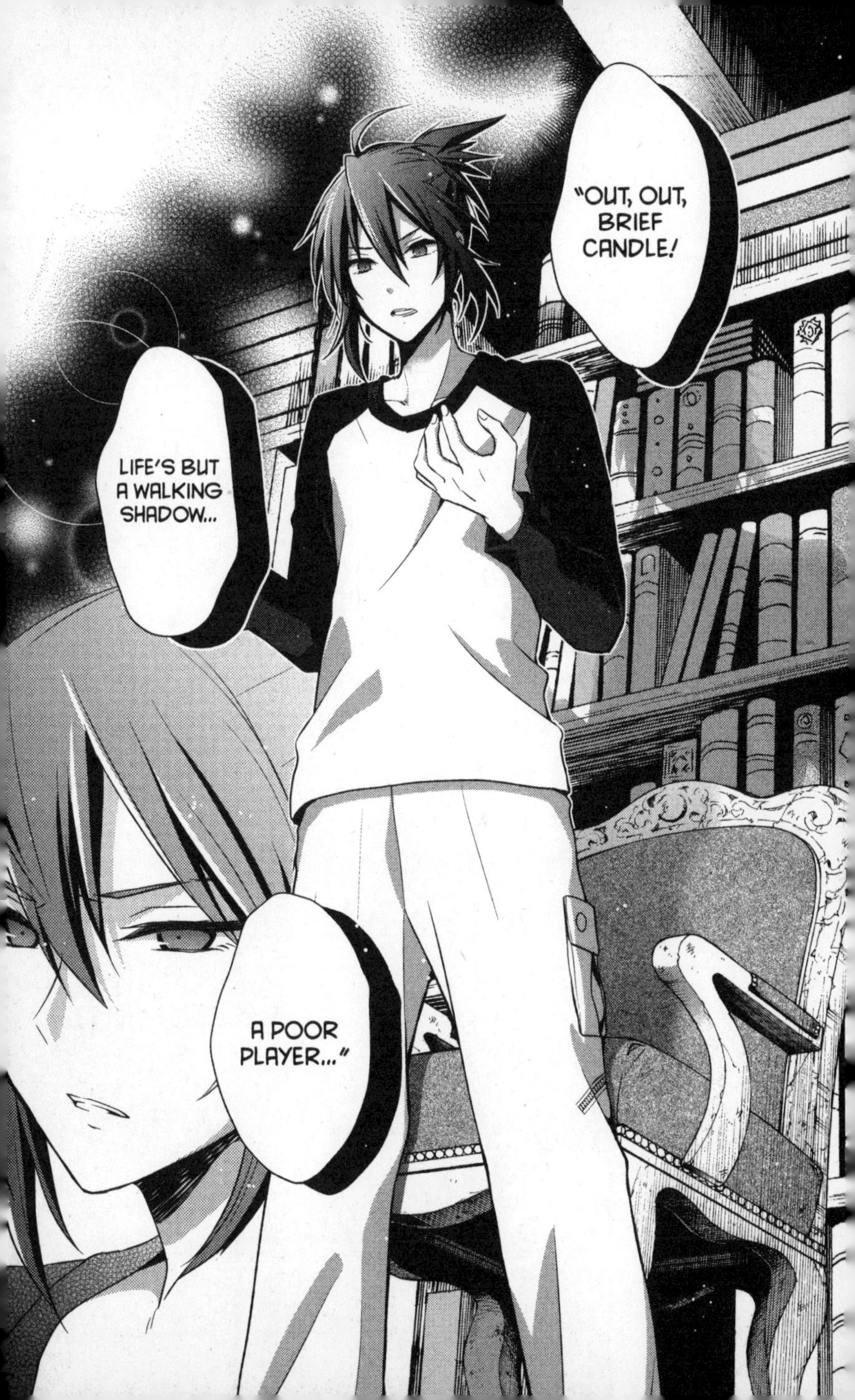
"OUT, OUT, BRIEF CANDLE!
LIFE'S BUT A WALKING SHADOW...
A POOR PLAYER..."

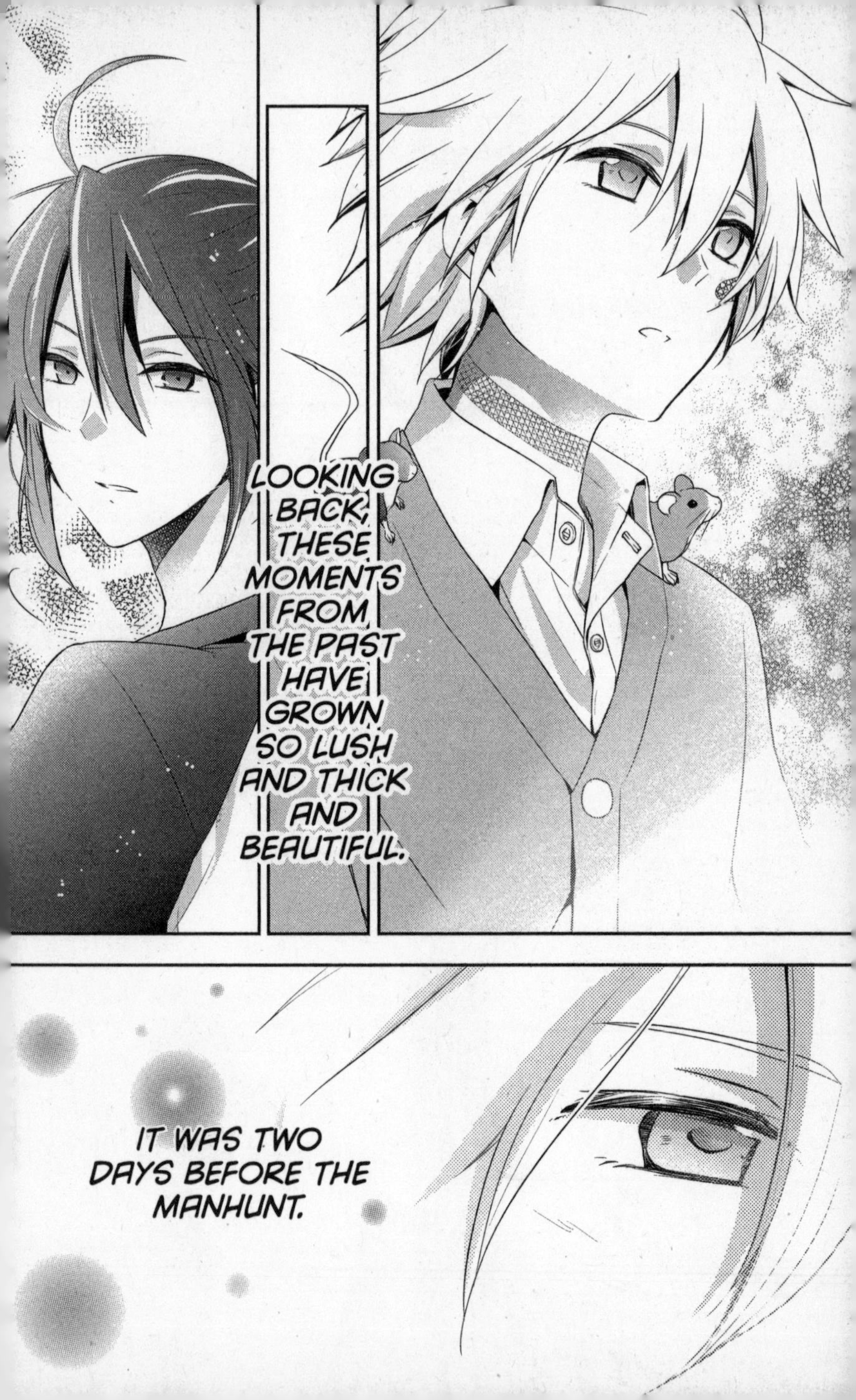
LOOKING BACK, THESE MOMENTS FROM THE PAST HAVE GROWN SO LUSH AND THICK AND BEAUTIFUL.
IT WAS TWO DAYS BEFORE THE MANHUNT.

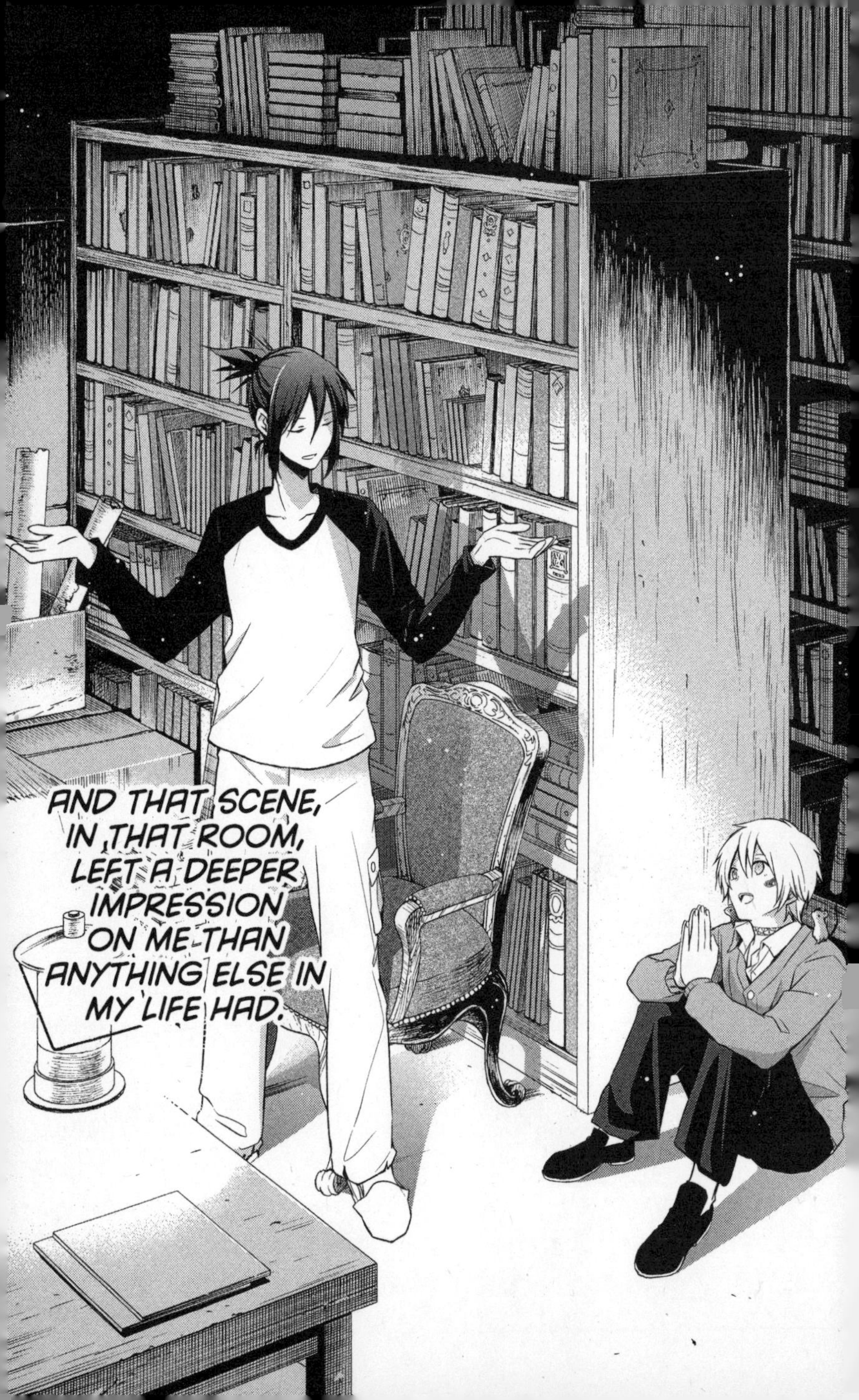
AND THAT SCENE, IN THAT ROOM, LEFT A DEEPER IMPRESSION ON ME THAN ANYTHING ELSE IN MY LIFE HAD.

Illustration from the Vault

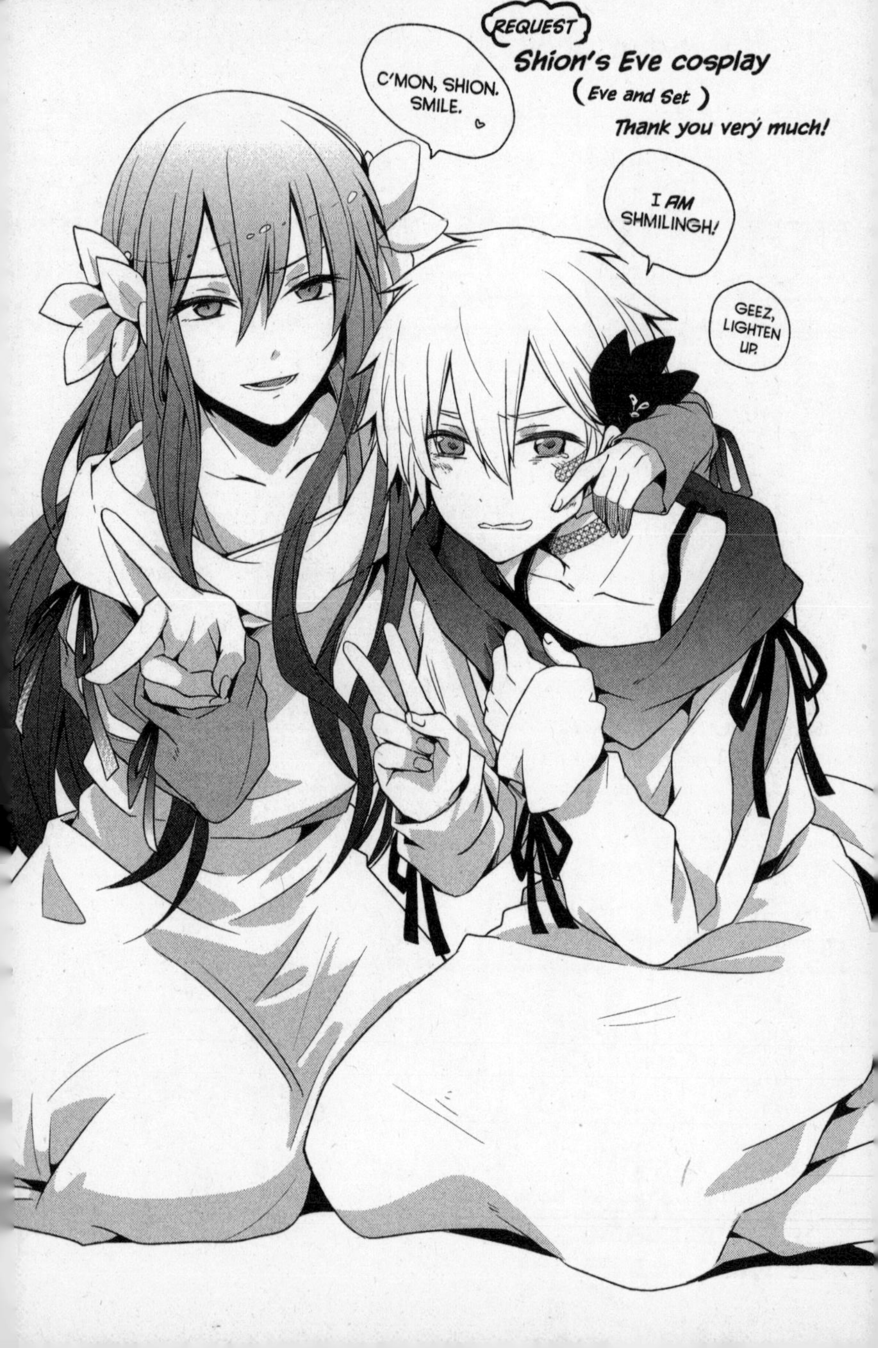
REQUEST
Shion's Eve cosplay
(Eve and Set)
Thank you very much!
C'MON, SHION. SMILE.
I AM SHMILINGH!
GEEZ, LIGHTEN UP.

Rat's room layout

Slightly different from the anime

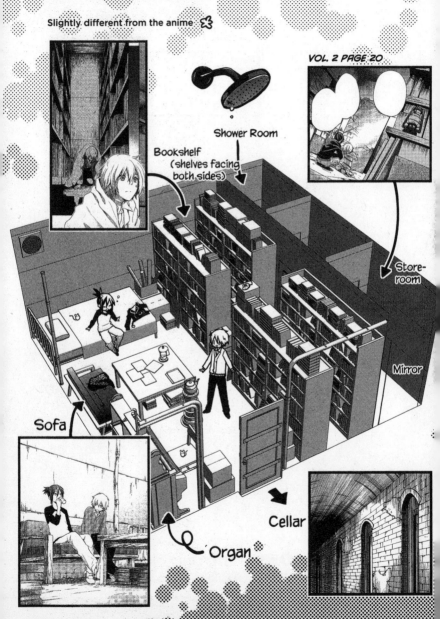

VOL. 2 PAGE 20

Shower Room

Bookshelf
(shelves facing
both sides)

Store-
room

Mirror

Sofa

Cellar

Organ

THANK YOU FOR BUYING THIS SPECIAL EDITION!

Thank you so much for reading this far. This is a story titled "Brief Candle." It was in the first scene of the novel version, Volume 8, Chapter 4. It's connected to the manga version Volume 8, Chapter 31, so please enjoy them together.

West Block Market and Rat's room! Because it's been a long time since there was such a peaceful, mellow atmosphere, it was very fun to draw. Depending on the translator, Macbeth Act 5, Scene 5 has so many different interpretations, so comparing them was really interesting.

The Eve Cosplay and Rat's Room were illustrations selected from requests via Twitter done a while back. Thanks for the input.

We hope you enjoy them.

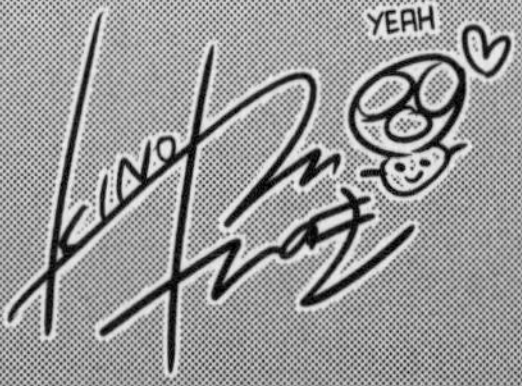
YEAH

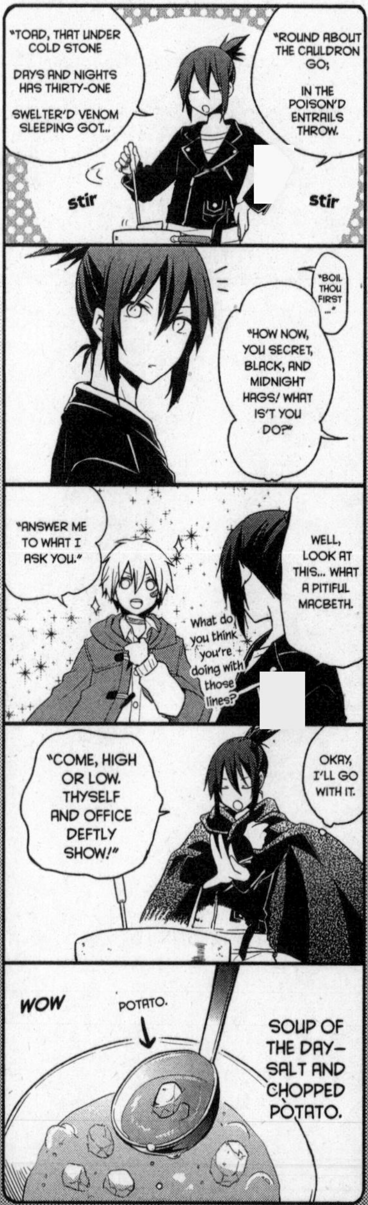
"ROUND ABOUT THE CAULDRON GO; IN THE POISON'D ENTRAILS THROW.
stir
"TOAD, THAT UNDER COLD STONE DAYS AND NIGHTS HAS THIRTY-ONE SWELTER'D VENOM SLEEPING GOT...
stir
"BOIL THOU FIRST ..."
"HOW NOW, YOU SECRET, BLACK, AND MIDNIGHT HAGS! WHAT IS'T YOU DO?"
WELL, LOOK AT THIS... WHAT A PITIFUL MACBETH.
"ANSWER ME TO WHAT I ASK YOU."
What do you think you're doing with those lines?
TRANSLATION: WHAT'S THE SOUP TODAY?
OKAY, I'LL GO WITH IT.
"COME, HIGH OR LOW. THYSELF AND OFFICE DEFTLY SHOW!"
SOUP OF THE DAY—SALT AND CHOPPED POTATO.
POTATO.
WOW

NO.6 plus

NO. 6 Vol. 7 bonus

Story: Atsuko Asano
Art: Hinoki Kino
Publisher: Kodansha
Format: Hiroshi Shinjo +
Yukiko Hamajima (NARTi;S)

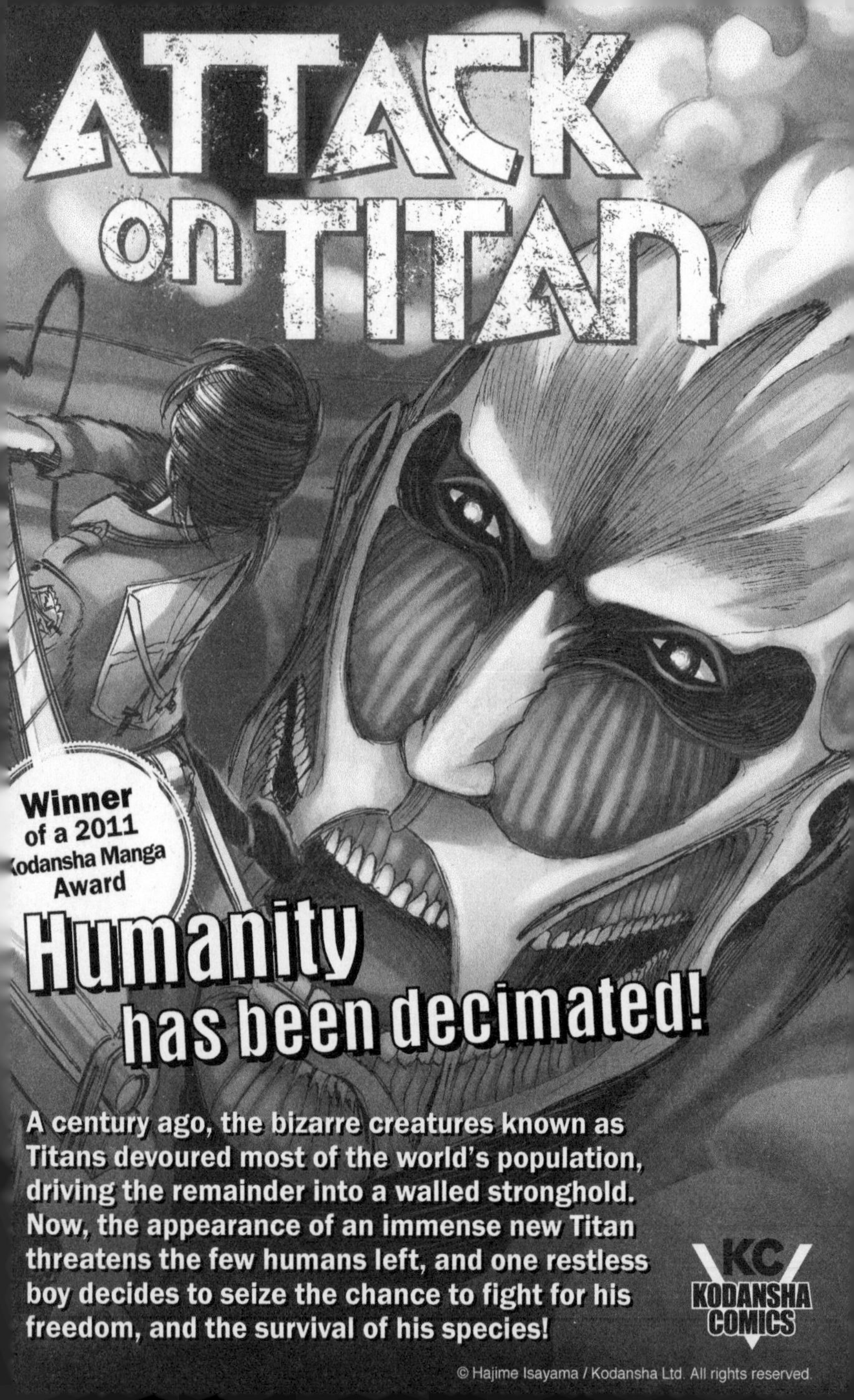
ATTACK on TITAN
Winner of a 2011 Kodansha Manga Award
Humanity has been decimated!
A century ago, the bizarre creatures known as Titans devoured most of the world's population, driving the remainder into a walled stronghold. Now, the appearance of an immense new Titan threatens the few humans left, and one restless boy decides to seize the chance to fight for his freedom, and the survival of his species!
KC KODANSHA COMICS
© Hajime Isayama / Kodansha Ltd. All rights reserved.

[redacted]

NO. 6 volume 7 is a work of fiction. Names, characters, places, and incidents are the products of the author's imagination or are used fictitiously. Any resemblance to actual events, locales, or persons, living or dead, is entirely coincidental.

A Kodansha Comics Trade Paperback Original.

Published in the United States by Kodansha Comics, an imprint of Kodansha USA Publishing, LLC, New York.

Publication rights for this English edition arranged through Kodansha Ltd., Tokyo.

First published in Japan in 2013 by Kodansha Ltd., Tokyo
ISBN 978-1-61262-553-9

Printed in the United States of America.

www.kodanshacomics.com

9 8 7 6 5 4 3 2 1

Translation: Jonathan Tarbox and Kazuko Shimizu
Lettering: Christy Sawyer
Editing: Ben Applegate